The Pillsbury
BAKE-OFF®
Cookbook

Pictured top to bottom: Choco-Peanut Toppers, page 112; Marshmallow Cookie Tarts, page 119

The Pillsbury
BAKE-OFF®
Cookbook

Doubleday
New York • London • Toronto • Sydney • Auckland

The Pillsbury Company
Pillsbury Publications

Managing Editor: Diane B. Anderson
Associate Editor: Elaine Christiansen
Recipe Copy Editor: Susanne Mattison
Home Economists: Bake-Off® Contest, Pillsbury Consumer Service and
  Publications
Nutrition Coordinators: Patricia Godfrey, R.D., Indra Mehrotra, R.D., Diane
  Christensen
Contributing Editor: S. J. Thoms & Associates, Inc.
Art Direction and Design: Lynne Dolan, Tad Ware & Company, Inc.
Food Stylists: Lynn C. Boldt, JoAnn Cherry, Sharon Harding, Barb Standal

Front Cover Photograph: Topsy Turvy Apple Pie, p. 162

PUBLISHED BY DOUBLEDAY
a division of Bantam Doubleday Dell Publishing Group, Inc.
666 Fifth Avenue, New York, New York 10103

DOUBLEDAY and the portrayal of an anchor with a dolphin
are registered trademarks of Doubleday,
a division of Bantam Doubleday Dell Publishing Group, Inc.

Library of Congress Cataloging-in-Publication Data

The Pillsbury bake-off cookbook.—1st paperback ed.
    p.   cm.
   Includes index.
   ISBN 0-385-42548-1
   1. Baking.   I. Pillsbury Company.
  TX765.P519   1992
  641.7'1—dc20   92-12013
                                             CIP

Contents

America's Premier Baking and Cooking Contest

The Bake-Off® Contest began modestly enough as an opportunity for women to share their treasured recipes. At the same time, the contest was intended to recognize the creativity of homemakers, paying them special honor for their baking skills.

Created by executives from Pillsbury's advertising agency, that first event—held in 1949—was called the Grand National Recipe and Baking Contest. Almost immediately media people dubbed it the Bake-Off® Contest. Contest finalists became overnight celebrities for skills they had honed to perfection in their own kitchens. So popular was the contest that Pillsbury executives decided to repeat it the next year, and the next year, until it became an institution. Today it is described as the granddaddy of cooking contests.

The Bake-Off® Contest remains popular today because it has kept pace with the changing needs and interests of American consumers. Entry rules and judging criteria have been revised often over the years. In 1966, the Bake-Off® Contest recognized the growing trend to convenience cooking by adding the theme "Busy Lady." Two years later, categories for convenience mixes and refrigerated fresh dough were introduced. And in 1973, the "Bake It Easy" theme stressed the need for simple recipes with strong family appeal.

For many people, the Bake-Off® Contest is a continuing source of fascination and intrigue. How do people become finalists? Who are they, and how do they come up with prizewinning recipes? What happens at the contest? How does it happen?

The pages that follow offer a peek into the intricate inner workings of the Bake-Off® Contest—how it began, how it has changed and what it is all about today.

In the Beginning

Eleanor Roosevelt was the honored guest at that first contest in 1949 and called it "an important part of the American scene." It was and has been ever since!

Held at New York's Waldorf-Astoria, an oversight almost kept the contest from happening. Just hours before the event, the staff discovered that the hotel's private electrical system was direct current, while the

From The First Pillsbury Grand National Baking Contest in 1949:

Above: Judges sampling cakes.

Above: Celebrities sharing the excitement.

Left: Winners enjoying top honors and checks.

electric ranges for the contest required alternating current. As the finalists slept, a hole was cut in the hotel's wall and a cable was dropped four stories to the street below. From there it descended via a manhole to the New York Central Railroad. A power cord was tapped into the railway's alternating current line, and the 100 ranges were ready to go in time.

With so many years of history, the Bake-Off® Contest is a treasury of funny anecdotes and poignant memories. And the unique charm of the contest is created by the finalists themselves, like . . .

- The farm housewife who, distrustful of city ways, brought eggs from her own chicken house to prepare her recipe.
- The Texas teenage finalist who hauled out a hammer to crack peppermint candy for her dessert entry.
- The contestant who sighted along a carpenter's level before committing her cake to the oven.

Stories like these reflect the depth and character of this remarkable event. It's about food, but more important, it's about people. It's a cherished vignette of Americana.

A Window on the Kitchens of America

Bake-Off® recipes are widely recognized as reflecting and even setting trends in American-style cooking. When the contest began, cooking was primarily the work of women, many of whom spent hours in the kitchen baking elaborate recipes. Homemakers who had experienced the rationing and shortages of World War II were taking new interest in cooking.

For Americans of the 1950s, home and family were all-important. The idea of "the good life" was evident in rich, filling meals topped off with sweet, often glamorous desserts and treats. Typical of these fancy mealtime finales were Snappy Turtle Cookies and "My Inspiration" Cake. Grand Prize winner in 1952, the cookies were cleverly shaped to look like turtles and featured the popular flavor combination we now know in turtle candy. "My Inspiration" Cake, the top winner just one year later, was layer upon layer of cake, chocolate and nuts.

As America moved into the 1960s, convenience of preparation became a greater concern than it had been previously. Women were entering the work force in larger numbers and needed recipes that could be made quickly. Reflecting this, entries included many one-step cakes, press-in-the-pan pie crusts, bar cookies and all-in-one main dishes. America—and its meals—went casual with quick and easy main dishes like Crafty Crescent Lasagne, a 1968 Bake-Off® favorite featuring refrigerated crescent dinner rolls. Good cooks also looked to the Bake-Off® Contest for new desserts that were inviting yet easy to make, such as the famous Tunnel of Fudge Cake and Magic Marshmallow Crescent Puffs.

In the 1970s, society's emphasis on nutrition was evident in the contestants' use of fruits and vegetables for everything from main dishes to desserts. Whole grain flours and cereals, nuts and seeds, plus honey and maple syrup for sweetening, became staple ingredients. Adventuresome cooks began to experiment with more herbs, spices and flavorings. Whole Wheat Raisin Loaf and other back-to-scratch baked goods were in vogue. Alongside were recipes like Chocolate Cherry Bars and Potato-Beef Quick Meal that made creative use of new convenience products like cake mixes and dried potato products.

What was trendy in the 1970s became a way of life in the 1980s—fresh vegetables, whole grain products and light, nutritious fare. Ethnic cuisine with an American twist became popular, as evidenced by such entries as Puffy Chiles Rellenos snacks, Streamlined Hungarian Torte and Italian Cheese Rustica Pie. Contestants also reached into their own heritage to prepare family heirloom recipes as well as regional favorites like Santa Fe Corn and Cheese Bake.

With the emphasis on fast meals, microwave cooking came into its own. Finalists used the new oven to prepare part or all of their recipes in a matter of minutes. They also continued to use small appliances, such as electric mixers, food processors and blenders, to help speed preparation of recipes.

Today's recipe entries combine the best of each Bake-Off® era. The ready availability of a wide variety of fresh ingredients makes it possible for American cooks to prepare virtually anything they desire any time of the year. Dishes like Italian Spinach Torta and Polish Poppy Swirl Loaf feature ethnic ideas adapted for American tastes. The concern about nutrition is reflected in light meal and mini-meal alternatives, such as Garden Chicken Salad and Ham and Cheese Biscuit Pockets. However, Americans still "pull out the stops" on cost, time and calories when it comes to desserts and sweet snacking, as evidenced by Chocolate Praline Layer Cake, the glamorous grand prize winner from 1988.

There is a new awareness of attractive food presentation, probably because of more frequent dining out. Main dishes, soups and side dishes might call for a special herb sprinkle or fresh vegetable garnish. And Bake-Off® dessert recipes often incorporate fancy pipped frosting or whipped cream plus chocolate curls.

Ask tens of thousands of creative cooks from around the country to share their favorite recipes, and you will get a good look at how America cooks today. That is the unique picture presented by entries in the Bake-Off® Contest.

Choosing the Bake-Off® Finalists

Have you ever wondered what happens to a Bake-Off® entry once it is dropped into a mailbox? How the recipes are selected for the finals?

To get a true picture, it's really necessary to back up about a year, to the time when the entry rules and judging criteria for the upcoming contest are written. In 1949, one rule was that all recipes had to use at least ½ cup of flour. During the 1960s, convenience mix and refrigerated dough categories were added. Over the years, various contest themes and recipe groups have been created to keep the contest in tune with the way Americans are cooking. They have covered ideas from Regional American Foods and Family Favorites to Quick and Easy Recipes and Ethnic Recipes.

About nine months before the contest, a promotional campaign is launched. Information begins to appear in supermarkets, magazines and newspapers throughout the country. The goal: to encourage America's best cooks to enter their favorite innovative recipes in the Bake-Off® Contest.

The Mailbags Arrive

Entries journey through the mail system and eventually arrive at the office of an independent judging agency. The agency's job is to screen all recipes, making sure the official rules and judging criteria are met. These judges also review the recipes for trends in food interests, which are incorporated into a report at the conclusion of the entry phase and used by Pillsbury home economists and marketing people, as well as newspaper and magazine food editors.

Eligible recipes are assigned a special code number, and the entrants' names and addresses are removed. This is a vitally important step in maintaining the integrity of the contest. Hundreds of these coded recipes are forwarded to Pillsbury test kitchens, where home economists read through them again. They continue the search for the most interesting food ideas, eliminating recipes that appear inaccurate or too involved, or that require unusual equipment or ingredients.

Test and Taste

Kitchen testing is the next step. Seasoned home economists sample and evaluate every possible detail of each recipe. Does it have family appeal? Is it a recipe most cooks would make often? Is it easy to prepare? Is the presentation appealing? And most important of all, does it taste good?

Meanwhile, a research team of home economists pore over a library of food publications. Their job is to make sure recipes have not been previously published by

Pillsbury home economists test and taste to assure reliable recipes.

national cookbooks, magazines or food companies nor chosen as winners in national contests.

The process of selecting the best 100 recipes is long and rigorous. Thousands of recipes are forwarded by the independent judging agency to Pillsbury, and each is read carefully for its special merits. Hundreds are prepared and evaluated by professional home economists in taste-test panels. The best are tested further, and finally, after months of work, the 100 winning entries are selected. Not until this time does the independent judging agency reveal the names and addresses of the people who submitted the recipes.

Next Step, Contest Preparations

As soon as the 100 recipes are selected, 100 finalists must be contacted and preparations for the Bake-Off® Contest begun. Countless details must be handled in order to make this "the experience of a lifetime" and to assure that every finalist has an equal opportunity to win prize money.

Calling All Finalists

A team of Pillsbury people goes to work contacting all finalists by phone to let them know of their newfound celebrity status. Locating the finalists can sometimes turn into a detective hunt. One contestant was traveling the country with no itinerary or plans to call home. So the highway patrols from several states, forest rangers and park officials joined in the chase! Another finalist without a phone in her home luckily "had her ears on" and responded to a CB message broadcast by her community's postmistress.

One by one, each of the finalists is contacted and congratulated. Certain papers must be signed and biographical information completed. Reading the biographies is like viewing a cross section of the American population. Bake-Off® finalists often seem familiar—like next-door neighbors. At the same time, they are all unique individuals.

- In addition to cooking and baking, their hobbies have ranged from "baby-sitting" orphaned sea otters to weight lifting.
- Many enjoy traveling and trying out the cuisine of exotic lands like Nepal, Poland, Monaco and the Fiji Islands. Still others have visited nearly every U.S. state.
- Among the finalists have been homemakers, students, physicians, teachers, military officers, bus drivers and musicians.
- Many men have counted among the finalists, with three qualifying for the earliest contest.
- The youngest to win the Grand Prize was a seventeen-year-old woman. A ten-year-old was the youngest finalist ever to compete in the contest.

With finalists coming from all corners of the United States, travel arrangements for the free trip to the contest site have involved a mix of transporation methods. Most fly, but a few have requested rail travel. Some simply drive from their nearby homes. The most unusual: a dogsled used for the first leg of the trip by a finalist living in a remote region of Alaska.

The World's Longest Shopping List

Once the finalists arrive at the contest site, Pillsbury supplies all of the groceries and cooking equipment needed for recipe preparation. Gathering these supplies is an immense organizational feat that involves a team of home economists. They call finalists to check and double-check the "shopping lists" so that everyone has exactly what they would use at home to prepare their winning recipe.

As with the recipes, the grocery and equipment lists reflect current cooking styles. For example, early contest recipes were prepared "by hand," but many contemporary finalists use microwave ovens, food processors, blenders and other small appliances. As part of their recipes, today's finalists even call for ingredients to add fancy garnishing, such as chocolate leaves or filigree or piped toppings.

How the Grocery List Has Changed!

With 3,000 items in a typical grocery store of 1949, the shopping list for the first contest was a relatively short one of 120 different ingredients.

Now this list contains more than 225 ingredients as Bake-Off® finalists choose from over 15,000 items in today's supermarket.

There's Nothing Like the Bake-Off® Contest

One hundred mini-kitchens in one great ballroom! Whether it's in Los Angeles, New York, Houston, or one of the many other sites chosen for the Bake-Off® Contest, the atmosphere is a marvelous melding of anticipation, excitement and fun combined with earnest and skilled competition for thousands of dollars in prize money.

Each contestant has an assigned work area complete with a range and preparation area plus ingredients and utensils. As finalists step to their areas to begin cooking, their "assistants" stand by. Chosen by Pillsbury, these assistants run errands for the finalists and escort them to the judges' area and to photography. They even help out with the dishwashing.

For each contest, 100 cooks in 100 mini-kitchens vie for prize money.

The Bake-Off® floor is a flurry of activity. Magazine and newspaper food editors as well as photographers and TV cameras record the action. Show business celebrities and dignitaries are on hand to greet the contestants and cheer them on. Special guests from the supermarket industry observe the hubbub. And Pillsbury officials roam the floor to ensure absolute integrity on the part of everyone involved.

Finalists work painstakingly to prepare their recipes. Even so, disasters can occur. One contestant accidentally dropped her finished cake just as she was taking it to the judges' area. Another set her fresh-baked pie on a chair to cool—and absentmindedly sat on it.

Other finalists seem totally unaffected by the near-chaos of the contest floor. A contestant from Hawaii danced the hula for photographers while she waited for her recipe to bake. One finalist was observed reading a book and commented that the setting was really quite peaceful compared to her kitchen at home with five children underfoot.

Some have likened the situation to a people traffic jam. Yet despite the commotion, finalists turn out wonderful foods—beautifully decorated and consistently delicious.

Great Cooks of America

On the Bake-Off® floor, finalists become celebrities for skills they have honed to perfection in their own kitchens. Many are uniquely talented cooks, enjoying all types of baking and cooking. Others have developed specialties, such as cake or bread baking as an all-consuming avocation. And there are novice cooks who have just recently discovered their own innate knack with food.

There's really no way to predict who will become a Bake-Off® contestant. Many enter multiple recipes, hoping that one will become a prizewinner. Some make the finals on their very first try, with only one recipe entry. At the 33rd contest, one of the first-time finalists was a senior citizen who had entered every Bake-Off® Contest since 1949. One woman entered many times but was never named a finalist. Then her husband entered and became a finalist on his first try.

Among the finalists are those who have made a "career" of entering all types of cooking contests. They join clubs and subscribe to newsletters that offer tips on how to win contests.

There are others for whom the Bake-Off® Contest is a family affair. Grandmothers and mothers pass along a heritage of Bake-Off® lore to the younger generations.

Many contestants express a long-standing love for food—an interest that endures beyond the excitement of the Bake-Off® experience. Young finalists have gone on to college to study food science. Other finalists have started bakeries and restaurants. Still others are now cookbook authors and food writers for magazines and newspapers.

The Tastes of Success

The inspirations for winning recipes are as varied and interesting as the finalists themselves. Sometimes the recipes are created specifically for the Bake-Off® Contest. One woman said that she sleeps with pen and paper next to her bed in case she gets a new recipe idea before going to sleep at night.

Many finalists draw inspiration from their own food heritage. They start with hand-me-down recipes and add a creative new twist. Newer citizens of the U.S. use American ingredients to re-create the essence of foods from their homelands. Well-traveled finalists develop recipes that replicate dishes from favorite restaurants of the world.

Choosing the Winners

Being part of the Bake-Off® Contest is reward enough, according to many finalists. But it also is an opportunity to win thousands of dollars in prize money. Therefore, the finalists are serious about their work on Bake-Off® day.

In years past, there was a rule stating that "you must be able to prepare the recipe in a day." Now, however, finalists are given six hours, and some are finished in less than an hour.

Finalists are supplied enough ingredients to prepare their recipes three times, and many do. They make one for photography, one to share with their newfound friends on the Bake-Off® floor and the best one for the judges.

Working in secrecy, the judges conduct their evaluation in a well-guarded room away from the contest area. Chosen for their knowledge of good food, the judges include newspaper and magazine food editors, cookbook authors and other noted food authorities.

The judges sample and discuss each recipe thoroughly, weighing the merits with no idea of the finalists' names or hometowns. Foods are taste-tested at their freshest best—hot foods are judged when hot and cold foods are kept chilled. Judging 100 wonderful recipes may seem like great duty, but it can be tiring. To prevent fatigue, the judges sip water, tea and clam broth and clear their palates with celery and carrot sticks.

Maintaining the secrecy of the judging process is vital to the integrity of the contest. So, finalists, media representatives, other Bake-Off® guests and Pillsbury personnel alike—all must await the judges' final decisions.

Esther Tomich WINS Grand Prize in 1978 for Nutty Graham Picnic Cake!

And the Winners Are . . .

The day after the official contest, finalists gather with other Bake-Off® guests for the awards ceremony. All are dressed in their Sunday best. The tables are graced with colorful flowers. As the music plays, a celebrity mounts the grand stage for the big moment—to announce who has won the top prizes in the nation's most famous cooking contest. The atmosphere is charged with eager anticipation, and as the winners are announced, cheers of congratulations go up from the crowd.

$ Prizes Galore $

Nearly $2,500,000 in prize money has been awarded to Bake-Off® finalists since 1949, the first contest.

Only a privileged few are among the big money winners but all finalists are celebrities. Their photos are in the newspapers. They appear on local and sometimes national television. Whole families, employer-companies and towns share in the excitement. Returning to her hometown, one finalist was greeted at the airport with crowd commotion like that for a winning football team returning from the Super Bowl. Another finalist said she was so busy making public appearances that she might not have time to return to her job.

Some Recipes Become Classics

Bake-Off® recipes gain celebrity status as well, and many have become culinary classics. These are recipes that have withstood the test of time, remaining popular for years and even decades. They have been incorporated into personal recipe collections across America and are enjoyed by literally thousands of families, who pass them on from one generation of good cooks to the next.

Some of the Bake-Off® recipes that have become favorites won the top prizes, but others are simply great recipes appreciated for their perfect fit with the way American families cook and eat. Among them are recipes like Cherry Wink Cookies, Peanut Blossoms and Dilly Casserole Bread, which have become so commonplace that their origins in the Bake-Off® Contest are often forgotten.

Also ranking as classics are recipes that caused quite a commotion in the marketplace when they became top prize winners. The 1954 Grand Prize winner, Open Sesame Pie, featured sesame seed in the crust. During the week that followed publication of the recipe, grocery stores around the country sold out their stock of this exotic little seed.

Many people puzzled over the selection of Magic Marshmallow Crescent Puffs as the top prize winner

in 1969. "It's so simple—just a marshmallow wrapped in dough," they said. The Puffs became a winner precisely because of this very simple way to achieve good taste. Each triangle of refrigerated crescent dough was wrapped around a marshmallow that "magically" melted during baking to create a hollow-centered sweet roll.

Product Inspirations

Certain recipes from among the "classics" have gone on to inspire new Pillsbury products. None is better-known than the 1966 prize winner, Tunnel of Fudge Cake, a rich, moist chocolate cake with a soft, fudgy center. So popular was the recipe that Pillsbury created a convenient mix version featuring the same delicious taste that made the original recipe a classic.

Great Recipes Made Better Than Ever

Pillsbury home economists return to the Bake-Off® files for often requested recipes and recipes they know are "winners." The best are retested and revised to ensure their appeal to today's consumers.

All of the recipes in this book have been thoroughly tested in the Pillsbury kitchens. And many of the old-favorite recipes have been updated so that contemporary consumers can enjoy the great tastes all over again. Here are some of the ways that the recipes have been retested and updated:

- Ingredients no longer made are replaced with readily available products.
- From-scratch steps are replaced with timesaving mixes as well as refrigerated and frozen products.
- Easy-to-follow preparation instructions and cooking terms are used.
- Oven temperatures and ingredient amounts are adjusted to ensure greater success.
- Fats and salt are reduced to suit current preferences.
- Flour sifting is eliminated.
- Microwave preparation is incorporated when it is a proven timesaver.

America's Fascination with Good Food

The best of Bake-Off® recipes are presented here for you to enjoy . . . to read and recall from your own memory . . . to prepare and share with family and friends. If you've never made these recipes, now is the time to try them out. They're guaranteed to become part of your family's collection of Bake-Off® favorites.

Harvest Fresh® Spinach Soup, page 14; Savory Crescent Chicken Squares, page 28

Soups, Sandwiches and Snacks

❧

The easy-to-prepare soups and stews, baked sandwiches and intriguing snacks of this chapter seem especially fitting for a nation on the go. You'll find hearty and wholesome fare as well as many foods for lighter eating and the increasingly popular mini-meals. Tuna Cheese Flips and Cheese Steak Crescent Braid demonstrate the versatility of refrigerated biscuit and crescent roll doughs, used by savvy finalists to wrap all manner of ingredients. And Italian Spinach Torta features all-ready pie crust, a wonderfully convenient way to make appetizers that look and taste as if they came from the best catering shop in town.

Everyday, off-the-shelf staples are combined with a new ingredient or two for deliciously wholesome yet quick meals. Frozen or canned vegetables are teamed with meats and seasonings for savory soups like Zesty Chicken Vegetable Bisque and Harvest Fresh® Spinach Soup. The microwave oven, the blender and other small appliances add to the convenience of these recipes.

While easy preparation is essential for today's meals-on-the-run, good taste, wholesomeness and imaginative presentation are qualities that set these Bake-Off® favorites apart from other "fast" food. Quesadilla Quiche is served with sour cream, salsa, chopped tomato and sliced ripe olives—ideal for a family supper and fine enough for a company meal. Chicken 'n Artichoke Crescent Sandwiches borrow an ingredient combination from gourmet cooking for a quick and neat-to-eat meal.

Creative touches like these make the recipes in this collection so appealing and so right for the way we cook and eat today. They're sure to be winners on your table, too!

Harvest Fresh®
Spinach Soup

Harvest Fresh®
Spinach Soup
❧

After entering every Bake-Off® Contest since the first one in 1949, this contestant finally became a finalist with this recipe for a delicately flavored, easy cream soup. It is delicious served hot or cold.

❧

Olga Jason, Massachusetts
Bake-Off® 33, 1988

¹/₄ cup chopped onion
¹/₄ cup margarine or butter, melted
¹/₄ cup all purpose or unbleached flour
1 teaspoon salt, if desired
¹/₂ teaspoon dry mustard
¹/₄ teaspoon nutmeg
10³/₄-ounce can condensed chicken broth
¹/₂ cup shredded carrots
9-ounce package frozen chopped spinach in a pouch
2¹/₂ cups milk
Lemon slices, if desired

In 2-quart saucepan over medium heat, cook onion in margarine until tender. Remove from heat; blend in flour, salt, dry mustard and nutmeg. Gradually stir in chicken broth. Bring to a boil, stirring constantly. Add carrots and spinach. Reduce heat to medium; simmer uncovered 10 minutes or until carrots are tender and spinach is thawed, stirring occasionally.* Cool to lukewarm. In blender container or food processor bowl with metal blade, puree spinach mixture until smooth. Stir in milk. Cover; refrigerate until thoroughly chilled. Garnish each serving with lemon slice. **5 (1-cup) servings.**

MICROWAVE DIRECTIONS: In 8-cup microwave-safe measuring cup or large bowl, combine onion and margarine. Microwave on HIGH for 45 to 60 seconds or until onion is tender. Blend in flour, salt, dry mustard and nutmeg; gradually stir in chicken broth. Microwave on HIGH for 4 to 5 minutes or until mixture comes to a boil, stirring once halfway through cooking. Add carrots and spinach. Microwave on HIGH for 8 to 9 minutes or until carrots are tender and spinach is thawed, stirring twice during cooking.* Continue as directed above.

TIP: *To serve soup warm: puree *hot* spinach mixture in blender container or food processor bowl with metal blade until smooth. Transfer mixture to saucepan; stir in milk. Heat gently, stirring frequently. Or, transfer mixture to 8-cup microwave-safe measuring cup. Microwave on HIGH for 2 to 3 minutes or until thoroughly heated.

NUTRIENTS PER 1/5 OF RECIPE

Calories	210	Protein	15% U.S. RDA
Protein	9g	Vitamin A	90% U.S. RDA
Carbohydrate	16g	Vitamin C	10% U.S. RDA
Fat	12g	Thiamine	8% U.S. RDA
Cholesterol	10mg	Riboflavin	20% U.S. RDA
Sodium	1160mg	Niacin	10% U.S. RDA
Potassium	570mg	Calcium	20% U.S. RDA
Dietary Fiber	2g	Iron	6% U.S. RDA

'Tater Tuna Chowder

❧

Lorraine Blahnik, Michigan
Bake-Off® 25, 1974

6 slices bacon
¹/₂ cup chopped onion
1 package au gratin or cheese scalloped potato mix
2 cups hot water
1¹/₂ cups milk
1¹/₄ cups chicken broth
17-ounce can whole kernel corn, undrained
1 bay leaf, if desired
1 to 2 (6¹/₂-ounce) cans tuna, drained
5.33-ounce can (²/₃ cup) evaporated milk or ²/₃ cup half-and-half

In large saucepan or skillet, cook bacon until crisp. Remove bacon from saucepan; drain, reserving 2 tablespoons drippings in saucepan. Add onion; cook until tender. Add potato slices, contents of seasoning mix envelope, water, milk, chicken broth, corn and bay leaf. Simmer uncovered 15 to 20 minutes or until potatoes are tender, stirring occasionally. Crumble bacon over potato mixture. Add tuna and evaporated milk; mix well. Heat gently, stirring frequently. *Do not boil.* Remove bay leaf before serving. **6 (1¹/₂-cup) servings.**

NUTRIENTS PER 1/6 OF RECIPE

Calories	280	Protein	40% U.S. RDA
Protein	27g	Vitamin A	8% U.S. RDA
Carbohydrate	27g	Vitamin C	15% U.S. RDA
Fat	7g	Thiamine	10% U.S. RDA
Cholesterol	50mg	Riboflavin	20% U.S. RDA
Sodium	1160mg	Niacin	50% U.S. RDA
Potassium	640mg	Calcium	20% U.S. RDA
Dietary Fiber	1g	Iron	10% U.S. RDA

'Tater Tuna Chowder

Mexican Vegetable Soup

Mexican Vegetable Soup
ᢒᣝᠪᣝ

Nancy Hindenach, Michigan
Bake-Off® 33, 1988

> 1 **pound ground beef**
> 1.25-**ounce package taco seasoning mix**
> 46-**ounce can (6 cups) tomato juice**
> 16-**ounce package frozen mixed vegetables**
> 15-**ounce can chili hot beans**
> 12-**ounce can tomato paste**
> 2 **cups crushed corn chips**
> 8 **ounces (2 cups) shredded Cheddar cheese**

In 5-quart Dutch oven, brown ground beef; drain. Add taco seasoning mix, tomato juice, vegetables, chili beans and tomato paste; mix well. Bring just to a boil. Reduce heat; simmer uncovered 20 to 25 minutes or until vegetables are tender, stirring occasionally. Top each serving with corn chips and cheese. **11 (1-cup) servings.**

NUTRIENTS PER 1/11 OF RECIPE

Calories	340	Protein	25% U.S. RDA
Protein	18g	Vitamin A	50% U.S. RDA
Carbohydrate	29g	Vitamin C	45% U.S. RDA
Fat	17g	Thiamine	10% U.S. RDA
Cholesterol	45mg	Riboflavin	15% U.S. RDA
Sodium	1210mg	Niacin	20% U.S. RDA
Potassium	840mg	Calcium	25% U.S. RDA
Dietary Fiber	6g	Iron	25% U.S. RDA

Creole Gumbo
ᢒᣝᠪᣝ

Elaine Thornton, Mississippi
Bake-Off® 6, 1954

GUMBO

> ³/₄ **cup chopped celery**
> ¹/₃ **cup chopped green bell pepper**
> ¹/₃ **cup chopped onion**
> 2 **garlic cloves, minced**
> 3 **tablespoons olive oil**
> ¹/₄ **cup all purpose or unbleached flour**
> 3 **cups water**
> 16-**ounce can tomatoes, undrained, cut up**
> 1 **tablespoon chopped parsley**
> 1 **teaspoon salt**
> ¹/₈ **teaspoon pepper**
> 1 **cup diced canned, frozen, or fresh okra**
> 6-**ounce can crab meat, drained**

CROUTONS

> 10-**ounce can refrigerated flaky biscuits**
> 1 **tablespoon margarine or butter, melted**
> 2 **tablespoons grated Parmesan cheese**
> **Paprika**

In large saucepan, cook celery, green pepper, onion and garlic in oil 5 minutes. Blend in flour; cook over medium heat about 10 minutes or until mixture browns, stirring constantly. Gradually add water and tomatoes, stirring constantly. Stir in remaining gumbo ingredients. Bring to a boil. Reduce heat, cover and simmer 1 hour.

Heat oven to 400°F. Separate dough into 10 biscuits; cut each into 4 pieces. Place on ungreased cookie sheet. Brush with margarine; sprinkle with Parmesan cheese and paprika. Bake at 400°F. for 6 to 9 minutes or until golden brown. Remove from cookie sheet immediately; cool on wire racks. Pour gumbo into individual serving bowls; top each serving with croutons.

4 (1¼-cup) servings.

NUTRIENTS PER 1/4 RECIPE

Calories	460	Protein	20% U.S. RDA
Protein	13g	Vitamin A	50% U.S. RDA
Carbohydrate	48g	Vitamin C	50% U.S. RDA
Fat	24g	Thiamine	30% U.S. RDA
Cholesterol	35mg	Riboflavin	20% U.S. RDA
Sodium	1850mg	Niacin	25% U.S. RDA
Potassium	600mg	Calcium	10% U.S. RDA
Dietary Fiber	4g	Iron	25% U.S. RDA

Zesty Chicken Vegetable Bisque

Taylor Arnold, Texas
Bake-Off® 33, 1988

3 whole chicken breasts, skinned, boned, halved
3 tablespoons margarine or butter
1 cup sliced onions
3 garlic cloves, minced
2 tablespoons all purpose or unbleached flour
2 (14½-ounce) cans (3½ cups) chicken broth
16-ounce can whole tomatoes, undrained, cut up
1 tablespoon chopped fresh parsley
1 teaspoon thyme leaves
½ to 1½ teaspoons salt
1 teaspoon hot pepper sauce
2 bay leaves
2 cups chopped green bell peppers
1 cup frozen whole kernel corn
1 cup frozen sweet peas
4.5-ounce jar sliced mushrooms, undrained
3 cups hot cooked rice

In large, deep skillet over medium heat, brown chicken breasts in margarine. Remove chicken breasts from skillet. Add onions and garlic; cook over medium heat until onions are tender, about 3 minutes. Remove from heat. Stir in flour. Add chicken broth, tomatoes, parsley, thyme, salt, hot pepper sauce and bay leaves; blend well. Add browned chicken breasts; cook over low heat 30 minutes, stirring occasionally. Add green peppers; cook an additional 10 minutes. Add corn, peas and mushrooms; cook 10 to 15 minutes more or until chicken is tender. Remove bay leaves before serving. To serve, place ½ cup rice in each individual serving bowl. Top with chicken breast half and generous 1 cup of bisque. **6 servings**

NUTRIENTS PER 1/6 OF RECIPE

Calories	420	Protein	50% U.S. RDA
Protein	34g	Vitamin A	20% U.S. RDA
Carbohydrate	45g	Vitamin C	100% U.S. RDA
Fat	10g	Thiamine	25% U.S. RDA
Cholesterol	70mg	Riboflavin	15% U.S. RDA
Sodium	1370mg	Niacin	80% U.S. RDA
Potassium	780mg	Calcium	8% U.S. RDA
Dietary Fiber	6g	Iron	25% U.S. RDA

Zesty Chicken Vegetable Bisque

This spicy chicken and vegetable one-dish meal is like Brunswick stew. Large pieces of boneless chicken, a variety of vegetables and a well-seasoned broth are spooned over rice in individual serving bowls.

Creole Gumbo

Tomatoes, crab meat and okra team up for a winning flavor combination in this marvelous gumbo from the '50s. It has been updated to use refrigerated flaky biscuit dough to speed up the preparation time for the cheesy crouton toppers.

Cheese Steak Crescent Braid

This attractive sandwich braid has flavors like the popular Philadelphia cheese steak sandwich.

Bacon Tomato Open-Faced Rounds

The popular BLT takes a new twist in this baked version that has a tender, flaky biscuit crust.

Cheese Steak Crescent Braid

Cindy Joy, California
Bake-Off® 33, 1988

4 portions frozen, thinly sliced sandwich steaks, cut crosswise into 1/2-inch strips
2 tablespoons margarine or butter
1/2 cup chopped onion
1 large green bell pepper, cut into strips (1 1/2 cups)
Salt and pepper to taste
2 (8-ounce) cans refrigerated crescent dinner rolls
4 ounces (1 cup) shredded mozzarella cheese
1 egg, beaten, if desired

Heat oven to 350°F. In large skillet over medium-high heat, stir-fry steak strips in margarine until no longer pink; remove from skillet. Add onion and green pepper; cook until crisp-tender, about 5 minutes. Return cooked steak to skillet; season with salt and pepper.

Unroll 1 can dough into 2 long rectangles. Place on ungreased cookie sheet with long sides overlapping 1/2 inch; firmly press edges and perforations to seal. Press or roll out to form 13 × 7-inch rectangle. Spoon heaping cupful of meat mixture in 2-inch strip lengthwise down center of dough to within 1/4 inch of each end. Sprinkle 1/2 cup of the cheese over meat mixture. Make cuts 1 inch apart on longest sides of rectangle just to edge of filling. To give braided appearance, fold strips of dough at an angle halfway across filling, alternating from side to side. Fold ends of braid under to seal. On second ungreased cookie sheet, repeat, using remaining can of dough, meat mixture and cheese. Brush braids with beaten egg. Bake at 350°F. for 16 to 22 minutes or until golden brown. Cool slightly; remove from cookie sheet. Cool 5 minutes before serving. **6 servings.**

NUTRIENTS PER 1/6 OF RECIPE

Calories	440	Protein	35% U.S. RDA
Protein	22g	Vitamin A	8% U.S. RDA
Carbohydrate	32g	Vitamin C	40% U.S. RDA
Fat	25g	Thiamine	20% U.S. RDA
Cholesterol	50mg	Riboflavin	20% U.S. RDA
Sodium	960mg	Niacin	20% U.S. RDA
Potassium	360mg	Calcium	15% U.S. RDA
Dietary Fiber	2g	Iron	20% U.S. RDA

Bacon Tomato Open-Faced Rounds

Helen Bridges, California
Bake-Off® 31, 1984

10-ounce can refrigerated flaky biscuits
10 slices bacon, cut into thirds, crisply cooked
10 thin slices tomato*
1/2 cup mayonnaise or salad dressing
1/2 cup chopped onion
2 ounces (1/2 cup) shredded Swiss cheese
1 teaspoon basil leaves

Heat oven to 400°F. Separate dough into 10 biscuits. On ungreased cookie sheets, press or roll out each biscuit to 4-inch circle, forming 1/4-inch rim around edge of each circle. Arrange 3 bacon pieces on each circle; top each with tomato slice. In small bowl combine mayonnaise, onion, cheese and basil. Spoon rounded tablespoonful of mayonnaise mixture over each tomato slice, spreading slightly. Bake at 400°F. for 11 to 16 minutes or until edges of biscuits are golden brown. **10 sandwiches.**

TIP: *If tomato slices are juicy, drain on paper towel before using.

To reheat, wrap loosely in foil; heat at 350°F. for 15 to 20 minutes or until warm.

NUTRIENTS PER 1 SANDWICH

Calories	240	Protein	8% U.S. RDA
Protein	6g	Vitamin A	4% U.S. RDA
Carbohydrate	14g	Vitamin C	6% U.S. RDA
Fat	18g	Thiamine	10% U.S. RDA
Cholesterol	20mg	Riboflavin	6% U.S. RDA
Sodium	490mg	Niacin	6% U.S. RDA
Potassium	100mg	Calcium	6% U.S. RDA
Dietry Fiber	1g	Iron	6% U.S. RDA

Bacon Tomato Open-Faced Rounds

Pictured top to bottom: Broccoli Ham and Swiss Rolls, Tex-Mex Biscuit Sandwiches

Broccoli Ham and Swiss Rolls

Angela Schlueter, California
Bake-Off® 33, 1988

2 tablespoons margarine or butter
2 tablespoons flour
¹/₂ cup milk
9-ounce package frozen cut broccoli in a pouch, thawed, drained
¹/₄ cup dairy sour cream
1 teaspoon lemon juice
¹/₄ teaspoon hot pepper sauce
4 (4-inch) Kaiser rolls, unsliced
4 thin slices cooked ham
4 tomato slices, ¹/₄ inch thick
4 thin slices Swiss cheese

In medium saucepan over low heat, melt margarine. Stir in flour; cook until mixture is smooth and bubbly, stirring frequently. Gradually stir in milk. Cook over medium heat until mixture thickens and boils, stirring constantly. Add broccoli, sour cream, lemon juice and hot pepper sauce. Cook until thoroughly heated, stirring occasionally.

Using sharp knife, remove about ¹/₂-inch slice from top of each roll; set aside. Remove bread from inside of rolls, leaving about ¹/₂-inch shell. Spoon about ¹/₃ cup of hot broccoli mixture into each roll. Place on ungreased cookie sheet or broiler pan. Top each with 1 slice ham, 1 slice tomato and 1 slice cheese. Broil 6 to 8 inches from heat for about 2 minutes or until cheese is melted. (Watch carefully.) Cover each with top of roll. **4 sandwiches.**

NUTRIENTS PER 1 SANDWICH

Calories	440	Protein	35% U.S. RDA
Protein	22g	Vitamin A	20% U.S. RDA
Carbohydrate	40g	Vitamin C	40% U.S. RDA
Fat	21g	Thiamine	30% U.S. RDA
Cholesterol	50mg	Riboflavin	25% U.S. RDA
Sodium	970mg	Niacin	15% U.S. RDA
Potassium	330mg	Calcium	40% U.S. RDA
Dietary Fiber	3g	Iron	10% U.S. RDA

Tex-Mex Biscuit Sandwiches

Elaine Schultz, Florida
Bake-Off® 33, 1988

2¹/₂ ounces (¹/₂ cup) deli roast beef, chopped
¹/₄ cup taco sauce
¹/₄ cup barbecue sauce
¹/₄ cup sliced green onions
¹/₄ cup sliced ripe olives, drained
2 ounces (¹/₂ cup) shredded Cheddar cheese
10-ounce can refrigerated flaky biscuits
2 tablespoons cornmeal
¹/₂ cup dairy sour cream
10 pimiento slices
10 ripe olive slices

Heat oven to 350°F. In medium bowl, combine roast beef, taco sauce, barbecue sauce, green onions, ¹/₄ cup olives and cheese; set aside.

Separate dough into 10 biscuits. Dip both sides of each biscuit in cornmeal. Press or roll out each to 5-inch circle. Place 5 circles on ungreased cookie sheet. Spoon about ¹/₄ cup of roast beef mixture onto center of each circle. Brush edges lightly with water. Place remaining 5 biscuit circles over roast beef mixture. Press edges with fork to seal. Using back of tablespoon, make indentation in center of each sandwich. Sprinkle sandwiches with remaining cornmeal.

Bake at 350°F. for 14 to 22 minutes or until golden brown. Remove from oven; gently repeat indentation if necessary. Fill each with heaping tablespoonful of sour cream. Garnish each with 2 pimiento slices and 2 ripe olive slices. **5 sandwiches.**

NUTRIENTS PER 1 SANDWICH

Calories	340	Protein	20% U.S. RDA
Protein	12g	Vitamin A	10% U.S. RDA
Carbohydrate	31g	Vitamin C	8% U.S. RDA
Fat	19g	Thiamine	15% U.S. RDA
Cholesterol	35mg	Riboflavin	15% U.S. RDA
Sodium	950mg	Niacin	10% U.S. RDA
Potassiuim	200mg	Calcium	15% U.S. RDA
Dietary Fiber	2g	Iron	15% U.S. RDA

Against all odds—

Although a few contestants have not been able to compete at the last minute—two had babies and two had serious health problems—many have competed under trying circumstances. One woman whose husband's dying wish was to have her attend the Bake-Off® did so the day after his funeral. Needless to say, when her indomitable spirit and creativity brought her a $2,000 prize for her efforts, the applause was long and from the hearts of admiring peers.

Pictured top to bottom: Chicken and Cheese Crescent Chimichangas, page 31, Quesadilla Quiche

Quesadilla Quiche

Laurie Keane, California
Bake-Off® 33, 1988

15-ounce package refrigerated pie
  crusts
1 teaspoon flour

FILLING

1 cup coarsely chopped onions
1 tablespoon margarine or butter
1 cup coarsely chopped tomatoes,
  drained
4-ounce can sliced ripe olives,
  drained
¼ teaspoon garlic powder or salt
¼ teaspoon cumin
⅛ teaspoon pepper
4-ounce can chopped green
  chiles, drained
2 eggs, beaten
2 to 3 drops hot pepper sauce
4 ounces (1 cup) shredded
  Monterey jack cheese
4 ounces (1 cup) shredded
  Cheddar cheese

Dairy sour cream, if desired
Salsa or picante sauce, if desired

Prepare pie crust according to package directions for *two-crust pie* using a 10-inch tart pan with removable bottom or a 9-inch pie pan. Place 1 prepared crust in pan; press in bottom and up sides of pan. Trim edges if necessary. Place oven rack at lowest position. Heat oven to 375°F.

In medium skillet, cook onions in margarine until tender. Reserve 1 tablespoon each tomatoes and olives. Stir remaining tomatoes and olives, garlic powder, cumin, pepper and chiles into cooked onions. In small bowl, beat eggs with hot pepper sauce; reserve 2 teaspoons of mixture. To remaining egg mixture, stir in ½ cup of the Monterey jack cheese and ½ cup of the Cheddar cheese. Sprinkle remaining cheeses over bottom of pie crust-lined pan. Spoon onion mixture evenly over cheese. Carefully pour egg mixture over onion mixture; spread to cover. Top with second crust; seal edges. With sharp knife, slit crust in decorative design in several places. Brush with reserved egg mixture.

Bake at 375°F. on lowest oven rack for 45 to 55 minutes or until golden brown. Let stand 5 minutes; remove sides of pan. Serve warm with sour cream, salsa and reserved tomatoes and olives. **6 servings.**

NUTRIENTS PER 1/6 OF RECIPE

Calories	600	Protein	20% U.S. RDA
Protein	15g	Vitamin A	50% U.S. RDA
Carbohydrate	39g	Vitamin C	20% U.S. RDA
Fat	43g	Thiamine	4% U.S. RDA
Cholesterol	140mg	Riboflavin	15% U.S. RDA
Sodium	1120mg	Niacin	2% U.S. RDA
Potassium	280mg	Calcium	35% U.S. RDA
Dietary Fiber	2g	Iron	6% U.S. RDA

Poppin' Fresh® Barbecups

Peter Russell, Kansas
Bake-Off® 19, 1968

1 pound ground beef
½ cup barbecue sauce
1 tablespooon instant minced
  onion or ¼ cup chopped onion
1 to 2 tablespoons brown sugar
10-ounce can refrigerated flaky
  biscuits
2 ounces (½ cup) shredded
  Cheddar or American cheese

Heat oven to 400°F. Grease 10 muffin cups. In large skillet, brown ground beef, drain. Stir in barbecue sauce, instant minced onion and brown sugar. Cook 1 minute to blend flavors, stirring constantly. Separate dough into 10 biscuits. Place 1 biscuit in each greased muffin cup; firmly press in bottom and up sides, forming ¼-inch rim. Spoon about ¼ cup of meat mixture into each biscuit-lined cup. Sprinkle each with cheese. Bake at 400°F. for 10 to 12 minutes or until edges of biscuits are golden brown. Cool 1 minute; remove from pan. **10 servings.**

TIP: To make ahead, prepare, cover and refrigerate up to 2 hours; bake as directed above.

NUTRIENTS PER 1/10 OF RECIPE

Calories	220	Protein	15% U.S. RDA
Protein	11g	Vitamin A	2% U.S. RDA
Carbohydrate	17g	Vitamin C	<2% U.S. RDA
Fat	12g	Thiamine	6% U.S. RDA
Cholesterol	35mg	Riboflavin	8% U.S. RDA
Sodium	460mg	Niacin	15% U.S. RDA
Potassium	150mg	Calcium	4% U.S. RDA
Dietary Fiber	<1g	Iron	8% U.S. RDA

Quesadilla Quiche

Cheese and chiles melted in a tortilla characterize quesadillas, a spicy Mexican cheese sandwich. That great combination becomes a main-dish pie in this recipe.

Poppin' Fresh® Barbecups

This Junior Prize-winning recipe was created by a twelve-year-old boy. He and his sister prepared this great-tasting, simple-to-do recipe for dinner on the nights his mother and dad worked late. Since its creation, Pillsbury has promoted many versions of this recipe.

Chicken 'n Artichoke Crescent Sandwiches

⋄⋄⋄

June Grayson, Oklahoma
Bake-Off® 33, 1988

1 whole chicken breast, skinned, boned, cut into bite-sized pieces*
1/2 teaspoon salt
1/8 teaspoon pepper
2.5-ounce jar sliced mushrooms, drained
1 tablespoon margarine or butter, melted
1 tablespoon oil
1/3 cup mayonnaise or salad dressing
1/8 to 1/4 teaspoon garlic powder
1/8 teaspoon hot pepper sauce
6-ounce jar marinated artichoke hearts, drained, chopped
2-ounce jar chopped pimiento, drained
8-ounce can refrigerated crescent dinner rolls
1 egg white, slightly beaten
1 tablespoon sesame seed
Dairy sour cream, if desired

Heat oven to 375°F. Sprinkle chicken with salt and pepper. In large skillet over medium heat, cook chicken and mushrooms in margarine and oil 3 to 5 minutes or until chicken is tender and slightly brown, stirring occasionally. Remove from heat.

In medium bowl, combine mayonnaise, garlic powder and hot pepper sauce. Stir in artichoke hearts, pimiento and chicken mixture; blend well. Separate dough into 4 rectangles; firmly press perforations to seal. Spoon about 1/2 cup of chicken mixture on half of each rectangle to within 1/4 inch of edges. Fold dough in half over filling; place on ungreased cookie sheet. Press edges with fork to seal. Brush beaten egg white over sandwiches; sprinkle with sesame seed. Bake at 375°F. for 15 to 20 minutes or until centers of sandwiches are golden brown. Serve warm with sour cream. **4 sandwiches.**

TIP: *Use about 1/2 pound skinned, boned chicken.

NUTRIENTS PER 1 SANDWICH

Calories	540	Protein	30% U.S. RDA
Protein	19g	Vitamin A	10% U.S. RDA
Carbohydrate	28g	Vitamin C	10% U.S. RDA
Fat	39g	Thiamine	15% U.S. RDA
Cholesterol	60mg	Riboflavin	15% U.S. RDA
Sodium	1010mg	Niacin	35% U.S. RDA
Potassium	390mg	Calcium	6% U.S. RDA
Dietary Fiber	3g	Iron	15% U.S. RDA

Reuben in the Round Crescents

⋄⋄⋄

Irene Dunn, Ohio
Bake-Off® 27, 1976

2 (8-ounce) cans refrigerated crescent dinner rolls
8-ounce package thinly sliced pastrami or corned beef
6-ounce package (4 slices) Swiss or mozzarella cheese
8-ounce can (1 cup) sauerkraut, drained
1/2 teaspoon caraway seed
1/2 teaspoon sesame seed

Heat oven to 400°F. Separate 1 can of dough into 4 rectangles. Place in ungreased 12-inch pizza pan or 13 × 9-inch pan; firmly press over bottom and 1/2 inch up sides to form crust. Seal perforations. Arrange pastrami, cheese and sauerkraut in layers over dough. Sprinkle with caraway seed. Separate remaining can of dough into 8 triangles. Arrange triangles spoke-fashion over filling with points toward center. Do not seal outer edges of triangles to bottom crust. Sprinkle with sesame seed. Bake at 400°F. for 15 to 25 minutes or until golden brown. Serve immediately. **6 to 8 servings.**

TIPS: To make ahead, prepare, cover and refrigerate up to 2 hours; bake as directed above.

To reheat, cover loosely with foil; heat at 375°F. for 15 to 18 minutes or until warm.

NUTRIENTS PER 1/8 OF RECIPE

Calories	380	Protein	25% U.S. RDA
Protein	15g	Vitamin A	4% U.S. RDA
Carbohydrate	24g	Vitamin C	4% U.S. RDA
Fat	25g	Thiamine	10% U.S. RDA
Cholesterol	50mg	Riboflavin	15% U.S. RDA
Sodium	1000mg	Niacin	15% U.S. RDA
Potassium	240mg	Calcium	20% U.S. RDA
Dietary Fiber	2g	Iron	10% U.S. RDA

Reuben in the Round Crescents

Chiles 'n Ham Cups

Chiles 'n Ham Cups

—◦✣◦—

Audeen Faller, Colorado
Bake-Off® 32, 1986

**10-ounce can refrigerated flaky
    biscuits**
 **3-ounce package cream cheese,
    softened**
 1 cup cubed cooked ham
 ¼ cup sliced ripe olives
 **4 ounces (1 cup) shredded
    Cheddar cheese**
 **4-ounce can chopped green
    chiles, drained***
**10 small pitted ripe olives, if
    desired**

Heat oven to 375°F. Grease 10 muffin
cups. Separate dough into 10 biscuits.
Place 1 biscuit in each greased muffin
cup; firmly press in bottom and up
sides, forming ¼-inch rim.

In large bowl, combine cream cheese,
ham, ¼ cup sliced olives, cheese and
chiles; blend well. Spoon about ¼ cup
of ham mixture into each biscuit-lined
cup. Bake at 375°F. for 20 to 25 minutes or until edges of biscuits are golden
brown. Cool 1 minute; remove from
pan. Garnish each with pitted olive. If
desired, serve with salsa or sour cream.
10 servings.

TIPS: *For a milder flavor, use ¼ cup
of the chopped green chiles.

To reheat, wrap loosely in foil; heat at
350°F. for 20 to 25 minutes or until
warm.

NUTRIENTS PER 1/10 OF RECIPE

Calories	190	Protein	10% U.S. RDA
Protein	8g	Vitamin A	25% U.S. RDA
Carbohydrate	13g	Vitamin C	25% U.S. RDA
Fat	12g	Thiamine	15% U.S. RDA
Cholesterol	30mg	Riboflavin	8% U.S. RDA
Sodium	620mg	Niacin	6% U.S. RDA
Potassium	110mg	Calcium	10% U.S. RDA
Dietary Fiber	1g	Iron	6% U.S. RDA

Potato-Topped Burger Cups

Lillian Cymbala, Connecticut
Bake-Off® 33, 1988

1 pound ground beef
3 tablespoons finely chopped onion
1 garlic clove, minced
1/4 to 1/2 teaspoon cayenne pepper
1/2 teaspoon salt, if desired
1/3 cup chili sauce
1 tablespoon vinegar
10-ounce can refrigerated flaky biscuits

TOPPING
1 1/2 cups water
3 tablespoons margarine or butter
1/2 teaspoon salt
1 1/2 cups mashed potato flakes
3-ounce package cream cheese, softened
1/2 cup coarsely crushed potato chips

Heat oven to 375°F. Grease 10 muffin cups. In large skillet, brown ground beef with onion, garlic and cayenne pepper; drain well. Stir in 1/2 teaspoon salt, chili sauce and vinegar; cook 1 minute to blend flavors, stirring constantly. Set aside. Separate dough into 10 biscuits. Place 1 biscuit in each greased muffin cup; firmly press in bottom and up sides forming 1/4-inch rim.

In medium saucepan, combine water, margarine and 1/2 teaspoon salt; bring to a rolling boil. Remove from heat. Using fork, stir in potato flakes until well blended. Add cream cheese; beat until mixture is smooth. (Mixture will be very thick.)

Spoon about 1/4 cup of meat mixture into each biscuit-lined cup. Spoon topping mixture over each filled cup; press to cover completely. Sprinkle each with potato chips. Bake at 375°F. for 25 to 30 minutes or until edges of biscuits are golden brown. Cool 1 minute; remove from pan. **10 servings.**

NUTRIENTS PER 1/10 OF RECIPE

Calories	300	Protein	15% U.S. RDA
Protein	11g	Vitamin A	8% U.S. RDA
Carbohydrate	23g	Vitamin C	6% U.S. RDA
Fat	18g	Thiamine	10% U.S. RDA
Cholesterol	40mg	Riboflavin	10% U.S. RDA
Sodium	740mg	Niacin	15% U.S. RDA
Potassium	320mg	Calcium	2% U.S. RDA
Dietary Fiber	2g	Iron	10% U.S. RDA

Savory Salmon-Filled Crescents

Carol DuVall, New York
Bake-Off® 26, 1975

16-ounce can salmon or 2 (6 1/2-ounce) cans tuna, drained, flaked
1 1/2 cups seasoned croutons
1/2 cup chopped onion
2 tablespoons chopped fresh parsley or 2 teaspoons parsley flakes
1 teaspoon dill weed
1/2 teaspoon garlic salt
1/4 teaspoon pepper
1/2 cup mayonnaise or salad dressing
1/2 cup dairy sour cream
4 hard-cooked eggs, coarsely chopped
2 (8-ounce) cans refrigerated crescent dinner rolls
1 to 2 tablespoons margarine or butter, melted
Parsley, if desired

Heat oven to 350°F. In medium bowl, combine salmon, croutons, onion, 2 tablespoons parsley, dill weed, garlic salt, pepper, mayonnaise, sour cream and eggs; toss lightly. Separate dough into 8 rectangles; firmly press perforations to seal. Spoon about 1/2 cup of salmon mixture onto center of each rectangle. Pull 4 corners of dough to center of salmon mixture; twist firmly. Pinch edges to seal. Place on ungreased cookie sheets. Brush each with margarine; sprinkle with parsley. Bake at 350°F. for 18 to 28 minutes or until golden brown. Serve immediately. **8 sandwiches.**

TIP: To reheat, wrap loosely in foil; heat at 350°F. for 15 to 20 minutes or until warm.

NUTRIENTS PER 1 SANDWICH

Calories	500	Protein	30% U.S. RDA
Protein	19g	Vitamin A	10% U.S. RDA
Carbohydrate	25g	Vitamin C	2% U.S. RDA
Fat	36g	Thiamine	15% U.S. RDA
Cholesterol	180mg	Riboflavin	20% U.S. RDA
Sodium	770mg	Niacin	30% U.S. RDA
Potassium	410mg	Calcium	20% U.S. RDA
Dietary Fiber	1g	Iron	15% U.S. RDA

Famous Faces at Bake-Off® since 1949

Bob Barker
Pat Boone
Joe E. Brown
Gary Collins
Duke and Duchess of Windsor
Irene Dunne
Greer Garson
Arthur Godfrey
Averell Harriman
Art Linkletter
Mary Ann Mobley
Garry Moore
Patricia Nixon
Tyrone Power
Ivy Baker Priest
Ronald Reagan
Eleanor Roosevelt
Red Skelton
Margaret Truman
Rudy Vallee
Tuesday Weld

Savory Crescent Chicken Squares

Doris Castle, Illinois
Bake-Off® 25, 1974

3-ounce package cream cheese, softened
1 tablespoon margarine or butter, softened
2 cups cubed cooked chicken*
1 tablespoon chopped chives or onion
¼ teaspoon salt
⅛ teaspoon pepper
2 tablespoons milk
1 tablespoon chopped pimiento, if desired
8-ounce can refrigerated crescent dinner rolls
1 tablespoon margarine or butter, melted
¾ cup seasoned croutons, crushed

Heat oven to 350°F. In medium bowl, beat cream cheese and 1 tablespoon softened margarine until smooth. Add chicken, chives, salt, pepper, milk and pimiento; mix well. Separate crescent dough into 4 rectangles; firmly press perforations to seal. Spoon ½ cup of chicken mixture onto center of each rectangle. Pull 4 corners of dough to center of chicken mixture; twist firmly. Pinch edges to seal. Place on ungreased cookie sheet. Brush tops of sandwiches with 1 tablespoon melted margarine; dip in crushed croutons. Bake at 350°F. for 20 to 25 minutes until golden brown. **4 sandwiches.**

TIP: *Two 5-ounce cans chunk chicken, drained and flaked, can be substituted for cubed cooked chicken.

NUTRIENTS PER 1 SANDWICH

Calories	500	Protein	40% U.S. RDA
Protein	27g	Vitamin A	15% U.S. RDA
Carbohydrate	28g	Vitamin C	4% U.S. RDA
Fat	30g	Thiamine	15% U.S. RDA
Cholesterol	110mg	Riboflavin	15% U.S. RDA
Sodium	890mg	Niacin	40% U.S. RDA
Potassium	350mg	Calcium	4% U.S. RDA
Dietary Fiber	1g	Iron	15% U.S. RDA

Ham and Cheese Biscuit Pockets

Carol J. Grass, Colorado
Bake-Off® 31, 1984

1 cup cubed cooked ham
4 ounces (1 cup) shredded Swiss cheese
½ cup finely chopped peeled apple
10-ounce can refrigerated flaky biscuits
1 egg, slightly beaten
1 teaspoon water

Alfalfa sprouts, if desired
Chopped tomato, if desired

Heat oven to 375°F. Lightly grease large cookie sheet. In small bowl, combine ham, cheese and apple. Separate dough into 10 biscuits. On greased cookie sheet, press or roll out 5 biscuits to 4-inch circles. Place about ½ cup of ham mixture onto center of each circle. Press or roll out remaining 5 biscuits to 5-inch circles. Place each over filling. Press edges with fork to seal. Combine egg and water; brush over filled biscuits.

Bake at 375°F. for 13 to 18 minutes or until golden brown. Cut each in half to form pocket sandwiches. To serve, garnish with alfalfa sprouts and tomato. Serve warm. **5 servings.**

TIP: To reheat, wrap loosely in foil; heat at 350°F. for 12 to 15 minutes or until warm.

NUTRIENTS PER 1/5 OF RECIPE

Calories	320	Protein	25% U.S. RDA
Protein	17g	Vitamin A	4% U.S. RDA
Carbohydrate	27g	Vitamin C	8% U.S. RDA
Fat	16g	Thiamine	25% U.S. RDA
Cholesterol	90mg	Riboflavin	20% U.S. RDA
Sodium	1000mg	Niacin	15% U.S. RDA
Potassium	170mg	Calcium	25% U.S. RDA
Dietary Fiber	1g	Iron	10% U.S. RDA

Chaos or calm—

At one event, a very relaxed contestant sat quietly reading a book while she waited for her entry to bake. When queried about her calm demeanor, she said that the Bake-Off® floor was peaceful compared to her home kitchen filled with the exuberance of her five children. In contrast, another finalist, who was used to cooking with only her cat looking on, found it extremely difficult to concentrate on the task at hand and deferred all interviews until she finished.

Ham and Cheese Biscuit Pockets

Crescent Three Cheese Calzone

Crescent Three Cheese Calzone

Irene McEwen, Arizona
Bake-Off® 32, 1986

2 eggs
15-ounce carton (1¾ cups) ricotta cheese
2 ounces (½ cup) shredded mozzarella cheese
¼ cup grated Parmesan cheese
½ teaspoon salt, if desired
½ teaspoon basil leaves
½ teaspoon oregano leaves
¼ teaspoon pepper
1 garlic clove, minced or ⅛ teaspoon instant minced garlic
2 (8-ounce) cans refrigerated crescent dinner rolls

SAUCE
2 (8-ounce) cans tomato sauce with mushrooms*
2 to 4 tablespoons red table wine, if desired
¼ teaspoon basil leaves
¼ teaspoon oregano leaves

Heat oven to 375°F. In large bowl, beat eggs slightly. Add ricotta cheese, mozzarella cheese, Parmesan cheese, salt, ½ teaspoon basil, ½ teaspoon oregano, pepper and garlic; blend well. Separate dough into 8 rectangles; firmly press perforations to seal. Press or roll out each to 7×5-inch rectangle. Spoon scant ⅓ cup of cheese mixture onto half of each rectangle to within 1 inch of edges. Fold dough in half over filling; firmly pinch edges to seal. Place on ungreased cookie sheet. With sharp knife, cut 3 slits in top of each filled rectangle. Bake at 375°F. for 14 to 17 minutes or until deep golden brown.

In small saucepan, combine all sauce ingredients; bring to a boil. Reduce heat; simmer uncovered for 15 minutes to blend flavors. Spoon over each serving. **8 servings.**

TIPS: *An 8-ounce can tomato sauce and a 2.5-ounce jar sliced mushrooms, drained, can be substituted for the tomato sauce with mushrooms.

To reheat, wrap loosely in foil; heat at 375°F. for 15 to 20 minutes or until warm.

NUTRIENTS PER 1/8 OF RECIPE

Calories	350	Protein	25% U.S. RDA
Protein	15g	Vitamin A	20% U.S. RDA
Carbohydrate	30g	Vitamin C	8% U.S. RDA
Fat	19g	Thiamine	15% U.S. RDA
Cholesterol	100mg	Riboflavin	20% U.S. RDA
Sodium	1030mg	Niacin	10% U.S. RDA
Potassium	450mg	Calcium	25% U.S. RDA
Dietary Fiber	2g	Iron	15% U.S. RDA

30 The Pillsbury Bake-Off® Cookbook

Chicken and Cheese Crescent Chimichangas

Marlene Zebleckis, California
Bake-Off® 33, 1988

    1/2 cup chopped onion
      2 garlic cloves, minced
      3 tablespoons oil
  2 1/2 cups shredded cooked chicken
      2 (8-ounce) cans refrigerated
        crescent dinner rolls
    1/2 cup salsa
      8 ounces (2 cups) shredded
        Cheddar cheese

        Dairy sour cream
        Salsa

Heat oven to 350°F. Grease large cookie sheet. In large skillet, cook onion and garlic in oil until onion is tender. Add chicken; cook over low heat until thoroughly heated, stirring occasionally. Remove from heat.

Separate dough into 8 rectangles; firmly press perforations to seal. Spread 2 teaspoonfuls of the salsa on each rectangle to within 1/2 inch of edge. Stir 1 cup of the cheese into chicken mixture. Spoon heaping 1/3 cup of chicken mixture onto half of each rectangle. Starting at shortest side of rectangle topped with chicken, roll up; firmly pinch ends to seal. Place seam side down on greased cookie sheet.

Bake at 350°F. for 16 to 21 minutes or until golden brown. Remove from oven; top each with about 2 tablespoonfuls of remaining cheese. Return to oven. Bake an additional 1 to 2 minutes or until cheese is melted. Serve with sour cream and additional salsa. **8 sandwiches.**

NUTRIENTS PER 1 SANDWICH

Calories	480	Protein	35% U.S. RDA
Protein	22g	Vitamin A	10% U.S. RDA
Carbohydrate	26g	Vitamin C	2% U.S. RDA
Fat	32g	Thiamine	15% U.S. RDA
Cholesterol	80mg	Riboflavin	20% U.S. RDA
Sodium	910mg	Niacin	25% U.S. RDA
Potassium	370mg	Calcium	25% U.S. RDA
Dietary Fiber	1g	Iron	10% U.S. RDA

Tuna Cheese Flips

Marilyn Belschner, Nebraska
Bake-Off® 27, 1976

      2 (6 1/2-ounce) cans tuna, drained,
        flaked
    1/8 teaspoon lemon pepper
        seasoning
    1/3 cup sliced ripe or green olives,
        drained
    1/3 cup mayonnaise or salad
        dressing
      2 ounces (1/2 cup) shredded
        Monterey jack or Cheddar
        cheese
  10-ounce can refrigerated flaky
        biscuits
      1 egg, beaten, or 2 tablespoons
        milk
      1 cup crushed potato chips

Heat oven to 375°F. In small bowl, combine tuna, lemon pepper seasoning, olives, mayonnaise and cheese. Separate dough into 10 biscuits. Press or roll out each to 5-inch circle. Spoon about 1/4 cup of tuna mixture onto center of each circle. Fold dough in half over filling; press edges with fork to seal. Brush both sides of each sandwich with egg; press both sides in chips. Place on ungreased cookie sheet. With sharp knife, make two or three 1/2-inch slits in top of each sandwich. Bake at 375°F. for 18 to 24 minutes or until deep golden brown. **10 sandwiches.**

TIP: To reheat, wrap loosely in foil; heat at 350°F. for 10 to 15 minutes or until warm.

NUTRIENTS PER 1 SANDWICH

Calories	250	Protein	20% U.S. RDA
Protein	14g	Vitamin A	2% U.S. RDA
Carbohydrate	16g	Vitamin C	2% U.S. RDA
Fat	14g	Thiamine	6% U.S. RDA
Cholesterol	60mg	Riboflavin	8% U.S. RDA
Sodium	460mg	Niacin	30% U.S. RDA
Potassium	210mg	Calcium	6% U.S. RDA
Dietary Fiber	1g	Iron	8% U.S. RDA

Chicken and Cheese Crescent Chimichangas

Chimichangas are made with a flour tortilla wrapped around a seasoned filling and fried until crisp. In this recipe, chimichangas are made easier when light, flaky crescents replace the tortilla and they are baked in the oven.

Crescent Chick-Be-Quicks

Rosemarie Berger, North Carolina
Bake-Off® 33, 1988

Crescent Chick-Be-Quicks

To create this hot chicken snack, fresh chicken pieces coated with french fried onions are baked in tiny crescent dough triangles. Serve them with sweet and sour sauce for dipping.

¾ cup crushed canned french fried onions
1 tablespoon flour
¼ teaspoon seasoned salt
8-ounce can refrigerated crescent dinner rolls
1 whole chicken breast, skinned, boned, cut into 16 pieces*
1 egg, beaten
Sesame or poppy seed

Heat oven to 375°F. Lightly grease cookie sheet. In small bowl, combine french fried onions, flour and salt; blend well. Set aside. Separate dough into 8 triangles. Cut each in half lengthwise to make 16 long triangles. Dip chicken pieces in beaten egg; coat with onion mixture. Place one coated piece on wide end of each triangle; roll to opposite point. Place point side down on greased cookie sheet. Brush tops with remaining beaten egg; sprinkle with sesame seed. Bake at 375°F. for 12 to 15 minutes or until golden brown. Serve warm or cold. **16 snacks.**

TIP: *About ½ pound, skinned and boned chicken.

NUTRIENTS PER 1 SNACK

Calories	100	Protein	8% U.S. RDA
Protein	5g	Vitamin A	<2% U.S. RDA
Carbohydrate	7g	Vitamin C	<2% U.S. RDA
Fat	5g	Thiamine	4% U.S. RDA
Cholesterol	30mg	Riboflavin	2% U.S. RDA
Sodium	160mg	Niacin	10% U.S. RDA
Potassium	75mg	Calcium	<2% U.S. RDA
Dietary Fiber	<1g	Iron	2% U.S. RDA

Shrimp Cocktail Crescent Snacks

Carole Ann (Flieller) Aktines, Texas
Bake-Off® 26, 1975

2 tablespoons margarine or butter, melted
1 tablespoon prepared horseradish
1 tablespoon ketchup
1 teaspoon lemon juice
3½-ounce can shrimp, rinsed, drained
8-ounce can refrigerated crescent dinner rolls
1 tablespoon grated Paramesan cheese
Sesame seed

Heat oven to 375°F. In small bowl, combine 1 tablespoon of the margarine, horseradish, ketchup, lemon juice and shrimp; mix well. Separate dough into 8 triangles; cut each in half diagonally to make 16 triangles. Place rounded teaspoonful of shrimp mixture onto center of each triangle. Fold short end of each triangle over filling; fold long end over all. Place on ungreased large cookie sheet. Brush each with remaining margarine; sprinkle with Parmesan cheese and sesame seed. Bake at 375°F. for 15 to 18 minutes or until golden brown. Serve warm. **16 snacks.**

TIP: To make ahead, prepare, cover and refrigerate up to 2 hours; bake as directed above.

NUTRIENTS PER 1 SNACK

Calories	80	Protein	4% U.S. RDA
Protein	3g	Vitamin A	<2% U.S. RDA
Carbohydrate	6g	Vitamin C	<2% U.S. RDA
Fat	5g	Thiamine	2% U.S. RDA
Cholesterol	10mg	Riboflavin	2% U.S. RDA
Sodium	160mg	Niacin	2% U.S. RDA
Potassium	50mg	Calcium	<2% U.S. RDA
Dietary Fiber	0g	Iron	2% U.S. RDA

Shrimp Cocktail Crescent Snacks

Puffy Chiles Rellenos

Helen Novak, California
Bake-Off® 29, 1980

2 (3-ounce) cans whole green chiles
8 ounces Monterey jack or Cheddar cheese
10-ounce can refrigerated flaky biscuits

TOPPING
3 eggs, separated
1/4 teaspoon salt
8 1/4-ounce jar chunky taco sauce

Heat oven to 375°F. Grease cookie sheet. Cut chiles lengthwise to make 10 pieces. Remove seeds and ribs; rinse and drain. Cut cheese into ten 3 × 1/2 × 1/2-inch pieces. Wrap each piece of cheese with piece of chile. Separate dough into 10 biscuits. Press or roll out each to 4-inch circle. Place 1 chile-wrapped cheese piece onto each circle; fold dough over to cover completely. Firmly pinch edges to seal. Form each into finger-shaped roll; place seam side up on greased cookie sheet.*

Bake at 375°F. for 10 to 12 minutes or until light golden brown. Meanwhile, prepare topping. In small bowl, beat egg whites until stiff peaks form. In second small bowl, beat egg yolks and salt. Gently fold egg yolk mixture into beaten egg whites until just blended. Spoon mounds of egg mixture over each partially baked roll, covering each completely. Bake an additional 12 to 15 minutes or until golden brown. In small saucepan, heat taco sauce. Spoon hot taco sauce over chiles rellenos.
10 servings.

TIP: *To make ahead, rellenos can be prepared to this point. Cover and refrigerate up to 2 hours. Continue as directed above.

NUTRIENTS PER 1/10 OF RECIPE

Calories	210	Protein	15% U.S. RDA
Protein	9g	Vitamin A	40% U.S. RDA
Carbohydrate	15g	Vitamin C	10% U.S. RDA
Fat	12g	Thiamine	8% U.S. RDA
Cholesterol	100mg	Riboflavin	10% U.S. RDA
Sodium	800mg	Niacin	4% U.S. RDA
Potassium	130mg	Calcium	20% U.S. RDA
Dietary Fiber	1g	Iron	8% U.S. RDA

Italian Spinach Torta

Torta *is an Italian term for cake or pie. In this recipe, torta is an impressive appetizer pie. Serve thin wedges as the first course at a dinner party.*

Italian Spinach Torta

Larry Elder, North Carolina
Bake-Off® 33, 1988

15-ounce package refrigerated pie crusts
1 teaspoon flour

FILLING
9-ounce package frozen chopped spinach in a pouch, thawed, squeezed to drain
1 cup ricotta cheese
1/2 cup grated Parmesan cheese
1/4 to 1/2 teaspoon garlic salt
1/4 teaspoon pepper
1 egg, separated
1 teaspoon water

Prepare pie crust according to package directions for *two-crust pie* using 10-inch tart pan with removable bottom or 9-inch pie pan. Place 1 prepared crust in pan; press in bottom and up sides of pan. Trim edges if necessary. Place oven rack at lowest position. Heat oven to 400°F.

In medium bowl, combine spinach, ricotta cheese, Parmesan cheese, garlic salt, pepper and egg yolk; blend well. Spread evenly over pie crust-lined pan.

To make lattice top, cut remaining crust into 3/4-inch wide strips. Arrange strips in lattice design over spinach mixture. Trim and seal edges. In small bowl, combine egg white and water; beat well. Gently brush over lattice. Bake at 400°F. on lowest oven rack for 45 to 50 minutes or until dark golden brown. Cool 10 minutes; remove sides of pan. Serve warm. **10 to 12 servings.**

TIP: Cover torta with foil during last 5 to 10 minutes of baking if necessary to prevent excessive browning.

NUTRIENTS PER 1/12 OF RECIPE

Calories	220	Protein	8% U.S. RDA
Protein	6g	Vitamin A	10% U.S. RDA
Carbohydrate	18g	Vitamin C	<2% U.S. RDA
Fat	14g	Thiamine	<2% U.S. RDA
Cholesterol	30mg	Riboflavin	6% U.S. RDA
Sodium	480mg	Niacin	<2% U.S. RDA
Potassium	135mg	Calcium	15% U.S. RDA
Dietary Fiber	1g	Iron	2% U.S. RDA

Italian Spinach Torta

Italian Biscuit Flat Bread

Italian Biscuit Flat Bread
꙳

Edith L. Shulman, Texas
Bake-Off® 32, 1986

⅓ cup mayonnaise or salad
   dressing
⅓ cup grated Parmesan cheese
¼ teaspoon basil leaves
¼ teaspoon oregano leaves
3 green onions, sliced
1 garlic clove, minced, or ⅛
   teaspoon garlic powder
10-ounce can refrigerated flaky
   biscuits

Heat oven to 400°F. In small bowl, combine mayonnaise and Parmesan cheese; stir in basil, oregano, green onions and garlic. Separate dough into 10 biscuits. On ungreased cookie sheets, press or roll out each biscuit to 4-inch circle. Spread about 1 tablespoonful of cheese mixture over each circle to within ¼ inch of edge. Bake at 400°F. for 10 to 13 minutes or until golden brown. Serve warm. **10 servings.**

NUTRIENTS PER 1/10 OF RECIPE

Calories	160	Protein	4% U.S. RDA
Protein	3g	Vitamin A	<2% U.S. RDA
Carbohydrate	12g	Vitamin C	<2% U.S. RDA
Fat	11g	Thiamine	<2% U.S. RDA
Cholesterol	6mg	Riboflavin	4% U.S. RDA
Sodium	390mg	Niacin	4% U.S. RDA
Potassium	35mg	Calcium	6% U.S. RDA
Dietary Fiber	1g	Iron	4% U.S. RDA

Crescent Oriental Egg Rolls
꙳

Judith Wilson Merritt, New York
Bake-Off® 32, 1986

PLUM SAUCE
4.75-ounce jar strained plums with
   tapioca baby food*
3 tablespoons brown sugar
2 tablespoons vinegar
¼ teaspoon instant minced onion
⅛ teaspoon garlic powder
⅛ teaspoon ginger

EGG ROLLS
1 cup finely shredded cabbage
½ cup shredded carrots
½ cup finely chopped celery
1 tablespoon oil
½ pound ground beef
1 teaspoon sugar
¼ teaspoon garlic powder
   Dash pepper
2 to 3 tablespoons peanut butter
2 to 4 teaspoons soy sauce
2 (8-ounce) cans refrigerated
   crescent dinner rolls**
1 egg, slightly beaten
1 tablespoon sesame seed

In small saucepan, combine all sauce ingredients; mix well. Bring to a boil, stirring constantly. Remove from heat; cool.

Heat oven to 375°F. Grease large cookie sheet. In large skillet, cook cabbage, carrots and celery in oil until crisp-tender, stirring constantly. Remove vegetables from skillet; set aside. In same skillet, brown ground beef; drain. Stir in sugar, ¼ teaspoon garlic powder, pepper, peanut butter and soy sauce; cook until peanut butter is melted, stirring frequently. Remove from heat; stir in cooked vegetables.

Separate 1 can dough into 4 rectangles; firmly press perforations to seal. Press or roll out each to 6 × 4-inch rectangle. Cut each rectangle crosswise into three 4 × 2-inch pieces. Spoon 1 tablespoonful of filling on half of each small rectangle to within ¼ inch of edges. Fold dough in half over filling; pinch edges to seal. Roll slightly to form 3-inch egg roll shape. Place on greased cookie sheet. Repeat with remaining can of dough. Brush beaten egg over rolls; sprinkle with sesame seed. Bake at 375°F. for 12 to 16 minutes or until golden brown. Serve warm with plum sauce. **24 egg rolls.**

TIPS: *One-half cup canned plums can be substituted for baby food. Drain and pit plums; puree in food processor.

**For best results, keep dough refrigerated until ready to use.

To make ahead, prepare, cover and refrigerate up to 2 hours; bake as directed above.

To reheat, wrap loosely in foil; heat at 375°F. for 15 to 18 minutes or until warm.

NUTRIENTS PER 1 EGG ROLL

Calories	120	Protein	6% U.S. RDA
Protein	4g	Vitamin A	10% U.S. RDA
Carbohydrate	11g	Vitamin C	2% U.S. RDA
Fat	7g	Thiamine	4% U.S. RDA
Cholesterol	20mg	Riboflavin	4% U.S. RDA
Sodium	240mg	Niacin	6% U.S. RDA
Potassium	115mg	Calcium	<2% U.S. RDA
Dietary Fiber	<1g	Iron	4% U.S. RDA

Mushroom Phyllo Tarts

❧

Melissa Daston, Maryland
Bake-Off® 33, 1988

3-ounce package cream cheese, softened
¼ cup dry bread crumbs
1 tablespoon dill weed
½ teaspoon salt
¾ cup dairy sour cream
1 to 2 tablespoons lemon juice
4.5-ounce jar sliced mushrooms, drained
1 garlic clove, minced
½ cup butter or margarine
8 (17 × 12-inch) frozen phyllo (fillo) pastry sheets, thawed
4.5-ounce jar whole mushrooms, drained

Heat oven to 350°F. In small bowl, combine cream cheese, bread crumbs, dill weed, salt, sour cream and lemon juice; blend well. Stir in sliced mushrooms. Set aside. In small skillet, over medium heat, cook garlic in butter, about 1 minute. Coat inside of 16 muffin cups with garlic butter; set aside.

Brush large cookie sheet with garlic butter. On work surface, unroll phyllo sheets; cover with plastic wrap or towel. Brush one phyllo sheet lightly with garlic butter; place buttered side up on buttered cookie sheet. Brush second phyllo sheet lightly with garlic butter; place buttered side up on top of first sheet. Repeat with remaining phyllo sheets. With sharp knife, cut through all layers of phyllo sheets to make sixteen 3 × 4¼-inch rectangles. Place one rectangle in each buttered muffin cup. Spoon heaping tablespoonful of cream cheese mixture into each cup. Top each with whole mushrooms, pushing stems into cream cheese mixture; drizzle with remaining garlic butter. Bake at 350°F. for 18 to 20 minutes or until light golden brown. **16 appetizers.**

NUTRIENTS PER 1 APPETIZER

Calories	120	Protein	2% U.S. RDA
Protein	2g	Vitamin A	8% U.S. RDA
Carbohydrate	5g	Vitamin C	2% U.S. RDA
Fat	10g	Thiamine	<2% U.S. RDA
Cholesterol	25mg	Riboflavin	4% U.S. RDA
Sodium	230mg	Niacin	2% U.S. RDA
Potassium	60mg	Calcium	2% U.S. RDA
Dietary Fiber	0g	Iron	2% U.S. RDA

Mushroom Phyllo Tarts

❧

Tender, flaky phyllo dough is placed in muffin cups, filled with a well-seasoned cream cheese mixture and topped with whole mushrooms to create this appetizer. These are easy to make and so impressive to serve!

Hungry Boy's Casserole, page 48

Main Dishes and Side Dishes

During the early years of the Bake-Off® Contest, it was not uncommon for a prizewinning main dish recipe to call for more than fifteen ingredients. Contest rules at that time required that each entry "must be able to be completed in one day."

Today's favorite Bake-Off® recipes have a more streamlined look. Also, vegetables and other fresh ingredients play an increasingly important role in meals. The familiar ingredients of Broccoli Cauliflower Tetrazzini take on a distinctive personality as they are combined in a new way. Easy yet glamorous one-dish meals like Chicken Prosciutto with Mushroom Sauce feature unique combinations of vegetables and other flavorful ingredients.

Yesteryear's favorite main dish staples—ground beef and ham—are flanked by today's choices, chicken and fish. Light 'n Easy Seafood Dinner and Chicken Broccoli Stroganoff demonstrate this trend. At the same time, recipes like Biscuit Stuffin' Atop Chops indicate an enduring love for hearty, down-home main dishes.

Flavor combinations are often reminiscent of old-time regional and foreign classics. Italian Cheese Rustica Pie, Oriental Cornish Chicks and Hearty Mexican Pizza are among the recipes that so deliciously incorporate foreign flavors with familiar American ingredients. But the recipe preparation techniques—with an emphasis on convenience products— are anything but old-time.

In this chapter, you'll find popular Bake-Off® recipes from decades past—often updated to add cooking convenience—as well as the best from recent contests. All are sure to become favorites in your file of special main dishes and side dishes.

Italian-Style Fish and Vegetables

Italian-Style Fish and Vegetables

Louise Bobzin, Florida
Bake-Off® 33, 1988

2 tablespoons olive or vegetable oil
1 medium onion, sliced
2.5-ounce jar sliced mushrooms, drained
½ teaspoon basil leaves
½ teaspoon fennel seed
2 cups frozen mixed vegetables
1½ pounds fresh or frozen catfish, orange roughy or sole fillets, thawed
¼ teaspoon salt
¼ teaspoon pepper
2 medium tomatoes, sliced
⅓ cup grated Parmesan cheese

In large skillet over medium heat, heat oil. Add onion, mushrooms, basil and fennel seed; cook 4 minutes or until onion is tender. Stir in frozen vegetables. Place fish over vegetables; sprinkle with salt and pepper. Arrange tomato slices over fish. Reduce heat to low; cover and cook 12 to 16 minutes or until fish flakes easily with fork. Remove from heat; sprinkle with Parmesan cheese. Cover; let stand about 3 minutes or until Parmesan cheese is melted. **6 servings.**

NUTRIENTS PER 1/6 OF RECIPE

Calories	240	Protein	40% U.S. RDA
Protein	25g	Vitamin A	60% U.S. RDA
Carbohydrate	11g	Vitamin C	10% U.S. RDA
Fat	10g	Thiamine	8% U.S. RDA
Cholesterol	70mg	Riboflavin	6% U.S. RDA
Sodium	400mg	Niacin	15% U.S. RDA
Potassium	590mg	Calcium	10% U.S. RDA
Dietary Fiber	3g	Iron	8% U.S. RDA

Crafty Crescent Lasagne

Betty Taylor, Texas
Bake-Off® 19, 1968

MEAT FILLING
½ pound pork sausage
½ pound ground beef
¾ cup chopped onions
1 tablespoon parsley flakes
½ teaspoon basil leaves
½ teaspoon oregano leaves
1 small garlic clove, minced
Dash pepper
6-ounce can tomato paste

CHEESE FILLING
¼ cup grated Parmesan cheese
1 cup creamed cottage cheese
1 egg

CRUST
2 (8-ounce) cans refrigerated crescent dinner rolls
2 (7 × 4-inch) slices mozzarella cheese
1 tablespoon milk
1 tablespoon sesame seed

In large skillet, brown sausage and ground beef; drain. Stir in remaining meat filling ingredients; simmer uncovered 5 minutes, stirring occasionally.

Heat oven to 375°F. In small bowl, combine all cheese filling ingredients; blend well. Unroll dough into 4 long rectangles. Place on ungreased cookie sheet with long sides overlapping ½ inch; firmly press edges and perforations to seal. Press or roll out to form 15 × 13-inch rectangle. Spoon half of meat filling mixture in 6-inch strip lengthwise down center of dough to within 1 inch of each end. Spoon cheese filling mixture over meat mixture; top with remaining meat mixture. Arrange mozzarella cheese slices over meat mixture. Fold shortest sides of dough 1 inch over filling. Fold long sides of dough tightly over filling, overlapping edges in center ¼ inch; firmly pinch center seam and ends to seal. Brush with milk; sprinkle with sesame seed. Bake at 375°F. for 23 to 27 minutes or until deep golden brown. **6 to 8 servings.**

TIP: To reheat, wrap loosely in foil; heat at 375°F. for 18 to 20 minutes or until warm.

NUTRIENTS PER 1/8 OF RECIPE

Calories	430	Protein	35% U.S. RDA
Protein	22g	Vitamin A	15% U.S. RDA
Carbohydrate	30g	Vitamin C	10% U.S. RDA
Fat	25g	Thiamine	20% U.S. RDA
Cholesterol	80mg	Riboflavin	20% U.S. RDA
Sodium	1070mg	Niacin	20% U.S. RDA
Potassium	520mg	Calcium	20% U.S. RDA
Dietary Fiber	2g	Iron	15% U.S. RDA

Crafty Crescent Lasagne

A crescent dough crust is stuffed with a well-seasoned meat and cheese filling. It's a crafty way to get to a great-tasting lasagne.

Oriental Cornish Chicks

Oriental Cornish Chicks

Lentsey M. Carlson, New York
Bake-Off® 31, 1984

**10-ounce package frozen long grain
rice with peas and mushrooms
in a pouch**
**¼ cup thinly sliced water
chestnuts**
**1 teaspoon finely chopped
candied ginger**
**8-ounce can (4 slices) sliced
pineapple, cut into bite-sized
pieces, drained, reserving
2 tablespoons liquid**
2 (1½-pound) Cornish game hens
3 tablespoons margarine or butter
1½ teaspoons paprika

Parsley, if desired
Fresh fruit, if desired

Heat oven to 450°F. Cook rice as directed on package. In small bowl, combine cooked rice, water chestnuts, ginger and pineapple; toss lightly. Spoon equal portions of rice mixture into body cavity of each hen. Secure openings with toothpicks or wooden skewers. Place hens breast side up on rack in shallow roasting pan. If desired, tie legs together and wings to body with string.

In small saucepan, melt margarine. Stir in paprika and reserved 2 tablespoons pineapple liquid. Brush half of margarine mixture over hens. Place hens in oven; immediately reduce oven temperature to 350°F. Bake 1 to 1¼ hours or until golden brown and tender, basting occasionally with remaining margarine mixture and pan drippings. (Remove string from legs after first 30 minutes of baking.) Let stand 5 minutes before serving. Garnish with parsley and fresh fruit. **2 to 4 servings.**

MICROWAVE DIRECTIONS: Make a small slit in center of rice pouch. Microwave on MEDIUM for 3 to 4 minutes to partially thaw. In small bowl, separate rice and vegetables. Add water chestnuts, ginger and pineapple; toss lightly. Spoon equal portions of rice mixture into body cavity of each hen. Secure openings with toothpicks or wooden skewers. If desired, tie legs together and wings to body with string.

Place margarine in small microwave-safe bowl. Microwave on HIGH for 30 to 45 seconds or until melted. Stir in paprika and reserved 2 tablespoons pineapple liquid. Brush half of margarine mixture over hens. Place hens breast side down in 12 × 8-inch or 8-inch (2 quart) square microwave-safe baking dish. Cover; microwave on HIGH for 18 minutes, rotating dish ½ turn halfway through cooking. Turn hens breast side up; baste with remaining margarine mixture. Microwave on HIGH for 6 minutes or until juices run clear when pierced with fork between thigh and body of hens. If juices are not clear, rotate dish and microwave on HIGH an additional 2 to 6 minutes. Let stand 5 minutes before serving.

TIP: Body cavities of hens vary in size. Any leftover rice mixture can be baked in oven or heated in microwave-safe container in microwave.

NUTRIENTS PER 1/4 OF RECIPE

Calories	460	Protein	50% U.S. RDA
Protein	35g	Vitamin A	25% U.S. RDA
Carbohydrate	37g	Vitamin C	110% U.S. RDA
Fat	19g	Thiamine	30% U.S. RDA
Cholesterol	100mg	Riboflavin	20% U.S. RDA
Sodium	370mg	Niacin	60% U.S. RDA
Potassium	740mg	Calcium	6% U.S. RDA
Dietary Fiber	1g	Iron	20% U.S. RDA

Biscuit-Topped Italian Casserole

Robert Wick, Florida
Bake-Off® 33, 1988

1 pound ground beef
½ cup chopped onion
1 tablespoon oil, if desired
¾ cup water
½ teaspoon salt, if desired
¼ teaspoon pepper
8-ounce can tomato sauce
6-ounce can tomato paste
8 ounces (2 cups) shredded mozzarella cheese
9-ounce package frozen mixed vegetables in a pouch, thawed
2 (10-ounce) cans refrigerated flaky biscuits
1 tablespoon margarine or butter, melted
½ teaspoon oregano leaves, crushed

Heat oven to 375°F. Grease 13 × 9-inch (3-quart) baking dish. In large skillet, brown ground beef and onion in oil; drain. Stir in water, salt, pepper, tomato sauce and tomato paste; simmer 15 minutes, stirring occasionally. Place half of *hot* meat mixture in greased baking dish; sprinkle with ⅔ cup of the cheese. Spoon mixed vegetables evenly over cheese; sprinkle an additional ⅔ cup cheese over vegetables. Spoon remaining *hot* meat mixture evenly over cheese and vegetables; sprinkle with remaining ⅔ cup cheese.

Separate dough into 20 biscuits. Separate each biscuit into 3 layers. Arrange layers over hot meat mixture, overlapping, in 3 rows of 20 layers each. Gently brush biscuits with margarine; sprinkle with oregano. Bake at 375°F. for 22 to 27 minutes or until biscuit topping is golden brown. **8 to 10 servings.**

NUTRIENTS PER 1/10 OF RECIPE

Calories	380	Protein	25% U.S. RDA
Protein	15g	Vitamin A	40% U.S. RDA
Carbohydrate	34g	Vitamin C	15% U.S. RDA
Fat	20g	Thiamine	25% U.S. RDA
Cholesterol	30mg	Riboflavin	20% U.S. RDA
Sodium	1340mg	Niacin	20% U.S. RDA
Potassium	420mg	Calcium	20% U.S. RDA
Dietary Fiber	3g	Iron	15% U.S. RDA

The great skillet hunt—

Pillsbury supplies all of the utensils as well as the ingredients needed by each contestant to bake the contest recipe. Occasionally the search for specialized cooking gear can lead to some exciting moments. On the eve of the 8th Bake-Off®, it was discovered that an iron skillet desired by a finalist had not been manufactured for many years. A task force of Pillsbury managers and advertising executives from the company's agency fanned out across Manhattan to suppliers of cooking utensils. Retailers and wholesalers were telephoned at their homes to lead the search through storage rooms, basements and musty warehouses. It was nearly 2 A.M. when Bake-Off® headquarters received a call that the proper skillet had been located in a warehouse in Brooklyn, putting an end to one of the greatest skillet hunts in history.

Chicken Prosciutto with Mushroom Sauce

Frances Kovar, New York
Bake-Off® 33, 1988

3 whole chicken breasts, skinned, boned, halved
5 tablespoons margarine or butter
¼ cup chopped onion
¼ cup all purpose or unbleached flour
2 tablespoons Dijon mustard
1 cup chicken broth
1 cup half-and-half
¼ cup dry white wine or water
3 (4.5-ounce) jars sliced mushrooms, drained
4 ounces (1 cup) shredded Swiss cheese
16-ounce package frozen cut broccoli
6 slices prosciutto or thinly sliced cooked ham
Paprika

Place 1 chicken breast half between 2 pieces of plastic wrap. Pound chicken with meat mallet or rolling pin until about ¼ inch thick; remove wrap. Repeat with remaining chicken breasts.

Heat oven to 400°F. In large skillet over medium heat, melt 2 tablespoons of the margarine. Cook chicken in margarine until lightly browned on both sides, about 5 minutes. Remove chicken. In same skillet, melt remaining 3 tablespoons margarine; add onion. Cook until onion is tender, about 2 minutes, stirring frequently. Remove from heat; stir in flour and mustard. Gradually stir in chicken broth, half-and-half and wine. Cook over low heat until mixture thickens and boils, stirring constantly. Add mushrooms and ½ cup of the cheese; stir until cheese is melted.

Arrange broccoli in bottom of ungreased 13 × 9-inch (3-quart) baking dish. Spoon half (2 cups) of sauce over broccoli. Alternate ham slices and chicken breasts, slightly overlapping, over sauce and broccoli down center of dish. Tuck ends of ham slices under chicken. Pour remaining sauce over chicken.

Bake at 400°F. for 20 to 30 minutes or until chicken is tender and no longer pink. Remove from oven; sprinkle with remaining ½ cup cheese and paprika. Bake an additional 2 minutes or until cheese is melted. **6 servings.**

NUTRIENTS PER 1/6 OF RECIPE

Calories	460	Protein	70% U.S. RDA
Protein	42g	Vitamin A	30% U.S. RDA
Carbohydrate	13g	Vitamin C	70% U.S. RDA
Fat	25g	Thiamine	25% U.S. RDA
Cholesterol	110mg	Riboflavin	30% U.S. RDA
Sodium	1040mg	Niacin	70% U.S. RDA
Potassium	680mg	Calcium	30% U.S. RDA
Dietary Fiber	3g	Iron	15% U.S. RDA

Grand Prize Winner

Chick-n-Broccoli Pot Pies

Linda Wood, Indiana
Bake-Off® 28, 1978

10-ounce can refrigerated flaky biscuits
3 ounces (⅔ cup) shredded Cheddar or American cheese
⅔ cup crisp rice cereal
9-ounce package frozen cut broccoli in a pouch, cooked, well drained
1 cup cubed cooked chicken or turkey
10¾-ounce can condensed cream of chicken or mushroom soup
⅓ cup slivered or sliced almonds

Heat oven to 375°F. Separate dough into 10 biscuits. Place 1 biscuit in each ungreased muffin cup; firmly press in bottom and up sides forming ½-inch rim over edge of muffin cup. Spoon about 1 tablespoonful each of cheese and cereal into each biscuit-lined cup. Press mixture into bottom of each cup. Cut large pieces of broccoli in half. In large bowl, combine broccoli, chicken and soup; mix well. Spoon about ⅓ cup of chicken mixture over cereal. Sprinkle with almonds. Bake at 375°F. for 20 to 25 minutes or until edges of biscuits are deep golden brown. **10 servings.**

NUTRIENTS PER 1/10 OF RECIPE

Calories	210	Protein	15% U.S. RDA
Protein	10g	Vitamin A	15% U.S. RDA
Carbohydrate	18g	Vitamin C	10% U.S. RDA
Fat	11g	Thiamine	10% U.S. RDA
Cholesterol	25mg	Riboflavin	10% U.S. RDA
Sodium	620mg	Niacin	15% U.S. RDA
Potassium	160mg	Calcium	8% U.S. RDA
Dietary Fiber	2g	Iron	8% U.S. RDA

Chicken Prosciutto with Mushroom Sauce

Zucchini Crescent Supper Torte

Zucchini Crescent Supper Torte

Kristy McMath, California
Bake-Off® 33, 1988

8-ounce can refrigerated crescent dinner rolls
4 slices bacon
4 cups thinly sliced zucchini
½ cup finely chopped onion
⅓ cup finely chopped green bell pepper
1 garlic clove, minced
1 cup tomatoes, chopped, seeded, drained
½ teaspoon salt
½ teaspoon Italian seasoning
¼ teaspoon pepper
8 ounces (2 cups) shredded Cheddar cheese

TOPPING
½ cup all purpose or unbleached flour
¼ cup grated Parmesan cheese
1 teaspoon baking powder
½ teaspoon salt
½ cup milk
8-ounce carton (1 cup) plain yogurt
2 eggs

Heat oven to 375°F. Separate dough into 8 triangles. Place in ungreased 9-inch springform pan or 9-inch square pan; press over bottom and ¾ of the way up sides to form crust. Seal perforations.

In large skillet, cook bacon until crisp. Remove bacon from skillet; drain, reserving 1 tablespoon drippings in skillet. Crumble bacon; set aside. Add zucchini, onion, green pepper and garlic to drippings in skillet; cook over medium heat until vegetables are tender.* Stir in cooked bacon, tomatoes, 1/2 teaspoon salt, Italian seasoning and pepper. Spoon into crust-lined pan; sprinkle with Cheddar cheese. Lightly spoon flour into measuring cup; level off. In medium bowl, combine all topping ingredients; beat until smooth. Pour over vegetable mixture.

Bake at 375°F. for 50 to 55 minutes or until top is puffed and deep golden brown around edges. Cool 10 minutes on wire rack. Carefully remove sides of pan. To serve, cut into wedges. Serve immediately. **8 servings.**

TIP: *If zucchini mixture is watery, drain well.

HIGH ALTITUDE—Above 3500 Feet: No change.

NUTRIENTS PER 1/8 OF RECIPE

Calories	340	Protein	25% U.S. RDA
Protein	17g	Vitamin A	15% U.S. RDA
Carbohydrate	24g	Vitamin C	20% U.S. RDA
Fat	20g	Thiamine	15% U.S. RDA
Cholesterol	110mg	Riboflavin	20% U.S. RDA
Sodium	880mg	Niacin	8% U.S. RDA
Potassium	440mg	Calcium	35% U.S. RDA
Dietary Fiber	2g	Iron	10% U.S. RDA

Italian Country Loaf Rustica
—✿—

Miranda Desantis, New Jersey
Bake-Off® 33, 1988

FILLING
- 1 pound sweet Italian sausage
- 1/2 cup chopped onion
- 2 to 4 garlic cloves, minced
- 8 ounces (2 cups) cubed mozzarella cheese
- 7-ounce jar mild roasted red peppers, drained, chopped*

BREAD
- 1 1/2 cups all purpose or unbleached flour**
- 1/2 cup whole wheat flour
- 1/2 cup yellow cornmeal
- 1 tablespoon sugar
- 1/2 teaspoon salt
- 1 package fast-acting dry yeast
- 1 1/4 cups hot water (120 to 130°F.)
- 2 teaspoons margarine or butter, softened
- 1 egg, beaten
- 2 to 3 teaspoons sesame seed

If sausage comes in casing, remove casing; break up. In large skillet, brown sausage, onion and garlic.*** Drain; set aside.

Lightly spoon flour into measuring cup; level off. In large bowl, combine 1/2 cup all purpose flour, whole wheat flour, cornmeal, sugar, salt and yeast; blend well. Stir in water and margarine; mix well. Stir in remaining 1 cup all purpose flour to form a stiff batter. Cover; let rest 10 minutes.

Grease 9 or 10-inch springform pan. Stir down dough. Spread about 2/3 of dough in bottom and 2 inches up sides of greased pan. Add cheese and peppers to meat mixture; spoon over dough. Gently pull dough on sides over meat mixture. Drop tablespoonfuls of remaining dough over filling. With back of spoon or buttered fingers, carefully spread to cover. (Top will appear rough.) Cover loosely with plastic wrap and cloth towel. Let rise in warm place (80 to 85°F.) until light, 20 to 30 minutes.

Heat oven to 400°F. Brush top of dough with beaten egg; sprinkle with sesame seed. Bake at 400°F. for 25 to 35 minutes or until bread begins to pull away from sides of pan and edges are deep golden brown. Cool 5 minutes. Loosen edges with knife; remove sides of pan. To serve, cut into wedges. Store in refrigerator. **8 servings.**

TIPS: *Two medium (1 1/4 cups) chopped red bell peppers can be substituted for roasted red peppers.

**Self-rising flour is not recommended.

***If using chopped red bell peppers, cook with sausage, onion and garlic. Continue as directed above.

HIGH ALTITUDE—Above 3500 Feet: No change.

NUTRIENTS PER 1/8 OF RECIPE

Calories	350	Protein	30% U.S. RDA
Protein	19g	Vitamin A	30% U.S. RDA
Carbohydrate	35g	Vitamin C	50% U.S. RDA
Fat	15g	Thiamine	30% U.S. RDA
Cholesterol	70mg	Riboflavin	20% U.S. RDA
Sodium	550mg	Niacin	15% U.S. RDA
Potassium	270mg	Calcium	25% U.S. RDA
Dietary Fiber	3g	Iron	15% U.S. RDA

Italian Country Loaf Rustica
—✿—

Savory Italian sausage, cheese and red peppers are baked inside batter bread to make a hearty, attractive main dish. Surprisingly easy to prepare, it is sliced into wedges to serve.

Zucchini Crescent Supper Torte
—✿—

An impressive main dish in a crust. Seasoned garden-fresh vegetables are the filling, and a souffle-like topping is the finishing touch. Superb!

Hungry Boy's Casserole

Mira Walilko, Michigan
Bake-Off® 15, 1963

Hungry Boy's Casserole

Light, tender biscuits top this beef-and-bean casserole. It is a Grand Prize winner that will satisfy the heartiest appetites.

1½ pounds ground beef
1 cup chopped celery
½ cup chopped onion
½ cup chopped green bell pepper
1 garlic clove, minced
6-ounce can tomato paste
¾ cup water
1 teaspoon paprika
½ teaspoon salt
16-ounce can pork and beans, undrained
15-ounce can garbanzo beans or lima beans, drained

BISCUITS
1½ cups all purpose, unbleached or self-rising flour*
2 teaspoons baking powder
½ teaspoon salt
¼ cup margarine or butter
½ to ¾ cup milk
2 tablespoons sliced stuffed green olives
1 tablespoon slivered almonds

In large skillet, combine ground beef, celery, onion, green pepper and garlic. Cook until meat is browned and vegetables are tender; drain. Stir in tomato paste, water, paprika and ½ teaspoon salt. Add pork and beans and garbanzo beans; simmer while preparing biscuits, stirring occasionally.

Heat oven to 425°F. Lightly spoon flour into measuring cup; level off. In large bowl, combine flour, baking powder and ½ teaspoon salt; mix well. Using pastry blender or fork, cut in margarine until mixture resembles coarse crumbs. Gradually stir in enough milk until mixture leaves sides of bowl and forms a soft, moist dough. On floured surface, gently knead dough 8 times. Roll dough to ¼-inch thickness; cut with floured 2½-inch doughnut cutter, saving holes.

Reserve ½ cup of hot meat mixture. Pour remaining hot meat mixture into ungreased 13×9-inch (3-quart) baking dish. Arrange biscuits without centers over hot meat mixture. Stir olives and almonds into reserved ½ cup meat mixture; spoon into hole of each biscuit. Top each with biscuit holes.

Bake at 425°F. for 15 to 25 minutes or until biscuits are golden brown.
6 to 8 servings.

TIP: *If using self-rising flour, omit baking powder and salt in biscuits.

HIGH ALTITUDE—Above 3500 Feet: No change.

NUTRIENTS PER 1/8 OF RECIPE

Calories	450	Protein	35% U.S. RDA
Protein	24g	Vitamin A	25% U.S. RDA
Carbohydrate	42g	Vitamin C	25% U.S. RDA
Fat	21g	Thiamine	15% U.S. RDA
Cholesterol	60mg	Riboflavin	20% U.S. RDA
Sodium	1010mg	Niacin	30% U.S. RDA
Potassium	740mg	Calcium	15% U.S. RDA
Dietary Fiber	7g	Iron	25% U.S. RDA

Potato-Beef Quick Meal

Ruth Emerson, Nebraska
Bake-Off® 25, 1974

2 pounds ground beef
1 cup chopped onions
¼ cup chopped green bell pepper
1 teaspoon brown sugar
Dash cayenne pepper, if desired
1¾ cups water
½ cup chili sauce or ketchup
½ teaspoon Worcestershire sauce
1 package au gratin or cheese scalloped potato mix
16-ounce can tomatoes, undrained, cut up
1 to 2 ounces (¼ to ½ cup) shredded mozzarella cheese

Heat oven to 350°F. In large ovenproof skillet, brown ground beef; drain. Add onions, green pepper, brown sugar, cayenne pepper, water, chili sauce, Worcestershire sauce, potato slices, contents of seasoning mix envelope and tomatoes; mix well. Bring mixture to a boil; stir. Carefully place skillet in oven. Bake at 350°F. for 35 to 45 minutes or until potatoes are tender, stirring occasionally. Sprinkle with cheese. Bake an additional 1 to 2 minutes or until cheese is melted. **8 (1-cup) servings.**

NUTRIENTS PER 1/8 OF RECIPE

Calories	300	Protein	35% U.S. RDA
Protein	22g	Vitamin A	20% U.S. RDA
Carbohydrate	13g	Vitamin C	25% U.S. RDA
Fat	18g	Thiamine	6% U.S. RDA
Cholesterol	70mg	Riboflavin	10% U.S. RDA
Sodium	410mg	Niacin	25% U.S. RDA
Potassium	510mg	Calcium	8% U.S. RDA
Dietary Fiber	3g	Iron	15% U.S. RDA

Potato-Beef Quick Meal

Chicken Picadillo Pie

Nina Reyes, Florida
Bake-Off® 32, 1986

15-ounce package refrigerated pie crusts
1 teaspoon flour

FILLING
1 tablespoon margarine or butter
1 tablespoon cornstarch
⅛ teaspoon ginger
Dash pepper
1 tablespoon prepared mustard
1 tablespoon soy sauce, if desired
1 tablespoon Worcestershire sauce
1 cup orange juice
2 tablespoons margarine or butter
2 large whole chicken breasts, skinned, boned, cut into bite-sized pieces
1 cup finely chopped onions
¼ cup finely chopped green bell pepper
2 garlic cloves, minced
½ cup coconut
¼ cup slivered almonds
¼ cup raisins
¼ to ½ cup chopped pimiento-stuffed green olives
2 tablespoons capers, drained, if desired

Prepare pie crust according to package directions for *two-crust pie* using 9-inch pie pan. Heat oven to 400°F.

In small saucepan, melt 1 tablespoon margarine. Blend in cornstarch, ginger, pepper, mustard, soy sauce and Worcestershire sauce. Gradually stir in orange juice. Bring to a boil; cook until mixture thickens, stirring constantly. Set aside.

In large skillet over medium heat, melt 2 tablespoons margarine. Cook chicken, onions, green pepper and garlic in margarine until chicken is completely cooked. Stir in coconut, almonds, raisins, olives, capers and the orange sauce. Reduce heat to low; cook until thoroughly heated, stirring occasionally. Spoon filling mixture into pie crust-lined pan. Top with second crust; seal and flute. Cut slits in several places. Bake at 400°F. for 30 to 40 minutes or until golden brown. Let stand 5 minutes before serving. **8 servings.**

NUTRIENTS PER 1/8 OF RECIPE

Calories	470	Protein	35% U.S. RDA
Protein	21g	Vitamin A	8% U.S. RDA
Carbohydrate	37g	Vitamin C	30% U.S. RDA
Fat	26g	Thiamine	6% U.S. RDA
Cholesterol	60mg	Riboflavin	6% U.S. RDA
Sodium	680mg	Niacin	40% U.S. RDA
Potassium	380mg	Calcium	4% U.S. RDA
Dietary Fiber	3g	Iron	8% U.S. RDA

Italian Cheese Rustica Pie

Gloria Bove, Pennsylvania
Bake-Off® 32, 1986

15-ounce package refrigerated pie crusts
1 tablespoon flour

FILLING
3 eggs
1 cup cubed cooked ham
1 cup ricotta or small curd cottage cheese
4 ounces (1 cup) shredded mozzarella cheese
4 ounces (1 cup) cubed provolone or Swiss cheese
4 tablespoons grated Parmesan cheese
1 tablespoon finely chopped fresh parsley or ½ teaspoon flakes
¼ teaspoon oregano leaves
Dash pepper
Beaten egg, if desired

Prepare pie crust according to package directions for *two-crust pie* using 9-inch pie pan. Place oven rack at lowest position. Heat oven to 375°F.

In large bowl, slightly beat 3 eggs. Add ham, ricotta cheese, mozzarella cheese, provolone cheese, 3 tablespoons of the Parmesan cheese, parsley, oregano and pepper; blend well. Spoon filling mixture into pie crust-lined pan. Top with second crust; seal edges and flute. Cut slits in crust in several places. Brush beaten egg over crust. Sprinkle with remaining 1 tablespoon Parmesan cheese. Bake at 375°F. for 50 to 60 minutes or until golden brown. Let stand 10 minutes before serving. **6 to 8 servings.**

NUTRIENTS PER 1/8 OF RECIPE

Calories	450	Protein	30% U.S. RDA
Protein	20g	Vitamin A	10% U.S. RDA
Carbohydrate	27g	Vitamin C	4% U.S. RDA
Fat	29g	Thiamine	10% U.S. RDA
Cholesterol	180mg	Riboflavin	15% U.S. RDA
Sodium	860mg	Niacin	4% U.S. RDA
Potassium	180mg	Calcium	35% U.S. RDA
Dietary Fiber	1g	Iron	6% U.S. RDA

Pictured top to bottom: Chicken Picadillo Pie, Italian Cheese Rustica Pie

Pictured left to right: Enchilada-Style Chicken Pie, Country Corn Pudding Pie

Country Corn Pudding Pie

Delores Rector, Indiana
Bake-Off® 32, 1986

15-ounce package refrigerated pie crusts
1 teaspoon flour

FILLING
3 tablespoons margarine or butter
2 tablespoons all purpose or unbleached flour
2 tablespoons sugar
1/2 to 1 teaspoon salt, if desired
1 cup milk
3 eggs
1/3 cup chopped green bell pepper
17-ounce can whole kernel corn, drained
4 slices bacon, crisply cooked, crumbled

MICROWAVE DIRECTIONS: Prepare pie crust according to package directions for *unfilled one-crust pie* using 9-inch microwave-safe pie pan. (Refrigerate remaining crust for later use.) Flute, if desired. Generously prick crust with fork. Microwave on HIGH for 6 to 8 minutes, rotating pan 1/2 turn every 2 minutes. Crust is done when surface appears dry and flaky. Cool.

In 1-quart microwave-safe bowl, microwave margarine on HIGH for 30 seconds or until melted. Blend in 2 tablespoons flour, sugar and salt. Stir in milk and eggs; blend well using wire whisk. Stir in green pepper and corn. Microwave on HIGH for 5 minutes, stirring every 1 1/2 minutes until smooth, using wire whisk. Pour filling mixture into cooked pie crust; sprinkle top with bacon. In microwave, elevate pie pan 1 to 2 inches by placing on inverted microwave-safe dish or on shelf provided. Microwave on HIGH for 4 to 6 minutes, rotating pan once halfway through cooking. Pie is done when knife inserted near center comes out clean. Let stand on flat surface for 5 minutes before serving. Garnish with additional green pepper or as desired. **6 to 8 servings.**

NUTRIENTS PER 1/8 OF RECIPE

Calories	280	Protein	10% U.S. RDA
Protein	6g	Vitamin A	10% U.S. RDA
Carbohydrate	28g	Vitamin C	10% U.S. RDA
Fat	16g	Thiamine	4% U.S. RDA
Cholesterol	110mg	Riboflavin	8% U.S. RDA
Sodium	630mg	Niacin	2% U.S. RDA
Potassium	200mg	Calcium	4% U.S. RDA
Dietary Fiber	1g	Iron	4% U.S. RDA

Enchilada-Style Chicken Pie

Nancy Jo Mathison, California
Bake-Off® 32, 1986

CRUST
 15-ounce package refrigerated pie crusts
 1 teaspoon flour
 1 egg
 1 teaspoon Worcestershire sauce

FILLING
 1 cup chopped onions
 5-ounce can chunk chicken, drained, chopped
 4-ounce can chopped green chiles, well drained
 3/4 cup sliced ripe olives, drained
 4 ounces (1 cup) shredded Monterey jack or Cheddar cheese*
 1/2 cup milk
 3 eggs
 1/2 teaspoon salt, if desired
 1/4 teaspoon cumin
 1/8 teaspoon garlic powder
 1/8 teaspoon pepper
 3 drops hot pepper sauce
 Chile salsa, sour cream, avocado slices and parsley, if desired

MICROWAVE DIRECTIONS: Prepare pie crust according to package directions for *unfilled one-crust pie* using 9-inch microwave-safe pie pan or 10-inch microwave-safe tart pan. (Refrigerate remaining crust for later use.) Flute, if desired. Generously prick crust with fork. In medium bowl, combine 1 egg and Worcestershire sauce; blend well. Brush lightly over pie crust. (Reserve any remaining egg mixture for filling.) Microwave on HIGH for 6 to 8 minutes, rotating pan 1/2 turn every 2 minutes. Crust is done when surface appears dry and flaky.

Place onions in small microwave-safe bowl. Cover with microwave-safe plastic wrap. Microwave on HIGH for 3 minutes or until crisp-tender. Drain well; set aside. To assemble pie, layer chicken, cooked onions, chiles, olives and cheese in cooked pie crust. To reserved egg mixture, add milk, 3 eggs, salt, cumin, garlic powder, pepper and hot pepper sauce; blend well. Pour mixture slowly over cheese. Microwave on HIGH for 8 to 11 minutes or until knife inserted near center comes out clean, rotating pan once halfway through cooking. Let stand on flat surface 5 minutes before serving. To serve, top each serving with salsa, sour cream, avocado slice and parsley. **6 to 8 servings.**

TIP: *A combination of Monterey jack and Cheddar cheese can be used.

NUTRIENTS PER 1/8 OF RECIPE

Calories	340	Protein	20% U.S. RDA
Protein	13g	Vitamin A	35% U.S. RDA
Carbohydrate	19g	Vitamin C	35% U.S. RDA
Fat	23g	Thiamine	4% U.S. RDA
Cholesterol	180mg	Riboflavin	15% U.S. RDA
Sodium	740mg	Niacin	8% U.S. RDA
Potassium	300mg	Calcium	20% U.S. RDA
Dietary Fiber	1g	Iron	10% U.S. RDA

Enchilada-Style Chicken Pie

Contemporary microwave preparation and refrigerated pie crusts are featured in this delicious Mexican-flavored pie.

California Casserole

California Casserole

--- ❧ ---

Savory poppy-seed dumplings bake on a flavorful veal stew mixture in this Grand Champion casserole. It's a wonderful entree for a dinner party.

California Casserole

--- ❧ ---

Mrs. H. H. Hatheway, California
Bake-Off® 8, 1956

⅓ cup all purpose or unbleached flour
1 teaspoon paprika
2 pounds boneless veal, cut into 1-inch pieces*
¼ cup oil
½ teaspoon salt
⅛ teaspoon pepper
1 cup water
10¾-ounce can condensed cream of chicken soup
1½ cups water
16-ounce can (1¾ cups) small onions, drained

DUMPLINGS
2 cups all purpose or unbleached flour
4 teaspoons baking powder
1 tablespoon poppy seed, if desired
1 teaspoon onion flakes
1 teaspoon celery seed
1 teaspoon poultry seasoning
¼ teaspoon salt
¾ to 1 cup milk
¼ cup oil
¼ cup margarine or butter, melted
1 cup dry bread crumbs

SAUCE
10¾-ounce can condensed cream of chicken soup
1 cup dairy sour cream
¼ cup milk

In small bowl or plastic bag, combine ⅓ cup flour and paprika. Add veal; coat well with flour mixture. In large skillet, brown veal in ¼ cup oil. Add ½ teaspoon salt, pepper and 1 cup water. Bring to a boil. Reduce heat; simmer uncovered 30 minutes or until veal is tender. Transfer veal mixture to ungreased 13 × 9-inch (3-quart) baking dish or 3-quart casserole.

In same skillet, combine 1 can cream of chicken soup and 1½ cups water; bring to a boil, stirring constantly. Pour over veal mixture in baking dish. Add onions; mix well.

Heat oven to 425°F. Lightly spoon flour into measuring cup; level off. In large bowl, combine 2 cups flour, baking powder, poppy seed, onion flakes, celery seed, poultry seasoning and ¼ teaspoon salt; mix well. Add milk and ¼ cup oil; stir until dry ingredients are just moistened. In small bowl, combine margarine and bread crumbs. Drop rounded tablespoons of dough into crumb mixture; roll to coat well. Arrange dumplings over warm veal mixture. Bake at 425°F. for 20 to 25 minutes or until dumplings are deep golden brown.

Meanwhile, in small saucepan combine all sauce ingredients. Bring just to a boil. Reduce heat; simmer 2 to 3 minutes or until thoroughly heated, stirring frequently. Serve sauce with veal casserole and dumplings. **8 to 10 servings.**

TIP: *Boneless pork, cut into 1-inch pieces, can be substituted for veal.

NUTRIENTS PER 1/10 OF RECIPE

Calories	560	Protein	40% U.S. RDA
Protein	26g	Vitamin A	15% U.S. RDA
Carbohydrate	40g	Vitamin C	2% U.S. RDA
Fat	33g	Thiamine	20% U.S. RDA
Cholesterol	100mg	Riboflavin	25% U.S. RDA
Sodium	960mg	Niacin	30% U.S. RDA
Potassium	440mg	Calcium	20% U.S. RDA
Dietary Fiber	2g	Iron	25% U.S. RDA

Quick-Topped Vegetable Chicken Casserole

Bernice Malinowski, Wisconsin
Bake-Off® 31, 1984

10³/₄-ounce can condensed cream of
   chicken soup
  3-ounce package cream cheese,
   softened
¹/₂ cup milk
¹/₂ cup chopped celery
¹/₂ cup chopped onion
¹/₄ cup Parmesan cheese
¹/₄ cup chopped green bell pepper
¹/₄ cup shredded carrot
¹/₂ teaspoon salt
  2 to 3 cups cubed cooked chicken
  9-ounce package frozen cut
   broccoli in a pouch, cooked,
   drained

TOPPING

  1 cup complete or buttermilk
   pancake mix
¹/₄ cup slivered almonds
  4 ounces (1 cup) shredded
   Cheddar cheese
¹/₄ cup milk
  1 tablespoon oil
  1 egg, slightly beaten

Heat oven to 375°F. In large saucepan, combine soup, cream cheese, milk, celery, onion, Parmesan cheese, green pepper, carrot and salt. Cook over medium heat until mixture is hot and cream cheese is melted, stirring frequently. Stir in chicken and broccoli. Pour into ungreased 2-quart casserole or 12 × 8-inch (2-quart) baking dish. In medium bowl, combine all topping ingredients; blend well. Spoon tablespoonfuls of topping over warm chicken mixture. Bake at 375°F. for 20 to 30 minutes or until topping is golden brown and chicken mixture bubbles around edges. **6 servings.**

HIGH ALTITUDE—Above 3500 Feet: No change.

NUTRIENTS PER 1/6 OF RECIPE

Calories	480	Protein	50% U.S. RDA
Protein	34g	Vitamin A	45% U.S. RDA
Carbohydrate	28g	Vitamin C	35% U.S. RDA
Fat	25g	Thiamine	15% U.S. RDA
Cholesterol	140mg	Riboflavin	25% U.S. RDA
Sodium	1310mg	Niacin	45% U.S. RDA
Potassium	500mg	Calcium	40% U.S. RDA
Dietary Fiber	3g	Iron	15% U.S. RDA

Chicken Broccoli Stroganoff

Patricia Kiewiet, Illinois
Bake-Off® 33, 1988

  2 cups frozen cut broccoli
  1 tablespoon margarine or butter
¹/₄ cup chopped onion
  3 tablespoons flour
10³/₄-ounce can condensed chicken
   broth
  2 cups cubed cooked chicken
  2.5-ounce jar sliced mushrooms,
   drained
  8-ounce carton (1 cup) dairy sour
   cream
   Hot cooked noodles
   Chopped fresh parsley

MICROWAVE DIRECTIONS: Cook broccoli in microwave until crisp-tender according to package directions. Drain; set aside. In 2-quart microwave-safe casserole, microwave margarine on HIGH for 20 seconds or until melted. Add onion; toss to coat. Cover with microwave-safe plastic wrap. Microwave on HIGH for 2 minutes or until crisp-tender. Add flour; blend well. Using wire whisk, stir chicken broth into onion mixture; blend well. Microwave on HIGH for 4 to 6 minutes or until mixture thickens and bubbles, stirring once halfway through cooking.* Add chicken, cooked broccoli, mushrooms and sour cream; blend well. Microwave on HIGH for 3 to 5 minutes or until mixture is thoroughly heated and bubbles around edges, stirring once halfway through cooking. Serve over noodles; garnish with parsley.
6 servings.

TIP: *For compact microwave ovens under 600 watts, microwave chicken broth-onion mixture on HIGH for 7 to 8 minutes or until mixture thickens and bubbles, stirring once halfway through cooking. Continue as directed above.

NUTRIENTS PER 1/6 OF RECIPE

Calories	490	Protein	40% U.S. RDA
Protein	26g	Vitamin A	25% U.S. RDA
Carbohydrate	58g	Vitamin C	40% U.S. RDA
Fat	17g	Thiamine	25% U.S. RDA
Cholesterol	120mg	Riboflavin	25% U.S. RDA
Sodium	445mg	Niacin	40% U.S. RDA
Potassium	510mg	Calcium	10% U.S. RDA
Dietary Fiber	3g	Iron	20% U.S. RDA

Quick-Topped Vegetable Chicken Casserole

Colorful vegetables and chicken are hidden under a topping made from pancake mix. So simple to prepare!

Chicken Broccoli Stroganoff

Chicken and broccoli in a light cream sauce create a new version of a popular family main dish. Make it in minutes in your microwave.

Hearty Mexican Pizza

❧❧

Linda Loda, Illinois
Bake-Off® 33, 1988

CRUST
1 tablespoon cornmeal
1 to 1½ cups self-rising flour*
1 cup whole wheat flour
¾ cup beer, room temperature
¼ cup oil

TOPPING
16-ounce can refried beans
1 pound ground beef
⅓ cup chopped onion
8-ounce can tomato sauce
4-ounce can chopped green chiles, undrained
8 ounces (2 cups) shredded Cheddar, Monterey jack or mozzarella cheese
1 medium red or green bell pepper, cut into strips
3 to 4 pitted ripe olives, sliced, if desired
Dairy sour cream, if desired
Taco or picante sauce, if desired

Heat oven to 400°F. Grease 14-inch pizza pan or 15 × 10 × 1-inch baking pan; sprinkle with cornmeal. Lightly spoon flour into measuring cup; level off. In large bowl, combine ½ cup self-rising flour, whole wheat flour, beer and oil; mix well. By hand, stir in ¼ to ½ cup self-rising flour to form a stiff dough. On floured surface, knead in remaining ¼ to ½ cup self-rising flour until dough is smooth and elastic, 2 to 3 minutes. On lightly floured surface, roll dough to 14-inch circle. Place over cornmeal in greased pan; press dough to fit pan evenly.

Spread refried beans over dough. In large skillet, brown ground beef; drain well. Add onion, tomato sauce and green chiles; blend well. Spoon meat mixture over refried beans; top with cheese, pepper strips and olives. Bake at 400°F. for 25 to 35 minutes or until crust is light golden brown. Let stand 5 minutes before serving. Garnish with sour cream or taco sauce. **8 servings.**

TIP: *All purpose or unbleached flour can be substituted for self-rising flour;

add 2 teaspoons baking powder and ½ teaspoon salt.

HIGH ALTITUDE—Above 3500 Feet: No change.

NUTRIENTS PER 1/8 OF RECIPE

Calories	560	Protein	40% U.S. RDA
Protein	25g	Vitamin A	35% U.S. RDA
Carbohydrate	42g	Vitamin C	80% U.S. RDA
Fat	31g	Thiamine	25% U.S. RDA
Cholesterol	70mg	Riboflavin	20% U.S. RDA
Sodium	1100mg	Niacin	25% U.S. RDA
Potassium	600mg	Calcium	35% U.S. RDA
Dietary Fiber	7g	Iron	25% U.S. RDA

Crab Meat Salad Pie

❧❧

Evelyn Robinson, Washington
Bake-Off® 11, 1959

CRUST
15-ounce package refrigerated pie crusts
1 teaspoon flour

FILLING
¾ cup dry bread crumbs
1 cup chopped celery
1 tablespoon finely chopped onion
1 tablespoon finely chopped green bell pepper
¾ to 1 cup mayonnaise or salad dressing
1 tablespoon lemon juice
6-ounce can crab meat, drained
2 ounces (½ cup) shredded Cheddar cheese

Heat oven to 450°F. Prepare pie crust according to package directions for *unfilled one-crust pie* using 9-inch pie pan. (Refrigerate remaining crust for later use.) Bake at 450°F. for 9 to 11 minutes or until light golden brown. Cool completely.

Reserve 2 tablespoons of the bread crumbs. In large bowl, combine remaining bread crumbs, celery, onion, green pepper, mayonnaise, lemon juice and crab meat; toss lightly. Spoon into cooled baked crust. Sprinkle with reserved 2 tablespoons bread crumbs and cheese. Bake at 450°F. for 8 to 10 minutes or until cheese is melted.

6 servings

NUTRIENTS PER 1/6 OF RECIPE

Calories	550	Protein	15% U.S. RDA
Protein	9g	Vitamin A	8% U.S. RDA
Carbohydrate	27g	Vitamin C	4% U.S. RDA
Fat	45g	Thiamine	4% U.S. RDA
Cholesterol	60mg	Riboflavin	6% U.S. RDA
Sodium	810mg	Niacin	6% U.S. RDA
Potassium	150mg	Calcium	10% U.S. RDA
Dietary Fiber	3g	Iron	6% U.S. RDA

Crab Meat Salad Pie

❧❧

When this tempting pie was a finalist the filling was spooned into a tender, flaky, made-from-scratch pie shell. In this updated recipe, the idea remains the same, but it all goes together in a flash using the convenience of refrigerated pie crusts.

Layered Italian Beef Pie

Ruth Boudreaux, Louisiana
Bake-Off® 32, 1986

15-ounce package refrigerated pie
  crusts
1 teaspoon flour

FILLING
1 pound ground beef
1 cup prepared spaghetti sauce
  with mushrooms and onions
2 eggs
1/4 cup grated Parmesan cheese
9-ounce package frozen chopped
  spinach in a pouch, thawed,
  well drained
8 ounces (2 cups) shredded
  mozzarella cheese
1/2 cup sliced ripe olives

Heat oven to 450°F. Prepare pie crust according to package directions for *unfilled one-crust pie* using 9-inch pie pan. (Refrigerate remaining crust for later use.) Bake at 450°F. for 9 to 11 minutes or until light golden brown; cool. Reduce oven temperature to 350°F.

Meanwhile, in large skillet brown ground beef; drain well. Add spaghetti sauce; simmer 10 minutes or until thoroughly heated. In medium bowl, beat eggs. Add Parmesan cheese and spinach; blend well. Spoon half of meat mixture into cooled baked crust; sprinkle with 1 cup of the mozzarella cheese and 1/4 cup of the olives. Spoon spinach mixture evenly over cheese; top with remaining meat mixture.

Bake at 350°F. for 25 to 35 minutes or until thoroughly heated. Sprinkle with remaining 1 cup mozzarella cheese and 1/4 cup olives. Bake an additional 1 to 2 minutes or until cheese is melted. Let stand 5 minutes before serving.
6 to 8 servings.

TIP: Cover edge of pie crust with strip of foil during last 10 to 15 minutes of baking if necessary to prevent excessive browning.

NUTRIENTS PER 1/8 OF RECIPE

Calories	410	Protein	30% U.S. RDA
Protein	20g	Vitamin A	25% U.S. RDA
Carbohydrate	19g	Vitamin C	4% U.S. RDA
Fat	28g	Thiamine	4% U.S. RDA
Cholesterol	140mg	Riboflavin	15% U.S. RDA
Sodium	720mg	Niacin	15% U.S. RDA
Potassium	410mg	Calcium	25% U.S. RDA
Dietary Fiber	2g	Iron	10% U.S. RDA

Broccoli Brunch Braid

Diane Tucker, Idaho
Bake-Off® 33, 1988

1/2 pound ground pork sausage
2 cups frozen cut broccoli
1 egg, beaten
1 tablespoon flour
1/4 teaspoon baking powder
1/2 cup ricotta cheese
4 ounces (1 cup) shredded
  Cheddar cheese
4.5-ounce jar sliced mushrooms,
  drained
8-ounce can refrigerated crescent
  dinner rolls
1 egg white, beaten
1/4 teaspoon caraway seed

In medium skillet, brown sausage. Drain well; set aside. Cook broccoli as directed on package. Drain; set aside.

Heat oven to 325°F. In large bowl, combine 1 beaten egg, flour and baking powder; beat well. Stir in ricotta cheese, Cheddar cheese, mushrooms, cooked sausage and broccoli. Unroll dough into 2 long rectangles. Place on large ungreased cookie sheet with long sides overlapping 1/2 inch; firmly press edges and perforations to seal. Press or roll out to form 14 × 10-inch rectangle. Spoon sausage mixture in 3 1/2-inch strip lengthwise down center of dough to within 1/4 inch of each end. Form sausage mixture into mounded shape. Make cuts 1 inch apart on longest sides of rectangle just to edge of filling. To give braided appearance, fold strips of dough at an angle halfway across filling, alternating from side to side with edges of strips slightly overlapping. Brush with beaten egg white; sprinkle with caraway seed.

Bake at 325°F. for 25 to 35 minutes or until deep golden brown. Cool 5 minutes; remove from cookie sheet. Cut into slices. **8 servings.**

NUTRIENTS PER 1/8 OF RECIPE

Calories	260	Protein	20% U.S. RDA
Protein	12g	Vitamin A	8% U.S. RDA
Carbohydrate	15g	Vitamin C	20% U.S. RDA
Fat	16g	Thiamine	10% U.S. RDA
Cholesterol	70mg	Riboflavin	15% U.S. RDA
Sodium	660mg	Niacin	8% U.S. RDA
Potassium	220mg	Calcium	20% U.S. RDA
Dietary Fiber	1g	Iron	8% U.S. RDA

"I haven't a thing to wear!"

A contestant, whose luggage was misplaced by the airline and who had nothing to wear but her traveling clothes, was taken on a hurried shopping trip by Sally Pillsbury, the wife of an executive, so she could face the awards presentation in a more suitable outfit.

Light 'n Easy Seafood Dinner

Light 'n Easy Seafood Dinner

━━━ ❧❧❧ ━━━

Creamy seafood-vegetable sauce is served over tender crescent pinwheels for a quick dinner idea.

━━━ ❧❧❧ ━━━

Nancy Signorelli, Florida
Bake-Off® 33, 1988

8-ounce can refrigerated crescent dinner rolls
4¼-ounce can tiny shrimp, drained, reserving liquid
1 pound frozen cod or haddock, thawed, cut into ½-inch cubes
4 green onions or scallions, sliced
⅓ cup all purpose or unbleached flour
1 cup milk
1 tablespoon dried parsley flakes
½ to 1 teaspoon garlic powder
1 cup dairy sour cream
3 tablespoons dry sherry, if desired
9-ounce package frozen sweet peas in a pouch, thawed, drained
8-ounce can sliced water chestnuts, drained
2.5-ounce jar sliced mushrooms, drained

Heat oven to 350°F. Remove dough from can in rolled sections; do not unroll. Cut each section into 6 slices. Place on ungreased cookie sheet; slightly flatten each slice. Bake at 350°F. for 13 to 16 minutes or until golden brown. Set aside.

In large skillet, combine reserved shrimp liquid, cod and green onions. Bring to a boil. Reduce heat; cover and simmer 3 to 5 minutes or until fish flakes easily with fork. Remove from heat; do not drain.

In medium saucepan, using wire whisk, stir flour into milk. Cook over medium heat about 2 minutes or until mixture thickens and boils, stirring constantly. Stir in parsley flakes, garlic powder, sour cream and sherry. Add shrimp, peas, water chestnuts and mushrooms; mix well. Gently blend sour cream mixture into fish mixture in skillet.* Heat over low heat about 5 minutes, stirring occasionally. To serve, place 2 baked crescent pinwheels on plate; spoon about 1 cup of fish mixture over pinwheels. **6 servings.**

TIP: *To make ahead, fish mixture can be prepared to this point. Cover and refrigerate. Just before serving, prepare crescent pinwheels as directed. Heat seafood mixture, covered, over low heat, stirring occasionally. Serve as directed above.

NUTRIENTS PER 1/6 OF RECIPE

Calories	410	Protein	40% U.S. RDA
Protein	25g	Vitamin A	10% U.S. RDA
Carbohydrate	37g	Vitamin C	10% U.S. RDA
Fat	17g	Thiamine	25% U.S. RDA
Cholesterol	90mg	Riboflavin	25% U.S. RDA
Sodium	580mg	Niacin	20% U.S. RDA
Potassium	740mg	Calcium	15% U.S. RDA
Dietary Fiber	2g	Iron	15% U.S. RDA

Biscuit Stuffin' Atop Chops

━━━ ❧❧❧ ━━━

Marilyn Ohl, Ohio
Bake-Off® 22, 1971

6 pork chops, ½ inch thick
1 tablespoon oil
10¾-ounce can condensed cream of chicken soup
1 cup chopped celery
1 cup chopped onions
¼ teaspoon pepper
⅛ teaspoon poultry seasoning or sage
1 egg
7.5-ounce can refrigerated biscuits

Heat oven to 350°F. In large skillet, brown pork chops in oil. Place in ungreased 13 × 9-inch pan. In medium bowl, combine soup, celery, onions, pepper, poultry seasoning and egg; mix well. Separate dough into 10 biscuits; cut each into 8 pieces. Stir biscuit pieces into soup mixture; spoon over pork chops. Bake at 350°F. for 45 to 55 minutes or until biscuit pieces are golden brown. **6 servings.**

NUTRIENTS PER 1/6 OF RECIPE

Calories	340	Protein	35% U.S. RDA
Protein	24g	Vitamin A	6% U.S. RDA
Carbohydrate	23g	Vitamin C	4% U.S. RDA
Fat	17g	Thiamine	50% U.S. RDA
Cholesterol	110mg	Riboflavin	25% U.S. RDA
Sodium	770mg	Niacin	30% U.S. RDA
Potassium	570mg	Calcium	4% U.S. RDA
Dietary Fiber	1g	Iron	10% U.S. RDA

Italian Zucchini Crescent Pie

Grand Prize Winner

Italian Zucchini Crescent Pie

Millicent Caplan, Florida
Bake-Off® 29, 1980

4 cups thinly sliced zucchini
1 cup chopped onions
2 tablespoons margarine or butter
2 tablespoons parsley flakes
¹/₂ teaspoon salt
¹/₂ teaspoon pepper
¹/₄ teaspoon garlic powder
¹/₄ teaspoon basil leaves
¹/₄ teaspoon oregano leaves
2 eggs, well beaten
8 ounces (2 cups) shredded Muenster or mozzarella cheese
8-ounce can refrigerated crescent dinner rolls
2 teaspoons prepared mustard

Heat oven to 375°F. In large skillet, cook zucchini and onions in margarine until tender, about 8 minutes. Stir in parsley flakes, salt, pepper, garlic powder, basil and oregano. In large bowl, combine eggs and cheese; mix well. Stir in cooked vegetable mixture.

Separate dough into 8 triangles.* Place in ungreased 10-inch pie pan, 12×8-inch (2-quart) baking dish or 11-inch quiche pan; press over bottom and up sides to form crust. Seal perforations. Spread crust with mustard. Pour egg-vegetable mixture evenly into prepared crust. Bake at 375°F. for 18 to 22 minutes or until knife inserted near center comes out clean.** Let stand 10 minutes before serving. **6 servings.**

TIPS: *If using 12×8-inch (2-quart) baking dish, unroll dough into 2 long rectangles; press over bottom and 1 inch up sides to form crust. Seal perforations. Continue as directed above.

**Cover edge of crust with strip of foil during last 10 minutes of baking if necessary to prevent excessive browning.

NUTRIENTS PER 1/6 OF RECIPE

Calories	360	Protein	25% U.S. RDA
Protein	15g	Vitamin A	20% U.S. RDA
Carbohydrate	20g	Vitamin C	10% U.S. RDA
Fat	25g	Thiamine	10% U.S. RDA
Cholesterol	130mg	Riboflavin	15% U.S. RDA
Sodium	820mg	Niacin	6% U.S. RDA
Potassium	440mg	Calcium	30% U.S. RDA
Dietary Fiber	2g	Iron	10% U.S. RDA

Garden Chicken Salad

Garden Chicken Salad

Edith Shulman, Texas
Bake-Off® 33, 1988

SALAD

2 cups frozen cut broccoli
4 cups cubed cooked chicken
1/3 cup chopped red or green bell pepper
3 tablespoons sliced ripe olives
2 tablespoons finely chopped red onion
1 large orange, peeled, chopped

DRESSING

3 tablespoons mango chutney
2/3 cup light mayonnaise or mayonnaise
1 tablespoon dry sherry, if desired
2 1/2 teaspoons garlic-flavored wine vinegar or red wine vinegar
1/4 cup sesame seed, toasted*
1/8 teaspoon pepper
Lettuce leaves

Cook broccoli until crisp-tender as directed on package. Drain; cool. In large bowl, combine cooked broccoli and remaining salad ingredients; blend well.

Place chutney in small bowl. Remove any large pieces and finely chop; return to bowl. Stir in remaining dressing ingredients; blend well. Pour dressing over salad; toss gently. Serve on lettuce leaves or in lettuce-lined bowl. Store in refrigerator. **6 (1 1/4-cup) servings.**

TIP: *To toast sesame seed, spread on cookie sheet; bake at 375°F. for about 5 minutes or until light golden brown, stirring occasionally. Or, spread in medium skillet; stir over medium heat for about 10 minutes or until light golden brown.

NUTRIENTS PER 1/6 OF RECIPE

Calories	340	Protein	45% U.S. RDA
Protein	30g	Vitamin A	20% U.S. RDA
Carbohydrate	14g	Vitamin C	90% U.S. RDA
Fat	18g	Thiamine	10% U.S. RDA
Cholesterol	90mg	Riboflavin	15% U.S. RDA
Sodium	290mg	Niacin	45% U.S. RDA
Potassium	450mg	Calcium	6% U.S. RDA
Dietary Fiber	3g	Iron	10% U.S. RDA

Hurry-Up Hot Potato Salad

Ike D. Fowler, Texas
Bake-Off® 19, 1968

3 cups water
1 package scalloped potato mix
3/4 cup mayonnaise or salad dressing
1/4 cup dairy sour cream
2 tablespoons parsley flakes
2 tablespoons Italian salad dressing
14.5-ounce can cut green beans, drained*
4-ounce jar sliced pimiento, drained
Paprika, if desired

Heat oven to 350°F. In medium saucepan, bring water to a boil; add potato slices. Return to a boil; boil 18 to 20 minutes or until tender. Drain. In ungreased 1 1/2-quart casserole, combine contents of seasoning mix envelope, mayonnaise, sour cream, parsley flakes and Italian dressing; blend well. Stir in cooked potato slices, green beans and pimiento; sprinkle with paprika. Bake at 350°F. for 15 to 20 minutes or until thoroughly heated; stir. Serve warm. **6 to 8 servings.**

TIP: An 8-ounce package frozen cut green beans in a pouch, cooked and drained, can be substituted for canned cut green beans.

NUTRIENTS PER 1/8 OF RECIPE

Calories	270	Protein	4% U.S. RDA
Protein	3g	Vitamin A	20% U.S. RDA
Carbohydrate	15g	Vitamin C	10% U.S. RDA
Fat	22g	Thiamine	2% U.S. RDA
Cholesterol	15mg	Riboflavin	4% U.S. RDA
Sodium	420mg	Niacin	4% U.S. RDA
Potassium	210mg	Calcium	4% U.S. RDA
Dietary Fiber	1g	Iron	6% U.S. RDA

Hurry-Up Hot Potato Salad

Shortly after this wonderful potato salad was a Bake-Off® recipe, an ingredient became obsolete. Today, almost twenty years later, Pillsbury's new scalloped potato mix makes it possible to serve this great-tasting recipe again.

Easy Vegetable Bulgur Salad

Easy Vegetable Bulgur Salad

Annette Erbeck, Ohio
Bake-Off® 33, 1988

1 cup bulgur wheat
2 cups boiling water
16-ounce package frozen broccoli, cauliflower and carrots
1/2 cup chopped fresh parsley
1/4 cup sliced green onions
1/2 to 1 cup Italian dressing

In medium bowl, combine bulgur and boiling water. Let stand 1 hour. Drain well. To thaw vegetables, place in colander under cold running water for 6 minutes. Drain well.

In large bowl, combine softened bulgur, thawed vegetables, parsley, green onions and Italian dressing; blend well. Cover; refrigerate 1 to 2 hours to blend flavors. Store in refrigerator.
12 (1/2-cup) servings.

NUTRIENTS PER 1/12 OF RECIPE

Calories	160	Protein	2% U.S. RDA
Protein	2g	Vitamin A	25% U.S. RDA
Carbohydrate	15g	Vitamin C	30% U.S. RDA
Fat	10g	Thiamine	2% U.S. RDA
Cholesterol	0mg	Riboflavin	2% U.S. RDA
Sodium	170mg	Niacin	4% U.S. RDA
Potassium	135mg	Calcium	2% U.S. RDA
Dietary Fiber	3g	Iron	6% U.S. RDA

Santa Fe Corn and Cheese Bake

Alda Menoni, California
Bake-Off® 33, 1988

2 eggs, beaten
1 cup creamed cottage cheese
1/2 cup dairy sour cream
1/3 cup chopped green chiles, drained
3 tablespoons flour
3 tablespoons milk
2 to 3 teaspoons sugar
1 teaspoon onion salt
1/4 to 1/2 teaspoon pepper
17-ounce can whole kernel corn, drained
3 tablespoons chopped ripe olives
1 ounce (1/4 cup) shredded Cheddar cheese

Heat oven to 350°F. In large bowl, combine eggs and cottage cheese; blend well. Stir in sour cream and chiles. In small bowl, combine flour and milk; beat until smooth. Add to cottage cheese mixture. Stir in sugar, onion salt, pepper and corn; blend well. Pour into ungreased 8-inch (2-quart) square baking dish or 2-quart casserole.

Bake at 350°F. for 30 to 40 minutes or until knife inserted near center comes out clean. Sprinkle top with olives and Cheddar cheese. Bake an additional 1 to 2 minutes or until cheese is melted. **6 to 8 servings.**

NUTRIENTS PER 1/8 OF RECIPE

Calories	160	Protein	10% U.S. RDA
Protein	8g	Vitamin A	25% U.S. RDA
Carbohydrate	15g	Vitamin C	8% U.S. RDA
Fat	8g	Thiamine	2% U.S. RDA
Cholesterol	80mg	Riboflavin	10% U.S. RDA
Sodium	580mg	Niacin	2% U.S. RDA
Potassium	180mg	Calcium	8% U.S. RDA
Dietary Fiber	1g	Iron	4% U.S. RDA

Easy Cheesy Potato Bake

Ruth Connelly, California
Bake-Off® 25, 1974

1 tablespoon margarine or butter
3 cups water
1 package au gratin potato mix
1/4 teaspoon salt, if desired
1 1/2 cups milk
1/8 teaspoon hot pepper sauce or cayenne pepper
3 eggs
1/2 cup finely chopped onion
8 ounces (2 cups) shredded Cheddar cheese

Heat oven to 350°F. Grease 10-inch deep-dish pie pan or 9-inch square pan with margarine. In medium saucepan, bring water to a boil; add potato slices. Return to a boil; boil 4 minutes. Drain. Arrange partially cooked potato slices over bottom and up sides of greased pan to form crust.

In medium bowl, combine contents of seasoning mix envelope, salt, milk, hot pepper sauce and eggs; stir until smooth. Stir in onion and cheese; pour into crust. Bake at 350°F. for 28 to 35 minutes or until center is set. Let stand 10 minutes before serving. To serve, cut into wedges or squares. **8 to 9 servings.**

NUTRIENTS PER 1/9 OF RECIPE

Calories	180	Protein	15% U.S. RDA
Protein	10g	Vitamin A	10% U.S. RDA
Carbohydrate	6g	Vitamin C	2% U.S. RDA
Fat	13g	Thiamine	2% U.S. RDA
Cholesterol	120mg	Riboflavin	10% U.S. RDA
Sodium	330mg	Niacin	<2% U.S. RDA
Potassium	150mg	Calcium	25% U.S. RDA
Dietary Fiber	1g	Iron	2% U.S. RDA

Hot 'n Spicy Sauteed Mushrooms

Gladys Randall, Texas
Bake-Off® 33, 1988

1/2 cup margarine or butter
1/2 cup chopped green bell pepper
1/2 cup chopped red bell pepper
1/4 cup sliced green onions
2 garlic cloves, minced
3 (6-ounce) jars sliced mushrooms, drained*
1/4 cup sherry
1/2 teaspoon creole or cajun seasoning
1/4 teaspoon cayenne pepper
1/4 teaspoon pepper

In large skillet, melt margarine. Add peppers, green onions and garlic; cook over medium heat until crisp-tender. Stir in remaining ingredients. Simmer 2 to 3 minutes or until thoroughly heated, stirring occasionally. **6 (1/2-cup) servings.**

MICROWAVE DIRECTIONS: Place margarine in medium microwave-safe bowl. Microwave on HIGH for 45 to 60 seconds or until melted. Stir in peppers, green onions and garlic. Cover with microwave-safe plastic wrap. Microwave on HIGH for 2 to 3 minutes or until peppers are crisp-tender. Stir in remaining ingredients. Microwave on HIGH for 2 to 3 minutes or until thoroughly heated, stirring once halfway through cooking.

TIP: *Four 4.5-ounce jars sliced mushrooms, drained, can be substituted for three 6-ounce jars.

NUTRIENTS PER 1/6 OF RECIPE

Calories	170	Protein	4% U.S. RDA
Protein	3g	Vitamin A	35% U.S. RDA
Carbohydrate	6g	Vitamin C	50% U.S. RDA
Fat	15g	Thiamine	2% U.S. RDA
Cholesterol	0mg	Riboflavin	10% U.S. RDA
Sodium	455mg	Niacin	6% U.S. RDA
Potassium	190mg	Calcium	<2% U.S. RDA
Dietary Fiber	1g	Iron	6% U.S. RDA

Hot 'n Spicy Sauteed Mushrooms

This spicy mushroom-vegetable side dish will add zest to any meal—try serving it on top of steaks or chops. It's sure to please your family or guests.

Microwave Vegetable Pie Supreme

Winnie Osborne, New York
Bake-Off® 33, 1988

2 tablespoons margarine or butter
1 cup coarsely chopped onions
¼ cup chopped green bell pepper
16-ounce package frozen broccoli, cauliflower and carrots
1 cup dry bread crumbs
2 tablespoons chopped fresh parsley
1 to 3 teaspoons basil leaves
½ teaspoon salt
¼ teaspoon pepper
4 ounces (1 cup) shredded Swiss cheese
¼ cup dairy sour cream
3 eggs, beaten

TOPPING
6 tomato slices
1 ounce (¼ cup) shredded Swiss cheese
Dairy sour cream, if desired

MICROWAVE DIRECTIONS: In 9 or 10-inch microwave-safe pie pan, combine margarine, onions and green pepper. Microwave on HIGH for 3 to 4 minutes or until onions and green pepper are crisp-tender, stirring once halfway through cooking.* Add frozen vegetables; cover with microwave-safe plastic wrap. Microwave on HIGH for 4 to 5 minutes or until frozen vegetables are thawed and separated, stirring once halfway through cooking. (Vegetables will feel cold.)

Meanwhile, reserve 1 tablespoon of the bread crumbs. In large bowl, combine remaining bread crumbs, parsley, basil, salt, pepper and 1 cup Swiss cheese; mix well. Stir in vegetable mixture, ¼ cup sour cream and eggs. Return mixture to pie pan; spread evenly. Arrange tomato slices over top of pie. Sprinkle with ¼ cup Swiss cheese and reserved 1 tablespoon bread crumbs.

Microwave on HIGH for 10 to 12 minutes or until knife inserted in center comes out clean, rotating pan ½ turn once halfway through cooking. Let stand on flat surface 5 minutes before serving. To serve, cut into wedges; top each serving with dollop of sour cream. **6 to 8 servings.**

TIP: *For compact microwave ovens under 600 watts, in 9 or 10-inch microwave-safe pie pan, combine margarine, onions and green pepper. Microwave on HIGH for 4 to 6 minutes or until onions and green pepper are crisp-tender, stirring once halfway through cooking. Add frozen vegetables; cover with microwave-safe plastic wrap. Microwave on HIGH for 5 to 6 minutes or until frozen vegetables are thawed and separated, stirring once halfway through cooking. (Vegetables will feel cold.) Continue ingredient preparation as directed above. Microwave on HIGH for 15 to 20 minutes or until knife inserted in center comes out clean, rotating pan ½ turn once halfway through cooking. Let stand on flat surface 5 minutes before serving.

NUTRIENTS PER 1/8 OF RECIPE

Calories	250	Protein	15% U.S. RDA
Protein	11g	Vitamin A	45% U.S. RDA
Carbohydrate	17g	Vitamin C	45% U.S. RDA
Fat	15g	Thiamine	8% U.S. RDA
Cholesterol	130mg	Riboflavin	15% U.S. RDA
Sodium	370mg	Niacin	4% U.S. RDA
Potassium	320mg	Calcium	25% U.S. RDA
Dietary Fiber	3g	Iron	10% U.S. RDA

Broccoli Cauliflower Tetrazzini

Broccoli Cauliflower Tetrazzini

Barbara Van Itallie, New York
Bake-Off® 33, 1988

8 ounces uncooked spaghetti, broken into thirds
16-ounce package frozen broccoli, cauliflower and carrots
2 tablespoons margarine or butter
3 tablespoons flour
2 cups skim or lowfat milk
½ cup grated Parmesan cheese
Dash pepper
4.5-ounce jar sliced mushrooms, drained
2 tablespoons grated Parmesan cheese

Cook spaghetti to desired doneness as directed on package. Drain; rinse with hot water. Keep warm; set aside. Cook vegetables until crisp-tender as directed on package. Drain; set aside.

Heat oven to 400°F. Grease 13 × 9-inch pan. In medium saucepan, melt margarine. Stir in flour until smooth. Gradually add milk; blend well. Cook over medium heat 6 to 10 minutes or until mixture thickens and boils, stirring constantly. Stir in ½ cup Parmesan cheese and pepper. Spoon cooked spaghetti into greased pan. Top with cooked vegetables and mushrooms. Pour milk mixture over mushrooms; sprinkle with 2 tablespoons Parmesan cheese. Bake at 400°F. for 15 to 20 minutes or until mixture is thoroughly heated and bubbles around edges.
8 servings.

NUTRIENTS PER 1/8 OF RECIPE

Calories	220	Protein	15% U.S. RDA
Protein	11g	Vitamin A	35% U.S. RDA
Carbohydrate	31g	Vitamin C	25% U.S. RDA
Fat	6g	Thiamine	20% U.S. RDA
Cholesterol	6mg	Riboflavin	20% U.S. RDA
Sodium	275mg	Niacin	10% U.S. RDA
Potassium	300mg	Calcium	20% U.S. RDA
Dietary Fiber	2g	Iron	8% U.S. RDA

Pictured top to bottom: Whole Wheat Raisin Loaf, page 68; Lemon Raspberry Muffins, page 81

Breads

❧✣❧

Breads of infinite variety have been part of the Bake-Off® repertoire since the beginning of the contest . . . Plump, golden-brown loaves of Whole Wheat Raisin Loaf, so crunchy on the outside, yet moist and tender within. Light and delicate Lemon Raspberry Muffins, fruity sweet and delicious. Dilly Casserole Bread, a Bake-Off® classic that's so easy to prepare.

At the first Bake-Off® Contest, breads were second only to cakes in popularity. The appeal of home-baked breads has continued over the years, with each decade offering its own unique inspirations. Traditional "from-scratch" yeast bread recipes have made way for no-knead varieties like Easy Cheese Batter Bread. Modern-day contestants streamline and simplify hand-me-down family recipes with hot roll mix, quick bread mixes and refrigerated fresh dough products. From the Old World come Italian Cheese Bread Ring and Polish Poppy Swirl Loaf, recipes that have been adapted for quick preparation by busy cooks.

What takes many of these recipes out of the ordinary is their distinctive flavoring, such as sesame seed, cheeses, garlic, and dry mustard. Anise and fennel seed and orange peel are unique seasonings that add a whiff of savory magic to Swedish Whole Wheat Dinner Rolls. And the growing ranks of health-conscious bakers have introduced a host of wholesome ingredients including bran, wheat germ and rolled oats as well as vegetables, like the shredded carrots featured in Golden Party Loaves.

This collection offers a glorious bounty of flavors, textures and shapes from the Bake-Off® bread basket. It's proof positive of America's ongoing love affair with home-baked breads.

Dilly Casserole Bread

Easy preparation and innovative flavor gave this soft-textured bread its winning qualities. For even easier preparation of this Bake-Off® classic recipe, food processor directions are now included.

Whole Wheat Raisin Loaf

Lenora Smith, Louisiana
Bake-Off® 27, 1976

3 to 3³/₄ cups all purpose or unbleached flour*
¹/₂ cup sugar
3 teaspoons salt
1 teaspoon cinnamon
¹/₂ teaspoon nutmeg
2 packages active dry yeast
2 cups milk
³/₄ cup water
¹/₄ cup oil
4 cups whole wheat flour
1 cup rolled oats
1 cup raisins
Oil or melted margarine, if desired
Sugar, if desired

Lightly spoon flour into measuring cup; level off. In large bowl, combine 1¹/₂ cups all purpose flour, ¹/₂ cup sugar, salt, cinnamon, nutmeg and yeast; blend well. In small saucepan, heat milk, water and ¹/₄ cup oil until very warm (120 to 130°F.). Add warm liquid to flour mixture. Blend at low speed until moistened; beat 3 minutes at medium speed. By hand, stir in whole wheat flour, rolled oats, raisins and 1 to 1¹/₂ cups all purpose flour until dough pulls cleanly away from sides of bowl.

On floured surface, knead in remaining ¹/₂ to ³/₄ cup all purpose flour until dough is smooth and elastic, about 5 minutes. Place dough in greased bowl; cover loosely with plastic wrap and cloth towel. Let rise in warm place (80 to 85°F.) until light and doubled in size, 20 to 30 minutes.

Grease two 9×5 or 8×4-inch loaf pans. Punch down dough several times to remove all air bubbles. Divide dough in half. Shape each half into a loaf. Place loaves in greased pans; brush tops with oil or margarine. Cover; let rise in warm place until light and doubled in size, 30 to 45 minutes.

Heat oven to 375°F. Uncover dough. Bake 40 to 50 minutes or until deep golden brown and loaves sound hollow when lightly tapped. If loaves become too brown, cover loosely with foil last 10 minutes of baking time. Remove from pans immediately; cool on wire racks. Brush top of warm loaves with oil or margarine; sprinkle with sugar. **2 (16-slice) loaves.**

TIP: *Bread flour can be substituted for all purpose or unbleached flour. Increase kneading time to 10 minutes and allow dough to rest 15 minutes before shaping.

HIGH ALTITUDE — Above 3500 Feet: No change.

NUTRIENTS PER 1 SLICE

Calories	170	Protein	6% U.S. RDA
Protein	5g	Vitamin A	<2% U.S. RDA
Carbohydrate	32g	Vitamin C	<2% U.S. RDA
Fat	3g	Thiamine	15% U.S. RDA
Cholesterol	0mg	Riboflavin	8% U.S. RDA
Sodium	210mg	Niacin	8% U.S. RDA
Potassium	150mg	Calcium	2% U.S. RDA
Dietary Fiber	3g	Iron	8% U.S. RDA

Dilly Casserole Bread

Leona P. Schnuelle, Nebraska
Bake-Off® 12, 1960

2 to 2²/₃ cups all purpose or unbleached flour
2 tablespoons sugar
2 to 3 teaspoons instant minced onion
2 teaspoons dill seed
1 teaspoon salt
¹/₄ teaspoon baking soda
1 package active dry yeast
¹/₄ cup water
1 tablespoon margarine or butter
8-ounce carton (1 cup) creamed cottage cheese
1 egg
Margarine or butter, melted
Coarse salt, if desired

Lightly spoon flour into measuring cup; level off. In large bowl, combine 1 cup flour, sugar, instant minced onion, dill seed, 1 teaspoon salt, baking soda and yeast; blend well. In small saucepan, heat water, 1 tablespoon margarine and cottage cheese until very warm (120 to 130°F.). Add warm liquid and egg to

Dilly Casserole Bread

flour mixture. Blend at low speed until moistened; beat 3 minutes at medium speed. By hand, stir in remaining 1 to 1⅔ cups flour to form a stiff batter. Cover loosely with plastic wrap and cloth towel. Let rise in warm place (80 to 85°F.) until light and doubled in size, 45 to 60 minutes.

Generously grease 1½ or 2-quart casserole. Stir down dough to remove all air bubbles. Turn into greased casserole. Cover; let rise in warm place until light and doubled in size, 30 to 45 minutes.

Heat oven to 350°F. Uncover dough. Bake 30 to 40 minutes or until deep golden brown and loaf sounds hollow when lightly tapped. Remove from casserole immediately; cool on wire rack. Brush warm loaf with melted margarine; sprinkle with coarse salt.
1 (18-slice) loaf.

FOOD PROCESSOR DIRECTIONS: In small bowl, soften yeast in ¼ cup warm water (105 to 115°F.). In food processor bowl with metal blade, combine *2 cups* flour, sugar, instant minced onion, dill seed, 1 teaspoon salt, baking soda and 1 tablespoon margarine. Cover; process 5 seconds. Add cottage cheese and egg. Cover; process about 10 seconds or until blended. With machine running, pour yeast mixture through feed tube. Continue processing until blended, about 20 seconds or until mixture pulls away from sides of bowl and forms a ball, adding additional flour if necessary. Carefully scrape dough from blade and bowl; place in lightly greased bowl. Cover loosely with plastic wrap and cloth towel. Let rise in warm place (80 to 85°F.) until light and doubled in size, 45 to 60 minutes. Continue as directed above.

HIGH ALTITUDE—Above 3500 Feet: Bake at 375°F. for 35 to 40 minutes.

NUTRIENTS PER 1 SLICE

Calories	90	Protein	6% U.S. RDA
Protein	4g	Vitamin A	<2% U.S. RDA
Carbohydrate	15g	Vitamin C	<2% U.S. RDA
Fat	2g	Thiamine	8% U.S. RDA
Cholesterol	15mg	Riboflavin	6% U.S. RDA
Sodium	240mg	Niacin	4% U.S. RDA
Potassium	40mg	Calcium	<2% U.S. RDA
Dietary Fiber	<1g	Iron	4% U.S. RDA

Golden Party Loaves

Golden Party Loaves

Effie Cato, Texas
Bake-Off® 31, 1984

4¹/₂ to 5¹/₂ cups bread flour*
1¹/₂ cups finely shredded carrots
  1 teaspoon salt
  1 package active dry yeast
  ³/₄ cup apricot nectar
  ¹/₂ cup plain yogurt
  ¹/₄ cup honey
  ¹/₄ cup margarine or butter
  1 egg
    Margarine or butter, softened

SPREAD
  8-ounce package cream cheese,
    softened
  ¹/₂ cup apricot preserves

Lightly spoon flour into measuring cup; level off. In large bowl, combine 2 cups flour, carrots, salt and yeast; blend well. In small saucepan, heat apricot nectar, yogurt, honey and ¹/₄ cup margarine until very warm (120 to 130°F.). Add warm liquid and egg to flour mixture. Blend at low speed until moistened; beat 3 minutes at medium speed. By hand, stir in 2 to 2¹/₂ cups flour to form a stiff dough. On floured surface, knead in remaining ¹/₂ to 1 cup flour until dough is smooth and elastic, about 10 minutes. Place dough in greased bowl; cover loosely with plastic wrap and cloth towel. Let rise in warm place (80 to 85°F.) until light and doubled in size, about 1¹/₄ hours.

Grease and flour two 9 × 5 or 8 × 4-inch loaf pans. Punch down dough several times to remove all air bubbles. Divide dough in half. Allow to rest on counter, covered with inverted bowl, for 15 minutes. Work dough with hands to remove large air bubbles. Divide each half into thirds. Shape each third into a small loaf. Spread sides of loaves with softened margarine. Place 3 loaves crosswise in greased and floured pan. Repeat with remaining dough. Cover; let rise in warm place until light and doubled in size, about 1 hour.

Heat oven to 375°F. Uncover dough. Bake 30 to 35 minutes or until deep golden brown and loaves sound hollow when lightly tapped. Remove from pans immediately; cool on wire racks. Brush warm loaves with softened margarine. In small bowl, combine spread ingredients; mix well. Serve with bread. **6 (7-slice) loaves.**

TIP: *All purpose or unbleached flour can be substituted for bread flour. Decrease kneading time to 5 minutes, omit resting period and decrease each rise time 15 minutes.

HIGH ALTITUDE—Above 3500 Feet: No change.

NUTRIENTS PER 1 SLICE

Calories	120	Protein	4% U.S. RDA
Protein	3g	Vitamin A	25% U.S. RDA
Carbohydrate	18g	Vitamin C	2% U.S. RDA
Fat	4g	Thiamine	8% U.S. RDA
Cholesterol	10mg	Riboflavin	6% U.S. RDA
Sodium	90mg	Niacin	4% U.S. RDA
Potassium	55mg	Calcium	<2% U.S. RDA
Dietary Fiber	<1g	Iron	4% U.S. RDA

Golden Party Loaves

Six wholesome mini-loaves are baked in two loaf pans and served with a tangy apricot spread.

Onion Lover's Twist

❧❧❧

Nan Robb, Arizona
Bake-Off® 21, 1970

Onion Lover's Twist

❧❧❧

This no-knead bread features fresh chopped onions rolled inside strips of dough that are braided together to create a light-textured onion bread. Serve it warm or cold with a favorite chicken or beef main dish and see why it took top honors!

3½ to 4½ cups all purpose or unbleached flour*
¼ cup sugar
1½ teaspoons salt
1 package active dry yeast
¾ cup water
½ cup milk
¼ cup margarine or butter
1 egg

FILLING
¼ cup margarine or butter
1 cup finely chopped onions or ¼ cup instant minced onion
1 tablespoon grated Parmesan cheese
1 tablespoon sesame or poppy seed
½ to 1 teaspoon garlic salt
1 teaspoon paprika

Lightly spoon flour into measuring cup; level off. In large bowl, combine 2 cups flour, sugar, salt and yeast; blend well. In small saucepan, heat water, milk and ¼ cup margarine until very warm (120 to 130°F.). Add warm liquid and egg to flour mixture. Blend at low speed until moistened; beat 3 minutes at medium speed. By hand, stir in remaining 1½ to 2½ cups flour to form a soft dough. Cover loosely with plastic wrap and cloth towel. Let rise in warm place (80 to 85°F.) until light and doubled in size, 45 to 60 minutes.

In small saucepan, melt ¼ cup margarine; stir in remaining filling ingredients. Set aside.

Grease large cookie sheet. Stir down dough to remove all air bubbles. On floured surface, toss dough until no longer sticky. Roll dough to 18 × 12-inch rectangle; spread with filling mixture. Cut rectangle in half crosswise to make two 9 × 12-inch rectangles. Cut each rectangle lengthwise into three 9 × 4-inch strips. Starting with 9-inch side, roll up each strip; pinch edges and ends to seal. On greased cookie sheet, braid 3 rolls together; pinch ends to seal. Repeat with remaining 3 rolls for second loaf. Cover; let rise in warm

place until light and doubled in size, 25 to 30 minutes.

Heat oven to 350°F. Uncover dough. Bake 27 to 35 minutes or until golden brown and loaves sound hollow when lightly tapped. Remove from cookie sheet immediately; cool on wire racks. **2 (16-slice) loaves.**

TIP: *Bread flour can be substituted for all purpose or unbleached flour. Allow dough to rest 15 minutes before shaping.

HIGH ALTITUDE—Above 3500 Feet: No change.

NUTRIENTS PER 1 SLICE

Calories	100	Protein	4% U.S. RDA
Protein	2g	Vitamin A	2% U.S. RDA
Carbohydrate	16g	Vitamin C	<2% U.S. RDA
Fat	3g	Thiamine	8% U.S. RDA
Cholesterol	8mg	Riboflavin	6% U.S. RDA
Sodium	200mg	Niacin	4% U.S. RDA
Potassium	40mg	Calcium	<2% U.S. RDA
Dietary Fiber	<1g	Iron	4% U.S. RDA

Cheesy Garlic Hot Roll Braid

❧❧❧

Gloria Bradfield, Kansas
Bake-Off® 20, 1969

1 package hot roll mix
¾ cup water heated to 120 to 130°F.
½ cup dairy sour cream
1 egg, separated, reserving white for topping

FILLING
⅓ cup Parmesan cheese
1 tablespoon instant minced onion
½ to ¾ teaspoon garlic powder
½ teaspoon Italian seasoning
¼ teaspoon paprika
2 tablespoons margarine or butter, softened

TOPPING
Reserved egg white
1 tablespoon water
1 tablespoon sesame seed

Grease large cookie sheet. In large bowl, combine flour mixture with yeast from foil packet; blend well. Stir in ¾ cup *hot* water, sour cream and egg yolk until dough pulls cleanly away from sides of bowl. Turn dough out

Cheesy Garlic Hot Roll Braid

onto lightly floured surface. With greased or floured hands, shape dough into a ball. Knead dough for 5 minutes until smooth. Cover with large bowl; let rest 5 minutes. In small bowl, combine all filling ingredients except margarine; mix well. Set aside.

On floured surface, roll dough to 13 × 11-inch rectangle. Spread with margarine; sprinkle evenly with filling mixture. Fold 13-inch sides to center, overlapping 1 inch. Press center seam and edges to seal. Place seam side up on greased cookie sheet. Make cuts 1 inch apart on longest sides of rectangle to within 1 inch of center. (Do not cut through center.) To give braided appearance, fold strips of dough at an angle halfway across filling, alternating from side to side. Pinch ends to seal. In small bowl, beat reserved egg white and 1 tablespoon water. Brush top of loaf

with egg white mixture. Sprinkle with sesame seed. Cover loosely with plastic wrap and cloth towel. Let rise in warm place (80 to 85°F.) until almost doubled in size, 25 to 30 minutes.

Heat oven to 375°F. Uncover dough. Bake 20 to 30 minutes or until deep golden brown. Remove from cookie sheet immediately; cool on wire rack. **1 (18-slice) loaf.**

TIP: Cover braid with foil during last 5 to 10 minutes of baking if necessary to prevent excessive browning.

HIGH ALTITUDE—Above 3500 Feet: No change.

NUTRIENTS PER 1 SLICE

Calories	130	Protein	6% U.S. RDA
Protein	4g	Vitamin A	2% U.S. RDA
Carbohydrate	19g	Vitamin C	<2% U.S. RDA
Fat	4g	Thiamine	10% U.S. RDA
Cholesterol	20mg	Riboflavin	10% U.S. RDA
Sodium	230mg	Niacin	8% U.S. RDA
Potassium	60mg	Calcium	4% U.S. RDA
Dietary Fiber	<1g	Iron	6% U.S. RDA

Swedish Whole Wheat Dinner Rolls

Swedish Whole Wheat Dinner Rolls

Patty Entringer, Minnesota
Bake-Off® 32, 1986

1 cup whole wheat flour
1/2 cup mashed potato flakes
2 tablespoons brown sugar
2 teaspoons salt
1 teaspoon anise seed, crushed
1 teaspoon fennel seed, crushed
1 1/2 teaspoons grated orange peel
1 package fast-acting dry yeast
1 1/3 cups water
1/4 cup margarine or butter
1 tablespoon instant coffee granules or crystals
2 tablespoons molasses
1 teaspoon orange extract, if desired
1 egg
2 1/2 to 3 1/2 cups bread flour
1 tablespoon margarine or butter, softened
1/2 teaspoon grated orange peel, if desired

Grease two 8 or 9-inch round cake pans. Lightly spoon flour into measuring cup; level off. In large bowl, combine whole wheat flour, potato flakes, brown sugar, salt, anise seed, fennel seed, 1 1/2 teaspoons orange peel and yeast; blend well. In small saucepan, heat water, 1/4 cup margarine, instant coffee, molasses and orange extract until very warm (120 to 130°F.). Add warm liquid and egg to flour mixture. Blend at low speed until moistened; beat 3 minutes at medium speed. Stir in 2 to 2 1/2 cups bread flour until dough pulls cleanly away from sides of bowl.

On floured surface, knead in remaining 1/2 to 1 cup bread flour until dough is smooth and elastic, about 10 minutes. Allow to rest on counter covered with inverted bowl for 10 minutes. Divide dough in half. Divide each half into 8 equal pieces; shape into balls. Place 8 balls in each greased pan. Cover loosely with plastic wrap and cloth towel. Let rise in warm place (80 to 85°F.) until light and doubled in size, about 1 hour.

Heat oven to 375°F. Uncover dough. Bake 20 to 25 minutes or until golden brown and rolls sound hollow when lightly tapped. Remove from pans immediately; cool on wire racks. Brush warm rolls with 1 tablespoon margarine; sprinkle with 1/2 teaspoon orange peel. **16 rolls.**

HIGH ALTITUDE—Above 3500 Feet: No change.

NUTRIENTS PER 1 ROLL

Calories	190	Protein	8% U.S. RDA
Protein	5g	Vitamin A	2% U.S. RDA
Carbohydrate	33g	Vitamin C	<2% U.S. RDA
Fat	4g	Thiamine	15% U.S. RDA
Cholesterol	15mg	Riboflavin	10% U.S. RDA
Sodium	320mg	Niacin	10% U.S. RDA
Potassium	140mg	Calcium	2% U.S. RDA
Dietary Fiber	2g	Iron	10% U.S. RDA

Easy Cheese Batter Bread

Frances Sisinni, Wisconsin
Bake-Off® 23, 1972

2½ cups all purpose or unbleached
　flour
2 teaspoons sugar
1½ teaspoons salt
1 package active dry yeast
4 ounces (1 cup) shredded
　Cheddar cheese
¾ cup milk
½ cup margarine or butter
3 eggs

Lightly spoon flour into measuring cup; level off. In large bowl, combine 1½ cups flour, sugar, salt and yeast; blend well. Stir in cheese. In small saucepan, heat milk and margarine until very warm (120 to 130°F.). Add warm liquid and eggs to flour mixture. Blend at low speed until moistened; beat 3 minutes at medium speed. By hand, stir in remaining 1 cup flour. Cover loosely with plastic wrap and cloth towel. Let rise in warm place (80 to 85°F.) until light and doubled in size, 45 to 60 minutes.

Generously grease 1½ or 2-quart casserole or 9 × 5-inch loaf pan. Stir down dough to remove all air bubbles. Turn into greased casserole. Cover; let rise in warm place until light and doubled in size, 20 to 25 minutes.

Heat oven to 350°F. Uncover dough. Bake 40 to 45 minutes or until deep golden brown. Remove from casserole immediately; cool on wire rack.
1 (18-slice) loaf.

HIGH ALTITUDE—Above 3500 Feet: Bake at 375°F. for 40 to 45 minutes.

NUTRIENTS PER 1 SLICE

Calories	150	Protein	8% U.S. RDA
Protein	5g	Vitamin A	6% U.S. RDA
Carbohydrate	15g	Vitamin C	<2% U.S. RDA
Fat	8g	Thiamine	8% U.S. RDA
Cholesterol	50g	Riboflavin	8% U.S. RDA
Sodium	290mg	Niacin	4% U.S. RDA
Potassium	60mg	Calcium	6% U.S. RDA
Dietary Fiber	<1mg	Iron	6% U.S. RDA

Graham Cracker Brown Bread

Grace M. Kain, Maine
Bake-Off® 10, 1958

2 cups (30 squares) finely crushed
　graham crackers or graham
　cracker crumbs
½ cup shortening
1¾ cups buttermilk*
¾ cup molasses
2 eggs, slightly beaten
1¾ cups all purpose or unbleached
　flour
2 teaspoons baking soda
1 teaspoon salt
¼ to ½ teaspoon nutmeg
1 cup raisins

Heat oven to 375°F. Grease and flour bottoms only of two 8 × 4-inch loaf pans. In large bowl, beat graham cracker crumbs and shortening until well blended. Add buttermilk, molasses and eggs; blend well. Lightly spoon flour into measuring cup; level off. In small bowl, combine flour, baking soda, salt and nutmeg; mix well. Add to graham cracker mixture; mix at low speed until well blended. Fold in raisins. Pour batter into greased and floured pans. Bake at 375°F. for 35 to 40 minutes or until toothpick inserted in center comes out clean. Cool 5 minutes; remove from pans. Cool on wire racks.
2 (16-slice) loaves.

TIP: *To substitute for buttermilk, use 1 tablespoon plus 2 teaspoons vinegar or lemon juice plus milk to make 1¾ cups.

HIGH ALTITUDE—Above 3500 Feet: Increase flour to 2¼ cups.

NUTRIENTS PER 1 SLICE

Calories	120	Protein	2% U.S. RDA
Protein	2g	Vitamin A	<2% U.S. RDA
Carbohydrate	18g	Vitamin C	<2% U.S. RDA
Fat	4g	Thiamine	4% U.S. RDA
Cholesterol	20mg	Riboflavin	6% U.S. RDA
Sodium	190mg	Niacin	2% U.S. RDA
Potassium	170mg	Calcium	4% U.S. RDA
Dietary Fiber	<1g	Iron	6% U.S. RDA

Easy Cheese Batter Bread

This moist, chewy casserole bread is even better the second day after baking.

Graham Cracker Brown Bread

Moist and flavorful, this quick bread tastes great spread with cream cheese or served with sausage and baked beans.

Easy English Muffins

Easy English Muffins

Julia Hauber, Kansas
Bake-Off® 19, 1968

2 packages active dry yeast
2 cups warm water
5 to 6 cups all purpose or
unbleached flour
1 tablespoon sugar
3 teaspoons salt
½ cup shortening
Cornmeal
Margarine or butter

In large bowl, dissolve yeast in warm water (105 to 115°F.). Lightly spoon flour into measuring cup; level off. Add 3 cups flour, sugar, salt and shortening to yeast mixture, stirring by hand until moistened. Stir vigorously by hand until smooth. Gradually add remaining 2 to 3 cups flour to form a stiff dough, beating well after each addition. On floured surface, gently knead dough 5 to 6 times until no longer sticky. Roll dough to ¼ to ⅜-inch thickness; cut with 3 to 4-inch floured round cutter. Sprinkle cornmeal evenly over 2 ungreased cookie sheets. Place cutout dough on cornmeal; sprinkle with additional cornmeal. Cover loosely with plastic wrap and cloth towel. Let rise in warm place until light, 30 to 45 minutes.

Heat griddle to 350°F. With wide spatula, invert dough rounds onto ungreased griddle. Bake 5 to 6 minutes on each side or until light golden brown; cool. Split, toast and butter. **18 to 26 muffins.**

HIGH ALTITUDE—Above 3500 Feet: No change.

NUTRIENTS PER 1 MUFFIN

Calories	250	Protein	4% U.S. RDA
Protein	3g	Vitamin A	8% U.S. RDA
Carbohydrate	24g	Vitamin C	<2% U.S. RDA
Fat	16g	Thiamine	10% U.S. RDA
Cholesterol	0mg	Riboflavin	8% U.S. RDA
Sodium	380mg	Niacin	8% U.S. RDA
Potassium	45mg	Calcium	<2% U.S. RDA
Dietary Fiber	<1g	Iron	8% U.S. RDA

Potato Chive Rolls

Susan H. Cox, Pennsylvania
Bake-Off® 27, 1976

4½ to 5 cups all purpose or
unbleached flour
1 cup mashed potato flakes
1 tablespoon sugar
3 to 4 teaspoons fresh chopped
chives or dried chives
2 teaspoons salt
2 packages active dry yeast
2 cups milk
½ cup dairy sour cream
2 eggs

Lightly spoon flour into measuring cup; level off. In large bowl, combine 1½ cups flour, potato flakes, sugar, chives, salt and yeast; blend well. In small saucepan, heat milk and sour cream until very warm (120 to 130°F.). Add warm liquid and eggs to flour mixture. Blend at low speed until moistened; beat 3 minutes at medium speed. By hand, stir in remaining 3 to 3½ cups flour to form a stiff dough. Cover loosely with plastic wrap and cloth towel. Let rise in warm place (80 to 85°F.) until light and doubled in size, 45 to 55 minutes.

Generously grease 13 × 9-inch pan. On well-floured surface, toss dough until no longer sticky. Divide dough into 24 equal pieces; shape into balls. Place in greased pan. Cover; let rise in warm place until light and doubled in size, 30 to 35 minutes.

Heat oven to 375°F. Uncover dough. Bake 25 to 35 minutes or until golden brown. Remove from pan immediately; cool on wire rack. If desired, lightly dust tops of rolls with flour. **24 rolls.**

HIGH ALTITUDE—Above 3500 Feet: No change.

NUTRIENTS PER 1 ROLL

Calories	130	Protein	6% U.S. RDA
Protein	4g	Vitamin A	2% U.S. RDA
Carbohydrate	24g	Vitamin C	<2% U.S. RDA
Fat	2g	Thiamine	10% U.S. RDA
Cholesterol	25mg	Riboflavin	10% U.S. RDA
Sodium	200mg	Niacin	8% U.S. RDA
Potassium	115mg	Calcium	4% U.S. RDA
Dietary Fiber	1g	Iron	8% U.S. RDA

Potato Chive Rolls

Mildly flavored with sour cream and chives, these light and airy pull-apart rolls are an excellent addition to any dinner.

Golden Sesame Loaves

Golden Sesame Loaves

᛬ᛣ᛬

Grayce Berggren, Pennsylvania
Bake-Off® 33, 1988

5 to 6 cups bread flour*
¹/₂ cup instant nonfat dry milk
¹/₂ cup oat bran
¹/₂ cup sesame seed, toasted**
1¹/₂ teaspoons salt
1 teaspoon sugar
2 packages active dry yeast
1³/₄ cups water
¹/₄ cup oil
¹/₄ cup honey
1 egg
1 egg white, beaten
1 tablespoon sesame seed

Lightly spoon flour into measuring cup; level off. In large bowl, combine 2 cups flour, instant nonfat dry milk, oat bran, ¹/₂ cup toasted sesame seed, salt, sugar and yeast; blend well. In small saucepan, heat water, oil and honey until very warm (120 to 130°F.). Add warm liquid and 1 egg to flour mixture. Blend at low speed until moistened; beat 3 minutes at medium speed. By hand, stir in 2³/₄ to 3¹/₂ cups flour until dough pulls cleanly away from sides of bowl.

On floured surface, knead in remaining ¹/₄ to ¹/₂ cup flour until dough is smooth and elastic, about 10 minutes. Place dough in greased bowl; cover loosely with plastic wrap and cloth towel. Let rise in warm place (80 to 85°F.) until light and doubled in size, about 1 hour.

Grease two 9×5 or three 7×3-inch loaf pans. Punch down dough several times to remove all air bubbles. Divide dough in half; shape into balls. Allow to rest on counter covered with inverted bowl for 15 minutes. Shape into 2 loaves by rolling each half into 12 × 8-inch rectangle. Starting with 8-inch side, roll up; pinch edges firmly to seal. Place seam side down in greased pans. Cover; let rise in warm place until dough fills pans and tops of loaves are about 1 inch above pan edges, about 45 minutes.

Heat oven to 350°F. Uncover dough. Carefully brush tops of loaves with beaten egg white. Sprinkle with 1 tablespoon sesame seed. Bake at 350°F. for 30 to 40 minutes or until loaves sound hollow when lightly tapped. Remove from pans immediately; cool on wire racks. **2 (16-slice) loaves.**

TIPS: *All purpose or unbleached flour can be substituted for bread flour. Self-rising flour is not recommended. Omit resting period and decrease each rise time by 10 to 15 minutes.

**To toast sesame seed, spread on cookie sheet; bake at 375°F. for about 5 minutes or until light golden brown, stirring occasionally. Or, spread in medium skillet; stir over medium heat for about 10 minutes or until light golden brown.

HIGH ALTITUDE—Above 3500 Feet: Decrease each rise time by about 15 minutes. Bake at 350°F. for 25 to 35 minutes.

NUTRIENTS PER 1 SLICE

Calories	140	Protein	6% U.S. RDA
Protein	5g	Vitamin A	<2% U.S. RDA
Carbohydrate	24g	Vitamin C	<2% U.S. RDA
Fat	3g	Thiamine	15% U.S. RDA
Cholesterol	8mg	Riboflavin	10% U.S. RDA
Sodium	115mg	Niacin	8% U.S. RDA
Potassium	80mg	Calcium	2% U.S. RDA
Dietary Fiber	1g	Iron	8% U.S. RDA

Cheese 'n Onion Sandwich Buns

Mariette A. Deutsch, Wisconsin
Bake-Off® 24, 1973

1 package hot roll mix
2 tablespoons dry onion soup mix
½ teaspoon dry mustard
4 ounces (1 cup) shredded Cheddar or American cheese
1 cup water heated to 120° to 130°F.
2 tablespoons margarine or butter, softened
1 egg

Grease cookie sheets. In large bowl, combine flour mixture with yeast from foil packet. Add soup mix, dry mustard and cheese; blend well. Stir in *hot* water, margarine and egg until dough pulls cleanly away from sides of bowl. Turn dough out onto lightly floured surface. With greased or floured hands, shape dough into a ball. Knead dough for 5 minutes until smooth. Cover with large bowl; let rest 5 minutes.

Divide dough into 8 equal pieces; shape into balls. Place on greased cookie sheets; flatten each ball slightly. Cover loosely with plastic wrap and cloth towel. Let rise in warm place (80 to 85°F.) until almost doubled in size, about 30 minutes.

Heat oven to 375°F. Uncover dough. Bake 12 to 17 minutes or until golden brown. Remove from cookie sheets immediately; cool on wire racks. **8 rolls.**

HIGH ALTITUDE—Above 3500 Feet: No change.

NUTRIENTS PER 1 ROLL

Calories	300	Protein	15% U.S. RDA
Protein	11g	Vitamin A	6% U.S. RDA
Carbohydrate	43g	Vitamin C	<2% U.S. RDA
Fat	9g	Thiamine	25% U.S. RDA
Cholesterol	50mg	Riboflavin	25% U.S. RDA
Sodium	740mg	Niacin	20% U.S. RDA
Potassium	120mg	Calcium	10% U.S. RDA
Dietary Fiber	1g	Iron	10% U.S. RDA

Golden Sesame Loaves

The sesame seed in the bread creates a delicious nutty flavor. You'll love this bread toasted!

Old Plantation Rolls

Old Plantation Rolls

First Lady Eleanor Roosevelt launched the Bake-Off® Contest when this recipe won recognition. Forty years later it continues to be a natural for today's busy cooks. The no-knead dough bakes into warm, tender rolls — or, if desired, refrigerate the dough overnight for fresh baked rolls the next day.

Lucile Baker, Colorado
Bake-Off® 1, 1949

5 to 6 cups all purpose or unbleached flour
¼ cup sugar
1 teaspoon baking powder
1 teaspoon salt
½ teaspoon baking soda
1 package active dry yeast
1 cup water
1 cup milk
½ cup shortening
1 egg

Grease 24 muffin cups. Lightly spoon flour into measuring cup; level off. In large bowl, combine 3 cups flour, sugar, baking powder, salt, baking soda and yeast; blend well. In small saucepan, heat water, milk and shortening until very warm (120 to 130°F.). Add warm liquid and egg to flour mixture. Blend at low speed until moistened; beat 3 minutes at medium speed. By hand, stir in remaining 2 to 3 cups flour to form a stiff dough. Cover loosely with greased plastic wrap and cloth towel. Let rise in warm place (80 to 85°F.) until light and doubled in size, about 1 hour.

Punch down dough several times to remove all air bubbles.* On well-floured surface, toss dough until no longer sticky. Divide dough into 24 equal pieces; shape into balls.** Place 1 ball in each greased muffin cup. With scissors or sharp knife, make X-shaped cut in each ball, forming 4 equal pieces. Cover; let rise in warm place until light and doubled in size, 35 to 45 minutes.

Heat oven to 400°F. Uncover dough. Bake 13 to 15 minutes or until golden brown. Remove from pans immediately. **24 rolls.**

TIPS: *Rolls can be prepared to this point, covered and refrigerated overnight. Increase second rise time to 1¼ hours.

**For a more traditional cloverleaf shape, divide dough into 72 pieces; shape into balls. Place 3 balls in each greased muffin cup. Cover; let rise in warm place until light and doubled in size, 35 to 45 minutes. Bake as directed above.

HIGH ALTITUDE—Above 3500 Feet: No change.

NUTRIENTS PER 1 ROLL
Calories	160	Protein	6% U.S. RDA
Protein	4g	Vitamin A	<2% U.S. RDA
Carbohydrate	25g	Vitamin C	<2% U.S. RDA
Fat	5g	Thiamine	10% U.S. RDA
Cholesterol	10mg	Riboflavin	8% U.S. RDA
Sodium	135mg	Niacin	8% U.S. RDA
Potassium	50mg	Calcium	2% U.S. RDA
Dietary Fiber	<1g	Iron	8% U.S. RDA

The Giant's Corn Muffins

Irene McEwen, Indiana
Bake-Off® 33, 1988

MUFFINS
½ cup all purpose, unbleached or self-rising flour*
½ cup whole wheat flour
1 cup cornmeal
1 teaspoon baking powder
1 teaspoon baking soda
½ teaspoon salt
¼ teaspoon nutmeg
1 cup plain yogurt or buttermilk
¼ cup margarine or butter, melted
3 tablespoons honey
1 egg
12-ounce can vacuum packed whole kernel corn with sweet peppers, drained
1 green onion, sliced

TOPPING
1 tablespoon all purpose, unbleached or self-rising flour
1 tablespoon cornmeal
Dash salt
4 teaspoons margarine or butter

Heat oven to 400°F. Grease bottoms only of six 6-oz. custard cups or 12 muffin cups.** Lightly spoon flour into measuring cup; level off. In large bowl, combine ½ cup all purpose flour, whole wheat flour, 1 cup cornmeal, baking powder, baking soda, ½ teaspoon salt and nutmeg; blend well. In medium bowl, combine yogurt, ¼ cup margarine, honey, egg, corn and green onion; mix well. Add to dry ingredients; stir until dry ingredients are just moistened. Spoon batter evenly into greased custard cups. (Cups will be full.) In small bowl, combine all topping ingredients; mix well. Crumble evenly over batter in each cup. Bake at 400°F. for 20 to 30 minutes or until toothpick inserted in center comes out clean. Cool 1 minute; remove from custard cups. **6 large or 12 regular sized muffins.**

TIPS: *If using self-rising flour, omit baking powder, baking soda and salt.

**For easier handling, place custard cups on cookie sheet.

HIGH ALTITUDE—Above 3500 Feet: No change.

NUTRIENTS PER 1 LARGE MUFFIN

Calories	380	Protein	15% U.S. RDA
Protein	9g	Vitamin A	20% U.S. RDA
Carbohydrate	56g	Vitamin C	6% U.S. RDA
Fat	13g	Thiamine	15% U.S. RDA
Cholesterol	50mg	Riboflavin	15% U.S. RDA
Sodium	760mg	Niacin	10% U.S. RDA
Potassium	320mg	Calcium	10% U.S. RDA
Dietary Fiber	2g	Iron	10% U.S. RDA

Dairyland Date Muffins

❀

Phyllis Saevre, Wisconsin
Bake-Off® 20, 1969

1 cup shreds of whole bran cereal
½ cup milk
2 (3-ounce) packages cream cheese
1 cup dairy sour cream
1 package date bread mix
1 egg

Heat oven to 400°F. Line with paper baking cups or grease bottoms only of 16 medium muffin cups or 12 large muffin cups. In large bowl, combine bran cereal and milk; let stand 10 minutes to soften. Cut each package of cream cheese into 6 to 8 equal cubes; set aside. Add sour cream, bread mix and egg to bran mixture; stir by hand 50 to 75 strokes until dry particles are moistened. Divide batter evenly among paper-lined muffin cups. Press cube of cream cheese into batter in each cup; spread batter to completely cover cream cheese. Bake at 400°F. for 19 to

21 minutes or until golden brown. Cool 1 minute; remove from pan.
12 to 16 muffins.

HIGH ALTITUDE—Above 3500 Feet: Add 1 tablespoon flour to dry bread mix.

NUTRIENTS PER 1 LARGE MUFFIN

Calories	200	Protein	6% U.S. RDA
Protein	4g	Vitamin A	8% U.S. RDA
Carbohydrate	27g	Vitamin C	2% U.S. RDA
Fat	9g	Thiamine	10% U.S. RDA
Cholesterol	35mg	Riboflavin	10% U.S. RDA
Sodium	190mg	Niacin	6% U.S. RDA
Potassium	140mg	Calcium	4% U.S. RDA
Dietary Fiber	2g	Iron	8% U.S. RDA

Lemon Raspberry Muffins

❀

Stephanie Luetkehans, Illinois
Bake-Off® 33, 1988

2 cups all purpose, unbleached or self-rising flour*
1 cup sugar
3 teaspoons baking powder
½ teaspoon salt
1 cup half-and-half
½ cup oil
1 teaspoon lemon extract
2 eggs
1 cup fresh or frozen raspberries without syrup (do not thaw)

Heat oven to 425°F. Line 12 large or 16 medium muffin cups with paper baking cups. Lightly spoon flour into measuring cup; level off. In large bowl, combine flour, sugar, baking powder and salt; mix well. In small bowl, combine half-and-half, oil, lemon extract and eggs; blend well. Add to dry ingredients; stir until dry ingredients are just moistened. Carefully fold in raspberries. Fill paper-lined muffin cups ¾ full. Bake at 425°F. for 18 to 23 minutes or until golden brown. Cool 5 minutes; remove from pan.
12 to 16 muffins.

TIP: *If using self-rising flour, omit baking powder and salt.

HIGH ALTITUDE—Above 3500 Feet: Decrease baking powder to 2 teaspoons.

NUTRIENTS PER 1 LARGE MUFFIN

Calories	200	Protein	4% U.S. RDA
Protein	3g	Vitamin A	2% U.S. RDA
Carbohydrate	26g	Vitamin C	2% U.S. RDA
Fat	9g	Thiamine	6% U.S. RDA
Cholesterol	40mg	Riboflavin	6% U.S. RDA
Sodium	140mg	Niacin	4% U.S. RDA
Potassium	55mg	Calcium	6% U.S. RDA
Dietary Fiber	<1g	Iron	4% U.S. RDA

Lemon Raspberry Muffins

❀

"After buying and eating dozens of bakery muffins, I decided to make my own," said the finalist who created these $2,000 prize-winning muffins. So rich, tender and flavorful, these muffins can easily be dessert.

Italian Cheese Bread Ring

Italian Cheese Bread Ring

Kayleen L. Sloboden, Washington
Bake-Off® 31, 1984

2 tablespoons sesame seed
4½ to 5¼ cups all purpose,
   unbleached or bread flour*
¼ cup sugar
1½ teaspoons salt
2 packages active dry yeast
1 cup milk
1 cup water
½ cup margarine or butter
2 eggs

FILLING

4 ounces (1 cup) shredded
   mozzarella cheese
½ teaspoon Italian seasoning
¼ teaspoon garlic powder
¼ cup margarine or butter,
   softened

Generously grease 12-cup fluted tube or 10-inch tube pan; sprinkle with sesame seed. Lightly spoon flour into measuring cup; level off. In large bowl, combine 2½ cups flour, sugar, salt and yeast; blend well. In small saucepan, heat milk, water and ½ cup margarine until very warm (120 to 130°F.). Add warm liquid and eggs to flour mixture. Blend at low speed until moistened; beat 3 minutes at medium speed. By hand, stir in remaining 2 to 2¾ cups flour to form a stiff batter.

In small bowl, combine all filling ingredients; mix well. Spoon half of batter over sesame seed in greased pan; spoon filling mixture evenly over batter to within ½ inch of sides of pan. Spoon remaining batter over filling. Cover loosely with plastic wrap and cloth towel. Let rise in warm place (80 to 85°F.) until light and doubled in size, about 30 minutes.

Heat oven to 350°F. Uncover dough. Bake 30 to 40 minutes or until golden brown and loaf sounds hollow when lightly tapped. Remove from pan immediately; cool on wire racks. Serve warm or cool. **1 (24-slice) loaf.**

HIGH ALTITUDE—Above 3500 Feet: No change.

NUTRIENTS PER 1 SLICE

Calories	190	Protein	8% U.S. RDA
Protein	5g	Vitamin A	6% U.S. RDA
Carbohydrate	24g	Vitamin C	<2% U.S. RDA
Fat	8g	Thiamine	15% U.S. RDA
Cholesterol	25mg	Riboflavin	10% U.S. RDA
Sodium	240mg	Niacin	8% U.S. RDA
Potassium	70mg	Calcium	6% U.S. RDA
Dietary Fiber	<1g	Iron	8% U.S. RDA

Banana-Wheat Quick Bread

Barbara Goldstein, California
Bake-Off® 24, 1973

1¼ cups all purpose or unbleached
   flour
½ cup whole wheat flour
1 cup sugar
1 teaspoon baking soda
1 teaspoon salt
1½ cups (3 medium) mashed
   bananas
¼ cup margarine or butter,
   softened
2 tablespoons orange juice
¼ teaspoon lemon juice, if desired
1 egg
¼ to ½ cup raisins

Heat oven to 350°F. Grease and flour bottom only of 9 × 5 or 8 × 4-inch loaf pan. Lightly spoon flour into measuring cup; level off. In large bowl, combine all purpose flour, whole wheat flour and remaining ingredients except raisins; beat 3 minutes at medium speed. Fold in raisins. Pour batter into greased and floured pan. Bake at 350°F. for 55 to 65 minutes or until toothpick inserted in center comes out clean. Cool 10 minutes; remove from pan. Cool on wire rack. **1 (16-slice) loaf.**

HIGH ALTITUDE—Above 3500 Feet: Increase all purpose flour to 1½ cups.

NUTRIENTS PER 1 SLICE

Calories	170	Protein	2% U.S. RDA
Protein	2g	Vitamin A	2% U.S. RDA
Carbohydrate	31g	Vitamin C	2% U.S. RDA
Fat	4g	Thiamine	6% U.S. RDA
Cholesterol	15mg	Riboflavin	4% U.S. RDA
Sodium	240mg	Niacin	4% U.S. RDA
Potassium	150mg	Calcium	<2% U.S. RDA
Dietary Fiber	1g	Iron	4% U.S. RDA

Each event is unique—

Elegant hotels and celebrity spokespeople are as much a part of the Bake-Off® as new recipes. The Duchess of Windsor, Ronald Reagan, Arthur Godfrey, Mamie Eisenhower, Pat Boone, Art Linkletter and Bob Barker have all lent it their names and personal appearances. Eleanor Roosevelt presented prizes at the first event and later wrote in her syndicated column, "This is a healthy contest and a highly American one. It may sell Pillsbury flour but it also reaches far down into the lives of the housewives of America." She hastened to add that three men had qualified for the trip to New York. One of their entries was called "Quick Man-Prepared Dinner." Since its birth in New York, the contest has been transported to different cities nationwide. Honolulu in 1971 drew a surge of entries.

Half-Time Spoon Rolls

Half-Time Spoon Rolls

Created in the '50s, this recipe is convenience-oriented for the '90s. These moist and light dinner rolls use just one bowl for both mixing and rising and require no kneading, rolling or shaping!

Virginia Walker, Wisconsin
Bake-Off® 2, 1950

3 to 3¹/₂ cups all purpose or unbleached flour
¹/₄ cup sugar
1 teaspoon salt
1 package active dry yeast
³/₄ cup milk
³/₄ cup water
¹/₃ cup margarine or butter
1 egg

Lightly spoon flour into measuring cup; level off. In large bowl, combine 1¹/₂ cups flour, sugar, salt and yeast; blend well. In small saucepan, heat milk, water and margarine until very warm (120 to 130°F.). Add warm liquid and egg to flour mixture. Blend at low speed until moistened; beat 3 minutes at medium speed. By hand, stir in remaining 1¹/₂ to 2 cups flour to form a stiff batter. Cover loosely with plastic wrap and cloth towel. Let rise in warm place (80 to 85°F.) until light and doubled in size, 45 to 50 minutes.

Grease 18 muffin cups. Stir down dough to remove all air bubbles. Spoon into greased muffin cups, filling about ²/₃ full. Cover loosely with greased plastic wrap and cloth towel; let rise in warm place until light and doubled in size, 25 to 35 minutes.

Heat oven to 400°F. Uncover dough. Bake 15 to 20 minutes or until golden brown. Remove from pans immediately; cool on wire racks. **18 rolls.**

HIGH ALTITUDE—Above 3500 Feet: No change.

NUTRIENTS PER 1 ROLL

Calories	140	Protein	4% U.S. RDA
Protein	3g	Vitamin A	2% U.S. RDA
Carbohydrate	22g	Vitamin C	<2% U.S. RDA
Fat	4g	Thiamine	10% U.S. RDA
Cholesterol	15mg	Riboflavin	8% U.S. RDA
Sodium	170mg	Niacin	6% U.S. RDA
Potassium	50mg	Calcium	<2% U.S. RDA
Dietary Fiber	<1g	Iron	6% U.S. RDA

Polish Poppy Swirl Loaf

Gene Swiderski, Minnesota
Bake-Off® 29, 1980

FILLING
³/₄ cup poppy seed, ground*
¹/₂ cup sugar
³/₄ cup milk
¹/₂ teaspoon vanilla
¹/₂ teaspoon almond extract
1 egg, separated, reserving yolk for bread

BREAD
1 package hot roll mix
2 tablespoons sugar
³/₄ cup water heated to 120 to 130°F.
2 tablespoons margarine or butter, softened
¹/₂ teaspoon vanilla
¹/₂ teaspoon almond extract
2 eggs
Reserved egg yolk

FROSTING
¹/₂ cup powdered sugar
1 tablespoon margarine or butter, softened
1 teaspoon water
¹/₂ teaspoon vanilla
¹/₂ teaspoon almond extract
1 tablespoon slivered almonds

In medium saucepan, combine poppy seed, ¹/₂ cup sugar and milk. Cook over medium heat until thick and milk is absorbed, about 15 minutes. Cool slightly; add ¹/₂ teaspoon vanilla, ¹/₂ teaspoon almond extract and egg white. Cool.

Grease 9×5-inch loaf pan. In large bowl, combine flour mixture with yeast from foil packet and 2 tablespoons sugar; blend well. Stir in *hot* water, 2 tablespoons margarine, ¹/₂ teaspoon vanilla, ¹/₂ teaspoon almond extract, 2 eggs and reserved egg yolk until dough pulls cleanly away from sides of bowl.

Polish Poppy Swirl Loaf

Turn dough out onto lightly floured surface. With greased or floured hands, shape dough into a ball. Knead dough for 5 minutes until smooth. Cover with large bowl; let rest 5 minutes.

On lightly floured surface, roll dough to 18 × 12-inch rectangle. Spread with cooled filling mixture. Starting with 18-inch side, roll up tightly; pinch edges and ends to seal. Fold roll in half, seam side down. Place seam side down in greased pan. Cover loosely with plastic wrap and cloth towel. Let rise in warm place (80 to 85°F.) until almost doubled in size, about 30 minutes.

Heat oven to 350°F. Uncover dough. Bake 30 to 45 minutes or until deep golden brown and loaf sounds hollow when lightly tapped. Remove from pan immediately; cool on wire rack. In small bowl, blend all frosting ingredients except almonds until smooth. Frost warm loaf; sprinkle with almonds. **1 (18-slice) loaf.**

TIP: *Poppy seed can be ground in blender at medium speed for 1 minute, scraping sides once.

HIGH ALTITUDE—Above 3500 Feet: No change.

NUTRIENTS PER 1 SLICE

Calories	190	Protein	8% U.S. RDA
Protein	5g	Vitamin A	2% U.S. RDA
Carbohydrate	30g	Vitamin C	<2% U.S. RDA
Fat	6g	Thiamine	15% U.S. RDA
Cholesterol	45mg	Riboflavin	10% U.S. RDA
Sodium	210mg	Niacin	8% U.S. RDA
Potassium	105mg	Calcium	10% U.S. RDA
Dietary Fiber	1g	Iron	8% U.S. RDA

Pictured top to bottom: No-Knead Water-Rising Twists, page 93; Magic Marshmallow Crescent Puffs, page 91; Country Apple Coffee Cake, page 103

Sweet Rolls and Coffee Cakes

No category of Bake-Off® recipes demonstrates greater creativity than this one. From ever-so-tender Country Apple Coffee Cake and Chocolate Almond Crescent Braid to old-fashioned Whole Wheat Caramel Rolls, so gooey and good—these are the tastes that make breakfast worth waking up for.

The sweet rolls and coffee cakes category was off to a spectacular start at the very first Bake-Off® Contest. Grand Prize honors went to No-Knead Water-Rising Twists, a sweet roll recipe featuring an unusual rising method and remarkably delicious results.

Classic from-scratch recipes, such as the Grand Prize-winning Ring-a-Lings, remain the choice of many baking enthusiasts. Others prefer the quick and easy methods used by Bake-Off® finalists to create the Grand Prize winners, Magic Marshmallow Crescent Puffs and Easy Crescent Danish Rolls. But whatever the method, the tantalizing treats in this collection look as though they belong in a showcase at the finest bakery.

Many of these recipes start simply with refrigerated dough or hot roll mix. Luscious fruit or nut fillings, crunchy toppings and flavorings, plus clever shapings turn these convenience products into mouth-watering delicacies.

Many Bake-Off® finalists draw on their own food heritage for recipe inspiration. Recipes like Quick Praline Rolls represent old family favorites that have become easy, any-day breakfast fare. Crescent Dutch Letter Pastries, Hot Roll Moravian Sugar Cake and Danish Almond Crescent Ring are recipes reminiscent of European bakery specialties—adapted for preparation by novice bakers. In short, the goodness of yesterday merges with the convenience of today, thanks to the creativity of Bake-Off® finalists.

Whole Wheat Caramel Rolls

Lorraine Edie, New York
Bake-Off® 9, 1957

1 to 2 cups all purpose or unbleached flour
1 cup whole wheat flour
3 tablespoons sugar
1 teaspoon salt
1 package active dry yeast
¾ cup milk
¼ cup water
2 tablespoons shortening
1 cup firmly packed brown sugar
⅓ cup margarine or butter, melted
½ cup chopped nuts

Lightly spoon flour into measuring cup; level off. In large bowl, combine ½ cup all purpose flour, whole wheat flour, sugar, salt and yeast; blend well. In small saucepan, heat milk, water and shortening until very warm (120 to 130°F.). Add warm liquid to flour mixture. By hand, stir until dry ingredients are moistened. Stir in ¼ to ¾ cup all purpose flour to form a stiff dough. On floured surface, knead in remaining ¼ to ¾ cup all purpose flour until dough is smooth and elastic, about 5 minutes. Place dough in greased bowl; cover loosely with plastic wrap and cloth towel. Let rise in warm place (80 to 85°F.) until light and doubled in size, about 1¼ hours.

Grease 9-inch square pan. Punch down dough several times to remove all air bubbles. On lightly floured surface, roll out dough to 16 × 12-inch rectangle. In small bowl, combine brown sugar and margarine; blend well. Spread evenly over dough; sprinkle with nuts. Starting with 16-inch side, roll up tightly; pinch edges to seal. Cut into 16 slices; place cut side down in greased pan. Cover; let rise in warm place until light and doubled in size, 45 to 60 minutes.

Heat oven to 350°F. Uncover dough. Bake 25 to 30 minutes or until golden brown. Cool 2 minutes; invert onto serving plate. **16 rolls.**

HIGH ALTITUDE—Above 3500 Feet: Bake at 375°F. for 25 to 30 minutes.

NUTRIENTS PER 1 ROLL

Calories	210	Protein	4% U.S. RDA
Protein	3g	Vitamin A	4% U.S. RDA
Carbohydrate	31g	Vitamin C	<2% U.S. RDA
Fat	8g	Thiamine	10% U.S. RDA
Cholesterol	0mg	Riboflavin	6% U.S. RDA
Sodium	190mg	Niacin	6% U.S. RDA
Potassium	135mg	Calcium	2% U.S. RDA
Dietary Fiber	2g	Iron	8% U.S. RDA

Twist-of-Honey Orange Rolls

Roxanne Frisbie, Oregon
Bake-Off® 33, 1988

1 tablespoon finely chopped nuts
1 tablespoon grated orange peel
3 tablespoons margarine or butter, softened
1 tablespoon honey
10-ounce can refrigerated flaky biscuits
½ cup sugar
¼ cup orange juice
1 teaspoon vanilla

Heat oven to 400°F. In small bowl, combine nuts, orange peel, margarine and honey; mix well. Separate dough into 10 biscuits. Separate each biscuit into 2 layers. Spread top of 10 layers with teaspoonful of honey-orange mixture. Top each with remaining layers; press together to form 10 filled biscuits. Gently pull and twist each filled biscuit 4 or 5 times to form 3½-inch twisted roll. Place rolls in ungreased 8 or 9-inch square pan.

In small saucepan, combine sugar, orange juice and vanilla. Cook over medium-high heat until sugar is melted and mixture begins to boil, stirring constantly. Spoon over rolls. (Mixture will glaze rolls while baking.) Bake at 400°F. for 16 to 22 minutes or until golden brown. Cool 2 minutes; invert onto serving plate. Serve warm. **10 rolls.**

NUTRIENTS PER 1 ROLL

Calories	180	Protein	2% U.S. RDA
Protein	2g	Vitamin A	2% U.S. RDA
Carbohydrate	25g	Vitamin C	4% U.S. RDA
Fat	8g	Thiamine	6% U.S. RDA
Cholesterol	0mg	Riboflavin	4% U.S. RDA
Sodium	330mg	Niacin	4% U.S. RDA
Potassium	35mg	Calcium	<2% U.S. RDA
Dietary Fiber	<1g	Iron	4% U.S. RDA

Whole Wheat Caramel Rolls

Bohemian Raisin Biscuit Kolachy

Bohemian Raisin Biscuit Kolachy

Margaret Kramer, Wisconsin
Bake-Off® 30, 1982

1 cup raisins or currants
¼ cup firmly packed brown sugar
¼ cup water
1 to 2 teaspoons lemon juice
½ cup sugar
½ teaspoon cinnamon
10-ounce can refrigerated flaky biscuits
¼ cup margarine or butter, melted

GLAZE
½ cup powdered sugar
½ teaspoon vanilla
2 to 4 teaspoons milk

Heat oven to 375°F. In small saucepan, combine raisins, brown sugar, water and lemon juice. Cook over medium heat about 7 minutes or until mixture thickens, stirring occasionally. Cool. In small bowl, combine sugar and cinnamon; set aside.

Separate dough into 10 biscuits. Dip both sides of each biscuit in margarine, then in sugar mixture. Place coated biscuits, sides touching, in ungreased 15×10×1-inch baking pan or 13×9-inch pan. With thumb, make wide imprint in center of each biscuit; fill with rounded tablespoonful of raisin mixture. Bake at 375°F. for 15 to 20 minutes or until golden brown. In small bowl, blend powdered sugar, vanilla and enough milk for desired drizzling consistency. Drizzle over warm rolls. **10 rolls.**

NUTRIENTS PER 1 ROLL

Calories	250	Protein	2% U.S. RDA
Protein	2g	Vitamin A	4% U.S. RDA
Carbohydrate	44g	Vitamin C	<2% U.S. RDA
Fat	8g	Thiamine	8% U.S. RDA
Cholesterol	0mg	Riboflavin	4% U.S. RDA
Sodium	350mg	Niacin	4% U.S. RDA
Potassium	150mg	Calcium	2% U.S. RDA
Dietary Fiber	1g	Iron	6% U.S. RDA

Grand Prize Winner

Magic Marshmallow Crescent Puffs

Edna (Holmgren) Walker, Minnesota
Bake-Off® 20, 1969

¼ cup sugar
2 tablespoons flour
1 teaspoon cinnamon
2 (8-ounce) cans refrigerated crescent dinner rolls
16 large marshmallows
¼ cup margarine or butter, melted

GLAZE
½ cup powdered sugar
½ teaspoon vanilla
2 to 3 teaspoons milk
¼ cup chopped nuts, if desired

Heat oven to 375°F. In small bowl, combine sugar, flour and cinnamon. Separate dough into 16 triangles. Dip 1 marshmallow in margarine; roll in sugar mixture. Place marshmallow on wide end of triangle. Roll up, starting at wide end of triangle and rolling to opposite point. Completely cover marshmallow with dough; firmly pinch edges to seal. Dip one end in remaining margarine; place margarine side down in ungreased large muffin cup or 6-ounce custard cup. Repeat with remaining marshmallows. Bake at 375°F. for 12 to 15 minutes or until golden brown. (Place foil or cookie sheet on rack below muffin cups during baking to catch any spillage.) Remove from muffin cups immediately; cool on wire racks. In small bowl, blend powdered sugar, vanilla and enough milk for desired drizzling consistency. Drizzle over warm rolls. Sprinkle with nuts. **16 rolls.**

NUTRIENTS PER 1 ROLL

Calories	190	Protein	2% U.S. RDA
Protein	2g	Vitamin A	2% U.S. RDA
Carbohydrate	23g	Vitamin C	<2% U.S. RDA
Fat	10g	Thiamine	6% U.S. RDA
Cholesterol	2mg	Riboflavin	4% U.S. RDA
Sodium	270mg	Niacin	4% U.S. RDA
Potassium	80mg	Calcium	<2% U.S. RDA
Dietary Fiber	<1g	Iron	4% U.S. RDA

Bohemian Raisin Biscuit Kolachy

This recipe has simplified the preparation of kolachy, a traditional Old World pastry, by using refrigerated flaky biscuits for the dough.

Magic Marshmallow Crescent Puffs

"Such a simple way to get great taste," people exclaim when they try this Bake-Off® classic recipe. It is created by wrapping refrigerated crescent roll dough around cinnamon-sugar-coated marshmallows. The marshmallows melt during baking, forming a sweet, hollow puff.

Lemon Nut Rolls

Lemon Nut Rolls

Betty May, Maryland
Bake-Off® 10, 1958

DOUGH

2½ to 3½ cups all purpose or
    unbleached flour
⅓ cup mashed potato flakes
⅓ cup sugar
1 teaspoon salt
½ teaspoon grated lemon peel
1 package active dry yeast
¾ cup water
½ cup milk
⅓ cup margarine or butter
1 tablespoon lemon juice
1 egg

FILLING

2 tablespoons margarine or butter,
    softened
¾ cup sugar
½ cup chopped pecans
1 teaspoon grated lemon peel

GLAZE

½ cup powdered sugar
½ teaspoon grated lemon peel
½ teaspoon lemon juice
2 to 3 teaspoons half-and-half or
    milk

Lightly spoon flour into measuring cup;
level off. In large bowl, combine 1 cup
flour, potato flakes, ⅓ cup sugar, salt,
½ teaspoon lemon peel and yeast;
blend well. In small saucepan, heat
water, milk and ⅓ cup margarine until
very warm (120 to 130°F.). Add warm
liquid, 1 tablespoon lemon juice and
egg to flour mixture. Blend at low speed
until moistened; beat 2 minutes at medium speed. By hand, stir in remaining
1½ to 2½ cups flour to form a stiff
dough. Cover loosely with plastic wrap
and cloth towel. Let rise in warm place
(80 to 85°F.) until light and doubled in
size, about 1 hour.

Grease two 8 or 9-inch round cake
pans. On well-floured surface, toss

dough until no longer sticky. Roll out dough to 16×12-inch rectangle. Spread with 2 tablespoons margarine. In small bowl, combine remaining filling ingredients; sprinkle evenly over buttered dough. Starting with 16-inch side, roll up tightly; pinch edges to seal. Cut into 16 slices; place cut side down in greased pans. Cover; let rise in warm place (80 to 85°F.) until light and doubled in size, 30 to 40 minutes.

Heat oven to 375°F. Uncover dough. Bake 20 to 30 minutes or until light golden brown. Remove from pans immediately; cool on wire racks. In small bowl, blend all glaze ingredients until smooth and of desired drizzling consistency. Drizzle over warm rolls. **16 rolls.**

HIGH ALTITUDE—Above 3500 Feet: No change.

NUTRIENTS PER 1 ROLL

Calories	250	Protein	6% U.S. RDA
Protein	4g	Vitamin A	4% U.S. RDA
Carbohydrate	40g	Vitamin C	2% U.S. RDA
Fat	9g	Thiamine	15% U.S. RDA
Cholesterol	20mg	Riboflavin	8% U.S. RDA
Sodium	210mg	Niacin	8% U.S. RDA
Potassium	85mg	Calcium	6% U.S. RDA
Dietary Fiber	1g	Iron	8% U.S. RDA

Grand Prize Winner

No-Knead Water-Rising Twists

Theodora Smafield, Michigan
Bake-Off® 1, 1949

2½ to 3½ cups all purpose or
   unbleached flour
½ cup sugar
 1 teaspoon salt
 1 package active dry yeast
¾ cup milk
½ cup margarine or butter
 1 teaspoon vanilla
 2 eggs
½ cup chopped nuts
½ cup sugar
 1 teaspoon cinnamon

Lightly spoon flour into measuring cup; level off. In large bowl, combine 1 cup flour, ½ cup sugar, salt and yeast; blend well. In small saucepan, heat milk and margarine until very warm (120 to 130°F.). Add warm liquid, vanilla and eggs to flour mixture. Blend at low speed until moistened; beat 2 minutes at medium speed. By hand, stir in remaining 1½ to 2½ cups flour to form a soft dough. Cover loosely with plastic wrap and cloth towel. Let rise in warm place (80 to 85°F.) until light and doubled in size, 30 to 40 minutes. *Dough will be sticky.*

Grease 2 large cookie sheets. In small bowl, combine nuts, ½ cup sugar and cinnamon; blend well. Drop about ¼ cup of dough into nut-sugar mixture; thoroughly coat. Stretch dough to about 8 inches in length; twist into desired shape. Place on greased cookie sheets. Repeat with remaining dough. Cover; let rise in warm place, 15 minutes.

Heat oven to 375°F. Uncover dough. Bake 8 to 16 minutes or until light golden brown. Remove from cookie sheet immediately; cool on wire racks. Serve warm. **12 rolls.**

HIGH ALTITUDE—Above 3500 Feet: No change.

NUTRIENTS PER 1 ROLL

Calories	320	Protein	8% U.S. RDA
Protein	6g	Vitamin A	8% U.S. RDA
Carbohydrate	47g	Vitamin C	<2% U.S. RDA
Fat	12g	Thiamine	20% U.S. RDA
Cholesterol	45mg	Riboflavin	10% U.S. RDA
Sodium	290mg	Niacin	10% U.S. RDA
Potassium	125mg	Calcium	10% U.S. RDA
Dietary Fiber	1g	Iron	10% U.S. RDA

No-Knead Water-Rising Twists

When first a finalist, this recipe had a unique rising method. In that procedure, the dough was wrapped in a tea towel and submerged in warm water to rise. In this updated recipe, we have streamlined the preparation of the dough and the rising method. Use your creativity and twist the cinnamon-sugar-coated dough into any pleasing shape when making these sweet rolls.

Lemon Nut Rolls

Soft, tender lemon rolls get extra lightness from potato flakes in the dough. A first-prize winner in the "bride category," these rolls are well worth the time it takes to make them from scratch.

Beehive Buns

Beehive Buns

Janis Chudleigh, Connecticut
Bake-Off® 32, 1986

2 cups whole wheat flour
2 packages active dry yeast
1 teaspoon salt
1 cup raisins
1 cup very hot water
1 cup milk
¹/₃ cup honey
¹/₃ cup margarine or butter
2 eggs
2 to 3¹/₄ cups all purpose or
**   unbleached flour**

GLAZE
**   3 tablespoons honey**
**   3 tablespoons margarine or butter**
1¹/₄ cups powdered sugar
**   1 teaspoon vanilla**

Lightly spoon flour into measuring cup; level off. In large bowl, combine whole wheat flour, yeast and salt; blend well. Cover raisins with water. Let stand for 1 minute; drain. In small saucepan, heat milk, ¹/₃ cup honey and ¹/₃ cup margarine until very warm (120 to 130°F.); stir into flour mixture. Beat in eggs, 1 at a time, beating well after each addition. By hand, stir in raisins. Stir in 1¹/₂ to 2 cups all purpose flour until dough pulls cleanly away from sides of bowl.

On floured surface, knead in remaining ¹/₂ to 1¹/₄ cups all purpose flour until dough is smooth and elastic, about 5 minutes. Place dough in greased bowl; cover loosely with plastic wrap and cloth towel. Let rise in warm place (80 to 85°F.) until light and doubled in size, 45 to 60 minutes.

Grease 24 muffin cups. Punch down dough several times to remove all air bubbles. Divide dough into 24 equal pieces. (Cover pieces with large bowl to prevent dough from drying out.) Using 1 piece of dough at a time, roll to form 10 to 12-inch rope. To form beehive shape, coil rope in greased muffin cup, tucking end into top center. Repeat with remaining pieces. Cover; let rise in warm place until light and doubled in size, 30 to 45 minutes.

Heat oven to 350°F. Uncover dough. Bake 15 to 20 minutes or until golden brown. Remove from pans immediately; cool on wire racks. In small saucepan, heat 3 tablespoons honey and 3 tablespoons margarine. Stir in powdered sugar and vanilla until smooth. Drizzle over warm rolls. **24 rolls.**

HIGH ALTITUDE—Above 3500 Feet: No change.

NUTRIENTS PER 1 ROLL

Calories	210	Protein	6% U.S. RDA
Protein	4g	Vitamin A	4% U.S. RDA
Carbohydrate	37g	Vitamin C	<2% U.S. RDA
Fat	5g	Thiamine	15% U.S. RDA
Cholesterol	25mg	Riboflavin	8% U.S. RDA
Sodium	150mg	Niacin	8% U.S. RDA
Potassium	140mg	Calcium	6% U.S. RDA
Dietary Fiber	2g	Iron	8% U.S. RDA

Quick Praline Rolls

Alic Houghtaling, California
Bake-Off® 14, 1962

FILLING

¾ cup firmly packed brown sugar
⅓ cup margarine or butter, softened
½ cup chopped walnuts

DOUGH

1¾ to 2¾ cups all purpose or unbleached flour
2 tablespoons sugar
1 teaspoon baking powder
½ teaspoon salt
1 package active dry yeast
⅓ cup milk
⅓ cup margarine or butter
¼ cup water
1 egg
¼ cup chopped walnuts

Grease cookie sheets. In small bowl, beat brown sugar and ⅓ cup margarine until light and fluffy. Stir in ½ cup walnuts; set aside.

Lightly spoon flour into measuring cup; level off. In large bowl, combine 1 cup flour, sugar, baking powder, salt and yeast; blend well. In small saucepan, heat milk, ⅓ cup margarine and water until very warm (120 to 130°F.). Add warm liquid and egg to flour mixture. Blend at low speed until moistened; beat 3 minutes at medium speed. Stir in remaining ¾ to 1¾ cups flour to form a soft dough.

On well-floured surface, toss dough until no longer sticky. Roll dough to 15 × 10-inch rectangle. Spread with half of filling mixture. Starting with 15-inch side, roll up tightly; pinch edges to seal. Cut into 15 slices. Place cut side down on greased cookie sheets; flatten each slice to ½-inch thickness. Spread tops of slices with remaining filling; sprinkle with ¼ cup walnuts. Cover loosely with greased plastic wrap and cloth towel. Let rise in warm place (80 to 85°F.) until light, about 45 minutes.

Heat oven to 400°F. Uncover dough. Bake 10 to 12 minutes or until light golden brown. Remove from cookie sheets immediately; cool on wire racks. Serve warm. **15 rolls.**

HIGH ALTITUDE—Above 3500 Feet: No change.

NUTRIENTS PER 1 ROLL

Calories	260	Protein	6% U.S. RDA
Protein	4g	Vitamin A	6% U.S. RDA
Carbohydrate	32g	Vitamin C	<2% U.S. RDA
Fat	13g	Thiamine	10% U.S. RDA
Cholesterol	20mg	Riboflavin	6% U.S. RDA
Sodium	200mg	Niacin	8% U.S. RDA
Potassium	125mg	Calcium	8% U.S. RDA
Dietary Fiber	1g	Iron	8% U.S. RDA

Beehive Buns

Shaped like miniature beehives, these honey-flavored raisin buns are perfect for breakfast. Serve warm with butter.

Quick Praline Rolls

The combined leavening action of yeast and baking powder gives these rolls a biscuit-like texture. After mixing and shaping, the dough rises only once before baking.

Ring-a-Lings

—— ❧❦❧ ——

Bertha Jorgensen, Oregon
Bake-Off® 7, 1955

Ring-a-Lings

—— ❧❦❧ ——

This no-knead sweet roll of the '50s has such a simple way to fill, twist and curl the dough. This innovative method and its refreshing orange flavor are the attributes that have earned this recipe a place on the list of Bake-Off® classics.

4 to 4½ cups all purpose or unbleached flour
⅓ cup sugar
2 teaspoons salt
2 teaspoons grated orange peel
2 packages active dry yeast
1 cup milk
⅓ cup margarine or butter
2 eggs

FILLING

1 cup powdered sugar
⅓ cup margarine or butter, softened
1 cup filberts, pecans or walnuts, ground

GLAZE

3 tablespoons sugar
¼ cup orange juice

Lightly spoon flour into measuring cup; level off. In large bowl, combine 2 cups flour, ⅓ cup sugar, salt, orange peel and yeast; blend well. In small saucepan, heat milk and ⅓ cup margarine until very warm (120 to 130°F.). Add warm liquid and eggs to flour mixture. Blend at low speed until moistened; beat 3 minutes at medium speed. By hand, stir in remaining 2 to 2½ cups flour to form a stiff dough. Place dough in greased bowl; cover loosely with plastic wrap and cloth towel. Let rise in warm place (80 to 85°F.) until light and doubled in size, 35 to 50 minutes.

In small bowl, blend powdered sugar and ⅓ cup margarine until smooth. Stir in filberts; set aside. In second small bowl, blend glaze ingredients; set aside.

Grease 2 large cookie sheets. Stir down dough to remove all air bubbles. On floured surface, toss dough until no longer sticky. Roll dough to 22 × 12-inch rectangle. Spread filling mixture lengthwise over half of dough. Fold dough over filling. Cut crosswise into 1-inch strips; twist each strip 4 to 5 times. To shape rolls, hold folded end of strip down on greased cookie sheet to form center; coil strip around center. Tuck loose end under. Repeat with remaining twisted strips. Cover; let rise in warm place until light and doubled in size, 30 to 45 minutes.

Heat oven to 375°F. Uncover dough. Bake 9 to 12 minutes or until light golden brown. Brush tops of rolls with glaze. Bake an addtional 3 to 5 minutes or until golden brown. Remove from cookie sheets immediately; cool on wire racks. **20 to 22 rolls.**

HIGH ALTITUDE—Above 3500 Feet: No change.

NUTRIENTS PER 1 ROLL

Calories	230	Protein	6% U.S. RDA
Protein	5g	Vitamin A	6% U.S. RDA
Carbohydrate	32g	Vitamin C	2% U.S. RDA
Fat	10g	Thiamine	10% U.S. RDA
Cholesterol	25mg	Riboflavin	10% U.S. RDA
Sodium	300mg	Niacin	8% U.S. RDA
Potassium	90mg	Calcium	2% U.S. RDA
Dietary Fiber	1g	Iron	6% U.S. RDA

Orange Date Crescent Claws

—— ❧❦❧ ——

Barbara Rhea, Ohio
Bake-Off® 33, 1988

½ cup chopped walnuts or pecans
¼ cup sugar
1 teaspoon grated orange peel
½ cup chopped dates
8-ounce can refrigerated crescent dinner rolls
2 tablespoons margarine or butter, melted

Heat oven to 375°F. In small bowl, combine walnuts, sugar and orange peel; mix well. Reserve ¼ cup of sugar-nut mixture for topping. Stir dates into remaining mixture; set aside.

Separate dough into 4 rectangles; firmly press perforations to seal. Cut each rectangle in half crosswise; press or roll out each to make eight 4-inch squares. Brush each with margarine. Spoon about 2 tablespoonfuls of date mixture in 1-inch strip across center of each square to within ¼ inch of each end. Fold dough over filling, overlapping in center; pinch center seam and ends to seal. Place seam side down on ungreased cookie sheet. Using scissors or sharp knife, make three ½-inch deep cuts in one folded side of each roll. To form claw shape, separate cut sections by gently curving each roll into crescent shape. Brush top of each claw with margarine; sprinkle with reserved

¼ cup sugar-nut mixture. Bake at 375°F. for 8 to 12 minutes or until golden brown. **8 rolls.**

NUTRIENTS PER 1 ROLL

Calories	240	Protein	4% U.S. RDA
Protein	3g	Vitamin A	2% U.S. RDA
Carbohydrate	27g	Vitamin C	<2% U.S. RDA
Fat	13g	Thiamine	8% U.S. RDA
Cholesterol	2mg	Riboflavin	4% U.S. RDA
Sodium	260mg	Niacin	4% U.S. RDA
Potassium	170mg	Calcium	<2% U.S. RDA
Dietary Fiber	2g	Iron	4% U.S. RDA

Grand Prize Winner

Easy Crescent Danish Rolls

❧

Barbara S. Gibson, Indiana
Bake-Off® 26, 1975

2 (3-ounce) packages cream
   cheese, softened
⅓ cup sugar
2 teaspoons lemon juice
2 (8-ounce) cans refrigerated
   crescent dinner rolls
4 teaspoons preserves

GLAZE
½ cup powdered sugar
1 teaspoon vanilla
2 to 3 teaspoons milk

Heat oven to 350°F. In small bowl, blend cream cheese, sugar and lemon juice until smooth. Separate dough into 8 rectangles; firmly press perforations to seal. Spread about 2 tablespoonfuls of cream cheese mixture on each rectangle to within ¼ inch of edges. Starting with longest side, roll up; firmly pinch edges to seal. Gently stretch each roll to about 10 inches in length. Coil loosely, seam side down, on ungreased cookie sheet. Seal ends. With thumb, make deep imprint in center of each roll; fill with ½ teaspoonful preserves.

Bake at 350°F. for 18 to 22 minutes or until golden brown. Remove from cookie sheet; cool on wire racks. In small bowl, blend powdered sugar, vanilla and enough milk for desired drizzling consistency. Drizzle over warm rolls. **8 rolls.**

NUTRIENTS PER 1 ROLL

Calories	350	Protein	8% U.S. RDA
Protein	5g	Vitamin A	6% U.S. RDA
Carbohydrate	39g	Vitamin C	<2% U.S. RDA
Fat	19g	Thiamine	10% U.S. RDA
Cholesterol	30mg	Riboflavin	10% U.S. RDA
Sodium	530mg	Niacin	8% U.S. RDA
Potassium	160mg	Calcium	2% U.S. RDA
Dietary Fiber	<1g	Iron	8% U.S. RDA

Crescent Dutch Letter Pastries

❧

Juddie Word, Alabama
Bake-Off® 32, 1986

1 cup (6 to 7 cookies) crushed
   crisp coconut macaroon cookies
¾ cup ground almonds
1 tablespoon margarine or butter,
   softened
3-ounce package cream cheese,
   softened
8-ounce can refrigerated crescent
   dinner rolls
1 egg yolk
1 tablespoon water

GLAZE
¾ to 1 cup powdered sugar
1 to 2 tablespoons milk

Heat oven to 375°F. Lightly grease large cookie sheet. In medium bowl, blend cookie crumbs, almonds, margarine and cream cheese until crumbly. Divide mixture into 8 equal portions; shape each into 8-inch rope.

Separate dough into 4 rectangles; firmly press perforations to seal. Press or roll out each to 8 × 4-inch rectangle; cut in half lengthwise to make eight 8 × 2-inch rectangles. Place 1 filling rope on each rectangle. Fold dough over filling, overlapping in center; pinch center seam and ends to seal. Shape into S shape on greased cookie sheet. In small bowl, blend egg yolk and water; brush over rolls.

Bake at 375°F. for 15 to 18 minutes or until golden brown. Remove from cookie sheet; cool on wire racks. In small bowl, blend enough powdered sugar and milk for desired drizzling consistency. Drizzle over warm rolls. **8 rolls.**

NUTRIENTS PER 1 ROLL

Calories	370	Protein	10% U.S. RDA
Protein	6g	Vitamin A	4% U.S. RDA
Carbohydrate	37g	Vitamin C	<2% U.S. RDA
Fat	22g	Thiamine	8% U.S. RDA
Cholesterol	70mg	Riboflavin	10% U.S. RDA
Sodium	290mg	Niacin	6% U.S. RDA
Potassium	250mg	Calcium	6% U.S. RDA
Dietary Fiber	2g	Iron	8% U.S. RDA

Crescent Dutch Letter Pastries

❧

These traditional pastries, made easy with refrigerated crescent roll dough, have an almond-macaroon filling and are shaped into a letter of the alphabet.

Apple Coffee Cake Supreme

Apple Coffee Cake Supreme

Nicole Plaut, Wisconsin
Bake-Off® 32, 1986

½ cup sugar
2 eggs
½ cup plain yogurt
3 tablespoons margarine or butter, melted
1 to 2 teaspoons grated lemon peel
1⅓ cups self-rising flour*
3 to 4 cups thinly sliced peeled apples
2 tablespoons sugar
½ to 1 cup sliced almonds

GLAZE
⅓ cup sugar
⅓ cup margarine or butter, melted
1 egg, beaten

Heat oven to 375°F. Grease 10-inch tart pan with removable bottom or 8-inch square pan. In small bowl, beat ½ cup sugar and 2 eggs until well blended; stir in yogurt, 3 tablespoons margarine and lemon peel. Lightly spoon flour into measuring cup; level off. Add flour to egg mixture; blend well. Pour batter into greased pan.

Arrange apple slices on top of batter, overlapping slightly. Sprinkle with 2 tablespoons sugar and almonds. Bake at 375°F. for 35 to 45 minutes or until golden brown and toothpick inserted in center comes out clean.**

As soon as coffee cake is removed from oven, increase oven temperature to *broil* and prepare glaze. In small bowl, combine all glaze ingredients; blend well. Slowly pour over hot cake; allow mixture to soak into cake. Broil 5 to 6 inches from heat for 1 to 2 minutes or until bubbly. Serve warm. Store in refrigerator. **6 to 8 servings.**

TIPS: *All purpose or unbleached flour can be substituted for self-rising flour; add 2 teaspoons baking powder and ½ teaspoon salt.

**If using 8-inch square pan, increase baking time 5 minutes.

HIGH ALTITUDE—Above 3500 Feet: No change.

NUTRIENTS PER 1/8 OF RECIPE

Calories	420	Protein	10% U.S. RDA
Protein	8g	Vitamin A	10% U.S. RDA
Carbohydrate	51g	Vitamin C	<2% U.S. RDA
Fat	21g	Thiamine	10% U.S. RDA
Cholesterol	100mg	Riboflavin	15% U.S. RDA
Sodium	400mg	Niacin	8% U.S. RDA
Potassium	220mg	Calcium	10% U.S. RDA
Dietary Fiber	2g	Iron	10% U.S. RDA

Maple Cream Coffee Treat

Reta Ebbink, California
Bake-Off® 28, 1978

1 cup firmly packed brown sugar
1/2 cup chopped nuts
1/3 cup maple-flavored syrup or dark corn syrup
1/4 cup margarine or butter, melted
8-ounce package cream cheese, softened
1/4 cup powdered sugar
2 tablespoons margarine or butter, softened
1/2 cup coconut
2 (10-ounce) cans refrigerated flaky biscuits

Heat oven to 350°F. In ungreased 13 × 9-inch pan, combine brown sugar, nuts, syrup and 1/4 cup margarine; spread evenly in bottom of pan. In small bowl, blend cream cheese, powdered sugar and 2 tablespoons margarine until smooth; stir in coconut. Separate dough into 20 biscuits. Press or roll out each to 4-inch circle. Spoon tablespoonful of cream cheese mixture down center of each circle to within 1/4 inch of edge. Overlap sides of dough over filling, forming finger-shaped rolls. Arrange rolls seam side down in 2 rows of 10 rolls each over brown sugar mixture in pan. Bake at 350°F. for 25 to 30 minutes or until deep golden brown. Cool 3 to 5 minutes; invert onto foil or waxed paper. **20 rolls.**

NUTRIENTS PER 1 ROLL

Calories	250	Protein	4% U.S. RDA
Protein	3g	Vitamin A	6% U.S. RDA
Carbohydrate	29g	Vitamin C	<2% U.S. RDA
Fat	14g	Thiamine	6% U.S. RDA
Cholesterol	10mg	Riboflavin	6% U.S. RDA
Sodium	370mg	Niacin	4% U.S. RDA
Potassium	90mg	Calcium	2% U.S. RDA
Dietary Fiber	<1g	Iron	6% U.S. RDA

Cinnamon-Crusted Zucchini Coffee Cake

Vickie L. Storey, Pennsylvania
Bake-Off® 32, 1986

1 tablespoon sugar
1/2 teaspoon cinnamon
1 3/4 cups whole wheat flour
1 cup sugar
1/2 cup chopped nuts, if desired
1 teaspoon baking soda
1 teaspoon cinnamon
2 cups shredded zucchini
1/2 cup buttermilk*
1/4 cup pineapple-orange or orange juice
1/4 cup oil
1 teaspoon vanilla
1 egg

MICROWAVE DIRECTIONS: Grease 12-cup microwave-safe fluted tube pan or 6-cup microwave-safe ring pan. In small bowl, blend 1 tablespoon sugar and 1/2 teaspoon cinnamon; coat inside of pan with mixture. Lightly spoon flour into measuring cup; level off. In large bowl, combine flour and all remaining ingredients. Blend at low speed until moistened; beat 2 minutes at medium speed. Pour into greased and sugared pan.

Microwave on HIGH for 10 to 14 minutes, rotating pan 1/4 turn every 4 minutes. Coffee cake is done when toothpick inserted in center comes out clean. Cool in pan on flat surface 2 minutes. Invert onto serving plate. Drizzle with powdered sugar glaze, if desired.** Store in refrigerator. **6 to 8 servings.**

TIPS: *To substitute for buttermilk, use 1 1/2 teaspoons vinegar or lemon juice plus milk to make 1/2 cup.

**Powdered Sugar Glaze: In small bowl, blend 1/2 cup powdered sugar and 2 to 3 teaspoons water until smooth and of desired glaze consistency.

HIGH ALTITUDE—Above 3500 Feet: No change.

NUTRIENTS PER 1/8 OF RECIPE

Calories	340	Protein	8% U.S. RDA
Protein	6g	Vitamin A	2% U.S. RDA
Carbohydrate	49g	Vitamin C	4% U.S. RDA
Fat	13g	Thiamine	10% U.S. RDA
Cholesterol	35mg	Riboflavin	4% U.S. RDA
Sodium	170mg	Niacin	6% U.S. RDA
Potassium	230mg	Calcium	4% U.S. RDA
Dietary Fiber	4g	Iron	8% U.S. RDA

Maple Cream Coffee Treat

Friends and family will praise the baker who serves these cream-filled, caramel-topped sweet rolls. The judges were also impressed and awarded the recipe first prize in its category.

Chocolate Almond Crescent Braid

Susie P. Dempsey, Illinois
Bake-Off® 29, 1980

2 ounces (2 squares) semi-sweet baking chocolate, melted, cooled
1/3 cup sugar
1/4 cup dairy sour cream
2 tablespoons chopped toasted almonds*
8-ounce can refrigerated crescent dinner rolls

GLAZE
1/2 cup powdered sugar
1/4 teaspoon almond extract
3 to 4 teaspoons milk
2 tablespoons chopped toasted almonds*

Heat oven to 350°F. In small bowl, combine chocolate, sugar and sour cream; mix until smooth. Stir in 2 tablespoons almonds. Unroll dough into 2 long rectangles. Place on ungreased cookie sheet with long sides overlapping 1/2 inch; roll out to 14 × 7-inch rectangle. Firmly press edges and perforations to seal. Spread chocolate mixture in 2-inch strip lengthwise down center of dough to within 1/4 inch of each end. Make cuts 2 inches apart on long sides of rectangle to within 1/2 inch of filling. To give braided appearance, fold strips of dough at an angle halfway across filling, alternating from side to side. Fold ends of braid under to seal.

Bake at 350°F. for 18 to 23 minutes or until golden brown. Cool 5 minutes; remove from cookie sheet. Cool on wire rack. In small bowl, blend powdered sugar, almond extract and enough milk for desired drizzling consistency. Drizzle over warm braid. Sprinkle with 2 tablespoons almonds. Cut into slices. **8 servings.**

TIP: *To toast almonds, spread on cookie sheet; bake at 375°F. for 3 to 5 minutes or until light golden brown, stirring occasionally. Or, spread in thin layer in microwave-safe pie pan; microwave on HIGH for 2 to 4 minutes or until light golden brown, stirring frequently.

NUTRIENTS PER 1/8 OF RECIPE

Calories	240	Protein	4% U.S. RDA
Protein	3g	Vitamin A	<2% U.S. RDA
Carbohydrate	31g	Vitamin C	<2% U.S. RDA
Fat	12g	Thiamine	6% U.S. RDA
Cholesterol	6mg	Riboflavin	6% U.S. RDA
Sodium	240mg	Niacin	4% U.S. RDA
Potassium	125mg	Calcium	2% U.S. RDA
Dietary Fiber	1g	Iron	4% U.S. RDA

Honeycomb Coffee Cake

This scrumptious coffee cake will melt in your mouth as you encounter warm pockets of honey throughout a moist and flaky bread.

Beverly A. Sebastian, Texas
Bake-Off® 30, 1982

1/4 cup firmly packed brown sugar
1 teaspoon cinnamon
1/4 teaspoon ground mace or nutmeg
1/4 cup margarine or butter, melted
1 tablespoon lemon juice
10-ounce can refrigerated flaky biscuits
1/4 to 1/3 cup (4 squares) finely crushed graham crackers or graham cracker crumbs
1/4 cup finely chopped nuts, if desired
2 to 4 tablespoons honey

Heat oven to 400°F. Grease 9 or 8-inch round cake pan. In small bowl, combine brown sugar, cinnamon and mace; mix well. In second small bowl, blend margarine and lemon juice.

Separate dough into 10 biscuits; cut each into 4 pieces. Place biscuit pieces and graham cracker crumbs in bag; toss gently to coat. Arrange coated pieces evenly in greased pan. With small wooden spoon handle, poke a deep hole in each biscuit piece. Sprinkle brown sugar mixture over pieces; drizzle with margarine mixture. Sprinkle with nuts. Bake at 400°F. for 12 to 18 minutes or until golden brown. Turn onto wire rack; invert onto serving plate. Fill holes with honey. Serve warm. **10 servings.**

NUTRIENTS PER 1/10 OF RECIPE

Calories	210	Protein	2% U.S. RDA
Protein	2g	Vitamin A	4% U.S. RDA
Carbohydrate	27g	Vitamin C	<2% U.S. RDA
Fat	10g	Thiamine	6% U.S. RDA
Cholesterol	0mg	Riboflavin	4% U.S. RDA
Sodium	370mg	Niacin	4% U.S. RDA
Potassium	70mg	Calcium	<2% U.S. RDA
Dietary Fiber	<1g	Iron	6% U.S. RDA

Honeycomb Coffee Cake

Lemon Almond Breakfast Pastry

Lemon Almond Breakfast Pastry

Sharon Richardson, Texas
Bake-Off® 33, 1988

FILLING
- ½ cup butter or margarine, softened
- 7-ounce tube almond paste, broken into small pieces
- 2 eggs
- 5 teaspoons flour
- 1 to 2 teaspoons grated lemon peel

CRUST
- 15-ounce package refrigerated pie crusts
- 1 teaspoon flour
- 1 egg, beaten
- 1 tablespoon milk
- 2 tablespoons sugar

In small bowl or food processor bowl with metal blade, combine butter and almond paste; beat or process until smooth. Add 2 eggs; mix well. By hand, stir in 5 teaspoons flour and lemon peel until just blended. Cover; place in freezer for 20 to 30 minutes or until mixture is thick.

Allow both crust pouches to stand at room temperature for 15 to 20 minutes. Heat oven to 400°F. Remove 1 crust from pouch. Unfold; remove top plastic sheet. Press out fold lines; sprinkle with 1 teaspoon flour. Place floured side down on ungreased 12-inch pizza pan or cookie sheet; remove remaining plastic sheet. Spread cold filling over crust to within 2 inches of edge. Brush edge with beaten egg. Refrigerate while preparing top crust.

Remove remaining crust from pouch. Unfold; remove both plastic sheets. Press out fold lines; cut 1-inch circle from center of crust. Using very sharp knife and curving motions, decoratively score crust in pinwheel design. (Do not cut through crust or filling will leak out.) Carefully place over filled bottom crust. Press edges to seal; flute. In small bowl, combine remaining beaten egg and milk. Brush over crust; sprinkle with sugar. Bake at 400°F. for 22 to 27 minutes or until golden brown. Serve warm. **12 to 16 servings.**

NUTRIENTS PER 1/16 OF RECIPE

Calories	250	Protein	4% U.S. RDA
Protein	3g	Vitamin A	4% U.S. RDA
Carbohydrate	20g	Vitamin C	<2% U.S. RDA
Fat	18g	Thiamine	2% U.S. RDA
Cholesterol	70mg	Riboflavin	8% U.S. RDA
Sodium	240mg	Niacin	2% U.S. RDA
Potassium	110mg	Calcium	4% U.S. RDA
Dietary Fiber	1g	Iron	2% U.S. RDA

One-Step Tropical Coffee Cake

Sharon Schubert, Ohio
Bake-Off® 24, 1973

CAKE

1½ cups all purpose or unbleached flour
1 cup sugar
2 teaspoons baking powder
½ teaspoon salt
½ cup oil
8-ounce carton pineapple or plain yogurt
2 eggs

TOPPING

1 cup coconut
⅓ cup sugar
1 teaspoon cinnamon

Heat oven to 350°F. Grease 9-inch square or 11×7-inch pan. Lightly spoon flour into measuring cup; level off. In large bowl, combine flour and all remaining cake ingredients; stir 70 to 80 strokes until well blended. Pour batter into greased pan. In small bowl, combine all topping ingredients; mix well. Sprinkle evenly over batter. Bake at 350°F. for 35 to 40 minutes or until toothpick inserted in center comes out clean. **9 servings.**

HIGH ALTITUDE—Above 3500 Feet: Decrease sugar to 1 cup minus 2 tablespoons. Decrease baking powder to 1½ teaspoons. Bake as directed above.

NUTRIENTS PER 1/9 OF RECIPE

Calories	390	Protein	6% U.S. RDA
Protein	5g	Vitamin A	<2% U.S. RDA
Carbohydrate	54g	Vitamin C	<2% U.S. RDA
Fat	17g	Thiamine	10% U.S. RDA
Cholesterol	60mg	Riboflavin	8% U.S. RDA
Sodium	220mg	Niacin	6% U.S. RDA
Potassium	125mg	Calcium	15% U.S. RDA
Dietary Fiber	1g	Iron	8% U.S. RDA

Country Apple Coffee Cake

Sue Porubcan, Wisconsin
Bake-Off® 31, 1984

2 tablespoons margarine or butter, softened
1½ cups chopped peeled apples
10-ounce can refrigerated flaky biscuits
⅓ cup firmly packed brown sugar
¼ teaspoon cinnamon
⅓ cup light corn syrup
1½ teaspoons whiskey, if desired
1 egg
½ cup pecan halves or pieces

GLAZE

⅓ cup powdered sugar
¼ teaspoon vanilla
1 to 2 teaspoons milk

Heat oven to 350°F. Using 1 tablespoon of the margarine, generously grease 9-inch round cake pan or 8-inch square pan. Spread 1 cup of the apples in greased pan. Separate dough into 10 biscuits; cut each into 4 pieces. Arrange biscuit pieces point side up over apples. Top with remaining ½ cup apples. In small bowl, combine remaining 1 tablespoon margarine, brown sugar, cinnamon, corn syrup, whiskey and egg; beat 2 to 3 minutes until sugar is partially dissolved. Stir in pecans; spoon over biscuit pieces and apples.

Bake at 350°F. for 35 to 45 minutes or until *deep* golden brown. Cool 5 minutes. In small bowl, blend powdered sugar, vanilla and enough milk for desired drizzling consistency. Drizzle over warm coffee cake. Store in refrigerator. **6 to 8 servings.**

TIP: If desired, serve as dessert with cream.

NUTRIENTS PER 1/8 OF RECIPE

Calories	300	Protein	4% U.S. RDA
Protein	3g	Vitamin A	2% U.S. RDA
Carbohydrate	43g	Vitamin C	<2% U.S. RDA
Fat	13g	Thiamine	10% U.S. RDA
Cholesterol	35mg	Riboflavin	6% U.S. RDA
Sodium	420mg	Niacin	6% U.S. RDA
Potassium	120mg	Calcium	2% U.S. RDA
Dietary Fiber	1g	Iron	10% U.S. RDA

Lemon Almond Breakfast Pastry

Filled with a light, lemon-flavored almond paste, this large round pastry is similar to pastries found in France and Switzerland. Cut in thin wedges to serve.

Hot Roll Moravian Sugar Cake

—◦ಶಿ—

Mary Simpson, South Carolina
Bake-Off® 29, 1980

1 package hot roll mix
1/3 cup sugar
1/3 cup instant nonfat dry milk
1/3 cup mashed potato flakes
1 cup water heated to 120 to 130°F.
1/3 cup margarine or butter, melted
2 eggs

TOPPING

2/3 cup firmly packed light brown sugar
1 teaspoon cinnamon
1/2 cup margarine or butter, melted
1/2 cup chopped nuts

Grease 13 × 9-inch pan. In large bowl, combine flour mixture with yeast from foil packet, sugar, instant nonfat dry milk and potato flakes; blend well. Stir in *hot* water, 1/3 cup margarine and eggs until well blended and dough forms. (Dough will be sticky.) Cover; let rest 5 minutes.

Press dough evenly in greased pan. Cover loosely with greased plastic wrap and cloth towel. Let rise in warm place (80 to 85°F.) until almost double in size, about 45 minutes.

Heat oven to 375°F. In small bowl, combine brown sugar and cinnamon; set aside. Make small pockets in dough by pressing lightly with floured fingertip. Sprinkle brown sugar mixture over dough. Drizzle with 1/2 cup margarine; sprinkle with nuts. Bake at 375°F. for 15 to 20 minutes or until golden brown. **15 servings.**

HIGH ALTITUDE—Above 3500 Feet: No change.

NUTRIENTS PER 1/15 OF RECIPE

Calories	300	Protein	8% U.S. RDA
Protein	6g	Vitamin A	10% U.S. RDA
Carbohydrate	39g	Vitamin C	<2% U.S. RDA
Fat	14g	Thiamine	15% U.S. RDA
Cholesterol	35mg	Riboflavin	15% U.S. RDA
Sodium	350mg	Niacin	10% U.S. RDA
Potassium	170mg	Calcium	6% U.S. RDA
Dietary Fiber	1g	Iron	8% U.S. RDA

—◦ಶಿ—

What next?

In 1949, *Life* magazine wanted a group photograph of the 100 final dishes in the first Grand National Baking and Cooking Contest. The magazine succeeded—almost. Someone couldn't resist and ate one of the desserts. The 99 others made the picture.

Quick Cheese Coffee Cake

—◦ಶಿ—

Joanna Yoakum, California
Bake-Off® 30, 1982

8-ounce package cream cheese, softened
1/2 cup sugar
1 tablespoon flour
1 egg
10-ounce can refrigerated flaky biscuits
1 1/2 teaspoons sugar
1/4 teaspoon cinnamon

Heat oven to 350°F. In small bowl, beat cream cheese, 1/2 cup sugar, flour and egg until smooth. Separate dough into 10 biscuits. Place in ungreased 8 or 9-inch round cake pan; press over bottom and 1 inch up sides to form crust. Pour cream cheese mixture into crust-lined pan. In second small bowl, blend 1 1/2 teaspoons sugar and cinnamon; sprinkle over cream cheese mixture. Bake at 350°F. for 24 to 30 minutes or until filling is set and edges of crust are deep golden brown. Cool 20 minutes. Serve warm or cool. Store in refrigerator. **6 to 8 servings.**

NUTRIENTS PER 1/8 OF RECIPE

Calories	270	Protein	8% U.S. RDA
Protein	5g	Vitamin A	8% U.S. RDA
Carbohydrate	30g	Vitamin C	<2% U.S. RDA
Fat	15g	Thiamine	8% U.S. RDA
Cholesterol	70mg	Riboflavin	8% U.S. RDA
Sodium	460mg	Niacin	6% U.S. RDA
Potassium	65mg	Calcium	2% U.S. RDA
Dietary Fiber	<1g	Iron	8% U.S. RDA

Quick Cheese Coffee Cake

Raspberry Ripple Crescent Coffee Cake

Raspberry Ripple Crescent Coffee Cake

Priscilla Yee, California
Bake-Off® 32, 1986

¾ cup sugar
¼ cup margarine, softened
2 eggs
¾ cup ground almonds
¼ cup all purpose or unbleached flour
1 teaspoon grated lemon peel
8-ounce can refrigerated crescent dinner rolls
8 teaspoons raspberry preserves
¼ cup sliced almonds

GLAZE
⅓ cup powdered sugar
1 to 2 teaspoons milk

Heat oven to 375°F. Grease 9-inch round cake pan or 9-inch pie pan. In small bowl, beat sugar, margarine and eggs until smooth. Stir in ground almonds, flour and lemon peel; set aside. Separate dough into 8 triangles.

Spread teaspoonful of the preserves on each triangle. Roll up, starting at shortest side of triangle and rolling to opposite point. Place rolls in greased pan in 2 circles, arranging 5 rolls around outside edge and 3 in center. Pour and carefully spread almond mixture evenly over rolls; sprinkle with almonds.

Bake at 375°F. for 25 to 35 minutes or until deep golden brown and knife inserted in center comes out clean. In small bowl, blend powdered sugar and enough milk for desired drizzling consistency. Drizzle over warm coffee cake. Serve warm. **8 servings.**

TIP: Cover coffee cake with foil during last 5 to 10 minutes of baking if necessary to prevent excessive browning.

NUTRIENTS PER 1/8 OF RECIPE

Calories	360	Protein	8% U.S. RDA
Protein	6g	Vitamin A	6% U.S. RDA
Carbohydrate	44g	Vitamin C	<2% U.S. RDA
Fat	18g	Thiamine	8% U.S. RDA
Cholesterol	70mg	Riboflavin	10% U.S. RDA
Sodium	320mg	Niacin	6% U.S. RDA
Potassium	170mg	Calcium	4% U.S. RDA
Dietary Fiber	2g	Iron	8% U.S. RDA

Quick Apple Pancake
꧁꧂

Eileen Thorston, Minnesota
Bake-Off® 31, 1984

¼ cup margarine or butter
1½ cups thinly sliced peeled apples
½ cup sugar
½ teaspoon cinnamon
¼ teaspoon nutmeg

BATTER
  1 cup complete or buttermilk
    complete pancake mix
  ½ teaspoon cinnamon
  ¼ teaspoon nutmeg
  ¾ cup water
  1 teaspoon vanilla

TOPPING
  1 tablespoon sugar
  ¼ teaspoon cinnamon

Heat oven to 350°F. In 9-inch pie pan or round cake pan, melt margarine in oven. Stir in apples, ½ cup sugar, ½ teaspoon cinnamon and ¼ teaspoon nutmeg. Bake at 350°F. for 10 minutes. In medium bowl, combine all batter ingredients; blend well. Pour evenly over cooked apples. In small bowl, blend topping ingredients; sprinkle over batter. Bake an additional 15 to 20 minutes or until toothpick inserted in center comes out clean. Let stand 2 minutes. Invert onto serving plate. To serve, cut into wedges. If desired, top with cheese slice or ice cream. **6 servings.**

MICROWAVE DIRECTIONS: In 9-inch microwave-safe pie pan or round cake pan, microwave margarine on HIGH for 30 to 45 seconds or until margarine is melted. Stir in apples, ½ cup sugar, ½ teaspoon cinnamon and ¼ teaspoon nutmeg. Cover; microwave on HIGH for 3 to 4 minutes or until apples are tender. In medium bowl, combine all batter ingredients; blend well. Pour evenly over cooked apples. In small bowl, blend topping ingredients; sprinkle over batter. Microwave on HIGH for 3 to 5 minutes or until toothpick inserted 1½ to 2 inches from edge comes out clean. Let stand 5 minutes on flat surface. Invert onto serving plate. Continue as directed above.

HIGH ALTITUDE—Above 3500 Feet: No change.

NUTRIENTS PER 1/6 OF RECIPE

Calories	240	Protein	2% U.S. RDA
Protein	2g	Vitamin A	6% U.S. RDA
Carbohydrate	39g	Vitamin C	2% U.S. RDA
Fat	9g	Thiamine	8% U.S. RDA
Cholesterol	0mg	Riboflavin	4% U.S. RDA
Sodium	390mg	Niacin	4% U.S. RDA
Potassium	55mg	Calcium	6% U.S. RDA
Dietary Fiber	1g	Iron	6% U.S. RDA

Danish Almond Crescent Ring
꧁꧂

Lynette Theodore, Wisconsin
Bake-Off® 33, 1988

¼ cup sugar
3 tablespoons margarine or butter, softened
3½-ounce tube almond paste, broken into small pieces
8-ounce can refrigerated crescent dinner rolls
1 egg, beaten
2 teaspoons sugar
¼ cup sliced almonds

Heat oven to 375°F. Lightly grease cookie sheet. In small bowl using fork, combine ¼ cup sugar, margarine and almond paste; mix well. Set aside.

Unroll dough into 2 long rectangles. Overlap long sides ½ inch; firmly press edges and perforations to seal. Press or roll out to form 16 × 8-inch rectangle; cut lengthwise into 3 equal strips. Place 3 tablespoonfuls of filling mixture evenly down center of each strip. Gently press filling to form 1-inch wide strip. Fold dough over filling, overlapping in center; firmly pinch center seam and ends to seal. On greased cookie sheet, loosely braid 3 filled strips. Form braid into ring; pinch ends of strips together to seal. Brush braid with beaten egg; sprinkle with 2 teaspoons sugar and almonds. Bake at 375°F. for 15 to 22 minutes or until golden brown. Cool 5 minutes; remove from cookie sheet. Serve warm. **8 servings.**

NUTRIENTS PER 1/8 OF RECIPE

Calories	250	Protein	6% U.S. RDA
Protein	5g	Vitamin A	4% U.S. RDA
Carbohydrate	24g	Vitamin C	<2% U.S. RDA
Fat	15g	Thiamine	8% U.S. RDA
Cholesterol	35mg	Riboflavin	10% U.S. RDA
Sodium	290mg	Niacin	6% U.S. RDA
Potassium	180mg	Calcium	4% U.S. RDA
Dietary Fiber	1g	Iron	6% U.S. RDA

Quick Apple Pancake
꧁꧂

This recipe, a microwave winner, can also be prepared in a conventional oven. It makes a great dessert when topped with ice cream.

Danish Almond Crescent Ring
꧁꧂

The contestant who created this recipe says, "I like this recipe because it's easy to make and uses only a few ingredients, yet it resembles pastries that are more time-consuming to prepare." Refrigerated crescent dinner roll dough is the easy-to-use pastry in this European-style coffee cake.

Pictured top to bottom: Cherry Winks, page 111; Salted Peanut Chews, page 123; Peanut Blossoms, page 124

Cookies and Bars

❧

Delectable cookies and bars of all shapes, sizes and flavors have filled the Bake-Off® cookie jar to overflowing. Recipes have ranged from indulgent, dessert-type sweets featuring chocolate and marshmallows to healthful snacks accented with the wholesome goodness of raisins, granola or oatmeal.

In the early days, recipe preparation was often time-consuming and complicated. Here's how one recipe from the 1950s was described: "Butter-rich coconut rounds topped with a chocolate layer, coated with coconut and crushed cereal and then easily shaped into a five-pointed star." By the 1970s, bar coookies outnumbered all other types of cookies. The 13×9-inch baking pan became standard equipment in all kitchens. And even with multiple layers and frostings or toppings, convenient mixes and refrigerated dough products made quick work of preparation.

While creative cooks have turned to inventive new ways of preparing cookies and bars, they still cherish the old favorite recipes from the early years of the Bake-Off® Contest. Several have become classics, although many people who treasure these recipes and use them often are unaware of their origin. Among these heritage recipes are Cherry Winks, Snappy Turtle Cookies, Peanut Blossoms and Oatmeal Carmelitas.

Flavors that were popular in cookies of those early Bake-Off® years are still favorites today—lemon, banana, peanut butter, coconut, cherry, and caramel. And at the top of the list is chocolate. At the first competition there were chocolate kisses, bits, shot, and mint wafers plus unsweetened baking chocolate and cocoa. Today the list has grown to include all of these and even more types of chocolate candies as well as white baking chocolate, as featured in the recipe for premium-style White Chocolate Chunk Cookies.

Within this chapter are ingenious recipes combining both familiar and unusual flavors. Some tuck special surprises inside. Others feature a creative blend of sweet and wholesome ingredients for marvelous new taste treats. And all are tantalizing additions to any family's cookie jar.

White Chocolate Chunk Cookies

White Chocolate Chunk Cookies

Dottie Due, Kentucky
Bake-Off® 33, 1988

1 cup shortening
¾ cup sugar
¾ cup firmly packed brown sugar
3 eggs
1 teaspoon vanilla
2½ cups all purpose, unbleached or self-rising flour*
1 teaspoon baking powder
1 teaspoon baking soda
½ teaspoon salt
1 cup flaked coconut
½ cup rolled oats
½ cup chopped walnuts
2 (6-ounce) packages white baking bars, cut into ¼ to ½-inch chunks**

Heat oven to 350°F. In large bowl, beat shortening, sugar and brown sugar until light and fluffy. Add eggs, 1 at a time, beating well after each addition. Add vanilla; blend well. Lightly spoon flour into measuring cup; level off. In small bowl, combine flour, baking powder, baking soda and salt; mix well. Add to sugar mixture; mix at low speed until well blended. By hand, stir in remaining ingredients. Drop by rounded tablespoonfuls 2 inches apart onto ungreased cookie sheets. Bake at 350°F. for 10 to 15 minutes or until light golden brown. Cool 1 minute; remove from cookie sheets. **5 dozen cookies.**

TIPS: *If using self-rising flour, omit baking powder, baking soda and salt.

**One 10-ounce package white baking pieces or 12-ounce package vanilla milk chips can be substituted for two 6-ounce packages white baking bars. Do not substitute almond bark or vanilla-flavored candy coating.

HIGH ALTITUDE—Above 3500 Feet: Decrease baking powder to ½ teaspoon. Decrease baking soda to ½ teaspoon. Bake at 375°F. for 8 to 12 minutes.

NUTRIENTS PER 1 COOKIE

Calories	120	Protein	2% U.S. RDA
Protein	1g	Vitamin A	<2% U.S. RDA
Carbohydrate	14g	Vitamin C	<2% U.S. RDA
Fat	6g	Thiamine	2% U.S. RDA
Cholesterol	15mg	Riboflavin	2% U.S. RDA
Sodium	60mg	Niacin	2% U.S. RDA
Potassium	45mg	Calcium	2% U.S. RDA
Dietary Fiber	<1g	Iron	2% U.S. RDA

Maple Oat Chewies

Kitty Cahill, Minnesota
Bake-Off® 32, 1986

1 cup sugar
1 cup firmly packed brown sugar
1 cup margarine or butter, softened
1 tablespoon molasses
2 teaspoons maple extract
2 eggs
1³/₄ cups all purpose or unbleached flour
2 teaspoons baking powder
1 teaspoon cinnamon
¹/₂ teaspoon salt
2 cups rolled oats
2 cups crisp rice cereal

Heat oven to 350°F. Grease cookie sheets. In large bowl, beat sugar, brown sugar and margarine until light and fluffy. Add molasses, maple extract and eggs; blend well. Lightly spoon flour into measuring cup; level off. Add flour, baking powder, cinnamon and salt; mix at medium speed until well blended. By hand, stir in rolled oats and cereal.* Drop by heaping teaspoonfuls 2 inches apart onto greased cookie sheets. Bake at 350°F. for 8 to 12 minutes or until light golden brown. Cool 2 minutes; remove from cookie sheets. **5 dozen cookies.**

TIP: *One cup butterscotch chips can be added with rolled oats and cereal, if desired.

HIGH ALTITUDE—Above 3500 Feet: No change.

NUTRIENTS PER 1 COOKIE

Calories	80	Protein	<2% U.S. RDA
Protein	1g	Vitamin A	2% U.S. RDA
Carbohydrate	13g	Vitamin C	<2% U.S. RDA
Fat	3g	Thiamine	4% U.S. RDA
Cholesterol	8mg	Riboflavin	2% U.S. RDA
Sodium	80mg	Niacin	<2% U.S. RDA
Potassium	35mg	Calcium	<2% U.S. RDA
Dietary Fiber	<1g	Iron	2% U.S. RDA

Cherry Winks

Ruth Derousseau, Wisconsin
Bake-Off® 2, 1950

1 cup sugar
³/₄ cup shortening
2 tablespoons milk
1 teaspoon vanilla
2 eggs
2¹/₄ cups all purpose or unbleached flour
1 teaspoon baking powder
¹/₂ teaspoon baking soda
¹/₂ teaspoon salt
1 cup chopped pecans
1 cup chopped dates
¹/₃ cup chopped maraschino cherries, well drained
1¹/₂ cups coarsely crushed cornflakes cereal
15 maraschino cherries, quartered, drained

Heat oven to 375°F. Grease cookie sheets. In large bowl, combine sugar, shortening, milk, vanilla and eggs at medium speed until well mixed. Lightly spoon flour into measuring cup; level off. In small bowl, combine flour, baking powder, baking soda and salt; mix well. Add to sugar mixture; mix at low speed until well blended. By hand, stir in pecans, dates and ¹/₃ cup chopped cherries.* Drop by rounded teaspoonfuls into cereal; thoroughly coat. Shape into balls; place 2 inches apart on greased cookie sheets. Gently press maraschino cherry piece into top of each ball. Bake at 375°F. for 10 to 15 minutes or until light golden brown. **5 dozen cookies.**

TIP: *If desired, cover and refrigerate dough for easier handling.

HIGH ALTITUDE—Above 3500 Feet: No change.

NUTRIENTS PER 1 COOKIE

Calories	90	Protein	<2% U.S. RDA
Protein	1g	Vitamin A	2% U.S. RDA
Carbohydrate	12g	Vitamin C	<2% U.S. RDA
Fat	4g	Thiamine	4% U.S. RDA
Cholesterol	8mg	Riboflavin	2% U.S. RDA
Sodium	60mg	Niacin	2% U.S. RDA
Potassium	40mg	Calcium	<2% U.S. RDA
Dietary Fiber	<1g	Iron	2% U.S. RDA

Cherry Winks

The cherry pressed in the top of each cookie gives these ever popular cookies their name. Their crunchy texture—from cornflakes cereal on the outside, and pecans, dates and cherries hidden inside—appeals to both young and old alike.

Choco-Peanut Toppers

Mary C. Berbano, New Jersey
Bake-Off® 12, 1960

COOKIES
- ½ cup sugar
- 1 cup margarine or butter, softened
- 1¾ cups all purpose or unbleached flour
- 2 teaspoons vanilla

TOPPING
- ⅓ cup firmly packed brown sugar
- ⅓ cup peanut butter
- ¼ cup margarine or butter, softened

GLAZE
- ⅓ cup semi-sweet chocolate chips
- ⅓ cup powdered sugar
- 3 to 4 tablespoons milk

Heat oven to 325°F. In large bowl, beat sugar and 1 cup margarine until light and fluffy. Lightly spoon flour into measuring cup; level off. Stir in flour and vanilla; mix well. Drop by teaspoonfuls 2 inches apart onto ungreased cookie sheets. Flatten to ¼-inch thickness with bottom of glass dipped in sugar. Bake at 325°F. for 10 to 15 minutes or until edges are light golden brown. Remove from cookie sheets.

In small bowl, beat brown sugar, peanut butter and ¼ cup margarine until light and fluffy. Spread over *warm* cookies.

In small saucepan over low heat, melt chocolate chips, stirring until smooth. Stir in powdered sugar and enough milk for desired drizzling consistency. Drizzle over cookies. Allow glaze to set before storing cookies.

3 dozen cookies.

HIGH ALTITUDE—Above 3500 Feet: No change.

NUTRIENTS PER 1 COOKIE

Calories	120	Protein	2% U.S. RDA
Protein	1g	Vitamin A	4% U.S. RDA
Carbohydrate	12g	Vitamin C	<2% U.S. RDA
Fat	8g	Thiamine	2% U.S. RDA
Cholesterol	0mg	Riboflavin	<2% U.S. RDA
Sodium	85mg	Niacin	2% U.S. RDA
Potassium	40mg	Calcium	<2% U.S. RDA
Dietary Fiber	<1g	Iron	2% U.S. RDA

Texan-Sized Almond Crunch Cookies

Barbara Hodgson, Indiana
Bake-Off® 30, 1982

- 1 cup sugar
- 1 cup powdered sugar
- 1 cup margarine or butter, softened
- 1 cup oil
- 1 teaspoon almond extract
- 2 eggs
- 3½ cups all purpose or unbleached flour
- 1 cup whole wheat flour
- 1 teaspoon baking soda
- 1 teaspoon cream of tartar
- 1 teaspoon salt
- 2 cups coarsely chopped almonds
- 6-ounce package almond brickle baking chips
- Sugar

Heat oven to 350°F. In large bowl, blend sugar, powdered sugar, margarine and oil until well mixed. Add almond extract and eggs; mix well. Lightly spoon flour into measuring cup; level off. In second large bowl, combine all purpose flour, whole wheat flour, baking soda, cream of tartar and salt; mix well. Add to sugar mixture; mix at low speed until well blended. By hand, stir in almonds and brickle chips.* Using large tablespoonfuls of dough, shape into balls. Roll in sugar. Place 5 inches apart on ungreased cookie sheets. With fork dipped in sugar, flatten in crisscross pattern. Bake at 350°F. for 12 to 18 minutes or until light golden brown around edges. Cool 1 minute; remove from cookie sheets. **3½ dozen (4-inch) cookies.**

TIP: *For easier handling, refrigerate dough about 30 minutes.

HIGH ALTITUDE—Above 3500 feet: No change.

NUTRIENTS PER 1 COOKIE

Calories	230	Protein	4% U.S. RDA
Protein	3g	Vitamin A	4% U.S. RDA
Carbohydrate	22g	Vitamin C	<2% U.S. RDA
Fat	15g	Thiamine	6% U.S. RDA
Cholesterol	10mg	Riboflavin	6% U.S. RDA
Sodium	135mg	Niacin	4% U.S. RDA
Potassium	70mg	Calcium	2% U.S. RDA
Dietary Fiber	1g	Iron	4% U.S. RDA

Everyone wants to bake a winner!

Late in January of 1950, a woman walked up to a clerk in a large drugstore in a Midwestern city, looking for Rockwood mint wafers. The clerk turned to his manager and said, "Mr. Jones, this lady must be the tenth person today asking for Rockwood Mint Wafers. We are out of them." The manager replied, "I'm sorry. I can't understand the sudden increase in sales of these mints." In 1950, the phenomenal sales of Rockwood Mint Wafers at first baffled the Rockwood people until they learned that the popularity and appeal were attributable to the Bake-Off® Contest $10,000 second-place prizewinner, Starlight Mint Surprise Cookies, page 122.

Peekaberry Boos

Peekaberry Boos

Margaret Gregg, Washington
Bake-Off® 10, 1958

1 cup firmly packed brown sugar
³/₄ cup sugar
1 cup margarine or butter,
    softened
¹/₂ cup water
1 teaspoon almond extract
2 eggs
3 cups all purpose or unbleached
    flour
2 cups quick-cooking rolled oats
1 teaspoon baking soda
¹/₂ teaspoon salt
¹/₂ teaspoon cinnamon
²/₃ cup raspberry preserves

Heat oven to 400°F. In large bowl, beat brown sugar, sugar and margarine until light and fluffy. Add water, almond extract and eggs; blend well. (Mixture will look curdled.) Lightly spoon flour into measuring cup; level off. In medium bowl, combine flour, rolled oats, baking soda, salt and cinnamon; mix well. Add to sugar mixture; mix at low speed until well blended. Drop by rounded teaspoonfuls 2 inches apart onto ungreased cookie sheets. With back of spoon, make depression in center of each cookie. Fill each depression with ¹/₂ teaspoonful of the preserves. Drop scant teaspoonful of dough over preserves on each cookie. Bake at 400°F. for 6 to 9 minutes or until light golden brown. Remove from cookie sheets immediately.

4¹/₂ to 5 dozen cookies.

HIGH ALTITUDE—Above 3500 Feet: Decrease sugar to ¹/₂ cup. Bake as directed above.

NUTRIENTS PER 1 COOKIE

Calories	100	Protein	2% U.S. RDA
Protein	1g	Vitamin A	2% U.S. RDA
Carbohydrate	15g	Vitamin C	<2% U.S. RDA
Fat	3g	Thiamine	4% U.S. RDA
Cholesterol	8mg	Riboflavin	2% U.S. RDA
Sodium	75mg	Niacin	<2% U.S. RDA
Potassium	35mg	Calcium	<2% U.S. RDA
Dietary Fiber	<1g	Iron	2% U.S. RDA

Sachertorte Cookies

Sachertorte Cookies

Phyllis Wolf, Oregon
Bake-Off® 30, 1982

1 cup margarine or butter, softened
4½-ounce package instant chocolate pudding and pie filling mix
1 egg
2 cups all purpose or unbleached flour
3 tablespoons sugar
½ cup apricot or cherry preserves
½ cup semi-sweet chocolate chips
3 tablespoons margarine or butter, melted

Heat oven to 325°F. In large bowl, beat margarine and pudding mix until light and fluffy; beat in egg. Lightly spoon flour into measuring cup; level off. Gradually blend in flour at low speed until dough forms. Shape into 1-inch balls; roll in sugar. Place 2 inches apart on ungreased cookie sheets. With thumb, make depression in center of each cookie.

Bake at 325°F. for 15 to 18 minutes or until firm to touch. Remove from cookie sheets immediately; cool on wire racks. Fill each depression with ½ teaspoonful of the preserves. In small saucepan over low heat, melt chocolate chips and margarine, stirring until smooth. Drizzle ½ teaspoonful over each cookie. **4 dozen cookies.**

HIGH ALTITUDE—Above 3500 Feet: Bake at 350°F. for 12 to 15 minutes.

NUTRIENTS PER 1 COOKIE

Calories	90	Protein	<2% U.S. RDA
Protein	1g	Vitamin A	4% U.S. RDA
Carbohydrate	11g	Vitamin C	<2% U.S. RDA
Fat	5g	Thiamine	2% U.S. RDA
Cholesterol	6mg	Riboflavin	<2% U.S. RDA
Sodium	65mg	Niacin	<2% U.S. RDA
Potassium	20mg	Calcium	2% U.S. RDA
Dietary Fiber	<1g	Iron	2% U.S. RDA

Lemon Kiss Cookies

Sandi Lamberton, California
Bake-Off® 33, 1988

1½ cups butter or margarine, softened
¾ cup sugar
1 tablespoon lemon extract
2¾ cups all purpose or unbleached flour
1½ cups finely chopped almonds
14-ounce package milk chocolate candy kisses
Powdered sugar
½ cup semi-sweet chocolate chips
1 tablespoon shortening

In large bowl, beat butter, sugar and lemon extract until light and fluffy. Lightly spoon flour into measuring cup; level off. Gradually blend in flour and almonds at low speed until well mixed. Cover; refrigerate at least 1 hour for easier handling.

Heat oven to 375°F. Using scant tablespoonful of dough, press around each candy kiss, covering completely. Roll in hands to form ball. Place on ungreased cookie sheets. Bake at 375°F. for 8 to 12 minutes or until set and bottom edges are light golden brown. Cool 1 minute; remove from cookie sheets. Cool completely.

Lightly sprinkle cooled cookies with powdered sugar. In small saucepan over low heat, melt chocolate chips and shortening, stirring until smooth. Drizzle over each cookie.

About 6 dozen cookies.

HIGH ALTITUDE—Above 3500 Feet: Decrease butter to 1¼ cups. Bake as directed above.

NUTRIENTS PER 1 COOKIE

Calories	120	Protein	2% U.S. RDA
Protein	2g	Vitamin A	2% U.S. RDA
Carbohydrate	10g	Vitamin C	<2% U.S. RDA
Fat	8g	Thiamine	2% U.S. RDA
Cholesterol	10mg	Riboflavin	2% U.S. RDA
Sodium	45mg	Niacin	<2% U.S. RDA
Potassium	50mg	Calcium	2% U.S. RDA
Dietary Fiber	<1g	Iron	2% U.S. RDA

Lemon Kiss Cookies

Delicate lemon-flavored cookie dough wraps up a chocolate kiss to make these cookies. They are special enough for entertaining.

Chocolate Almond Bonbons

Mrs. J. Rosoff, California
Bake-Off® 4, 1952

4-ounce bar sweet cooking chocolate
2 tablespoons milk
1/4 cup sugar
3/4 cup margarine or butter, softened
2 teaspoons vanilla
2 cups all purpose or unbleached flour
1/4 teaspoon salt
3 1/2-ounce tube almond paste
Sugar

Heat oven to 350°F. In small saucepan over low heat, melt chocolate in milk, stirring until smooth. In large bowl, beat 1/4 cup sugar and margarine until light and fluffy. Blend in chocolate mixture and vanilla. Lightly spoon flour into measuring cup; level off. Stir in flour and salt; mix well. Using rounded teaspoonfuls of dough, shape into balls. Place 2 inches apart on ungreased cookie sheets. Make a depression in center of each ball. Fill each with scant 1/4 teaspoonful of the almond paste; press dough around filling, covering completely. Bake at 350°F. for 9 to 11 minutes or until set. Remove from cookie sheets; roll in sugar.
4 dozen cookies.

HIGH ALTITUDE—Above 3500 Feet: No change.

NUTRIENTS PER 1 COOKIE

Calories	70	Protein	<2% U.S. RDA
Protein	1g	Vitamin A	2% U.S. RDA
Carbohydrate	8g	Vitamin C	<2% U.S. RDA
Fat	4g	Thiamine	2% U.S. RDA
Cholesterol	0mg	Riboflavin	2% U.S. RDA
Sodium	45mg	Niacin	<2% U.S. RDA
Potassium	25mg	Calcium	<2% U.S. RDA
Dietary Fiber	<1g	Iron	<2% U.S. RDA

Swedish Heirloom Cookies

Bernice Wheaton, Minnesota
Bake-Off® 3, 1951

2 cups all purpose or unbleached flour
1 cup powdered sugar
1/4 teaspoon salt
1 cup butter or margarine
1 cup finely chopped almonds
1 tablespoon vanilla
Powdered sugar

Heat oven to 325°F. Lightly spoon flour into measuring cup; level off. In large bowl, combine flour, 1 cup powdered sugar and salt; mix well. Using pastry blender or fork, cut in butter until mixture resembles coarse crumbs. Add almonds and vanilla; knead by hand to form a smooth dough. Using rounded teaspoonfuls of dough, shape into balls or crescents. Place 1 inch apart on ungreased cookie sheets. Bake at 325°F. for 12 to 15 minutes or until set. *Do not brown.* Remove from cookie sheets; roll in powdered sugar.
4 to 5 dozen cookies.

HIGH ALTITUDE—Above 3500 Feet: No change.

NUTRIENTS PER 1 COOKIE

Calories	60	Protein	<2% U.S. RDA
Protein	1g	Vitamin A	2% U.S. RDA
Carbohydrate	5g	Vitamin C	<2% U.S. RDA
Fat	4g	Thiamine	2% U.S. RDA
Cholesterol	8mg	Riboflavin	2% U.S. RDA
Sodium	40mg	Niacin	<2% U.S. RDA
Potassium	20mg	Calcium	<2% U.S. RDA
Dietary Fiber	<1g	Iron	<2% U.S. RDA

Sweet success—

Sweet treats have always counted strongly among Bake-Off® entries. Since 1949, finalist recipes have included a total of 1,903 sweets: 597 cakes, 283 pies, 340 desserts and 683 cookies and bars.

Pictured left to right: Chocolate Almond Bonbons, Swedish Heirloom Cookies

Pictured top to bottom: Orange and Oats Chewies, page 119; Chewy Microwave Granola Bars, page 127.

Orange and Oats Chewies

Maryann Goschka, Michigan
Bake-Off® 31, 1984

2 cups firmly packed brown sugar
1 cup shortening
1 tablespoon grated orange peel
3 tablespoons frozen orange juice concentrate, thawed
2 eggs
2 cups all purpose, unbleached or self-rising flour*
1 teaspoon baking soda
3/4 teaspoon salt
2 cups rolled oats
1 cup chopped nuts
1/3 cup coconut

Heat oven to 350°F. Grease cookie sheets. In large bowl, combine brown sugar, shortening, orange peel, orange juice concentrate and eggs at medium speed until well mixed. Lightly spoon flour into measuring cup; level off. In small bowl, combine flour, baking soda and salt; mix well. Add to sugar mixture; mix at low speed until well blended. By hand, stir in rolled oats, nuts and coconut. Drop by rounded teaspoonfuls 2 inches apart onto greased cookie sheets. Bake at 350°F. for 10 to 12 minutes or until light golden brown. Cool 1 minute; remove from cookie sheets. **5 dozen cookies.**

TIP: *If using self-rising flour, omit baking soda and salt.

HIGH ALTITUDE—Above 3500 Feet: Increase flour to 2 1/2 cups. Bake at 375°F. for 9 to 12 minutes.

NUTRIENTS PER 1 COOKIE

Calories	100	Protein	2% U.S. RDA
Protein	1g	Vitamin A	2% U.S. RDA
Carbohydrate	13g	Vitamin C	<2% U.S. RDA
Fat	5g	Thiamine	6% U.S. RDA
Cholesterol	8mg	Riboflavin	2% U.S. RDA
Sodium	75mg	Niacin	4% U.S. RDA
Potassium	60mg	Calcium	2% U.S. RDA
Dietary Fiber	<1g	Iron	6% U.S. RDA

Marshmallow Cookie Tarts

Susan McCray, Nebraska
Bake-Off® 13, 1961

TARTS
20-ounce package refrigerated sliceable sugar cookie dough
3/4 cup coconut
1 to 1 1/2 cups marshmallow creme

TOPPINGS
Chocolate chips
Chocolate mint candy wafers
Chopped nuts
Peanut butter
Preserves
Toasted Coconut

Heat oven to 325°F. Generously grease 36 muffin cups. Slice cookie dough into 1/4-inch slices. Place one slice in bottom of each greased muffin cup. Sprinkle each with 1 teaspoon of the coconut. Bake at 325°F. for 12 to 15 minutes or until edges are golden brown. Cool 5 minutes; remove from pans. Cool completely. Fill each tart with 1 to 2 teaspoonfuls of the marshmallow creme. Top each with desired toppings. **3 dozen tarts.**

NUTRIENTS PER 1 TART (NO TOPPING)

Calories	90	Protein	<2% U.S. RDA
Protein	1g	Vitamin A	<2% U.S. RDA
Carbohydrate	14g	Vitamin C	<2% U.S. RDA
Fat	3g	Thiamine	2% U.S. RDA
Cholesterol	0mg	Riboflavin	2% U.S. RDA
Sodium	65mg	Niacin	<2% U.S. RDA
Potassium	30mg	Calcium	<2% U.S. RDA
Dietary Fiber	<1g	Iron	<2% U.S. RDA

Marshmallow Cookie Tarts

Marshmallow creme and a choice of toppings fill these delightful cookie tarts. This updated version uses refrigerated sugar cookie dough for the crust, making this favorite from 1961 even quicker to prepare today.

Candy Bar Cookies

To make this champion cookie more convenient, we replaced rolling and cutting out the cookie dough with a tender, buttery, press-in-the-pan crust. The baked crust is topped, as in the original recipe, with a turtle-like mixture of caramel, chocolate and pecans.

Split Seconds

Jelly-filled strips of dough are baked and cut to form an attractive shortbread cookie. Use your favorite flavor of jelly or preserves.

Grand Prize Winner

Candy Bar Cookies

Alice Reese, Minnesota
Bake-Off® 13, 1961

BASE

2 cups all purpose or unbleached flour
3/4 cup powdered sugar
3/4 cup margarine or butter, softened
2 tablespoons whipping cream
1 teaspoon vanilla

FILLING

28 caramels
1/4 cup whipping cream
1/4 cup margarine or butter
1 cup powdered sugar
1 cup chopped pecans

GLAZE

1/2 cup semi-sweet chocolate chips
2 tablespoons whipping cream
1 tablespoon margarine or butter
1/4 cup powdered sugar
1 teaspoon vanilla
Pecan halves, if desired

Heat oven to 325°F. Lightly spoon flour into measuring cup; level off. In large bowl, blend flour and all remaining base ingredients at low speed until crumbly. Press crumb mixture into ungreased 15 × 10 × 1-inch baking pan. Bake at 325°F. for 15 to 20 minutes or until light golden brown.

In small saucepan over low heat, melt caramels with 1/4 cup whipping cream and 1/4 cup margarine, stirring until smooth. Remove from heat; stir in 1 cup powdered sugar and pecans. (Add additional cream if necessary for spreading consistency.) Spread filling mixture over base.

In small saucepan over low heat, melt chocolate chips with 2 tablespoons whipping cream and 1 tablespoon margarine, stirring until smooth. Remove from heat; stir in 1/4 cup powdered sugar and vanilla. Drizzle glaze over filling. Cut into bars. Decorate each bar with pecan half. **48 cookies.**

HIGH ALTITUDE—Above 3500 Feet: No change.

NUTRIENTS PER 1 COOKIE

Calories	140	Protein	<2% U.S. RDA
Protein	1g	Vitamin A	4% U.S. RDA
Carbohydrate	14g	Vitamin C	<2% U.S. RDA
Fat	9g	Thiamine	4% U.S. RDA
Cholesterol	2mg	Riboflavin	2% U.S. RDA
Sodium	60mg	Niacin	<2% U.S. RDA
Potassium	40mg	Calcium	<2% U.S. RDA
Dietary Fiber	<1g	Iron	2% U.S. RDA

Split Seconds

Karin Fellows, Maryland
Bake-Off® 6, 1954

2/3 cup sugar
3/4 cup margarine or butter, softened
2 teaspoons vanilla
1 egg
2 cups all purpose or unbleached flour
1/2 teaspoon baking powder
1/2 cup red jelly or preserves

Heat oven to 350°F. In large bowl, beat sugar and margarine until light and fluffy. Blend in vanilla and egg. Lightly spoon flour into measuring cup; level off. Stir in flour and baking powder; mix well. Divide dough into 4 equal parts. On lightly floured surface, shape each part into 12 × 3/4-inch roll; place on ungreased cookie sheets. Using handle of wooden spoon or finger, make a depression about 1/2 inch wide and 1/4 inch deep, lengthwise down center of each roll. Fill each with 2 tablespoonfuls of the jelly. Bake at 350°F. for 15 to 20 minutes or until light golden brown. Cool slightly; cut diagonally into bars. Cool on wire racks.
4 dozen cookies.

HIGH ALTITUDE—Above 3500 Feet: No change.

NUTRIENTS PER 1 COOKIE

Calories	70	Protein	<2% U.S. RDA
Protein	1g	Vitamin A	2% U.S. RDA
Carbohydrate	9g	Vitamin C	<2% U.S. RDA
Fat	3g	Thiamine	2% U.S. RDA
Cholesterol	6mg	Riboflavin	<2% U.S. RDA
Sodium	40mg	Niacin	<2% U.S. RDA
Potassium	10mg	Calcium	<2% U.S. RDA
Dietary Fiber	<1g	Iron	<2% U.S. RDA

Split Seconds

Snappy Turtle Cookies

Beatrice Harlib, Illinois
Bake-Off® 4, 1952

Snappy Turtle Cookies

These rich brown sugar cookies resemble the well-known turtle-shaped candies. This is another recipe that has earned the rank of Bake-Off® classic.

Starlight Mint Surprise Cookies

The idea for this cookie came to the originator when she was given a package of mint-flavored chocolate candies. Brown sugar cookie dough is pressed around each candy so each cookie has a surprise chocolate mint in the center.

COOKIES

¹/₂ cup firmly packed brown sugar
¹/₂ cup margarine or butter, softened
¹/₄ teaspoon vanilla
¹/₈ teaspoon maple flavoring, if desired
1 egg
1 egg, separated
1¹/₂ cups all purpose or unbleached flour
¹/₄ teaspoon baking soda
¹/₄ teaspoon salt
1¹/₂ to 2 cups split pecan halves

FROSTING

¹/₃ cup semi-sweet chocolate chips
3 tablespoons milk
1 tablespoon margarine or butter
1 cup powdered sugar

In large bowl, beat brown sugar and ¹/₂ cup margarine until light and fluffy. Blend in vanilla, maple flavoring, 1 whole egg and 1 egg yolk. Lightly spoon flour into measuring cup; level off. Add flour, baking soda and salt; mix at low speed until well blended. Cover; refrigerate for easier handling.

Heat oven to 350°F. Grease cookie sheets. Arrange pecan pieces in groups of 5 on greased cookie sheets to resemble head and legs of turtle. In small bowl, beat 1 egg white. Using rounded teaspoonfuls of dough, shape into balls. Dip bottoms into beaten egg white; gently press onto pecans. (Tips of pecans should show.) Bake at 350°F. for 10 to 12 minutes or until light golden brown around edges. *Do not overbake.* Remove from cookie sheets immediately. Cool on wire racks.

In small saucepan over low heat, melt chocolate chips with milk and 1 tablespoon margarine, stirring until smooth. Remove from heat; stir in powdered sugar. Add additional powdered sugar if necessary for desired spreading consistency. Frost cookies. **42 cookies.**

HIGH ALTITUDE—Above 3500 Feet: No change.

NUTRIENTS PER 1 COOKIE.

Calories	110	Protein	<2% U.S. RDA
Protein	1g	Vitamin A	2% U.S. RDA
Carbohydrate	10g	Vitamin C	<2% U.S. RDA
Fat	7g	Thiamine	4% U.S. RDA
Cholesterol	10mg	Riboflavin	<2% U.S. RDA
Sodium	50mg	Niacin	<2% U.S. RDA
Potassium	45mg	Calcium	<2% U.S. RDA
Dietary Fiber	<1g	Iron	2% U.S. RDA

Starlight Mint Surprise Cookies

Laura Rott, Illinois
Bake-Off® 1, 1949

1 cup sugar
¹/₂ cup firmly packed brown sugar
³/₄ cup margarine or butter, softened
2 tablespoons water
1 teaspoon vanilla
2 eggs
3 cups all purpose or unbleached flour
1 teaspoon baking soda
¹/₂ teaspoon salt
2 (6-ounce) packages solid chocolate mint candy wafers, unwrapped
60 walnut halves

In large bowl, blend sugar, brown sugar, margarine, water, vanilla and eggs until well mixed. Lightly spoon flour into measuring cup; level off. In medium bowl, combine flour, baking soda and salt; mix well. Add to sugar mixture; mix at low speed until well blended. Cover; refrigerate at least 2 hours for easier handling.

Heat oven to 375°F. Using about 1 tablespoonful of dough, press around each candy wafer to cover completely. Place 2 inches apart on ungreased cookie sheets. Top each with walnut half. Bake at 375°F. for 7 to 9 minutes or until light golden brown.
5 dozen cookies.

HIGH ALTITUDE—Above 3500 Feet: No change.

NUTRIENTS PER 1 COOKIE

Calories	100	Protein	<2% U.S. RDA
Protein	1g	Vitamin A	2% U.S. RDA
Carbohydrate	13g	Vitamin C	<2% U.S. RDA
Fat	5g	Thiamine	2% U.S. RDA
Cholesterol	8mg	Riboflavin	<2% U.S. RDA
Sodium	65mg	Niacin	<2% U.S. RDA
Potassium	40mg	Calcium	<2% U.S. RDA
Dietary Fiber	<1g	Iron	2% U.S. RDA

Salted Peanut Chews

Gertrude Schweitzerhof, California
Bake-Off® 29, 1980

CRUST
- 1½ cups all purpose or unbleached flour
- ⅔ cup firmly packed brown sugar
- ½ teaspoon baking powder
- ½ teaspoon salt
- ¼ teaspoon baking soda
- ½ cup margarine or butter, softened
- 1 teaspoon vanilla
- 2 egg yolks
- 3 cups miniature marshmallows

TOPPING
- ⅔ cup corn syrup
- ¼ cup margarine or butter
- 2 tablespoons vanilla
- 12-ounce package (2 cups) peanut butter chips
- 2 cups crisp rice cereal
- 2 cups salted peanuts

Heat oven to 350°F. Lightly spoon flour into measuring cup; level off. In large bowl, combine flour and remaining crust ingredients except marshmallows on low speed until crumbly. Press firmly in bottom of ungreased 13×9-inch pan. Bake at 350°F. for 12 to 15 minutes or until light golden brown. Immediately sprinkle marshmallows over top. Bake an additional 1 to 2 minutes or until marshmallows just begin to puff. Cool while preparing topping.

In large saucepan over low heat, heat corn syrup, ¼ cup margarine, 2 teaspoons vanilla and peanut butter chips just until chips are melted and mixture is smooth, stirring constantly. Remove from heat. Stir in cereal and peanuts. Immediately spoon warm topping over marshmallows; spread to cover. Refrigerate until firm. Cut into bars. **36 bars.**

MICROWAVE DIRECTIONS Combine all crust ingredients as directed above. Press in bottom of ungreased 13×9-inch (3-quart) microwave-safe baking dish. Microwave on HIGH for 4 to 5½ minutes, rotating pan ½ turn halfway through cooking. Immediately sprinkle with marshmallows. Microwave on HIGH for 1 to 1½ minutes or until marshmallows begin to puff.

In 2-quart microwave-safe casserole, combine corn syrup, ¼ cup margarine, 2 teaspoons vanilla and peanut butter chips. Microwave on HIGH for 2 to 2½ minutes or until chips are melted, stirring once. Stir in cereal and peanuts. Immediately spoon warm topping over marshmallows; spread to cover. Refrigerate until firm. Cut into bars.

HIGH ALTITUDE—Above 3500 Feet: No change.

NUTRIENTS PER 1 BAR

Calories	210	Protein	6% U.S. RDA
Protein	5g	Vitamin A	4% U.S. RDA
Carbohydrate	23g	Vitamin C	<2% U.S. RDA
Fat	11g	Thiamine	6% U.S. RDA
Cholesterol	15mg	Riboflavin	4% U.S. RDA
Sodium	200mg	Niacin	10% U.S. RDA
Potassium	125mg	Calcium	2% U.S. RDA
Dietary Fiber	<1g	Iron	6% U.S. RDA

Lemon-Go-Lightly Cookies

Margaret Conway, California
Bake-Off® 27, 1976

- 2 cups all purpose or unbleached flour
- 2 cups mashed potato flakes
- 1 cup sugar
- 1 cup firmly packed brown sugar
- ½ to ¾ cup finely chopped nuts
- 1 teaspoon baking soda
- ¾ cup margarine or butter, melted
- 1 teaspoon grated lemon peel
- 2 eggs
- ¼ cup sugar

Heat oven to 350°F. Lightly spoon flour into measuring cup; level off. In large bowl, blend flour and remaining ingredients except ¼ cup sugar until well mixed. (Mixture will be crumbly.) Firmly press mixture into 1-inch balls; roll in ¼ cup sugar. Place 2 inches apart on ungreased cookie sheets. Bake at 350°F. for 9 to 12 minutes or until golden brown. Cool 1 minute; remove from cookie sheets.
6 dozen cookies.

HIGH ALTITUDE—Above 3500 Feet: No change.

NUTRIENTS PER 1 COOKIE

Calories	70	Protein	<2% U.S. RDA
Protein	1g	Vitamin A	<2% U.S. RDA
Carbohydrate	11g	Vitamin C	<2% U.S. RDA
Fat	3g	Thiamine	2% U.S. RDA
Cholesterol	8mg	Riboflavin	<2% U.S. RDA
Sodium	45mg	Niacin	<2% U.S. RDA
Potassium	45mg	Calcium	<2% U.S. RDA
Dietary Fiber	<1g	Iron	<2% U.S. RDA

Salted Peanut Chews

This frequently made bar cookie, reminiscent of a popular candy bar, is equally successful when baked in microwave or conventional oven.

Lemon-Go-Lightly Cookies

Potato flakes are the secret ingredient in these soft, chewy, delicately flavored cookies.

Peanut Blossoms

Freda Smith, Ohio
Bake-Off® 9, 1957

Peanut Blossoms

Have you ever wondered where old-fashioned cookie favorites such as these originated? This cookie made its first appearance as a prizewinner in a Bake-Off® Contest.

1³/4 cups all purpose or unbleached flour
¹/2 cup sugar
¹/2 cup firmly packed brown sugar
1 teaspoon baking soda
¹/2 teaspoon salt
¹/2 cup shortening
¹/2 cup peanut butter
2 tablespoons milk
1 teaspoon vanilla
1 egg
Sugar
About 48 milk chocolate candy kisses

Heat oven to 375°F. Lightly spoon flour into measuring cup; level off. In large bowl, blend flour, ¹/2 cup sugar, brown sugar, baking soda, salt, shortening, peanut butter, milk, vanilla and egg at low speed until stiff dough forms. Shape into 1-inch balls; roll in sugar. Place 2 inches apart on ungreased cookie sheets. Bake at 375°F. for 10 to 12 minutes or until golden brown. Immediately top each cookie with a candy kiss, pressing down firmly so cookie cracks around edge; remove from cookie sheets. **About 4 dozen cookies.**

HIGH ALTITUDE—Above 3500 Feet: No change.

NUTRIENTS PER 1 COOKIE

Calories	100	Protein	2% U.S. RDA
Protein	2g	Vitamin A	<2% U.S. RDA
Carbohydrate	12g	Vitamin C	<2% U.S. RDA
Fat	5g	Thiamine	2% U.S. RDA
Cholesterol	6mg	Riboflavin	2% U.S. RDA
Sodium	65mg	Niacin	2% U.S. RDA
Potassium	55mg	Calcium	<2% U.S. RDA
Dietary Fiber	<1g	Iron	2% U.S. RDA

Easy Lemon Sours

Irene E. Souza, California
Bake-Off® 30, 1982

BASE
1 package pudding-included yellow cake mix
2 cups crushed cornflakes cereal
¹/2 cup firmly packed brown sugar
¹/3 cup chopped nuts
¹/2 cup margarine or butter, softened

FILLING
3-ounce package lemon pudding and pie filling mix (not instant)
14-ounce can sweetened condensed milk (not evaporated)
³/4 teaspoon lemon extract

GLAZE
1 cup powdered sugar, sifted
¹/4 teaspoon lemon extract
3 to 5 teaspoons water

Heat oven to 350°F. Generously grease 15×10×1-inch baking pan. In large bowl, combine all base ingredients at low speed until crumbly. Reserve 1¹/2 cups of crumb mixture for topping. Press remaining mixture in bottom of greased pan. In small bowl, combine all filling ingredients; mix well. Pour filling mixture evenly over base; gently spread. Sprinkle with reserved 1¹/2 cups crumb mixture.

Bake at 350°F. for 20 to 30 minutes or until golden brown. Loosen edges. In small bowl, blend powdered sugar, ¹/4 teaspoon lemon extract and enough water for desired drizzling consistency. Drizzle over warm bars. Cool completely. Cut into bars. **48 bars.**

HIGH ALTITUDE—Above 3500 Feet: No change.

NUTRIENTS PER 1 BAR

Calories	140	Protein	2% U.S. RDA
Protein	2g	Vitamin A	4% U.S. RDA
Carbohydrate	23g	Vitamin C	2% U.S. RDA
Fat	5g	Thiamine	6% U.S. RDA
Cholesterol	4mg	Riboflavin	6% U.S. RDA
Sodium	150mg	Niacin	4% U.S. RDA
Potassium	65mg	Calcium	4% U.S. RDA
Dietary Fiber	<1g	Iron	2% U.S. RDA

Easy Lemon Sours

Oatmeal Carmelitas

Erlyce Larson, Minnesota
Bake-Off® 18, 1967

Oatmeal Carmelitas

This layered oatmeal bar cookie with its indulgent chocolate-caramel filling is a time-tested favorite.

CRUST

2 cups all purpose or unbleached flour
2 cups quick-cooking rolled oats
1½ cups firmly packed brown sugar
1 teaspoon baking soda
½ teaspoon salt
1¼ cups margarine or butter, softened

FILLING

6-ounce package (1 cup) semi-sweet chocolate chips
½ cup chopped nuts
12-ounce jar (1 cup) caramel ice cream topping
3 tablespoons flour

Heat oven to 350°F. Grease 13 × 9-inch pan. Lightly spoon flour into measuring cup; level off. In large bowl, blend flour and all remaining crust ingredients at low speed until crumbly. Press half (about 3 cups) of crumb mixture in bottom of greased pan. Reserve remaining crumb mixture for topping. Bake at 350°F. for 10 minutes.

Sprinkle warm crust with chocolate chips and nuts. In small bowl, combine caramel topping and 3 tablespoons flour; drizzle evenly over chocolate chips and nuts. Sprinkle with reserved crumb mixture. Bake an additional 18 to 22 minutes or until golden brown. Cool completely. Refrigerate 1 to 2 hours or until filling is set. Cut into bars. **36 bars.**

HIGH ALTITUDE—Above 3500 Feet: No change.

NUTRIENTS PER 1 BAR

Calories	200	Protein	4% U.S. RDA
Protein	2g	Vitamin A	10% U.S. RDA
Carbohydrate	26g	Vitamin C	<2% U.S. RDA
Fat	9g	Thiamine	8% U.S. RDA
Cholesterol	0mg	Riboflavin	4% U.S. RDA
Sodium	200mg	Niacin	6% U.S. RDA
Potassium	80mg	Calcium	4% U.S. RDA
Dietary Fiber	1g	Iron	10% U.S. RDA

Apricot Almond Squares

Sandy Munson, Colorado
Bake-Off® 32, 1986

BASE

1 package pudding-included yellow or white cake mix
½ cup margarine or butter, melted
½ cup finely chopped almonds
1 cup apricot preserves

FILLING

8-ounce package cream cheese, softened
¼ cup sugar
2 tablespoons flour
⅛ teaspoon salt
1 teaspoon vanilla
1 egg
⅓ cup apricot preserves
½ cup coconut

Heat oven to 350°F. Generously grease 13 × 9-inch pan. In large bowl, combine cake mix and margarine at low speed until crumbly. Stir in almonds. Reserve 1 cup of crumb mixture for filling. Press remaining mixture in bottom of greased pan. Carefully spread 1 cup preserves over base.*

In same bowl, beat cream cheese, sugar, flour, salt, vanilla and egg until well blended. Stir in ⅓ cup preserves at low speed. Carefully spread filling mixture over base. In small bowl, combine reserved 1 cup crumb mixture and coconut; mix well. Sprinkle over filling. Bake at 350°F. for 30 to 40 minutes or until golden brown and center is set. Cool completely. Store in refrigerator. **36 bars.**

TIP: *For ease in spreading, preserves can be warmed slightly.

HIGH ALTITUDE—Above 3500 Feet: No change.

NUTRIENTS PER 1 BAR

Calories	170	Protein	2% U.S. RDA
Protein	2g	Vitamin A	4% U.S. RDA
Carbohydrate	22g	Vitamin C	<2% U.S. RDA
Fat	8g	Thiamine	2% U.S. RDA
Cholesterol	15mg	Riboflavin	2% U.S. RDA
Sodium	150mg	Niacin	2% U.S. RDA
Potassium	45mg	Calcium	2% U.S. RDA
Dietary Fiber	<1g	Iron	2% U.S. RDA

White Chocolate Almond Brownies

ᗡᏦᏘ

Sally Vog, Oregon
Bake-Off® 33, 1988

BARS

  2 (5-ounce) Alpine White® candy
     bars with chopped almonds
  1/4 cup margarine or butter
  1/2 cup sugar
  1/8 teaspoon salt
  2 eggs
  1 teaspoon vanilla
  1/4 teaspoon almond extract
  1 cup all purpose or unbleached
     flour
  1/4 teaspoon baking powder

GLAZE

  1 teaspoon shortening
  1 ounce (1 square) semi-sweet
     chocolate, cut into pieces

Heat oven to 350°F. Grease 8 or 9-inch square pan. Cut 1 of the candy bars into 3/8-inch pieces; set aside. In small saucepan over low heat, melt second candy bar and margarine, stirring until smooth. In large bowl, combine sugar, salt and eggs; beat at high speed until light in color, about 4 minutes. Add melted candy bar mixture, vanilla and almond extract; mix at medium speed until well blended. Lightly spoon flour into measuring cup; level off. By hand, stir in flour and baking powder until just combined. Fold in candy bar pieces. Pour into greased pan. Bake at 350°F. for 25 to 30 minutes or until center is set and top is light golden brown. Cool completely.

In small saucepan over low heat, melt shortening and semi-sweet chocolate, stirring until smooth. Drizzle over cooled bars. Allow glaze to set before cutting into bars. Cut into bars.
24 to 36 bars.

HIGH ALTITUDE—Above 3500 Feet: No change.

NUTRIENTS PER 1 BAR

Calories	90	Protein	2% U.S. RDA
Protein	1g	Vitamin A	<2% U.S. RDA
Carbohydrate	11g	Vitamin C	<2% U.S. RDA
Fat	5g	Thiamine	<2% U.S. RDA
Cholesterol	15mg	Riboflavin	2% U.S. RDA
Sodium	35mg	Niacin	<2% U.S. RDA
Potassium	40mg	Calcium	2% U.S. RDA
Dietary Fiber	<1g	Iron	<2% U.S. RDA

Chewy Microwave Granola Bars

ᗡᏦᏘ

Ann Scates, Illinois
Bake-Off® 31, 1984

  1 cup firmly packed brown sugar
  1/4 cup sugar
  1/2 cup margarine or butter,
     softened
  2 tablespoons honey
  1/2 teaspoon vanilla
  1 egg
  1 cup all purpose or unbleached
     flour
  1 teaspoon cinnamon
  1/2 teaspoon baking powder
  1/4 teaspoon salt
  1 1/2 cups rolled oats
  1 1/4 cups crisp rice cereal
  1 cup chopped almonds
  1 cup semi-sweet chocolate chips
  1/2 cup wheat germ

MICROWAVE DIRECTIONS: Grease 12 × 8-inch (2-quart) or 13 × 9-inch (3-quart) microwave-safe dish. In large bowl, beat brown sugar, sugar and margarine until light and fluffy. Blend in honey, vanilla and egg. Lightly spoon flour into measuring cup; level off. Gradually blend in flour, cinnamon, baking powder and salt at low speed until well mixed. By hand, stir in remaining ingredients. Press firmly in bottom of greased dish. Microwave on MEDIUM for 7 to 9 minutes or until set, rotating dish 1/2 turn every 3 minutes during cooking. (Bars will firm up as they stand.) Cool completely. **24 bars.**

CONVENTIONAL DIRECTIONS: Heat oven to 350°F. Grease 13 × 9-inch pan. In large bowl, combine ingredients as directed above. Press firmly in bottom of greased pan. Bake at 350°F. for 20 to 25 minutes or until edges are light golden brown and center appears set. Cool completely. Cut into bars.

HIGH ALTITUDE—Above 3500 Feet: No change.

NUTRIENTS PER 1 BAR

Calories	210	Protein	4% U.S. RDA
Protein	3g	Vitamin A	10% U.S. RDA
Carbohydrate	27g	Vitamin C	<2% U.S. RDA
Fat	10g	Thiamine	10% U.S. RDA
Cholesterol	10mg	Riboflavin	8% U.S. RDA
Sodium	160mg	Niacin	8% U.S. RDA
Potassium	135mg	Calcium	6% U.S. RDA
Dietary Fiber	1g	Iron	10% U.S. RDA

ᗡᏦᏘ

Persistence pays off!

Food editors, reporters and cameras all contribute to the hubbub of the contest area. One flustered contestant, trying politely to answer a reporter's questions, omitted an important ingredient in his cake and didn't discover the error until it came out of the oven. His next try was completed just seconds before the contest time officially ended. But persistence paid off—he was a $2,000-prize winner.

Peanut Butter 'n Fudge Brownies

Peanut Butter 'n Fudge Brownies

—◦ஃ◦—

Jeannie Hobel, California
Bake-Off® 31, 1984

BROWNIES

  2 cups sugar

  1 cup margarine or butter, softened

  4 eggs

  2 teaspoons vanilla

  1½ cups all purpose or unbleached flour

  ¾ cup unsweetened cocoa

  1 teaspoon baking powder

  ½ teaspoon salt

  1 cup peanut butter chips

  ¾ peanut butter

  ⅓ cup margarine or butter, softened

  ⅓ cup sugar

  2 tablespoons flour

  ¾ teaspoon vanilla

  2 eggs

FROSTING

  3 tablespoons margarine or butter

  3-ounces (3 squares) unsweetened chocolate

  2⅔ cups powdered sugar

  ¼ teaspoon salt

  ¾ teaspoon vanilla

  4 to 5 tablespoons water

Heat oven to 350°F. Grease 13 × 9-inch pan. In large bowl, beat 2 cups sugar and 1 cup margarine until light and fluffy. Add 4 eggs, 1 at a time, beating well after each addition. Add 2 teaspoons vanilla; mix well. Lightly spoon flour into measuring cup; level off. In small bowl, combine 1½ cups flour, cocoa, baking powder and ½ teaspoon salt; mix well. Add to sugar mixture; mix at low speed until well blended. By hand, stir in peanut butter chips.

In small bowl, beat peanut butter and ⅓ cup margarine until smooth. Add ⅓ cup sugar and 2 tablespoons flour; mix well. Add ¾ teaspoon vanilla and 2 eggs; beat until smooth. Spread half of chocolate mixture in greased pan. Spread peanut butter mixture evenly over chocolate mixture. Spread remaining chocolate mixture evenly over peanut butter mixture. To marble, pull knife through layers in wide curves. Bake at 350°F. for 40 to 50 minutes or until top springs back when touched lightly in center and brownies begin to pull away from sides of pan. Cool completely.

In medium saucepan over low heat, melt 3 tablespoons margarine and chocolate, stirring until smooth. Remove from heat. Blend in powdered sugar, 1/4 teaspoon salt, 3/4 teaspoon vanilla and enough water for desired spreading consistency. Frost cooled brownies. Cut into bars. **36 bars.**

HIGH ALTITUDE—Above 3500 Feet: No change.

NUTRIENTS PER 1 BAR

Calories	260	Protein	6% U.S. RDA
Protein	5g	Vitamin A	6% U.S. RDA
Carbohydrate	29g	Vitamin C	<2% U.S. RDA
Fat	14g	Thiamine	4% U.S. RDA
Cholesterol	45mg	Riboflavin	4% U.S. RDA
Sodium	200mg	Niacin	8% U.S. RDA
Potassium	115mg	Calcium	2% U.S. RDA
Dietary Fiber	1g	Iron	4% U.S. RDA

Chocolate Mint Parfait Bars

꽃

Cheryl Wolf, Oregon
Bake-Off® 30, 1982

BASE
1 package pudding-included devil's food cake mix
1/3 cup margarine or butter, softened
1 egg

FILLING
1 envelope unflavored gelatin
1/4 cup boiling water
4 cups powdered sugar
1/2 cup margarine or butter, softened
1/2 cup shortening
1/4 teaspoon peppermint extract
2 to 3 drops green food coloring

FROSTING
3 tablespoons margarine or butter
6-ounce package (1 cup) semi-sweet chocolate chips

Heat oven to 350°F. Grease 15 × 10 × 1-inch baking pan. In large bowl, combine all base ingredients at low speed until crumbly. Press in bottom of greased pan. Bake at 350°F. for 10 minutes. Cool completely.

Dissolve gelatin in water; cool slightly. In large bowl, combine dissolved gelatin and 2 cups of the powdered sugar; mix well. Add 1/2 cup margarine, shortening, peppermint extract and food coloring; beat 1 minute at medium speed until smooth. Blend in remaining 2 cups powdered sugar at low speed until well mixed. Spread filling mixture evenly over cooled base.

In small saucepan over low heat, melt 3 tablespoons margarine and chocolate chips, stirring until smooth. Spoon frosting evenly over filling, carefully spreading to cover. Refrigerate until firm. Cut into bars. Let stand at room temperature about 20 minutes before serving. Store in refrigerator. **48 bars.**

HIGH ALTITUDE—Above 3500 Feet: No change.

NUTRIENTS PER 1 BAR

Calories	160	Protein	<2% U.S. RDA
Protein	1g	Vitamin A	2% U.S. RDA
Carbohydrate	18g	Vitamin C	<2% U.S. RDA
Fat	9g	Thiamine	<2% U.S. RDA
Cholesterol	6mg	Riboflavin	<2% U.S. RDA
Sodium	135mg	Niacin	<2% U.S. RDA
Potassium	35mg	Calcium	2% U.S. RDA
Dietary Fiber	<1g	Iron	<2% U.S. RDA

Chocolate Mint Parfait Bars

꽃

Layers of chocolate frosting, refreshing mint filling, and devil's food cake make this bar one of the most requested Bake-Off® recipes.

◦◦◦

Marie Hammons, Kansas
Bake-Off® 14, 1962

◦◦◦

Annette Erbeck, Ohio
Bake-Off® 29, 1980

Quick Crescent Baklava

◦◦◦

This ingenious contestant borrowed an idea from the Greeks, simplified it by using refrigerated crescent roll dough and created a delightful dessert bar.

BARS

2 cups all purpose or unbleached flour
½ cup sugar
½ cup firmly packed brown sugar
1½ teaspoons baking powder
Dash salt
¾ cup milk
½ cup margarine or butter, softened
1 teaspoon vanilla
2 eggs
3 (1.45-ounce) bars milk chocolate candy, cut into small pieces
1 cup maraschino cherries, drained, halved
1 cup coarsely chopped mixed nuts

ICING

¼ cup butter
2 cups powdered sugar
½ teaspoon vanilla
2 to 3 tablespoons milk

Heat oven to 350°F. Grease and flour 15 × 10 × 1-inch baking pan. Lightly spoon flour into measuring cup; level off. In large bowl, combine flour and remaining ingredients except chocolate, cherries and nuts. Blend 2 minutes at medium speed or until smooth. By hand, stir in chocolate, cherries and nuts. Spread in greased and floured pan. Bake at 350°F. for 25 to 30 minutes or until light golden brown.

In small heavy saucepan over medium heat, brown butter until light golden brown, stirring constantly. Remove from heat. Blend in powdered sugar, ½ teaspoon vanilla and enough milk for desired spreading consistency. Spread over warm bars. Cool completely. Cut into bars. **48 bars.**

HIGH ALTITUDE—Above 3500 Feet: No change.

NUTRIENTS PER 1 BAR

Calories	120	Protein	2% U.S. RDA
Protein	2g	Vitamin A	2% U.S. RDA
Carbohydrate	15g	Vitamin C	<2% U.S. RDA
Fat	6g	Thiamine	2% U.S. RDA
Cholesterol	15mg	Riboflavin	2% U.S. RDA
Sodium	55mg	Niacin	2% U.S. RDA
Potassium	55mg	Calcium	2% U.S. RDA
Dietary Fiber	<1g	Iron	2% U.S. RDA

2 (8-ounce) cans refrigerated crescent dinner rolls
3 to 4 cups walnuts, finely chopped
½ cup sugar
1 teaspoon cinnamon

GLAZE

¼ cup sugar
½ cup honey
2 tablespoons margarine or butter
2 teaspoons lemon juice

Heat oven to 350°F. Unroll 1 can of dough into 2 long rectangles. Place in ungreased 13 × 9-inch pan; press over bottom and ½ inch up sides to form crust. Seal perforations. Bake at 350°F. for 5 minutes.

In large bowl, combine walnuts, ½ cup sugar and cinnamon; mix well. Spoon walnut mixture evenly over partially baked crust. Unroll remaining can of dough into 2 long rectangles. Place over walnut mixture; press out to edges of pan. With tip of sharp knife and using dough edges and perforations as a guide, score dough with 5 lengthwise and 7 diagonal markings to form 28 diamond-shaped pieces.

In small saucepan, combine all glaze ingredients. Bring to a boil; remove from heat. Spoon half of glaze evenly over dough. Bake an additional 25 to 30 minutes or until golden brown. Spoon remaining glaze evenly over hot baklava. Cool completely. Refrigerate until thoroughly chilled. Cut into diamond-shaped pieces. **28 servings.**

NUTRIENTS PER 1/28 OF RECIPE

Calories	230	Protein	4% U.S. RDA
Protein	3g	Vitamin A	<2% U.S. RDA
Carbohydrate	20g	Vitamin C	<2% U.S. RDA
Fat	15g	Thiamine	6% U.S. RDA
Cholesterol	0mg	Riboflavin	2% U.S. RDA
Sodium	140mg	Niacin	2% U.S. RDA
Potassium	125mg	Calcium	2% U.S. RDA
Dietary Fiber	1g	Iron	4% U.S. RDA

Quick Crescent Baklava

Rocky Road Fudge Bars

Rocky Road Fudge Bars
—⁂—

Mary Wilson, Georgia
Bake-Off® 23, 1972

BASE

 1/2 cup margarine or butter
 1 ounce (1 square) unsweetened
 chocolate, chopped
 1 cup all purpose or unbleached
 flour
 1 cup sugar
 3/4 cup chopped nuts
 1 teaspoon baking powder
 1 teaspoon vanilla
 2 eggs

FILLING

 8-ounce package cream cheese,
 softened, reserving 2 ounces for
 frosting
 1/4 cup margarine or butter,
 softened
 1/2 cup sugar
 2 tablespoons flour
 1/2 teaspoon vanilla
 1 egg
 1/4 cup chopped nuts
 6-ounce package (1 cup) semi-
 sweet chocolate chips

FROSTING

 2 cups miniature marshmallows
 1/4 cup margarine or butter
 1/4 cup milk
 1 ounce (1 square) unsweetened
 chocolate, chopped
 3 cups powdered sugar, sifted
 1 teaspoon vanilla

Heat oven to 350°F. Grease and flour
13 × 9-inch pan. In large saucepan over
low heat, melt 1/2 cup margarine and
1 ounce unsweetened chocolate, stirring
until smooth. Lightly spoon flour into
measuring cup; level off. Add 1 cup
flour and remaining base ingredients;
mix well. Spread in greased and floured
pan.

In small bowl, combine all filling ingredients except 1/4 cup nuts and chocolate chips. Beat 1 minute at medium
speed until smooth and fluffy. By hand,
stir in nuts. Spread over chocolate mixture; sprinkle evenly with chocolate
chips. Bake at 350°F. for 25 to 35 minutes or until toothpick inserted in center comes out clean.

Immediately sprinkle marshmallows
over top. Bake an additional 2 minutes.
In large saucepan over low heat, combine 1/4 cup margarine, milk, 1 ounce

unsweetened chocolate and reserved 2 ounces cream cheese; stir until well blended. Remove from heat. Stir in powdered sugar and 1 teaspoon vanilla; blend until smooth. Immediately spoon warm frosting over marshmallows. To marble, lightly pull knife through frosting and marshmallows in wide curves. Refrigerate until firm. Cut into bars. **48 bars.**

HIGH ALTITUDE—Above 3500 Feet: No change.

Grand Prize Winner

Chocolate Cherry Bars

—∘❦∘—

Frances Jerzak, Minnesota
Bake-Off® 25, 1974

BARS
1 package pudding-included
  devil's food cake mix
21-ounce can cherry fruit pie filling
1 teaspoon almond extract
2 eggs, beaten

FROSTING
1 cup sugar
1/3 cup milk
5 tablespoons margarine or butter
6-ounce package (1 cup) semi-
  sweet chocolate chips

Heat oven to 350°F. Grease and flour 15 × 10 × 1-inch baking pan or 13 × 9-inch pan. In large bowl, combine all bar ingredients; stir until well blended. Pour into greased and floured pan. Bake at 350°F. in 15 × 10 × 1-inch pan for 20 to 30 minutes or in 13 × 9-inch pan for 25 to 30 minutes or until toothpick inserted in center comes out clean.

In small saucepan, combine sugar, milk and margarine. Bring to a boil; boil 1 minute, stirring constantly. Remove from heat; stir in chocolate chips until smooth. Pour and spread over warm bars. Cool completely. **36 to 48 bars.**

HIGH ALTITUDE—Above 3500 Feet: Bake at 375°F. in 15 × 10 × 1-inch pan for 20 to 30 minutes or in 13 × 9-inch pan for 25 to 30 minutes.

Grand Prize Winner

Pecan Pie Surprise Bars

—∘❦∘—

Pearl Hall, Washington
Bake-Off® 22, 1971

BASE
1 package pudding-included
  yellow or butter flavor cake mix
1/3 cup margarine or butter,
  softened
1 egg

FILLING
1/2 cup firmly packed brown sugar
1 1/2 cups dark corn syrup
1 teaspoon vanilla
3 eggs
1 cup chopped pecans

Heat oven to 350°F. Grease 13 × 9-inch pan. Reserve 2/3 cup of the dry cake mix for filling. In large bowl, combine remaining dry cake mix, margarine and 1 egg at low speed until well blended. Press in bottom of greased pan. Bake at 350°F. for 15 to 20 minutes or until light golden brown.

In large bowl, combine reserved 2/3 cup dry cake mix, brown sugar, corn syrup, vanilla and 3 eggs at low speed until moistened. Beat 1 minute at medium speed until well blended. Pour filling mixture over warm base; sprinkle with pecans. Bake an additional 30 to 35 minutes or until filling is set. Cool completely. Cut into bars. Store in refrigerator. **36 bars.**

HIGH ALTITUDE—Above 3500 Feet: Add 1/3 cup flour to dry cake mix. Decrease dark corn syrup to 1 1/4 cups. Bake as directed above.

Pecan Pie Surprise Bars

—∘❦∘—

The surprise is pecan pie in a convenient bar cookie.

Pictured top to bottom: Orange Kiss-Me Cake, page 153; Caramel Apple Cake, page 153; Double Lemon Streusel Cake, page 152

Cakes and Tortes

꧁꧂

It's been said that a great meal without dessert is a contradiction in terms. And what could be a more fitting mealtime finale than a taste-tempting cake or torte, especially if it ranks among the best of Bake-Off® recipes. In fact, cakes have won more Grand Prizes than any other type of food since the beginning of the Bake-Off® Contest.

Although this category has remained ever popular, it has undergone tremendous change over the years. Fancy, elaborately decorated cakes made up the largest category of entries in the 1950s. And several gorgeous multilayered productions of that time, including "My Inspiration" Cake and Mardi Gras Party Cake, have become Bake-Off® classics.

During the ensuing years, cake and frosting mixes came into the limelight. The emphasis on shortcut baking resulted in simple sensations like self-frosted cakes and others with no topping at all. Ring-of-Coconut Fudge Cake and Banana Crunch Cake were typical of those featuring multiple baked-in layers. And with the famous Tunnel of Fudge Cake, a soft, fudgy center "magically" appeared after baking.

Sweets lovers today are showing renewed interest in glamorous desserts. Traditional from-scratch ideas are often coupled with the convenience of mixes to create special occasion desserts, such as Chocolate Orange Cream Torte and Chocolate Praline Layer Cake.

Imaginative toppings, fillings and garnishes create eye-catching presentations. One cake is topped with fruit preserves and then cream cheese frosting. Another features chocolate curls and pecan halves, artistically arranged on whipped cream topping. Still another is carefully drizzled with glaze to create a complex lattice-work design.

Other special touches include baking in pans that add glamour and sophistication. Nutty Graham Picnic Cake, Very Berry Lemon Cake and others bake in a fluted tube pan, while the Swiss Almond Apple Cake recipe calls for a springform pan. Liqueur in Almond Mocha Cake and the fruit filling of Heavenly Hawaiian Cake Roll are among the special ingredients featured in this chapter's artistic centerpiece desserts.

For all those occasions when nothing but the most wonderful dessert will do, these cakes and tortes say it all!

Chocolate Praline Layer Cake

~•ᵉᵇᵉᵇ•~

Julie Konecne, Minnesota
Bake-Off® 33, 1988

NUTRIENTS PER 1/12 OF RECIPE			
Calories	610	Protein	8% U.S. RDA
Protein	5g	Vitamin A	20% U.S. RDA
Carbohydrate	56g	Vitamin C	<2% U.S. RDA
Fat	41g	Thiamine	10% U.S. RDA
Cholesterol	140mg	Riboflavin	10% U.S. RDA
Sodium	470mg	Niacin	4% U.S. RDA
Potassium	230mg	Calcium	15% U.S. RDA
Dietary Fiber	1g	Iron	10% U.S. RDA

Chocolate Praline Layer Cake

~•ᵉᵇᵉᵇ•~

Created by a university professor of music, this easy-to-prepare cake is spectacular to serve and marvelous to eat. It's best if made a few hours ahead and refrigerated before serving.

Very Berry Lemon Cake

~•ᵉᵇᵉᵇ•~

Bake-Off® recipes have inspired new Pillsbury products. Among them is the line of Bundt-style cake mixes. The refreshing flavor combination of this cake was the first flavor to be introduced in this line of mixes.

CAKE
¹/₂ cup butter or margarine
¹/₄ cup whipping cream
1 cup firmly packed brown sugar
³/₄ cup coarsely chopped pecans
1 package pudding-included devil's food cake mix
1¹/₄ cups water
¹/₃ cup oil
3 eggs

TOPPING
1³/₄ cups whipping cream
¹/₄ cup powdered sugar
¹/₄ teaspoon vanilla
Whole pecans, if desired
Chocolate curls, if desired

Heat oven to 325°F. In small heavy saucepan, combine butter, ¹/₄ cup whipping cream and brown sugar. Cook over low heat just until butter is melted, stirring occasionally. Pour into two 9 or 8-inch round cake pans; sprinkle evenly with chopped pecans. In large bowl, combine cake mix, water, oil and eggs at low speed until moistened; beat 2 minutes at *highest* speed. Carefully spoon batter over pecan mixture in pans. Bake at 325°F. for 35 to 45 minutes or until top springs back when touched lightly in center. Cool 5 minutes; remove from pans. Cool completely.

In small bowl, beat 1³/₄ cups whipping cream until soft peaks form. Add powdered sugar and vanilla; beat until stiff peaks form.

To assemble cake, place 1 cake layer praline side up on serving plate. Spread top with ¹/₂ of whipped cream mixture. Top with remaining layer, praline side up. Spread top with remaining whipped cream. Garnish top of cake with whole pecans and chocolate curls. Store in refrigerator. **12 servings.**

HIGH ALTITUDE—Above 3500 Feet: Add 2 tablespoons flour to dry cake mix. Increase water to 1¹/₃ cups. Bake at 350°F. for 30 to 35 minutes. Remove from pans immediately.

Very Berry Lemon Cake

~•ᵉᵇᵉᵇ•~

Alice Wyman, North Dakota
Bake-Off® 20, 1969

CAKE
16¹/₂-ounce can blueberries, drained, reserving 1 cup liquid for sauce
1 package pudding-included lemon cake mix
8-ounce carton (1 cup) plain yogurt or dairy sour cream
4 eggs
Powdered sugar

BLUEBERRY SAUCE
¹/₄ cup sugar
1 tablespoon cornstarch
Reserved 1 cup blueberry liquid

Heat oven to 350°F. Grease and flour 12-cup fluted tube pan or 10-inch tube pan. Rinse blueberries with cold water; drain on paper towel. In large bowl, blend cake mix, yogurt and eggs at low speed until moistened; beat 2 minutes at *medium* speed. Carefully fold in blueberries. Pour batter into greased and floured pan. Bake at 350°F. for 35 to 45 minutes or until toothpick inserted in center comes out clean. Cool upright in pan 15 minutes; remove from pan. Cool completely. Sprinkle with powdered sugar.

In small saucepan, blend sugar and cornstarch. If necessary, add enough water to reserved blueberry liquid to make 1 cup. Gradually stir blueberry liquid into sugar mixture. Bring to a boil. Reduce heat to low; cook until mixture thickens, stirring constantly. Serve sauce with cake. **16 servings.**

HIGH ALTITUDE—Above 3500 Feet: Add ¹/₄ cup flour to dry cake mix.

NUTRIENTS PER 1/16 OF RECIPE			
Calories	200	Protein	6% U.S. RDA
Protein	4g	Vitamin A	<2% U.S. RDA
Carbohydrate	37g	Vitamin C	<2% U.S. RDA
Fat	4g	Thiamine	6% U.S. RDA
Cholesterol	70mg	Riboflavin	8% U.S. RDA
Sodium	230mg	Niacin	2% U.S. RDA
Potassium	70mg	Calcium	6% U.S. RDA
Dietary Fiber	<1g	Iron	4% U.S. RDA

Chocolate Praline Layer Cake

Kentucky Butter Cake

Kentucky Butter Cake

Nell Lewis, Missouri
Bake-Off® 15, 1963

CAKE
- 3 cups all purpose or unbleached flour
- 2 cups sugar
- 1 teaspoon baking powder
- 1 teaspoon salt
- ½ teaspoon baking soda
- 1 cup buttermilk*
- 1 cup butter or margarine, softened
- 2 teaspoons vanilla or rum extract
- 4 eggs

BUTTER SAUCE
- ¾ cup sugar
- ⅓ cup butter or margarine
- 3 tablespoons water
- 1 to 2 teaspoons vanilla or rum extract
- Powdered sugar
- Whipped cream, if desired

Heat oven to 325°F. Generously grease and lightly flour 12-cup fluted tube pan or 10-inch tube pan. Lightly spoon flour into measuring cup; level off. In large bowl, combine flour and all remaining cake ingredients at low speed until moistened; beat 3 minutes at medium speed. Pour batter into greased and floured pan. Bake at 325°F. for 55 to 70 minutes or until toothpick inserted in center comes out clean. Do not remove cake from pan.

In small saucepan, combine all sauce ingredients; cook over low heat until butter melts, stirring occasionally. *Do not boil.* Using long-tined fork, pierce hot cake in pan 10 to 12 times. Slowly pour hot sauce over cake. Remove cake from pan immediately after sauce has been absorbed, 5 to 10 minutes. Cool completely. Just before serving, sprinkle with powdered sugar. Serve with whipped cream. **12 to 16 servings.**

TIP: *To substitute for buttermilk, use 1 tablespoon vinegar or lemon juice plus milk to make 1 cup.

HIGH ALTITUDE—Above 3500 Feet: Decrease sugar to 1¾ cups; increase buttermilk to 1 cup plus 2 tablespoons. Bake at 350°F. for 60 to 70 minutes.

NUTRIENTS PER 1/16 OF RECIPE

Calories	410	Protein	6% U.S. RDA
Protein	5g	Vitamin A	15% U.S. RDA
Carbohydrate	54g	Vitamin C	<2% U.S. RDA
Fat	20g	Thiamine	10% U.S. RDA
Cholesterol	120mg	Riboflavin	10% U.S. RDA
Sodium	380mg	Niacin	6% U.S. RDA
Potassium	75mg	Calcium	4% U.S. RDA
Dietary Fiber	<1g	Iron	8% U.S. RDA

Grand Prize Winner

Nutty Graham Picnic Cake

Esther V. Tomich, California
Bake-Off® 28, 1978

CAKE
    2 cups all purpose or unbleached
        flour
    1 cup (14 squares) finely crushed
        graham crackers or graham
        cracker crumbs
    1 cup firmly packed brown sugar
½ cup sugar
    1 teaspoon baking powder
    1 teaspoon baking soda
    1 teaspoon salt
½ teaspoon cinnamon
    1 cup margarine or butter,
        softened
    1 cup orange juice
    1 tablespoon grated orange peel
    3 eggs
    1 cup chopped nuts

GLAZE
    2 tablespoons brown sugar
    5 teaspoons milk
    1 tablespoon margarine or butter
¾ cup powdered sugar
¼ cup chopped nuts

Heat oven to 350°F. Generously grease and flour 12-cup fluted tube pan or 10-inch tube pan. Lightly spoon flour into measuring cup; level off. In large bowl, combine flour and remaining cake ingredients except nuts at low speed until moistened; beat 3 minutes at medium speed. By hand, stir in 1 cup nuts. Pour batter into greased and floured pan. Bake at 350°F. for 40 to 60 minutes or until toothpick inserted in center comes out clean. Cool upright in pan 15 minutes; invert onto serving plate. Cool completely.

In small saucepan over low heat, combine 2 tablespoons brown sugar, milk and 1 tablespoon margarine; heat just until sugar is dissolved, stirring constantly. Remove from heat. Stir in powdered sugar; blend until smooth. Drizzle over cake; sprinkle with ¼ cup nuts. **12 to 16 servings.**

HIGH ALTITUDE—Above 3500 Feet: Bake at 350°F. for 50 to 55 minutes.

NUTRIENTS PER 1/16 OF RECIPE

Calories	380	Protein	6% U.S. RDA
Protein	5g	Vitamin A	10% U.S. RDA
Carbohydrate	46g	Vitamin C	8% U.S. RDA
Fat	20g	Thiamine	10% U.S. RDA
Cholesterol	50mg	Riboflavin	8% U.S. RDA
Sodium	420mg	Niacin	6% U.S. RDA
Potassium	190mg	Calcium	4% U.S. RDA
Dietary Fiber	1g	Iron	10% U.S. RDA

A new cake shape sweeps the country!

In 1966, the 17th Bake-Off® Contest, the chocolate beauty, Tunnel of Fudge Cake, popularized the little-known Bundt-shaped cake pan into kitchen prominence. The Pillsbury Company received over 200,000 consumer requests for help in locating the 12-cup fluted tube pan following the contest. More than twenty years later Tunnel of Fudge Cake continues to be a recipe most frequently requested. It was also a recipe that stimulated the development of a new line of Bundt cake mixes featuring tempting fillings.

Swiss Almond Apple Cake

Swiss Almond Apple Cake

Stephen Hill, California
Bake-Off® 33, 1988

CAKE
- ²/₃ cup sugar
- ½ cup butter or margarine, softened
- 2 eggs
- 2 tablespoons lemon juice
- 2 cups all purpose or unbleached flour
- 2 teaspoons baking powder
- ¼ teaspoon salt
- ¼ cup raspberry preserves
- 3½ cups (about 4 medium) thinly sliced peeled apples

TOPPING
- 1 cup ground almonds
- ½ cup sugar
- 2 tablespoons flour
- ½ cup dairy sour cream
- 1 teaspoon grated lemon peel
- 2 eggs, beaten

GLAZE
- ¼ cup powdered sugar
- 1 to 2 teaspoons lemon juice

Heat oven to 350°F. Grease and flour 9 or 10-inch springform pan. In large bowl, beat ²/₃ cup sugar and butter until light and fluffy. Add 2 eggs and 2 tablespoons lemon juice; beat until well blended. Lightly spoon flour into measuring cup; level off. In small bowl, combine 2 cups flour, baking powder and salt; mix well. Add to sugar mixture; beat at low speed until well blended. Spread batter in greased and floured pan. Spoon preserves over batter; carefully spread to cover. Top with apple slices; slightly press into batter. In medium bowl, combine all topping ingredients; blend well. Pour over apples.

Bake at 350°F. for 55 to 65 minutes or until apples are tender, edges of cake are light golden brown and toothpick inserted in center comes out clean. Cool 10 minutes; carefully remove sides of pan. In small bowl, blend powdered sugar and enough lemon juice for desired drizzling consistency. Drizzle over warm cake. Serve warm or cold. **16 servings.**

HIGH ALTITUDE — Above 3500 Feet: No change.

NUTRIENTS PER 1/16 OF RECIPE

Calories	280	Protein	6% U.S. RDA
Protein	5g	Vitamin A	6% U.S. RDA
Carbohydrate	39g	Vitamin C	4% U.S. RDA
Fat	12g	Thiamine	8% U.S. RDA
Cholesterol	90mg	Riboflavin	8% U.S. RDA
Sodium	150mg	Niacin	6% U.S. RDA
Potassium	125mg	Calcium	6% U.S. RDA
Dietary Fiber	2g	Iron	6% U.S. RDA

Ring-of-Coconut Fudge Cake

Rita Glomb, Pennsylvania
Bake-Off® 22, 1971

FILLING

8-ounce package cream cheese, softened
¼ cup sugar
1 teaspoon vanilla
1 egg
½ cup flaked coconut
6-ounce package (1 cup) semi-sweet or milk chocolate chips

CAKE

3 cups all purpose, unbleached or self-rising flour*
¾ cup unsweetened cocoa
2 teaspoons baking soda
2 teaspoons baking powder
1½ teaspoons salt
2 cups sugar
1 cup cooking oil
2 eggs
1 cup hot coffee or water
1 cup buttermilk**
1 teaspoon vanilla
½ cup chopped nuts

GLAZE

1 cup powdered sugar
3 tablespoons unsweetened cocoa
2 tablespoons margarine or butter, softened
2 teaspoons vanilla
1 to 3 tablespoons hot water

Heat oven to 350°F. Generously grease and lightly flour 12-cup fluted tube pan or 10-inch tube pan. In small bowl, beat cream cheese, ¼ cup sugar, 1 teaspoon vanilla and 1 egg until smooth. By hand, stir in coconut and chocolate chips; set aside.

Lightly spoon flour into measuring cup; level off. In medium bowl, combine flour, ¾ cup cocoa, baking soda, baking powder and salt; mix well. In large bowl, combine 2 cups sugar, oil and 2 eggs; beat 1 minute at high speed. Add flour mixture, coffee, buttermilk and 1 teaspoon vanilla to sugar mixture. Blend at low speed until moistened; beat 3 minutes at medium speed. By hand, stir in nuts. Pour half of batter into greased and floured pan. Carefully spoon cream cheese filling over batter. (Filling should not touch sides or center of pan.) Spoon remaining batter over filling. Bake at 350°F. for 70 to 75 minutes or until top springs back when touched lightly in center. Cool upright in pan 15 minutes; invert onto serving plate. Cool completely.

In small bowl, blend powdered sugar, 3 tablespoons cocoa, margarine, 2 teaspoons vanilla and enough water for desired glaze consistency. Spoon over cake, allowing some to run down sides. Store in refrigerator. **16 servings.**

TIPS: *If using self-rising flour, decrease baking soda to 1 teaspoon; omit baking powder and salt.

**To substitute for buttermilk, use 1 tablespoon vinegar or lemon juice plus milk to make 1 cup.

HIGH ALTITUDE — Above 3500 Feet: Increase flour to 3½ cups. Decrease sugar in cake to 1⅔ cups.

NUTRIENTS PER 1/16 OF RECIPE

Calories	510	Protein	10% U.S. RDA
Protein	7g	Vitamin A	4% U.S. RDA
Carbohydrate	57g	Vitamin C	<2% U.S. RDA
Fat	28g	Thiamine	10% U.S. RDA
Cholesterol	70mg	Riboflavin	10% U.S. RDA
Sodium	480mg	Niacin	6% U.S. RDA
Potassium	170mg	Calcium	6% U.S. RDA
Dietary Fiber	3g	Iron	10% U.S. RDA

Ring-of-Coconut Fudge Cake

This chocolate cake with its macaroon-like tunnel of cream cheese, coconut and chocolate chips has certainly made its mark. Its popularity encouraged Pillsbury to add a pudding-filled version to its line of Bundt-style cake mixes.

Swiss Almond Apple Cake

Serve this European-style cake for dessert or anytime with coffee or tea. Sliced apples, a rippling of raspberry preserves and ground almonds make this an extra-special cake.

Golden Apricot Cake

This golden layer cake, filled with tangy apricot preserves and frosted with a cream cheese frosting, was a winning recipe for a retired lieutenant commander in the U.S. Navy.

"My Inspiration" Cake

This cake could inspire a party! Each layer has a ribbon of chocolate running through it and a toasted nut topping baked right in. The layers are attractively put together with buttery chocolate and white frostings. The bonus is that the recipe is even easier to make now, using a cake mix.

Golden Apricot Cake

Dale P. Grant, Texas
Bake-Off® 32, 1986

CAKE
> 1 package pudding-included yellow cake mix
> 1 cup apricot nectar
> 1/3 cup oil
> 1/4 cup honey
> 3 eggs

FILLING AND FROSTING
> 10-ounce jar apricot preserves
> 3-ounce package cream cheese, softened
> 1/4 cup margarine or butter, softened
> 2 1/2 cups powdered sugar
> 1/3 cup chopped pecans or walnuts

Heat oven to 350°F. Grease and flour two 8 or 9-inch round cake pans. In large bowl, combine all cake ingredients at low speed until moistened; beat 2 minutes at *highest* speed. Pour batter into greased and floured pans. Bake at 350°F. for 25 to 35 minutes or until toothpick inserted in center comes out clean. Cool 10 minutes; remove from pans. Cool completely.

Reserve 2/3 cup of the preserves. In small saucepan, heat remaining preserves until melted, stirring occasionally. Set aside.

In small bowl, beat cream cheese and margarine until smooth. Add powdered sugar; beat at low speed until well blended. Add enough warm preserves to cream cheese mixture for desired spreading consistency. Stir in pecans.

To assemble cake, place 1 cake layer on serving plate. Spread top with reserved 2/3 cup preserves. Top with remaining layer. Frost sides and top of cake with frosting mixture. Refrigerate before serving. Store in refrigerator.
12 servings.

HIGH ALTITUDE—Above 3500 Feet: Add 5 tablespoons flour to dry cake mix. Decrease apricot nectar to 1/2 cup and honey to 1 tablespoon. Add 1/2 cup water. Bake at 375°F. for 30 to 40 minutes.

NUTRIENTS PER 1/12 OF RECIPE

Calories	520	Protein	6% U.S. RDA
Protein	4g	Vitamin A	10% U.S. RDA
Carbohydrate	80g	Vitamin C	20% U.S. RDA
Fat	21g	Thiamine	10% U.S. RDA
Cholesterol	80mg	Riboflavin	8% U.S. RDA
Sodium	360mg	Niacin	4% U.S. RDA
Potassium	105mg	Calcium	6% U.S. RDA
Dietary Fiber	<1g	Iron	8% U.S. RDA

Grand Prize Winner

"My Inspiration" Cake

Lois Kanago, South Dakota
Bake-Off® 5, 1953

CAKE
> 1 cup finely chopped pecans
> 1 package pudding-included white cake mix
> 1 1/4 cups water
> 1/3 cup oil
> 3 egg whites
> 2 ounces (2 squares) semi-sweet chocolate, grated

FROSTING
> 1/2 cup sugar
> 2 ounces (2 squares) unsweetened chocolate
> 1/4 cup water
> 1/2 cup margarine or butter, softened
> 1 teaspoon vanilla
> 2 1/4 cups powdered sugar

Heat oven to 350°F. Grease and flour two 8 or 9-inch round cake pans. Sprinkle pecans evenly over bottom of both greased and floured pans. In large bowl, combine cake mix, 1 1/4 cups water, oil and egg whites at low speed until moistened; beat 2 minutes at *highest* speed. Carefully spoon 1/4 of batter into each nut-lined pan; sprinkle with grated chocolate. Spoon remaining batter over grated chocolate; spread carefully. Bake at 350°F. for 20 to 28 minutes or until toothpick inserted in center comes out clean. Cool 15 minutes; remove from pans. Cool completely.

In small saucepan over low heat, melt

"My Inspiration" Cake

sugar and unsweetened chocolate in ¼ cup water, stirring until smooth. Remove from heat; cool. In small bowl, beat margarine and vanilla until smooth. Gradually add powdered sugar at low speed until well blended. Reserve ⅓ cup of frosting mixture. Add cooled chocolate mixture to remaining frosting; beat until smooth.

To assemble cake, place 1 cake layer nut side up on serving plate. Spread top with ⅓ (about ½ cup) of chocolate frosting. Top with remaining layer, nut side up. Frost sides and ½ inch around top edge of cake with remaining chocolate frosting. Pipe reserved white frosting around edge of chocolate frosting and nuts on top of cake.*
12 servings.

TIP: *If necessary, add water, 1 drop at a time, to white frosting for desired piping consistency.

HIGH ALTITUDE—Above 3500 Feet: Add 3 tablespoons flour to dry cake mix and increase water to 1⅓ cups.

NUTRIENTS PER 1/12 OF RECIPE

Calories	530	Protein	6% U.S. RDA
Protein	4g	Vitamin A	6% U.S. RDA
Carbohydrate	68g	Vitamin C	<2% U.S. RDA
Fat	29g	Thiamine	8% U.S. RDA
Cholesterol	0mg	Riboflavin	4% U.S. RDA
Sodium	390mg	Niacin	4% U.S. RDA
Potassium	170mg	Calcium	4% U.S. RDA
Dietary Fiber	2g	Iron	4% U.S. RDA

Tunnel of Fudge Cake

Tunnel of Fudge Cake
—◦⅋◦—

The popularity of Bundt[†] shaped fluted tube pans was heightened after this recipe won Bake-Off® judges' approval. The original recipe called for dry frosting mix that is no longer available. Updated and revised, this version still has a soft tunnel of fudge surrounded by delicious chocolate cake.

[†] Registered trademark of Northland Aluminum Products, Inc., Minneapolis, MN

Tunnel of Fudge Cake
—◦⅋◦—
Ella Helfrich, Texas
Bake-Off® 17, 1966

CAKE
- 1³/₄ cups sugar
- 1³/₄ cups margarine or butter, softened
- 6 eggs
- 2 cups powdered sugar
- 2¹/₄ cups all purpose or unbleached flour
- 2 cups chopped walnuts*
- ³/₄ cup unsweetened cocoa

GLAZE
- ³/₄ cup powdered sugar
- ¹/₄ cup unsweetened cocoa
- 1¹/₂ to 2 tablespoons milk

Heat oven to 350°F. Grease and flour 12-cup fluted tube pan or 10-inch tube pan. In large bowl, beat sugar and margarine until light and fluffy. Add eggs, 1 at a time, beating well after each addition. Gradually add 2 cups powdered sugar; blend well. Lightly spoon flour into measuring cup; level off. By hand, stir in flour and remaining cake ingredients until well blended. Spoon batter into greased and floured pan; spread evenly. Bake at 350°F. for 58 to 62 minutes.** Cool upright in pan on wire rack 1 hour; invert onto serving plate. Cool completely.

In small bowl, blend ³/₄ cup powdered sugar, ¹/₄ cup cocoa and enough milk for desired drizzling consistency. Spoon over cake, allowing some to run down sides. Store tightly covered.
16 servings.

TIPS: *Nuts are essential for the success of this recipe.

**Since this cake has a soft tunnel of fudge, an ordinary doneness test cannot be used. Accurate oven temperature and baking time are essential.

HIGH ALTITUDE—Above 3500 Feet: Increase flour to 2¹/₄ cups plus 3 tablespoons. Bake as directed above.

NUTRIENTS PER 1/16 OF RECIPE

Calories	560	Protein	10% U.S. RDA
Protein	7g	Vitamin A	20% U.S. RDA
Carbohydrate	58g	Vitamin C	<2% U.S. RDA
Fat	33g	Thiamine	10% U.S. RDA
Cholesterol	100mg	Riboflavin	10% U.S. RDA
Sodium	300mg	Niacin	6% U.S. RDA
Potassium	170mg	Calcium	4% U.S. RDA
Dietary Fiber	2g	Iron	10% U.S. RDA

Almond Mocha Cake

Debbie Russell, Colorado
Bake-Off® 33, 1988

½ cup chopped almonds
1¼ cups strong coffee
½ cup margarine or butter
12-ounce package (2 cups) semi-sweet chocolate chips
1 cup sugar
¼ cup amaretto*
2 cups all purpose or unbleached flour**
1 teaspoon baking soda
1 teaspoon vanilla
2 eggs
Powdered sugar

Heat oven to 325°F. Generously grease 12-cup fluted tube pan or 10-inch tube pan. Press almonds in bottom and halfway up sides of greased pan. In medium saucepan over low heat, warm coffee. Add margarine and chocolate chips; cook until mixture is smooth, stirring constantly. Remove from heat; stir in sugar and amaretto. Place in large bowl; cool 5 minutes.

Lightly spoon flour into measuring cup; level off. Gradually blend flour and baking soda into chocolate mixture at low speed until moistened. Add vanilla and eggs; beat at medium speed about 30 seconds or just until well blended. Pour batter over almonds in greased pan.

Bake at 325°F. for 60 to 75 minutes or until toothpick inserted in center comes out clean. Cool upright in pan 25 minutes; invert onto serving plate. Cool completely. Sprinkle with powdered sugar. **16 servings.**

TIPS: *Two teaspoons almond extract can be substituted for amaretto. Increase coffee to 1½ cups.

**Self-rising flour is not recommended.

HIGH ALTITUDE—Above 3500 Feet: No change.

NUTRIENTS PER 1/16 OF RECIPE

Calories	320	Protein	6% U.S. RDA
Protein	4g	Vitamin A	4% U.S. RDA
Carbohydrate	41g	Vitamin C	<2% U.S. RDA
Fat	16g	Thiamine	8% U.S. RDA
Cholesterol	35mg	Riboflavin	8% U.S. RDA
Sodium	50mg	Niacin	4% U.S. RDA
Potassium	130mg	Calcium	2% U.S. RDA
Dietary Fiber	2g	Iron	8% U.S. RDA

Grand Prize Winner

Banana Crunch Cake

Bonnie Brooks, Maryland
Bake-Off® 24, 1973

½ cup all purpose or unbleached flour
1 cup coconut
1 cup rolled oats
¾ cup firmly packed brown sugar
½ cup chopped pecans
½ cup margarine or butter
1½ cups (2 large) sliced *very ripe* bananas
½ cup dairy sour cream
4 eggs
1 package pudding-included yellow cake mix

Heat oven to 350°F. Grease and flour 10-inch tube pan. Lightly spoon flour into measuring cup; level off. In medium bowl, combine flour, coconut, rolled oats, brown sugar and pecans; mix well. Using pastry blender or fork, cut in margarine until mixture is crumbly; set aside.

In large bowl, combine bananas, sour cream and eggs; blend until smooth. Add cake mix; beat 2 minutes at *highest* speed. Spread ⅓ of batter in greased and floured pan; sprinkle with ⅓ of coconut mixture. Repeat layers twice, using remaining batter and coconut mixture and ending with coconut mixture. Bake at 350°F. for 50 to 60 minutes or until toothpick inserted in center comes out clean. Cool upright in pan 15 minutes; remove from pan. Place on serving plate, coconut side up. **16 servings.**

HIGH ALTITUDE—Above 3500 Feet: Add 3 tablespoons flour to dry cake mix. Bake at 375°F. for 45 to 55 minutes.

NUTRIENTS PER 1/16 RECIPE

Calories	360	Protein	6% U.S. RDA
Protein	5g	Vitamin A	8% U.S. RDA
Carbohydrate	50g	Vitamin C	<2% U.S. RDA
Fat	16g	Thiamine	10% U.S. RDA
Cholesterol	70mg	Riboflavin	8% U.S. RDA
Sodium	310mg	Niacin	6% U.S. RDA
Potassium	220mg	Calcium	6% U.S. RDA
Dietary Fiber	2g	Iron	8% U.S. RDA

Almond Mocha Cake

"It melts in your mouth" describes the texture of this brownie-like chocolate cake. Coffee and amaretto enhance its deep dark chocolate flavor.

Banana Crunch Cake

This recipe originally used a dry frosting mix that is no longer available for the streusel layer. Now that crunchy layer is made from scratch to create the same great winning taste.

Banana Split Cake

—◦◦❧—

Sally Kraywiecki, Michigan
Bake-Off® 11, 1959

Banana Split Cake

—◦◦❧—

An impressive dessert is created with three layers of milk chocolate banana cake filled with banana-pecan pudding and topped with a chocolate glaze. Use fully ripened bananas that have skins with brown flecks for the best flavor and texture.

CAKE

4-ounce bar sweet cooking chocolate
¼ cup water
2½ cups all purpose or unbleached flour
1 teaspoon baking soda
1 teaspoon salt
¾ cup shortening
1½ cups sugar
2 eggs
2 eggs, separated, reserving yolks for filling
1 cup mashed ripe bananas
1 teaspoon vanilla
1 cup buttermilk*
¾ cup chopped pecans or nuts

FILLING

¾ cup sugar
¾ cup evaporated milk
3 tablespoons butter or margarine
Reserved 2 egg yolks
¾ cup chopped pecans or nuts
¼ cup mashed ripe banana
1 teaspoon vanilla

GLAZE

1 ounce (1 square) unsweetened chocolate
2 tablespoons butter or margarine
1 cup powdered sugar
½ teaspoon vanilla
3 to 4 tablespoons milk
Chopped pecans, if desired

Heat oven to 375°F. Grease and flour three 8 or 9-inch round cake pans. In small saucepan over low heat, melt sweet cooking chocolate in water, stirring until smooth. Remove from heat; set aside. Lightly spoon flour into measuring cup; level off. In medium bowl, combine flour, baking soda and salt; mix well. In large bowl, beat shortening and 1½ cups sugar until light and fluffy. Beat in 2 whole eggs, 1 at a time, beating well after each addition. Beat in 2 egg whites. Blend in melted chocolate, 1 cup mashed bananas and 1 teaspoon vanilla. Add flour mixture and buttermilk alternately to chocolate mixture, beginning and ending with flour mixture. Blend well after each

addition. By hand, stir in ¾ cup pecans. Pour batter evenly into greased and floured pans. Bake at 375°F. for 25 to 30 minutes or until toothpick inserted in center comes out clean. Cool 5 minutes; remove from pan. Cool completely.

In medium saucepan, combine ¾ cup sugar, evaporated milk, 3 tablespoons butter and reserved egg yolks; mix well. Cook over medium heat 10 to 14 minutes or until mixture thickens, stirring constantly. Stir in ¾ cup pecans, ¼ cup mashed bananas and 1 teaspoon vanilla. Cool to spreading consistency, stirring occasionally.

In small saucepan over low heat, melt unsweetened chocolate and 2 tablespoons butter, stirring until smooth. Remove from heat. Blend in powdered sugar, ½ teaspoon vanilla and enough milk for desired glaze consistency.

To assemble cake, place 1 cake layer on serving plate. Spread top with half of filling mixture. Repeat with second layer and remaining filling. Top with third layer. Spoon glaze over top of cake, allowing some to run down sides. Sprinkle pecans over top of cake. Store in refrigerator. **16 servings.**

TIP: *To substitute for buttermilk, use 1 tablespoon vinegar or lemon juice plus enough milk to make 1 cup.

HIGH ALTITUDE—Above 3500 Feet: Add 3 tablespoons flour to cake ingredients.

NUTRIENTS PER 1/16 OF RECIPE

Calories	510	Protein	10% U.S. RDA
Protein	7g	Vitamin A	6% U.S. RDA
Carbohydrate	63g	Vitamin C	2% U.S. RDA
Fat	26g	Thiamine	10% U.S. RDA
Cholesterol	80mg	Riboflavin	10% U.S. RDA
Sodium	290mg	Niacin	6% U.S. RDA
Potassium	250mg	Calcium	8% U.S. RDA
Dietary Fiber	2g	Iron	10% U.S. RDA

Banana Split Cake

Apricot Fantasia Cake

Marge Walker, Indiana
Bake-Off® 32, 1986

Apricot Fantasia Cake

Sweet orange cream sauce tops a tart and tangy apricot "steamed pudding" cake that's easily made in the microwave.

CAKE

- ³/₄ to 1 cup chopped dried apricots
- 1¹/₂ cups apricot nectar
- ¹/₂ cup margarine or butter, cut into pieces
- 1³/₄ cups all purpose, unbleached or self-rising flour*
- 1 cup firmly packed brown sugar
- ¹/₄ cup whole wheat flour
- 1¹/₂ teaspoons baking powder
- ¹/₂ teaspoon baking soda
- ¹/₂ teaspoon salt
- ¹/₂ teaspoon cinnamon
- ¹/₂ teaspoon nutmeg
- ¹/₄ teaspoon ginger
- 1 teaspoon vanilla
- 2 eggs

SAUCE

- 1 cup ready-to-spread cream cheese frosting
- 2 tablespoons orange juice
- 2 teaspoons grated orange peel

MICROWAVE DIRECTIONS: Grease 4-cup microwave-safe measuring cup; line bottom with waxed paper and grease again.** In medium microwave-safe bowl, combine apricots, apricot nectar and margarine. Cover loosely with waxed paper; microwave on HIGH for 3 minutes. Let stand 3 minutes.

Lightly spoon flour into measuring cup; level off. In large bowl, combine all purpose flour, brown sugar, whole wheat flour and all remaining cake ingredients; mix well. Add warm apricot mixture; mix until well blended. Pour half of batter, about 2¹/₂ cups, into greased measuring cup; cover tightly with microwave-safe plastic wrap.

Microwave on MEDIUM for 9 to 11 minutes, rotating measuring cup once halfway through cooking. Cake is done when toothpick inserted in center comes out clean and bottom of cake is no longer wet. Uncover; let stand on flat surface 5 minutes. Loosen cake from sides of measuring cup; invert onto serving plate. Remove waxed paper. Repeat cooking steps with remaining batter.

In small bowl, combine all sauce ingredients; mix well. Spoon over warm cakes. Garnish as desired. Cut into wedges to serve. Serve with remaining sauce. Store in refrigerator.

2 (6-serving) cakes.

TIPS: *If using self-rising flour, omit baking powder and salt. Reduce baking soda to ¹/₄ teaspoon.

**A 12-cup microwave-safe fluted tube pan can be substituted for measuring cup; omit lining with waxed paper. *Grease and sugar pan.* Prepare cake batter as directed above; pour *all of batter* into greased and sugared pan. Cover tightly with microwave-safe plastic wrap. Microwave on MEDIUM for 10 minutes. Rotate pan ¹/₂ turn. Microwave on HIGH for 5 to 6 minutes or until toothpick inserted in center comes out clean, rotating pan once halfway through cooking. Continue as directed above.

HIGH ALTITUDE—Above 3500 Feet: No change.

NUTRIENTS PER 1/12 OF RECIPE

Calories	360	Protein	6% U.S. RDA
Protein	4g	Vitamin A	30% U.S. RDA
Carbohydrate	59g	Vitamin C	2% U.S. RDA
Fat	12g	Thiamine	10% U.S. RDA
Cholesterol	45mg	Riboflavin	8% U.S. RDA
Sodium	340mg	Niacin	8% U.S. RDA
Potassium	310mg	Calcium	6% U.S. RDA
Dietary Fiber	2g	Iron	10% U.S. RDA

Apricot Fantasia Cake

Spicy Raisin Brunch Cake

Spicy Raisin Brunch Cake

—❀❀—

Shirley Domeier, Minnesota
Bake-Off® 32, 1986

¼ cup graham cracker crumbs
1½ cups all purpose or unbleached flour
½ cup raisins
½ cup chopped walnuts
½ teaspoon baking soda
1½ teaspoons pumpkin pie spice
¼ to ½ teaspoon cloves
1 cup firmly packed brown sugar
½ cup apricot preserves
½ cup margarine or butter, softened
2 tablespoons rum or ½ teaspoon rum extract
4 eggs
⅔ cup buttermilk*

GLAZE

1 cup powdered sugar
1 teaspoon margarine or butter
½ teaspoon rum, if desired
5 to 6 teaspoons milk

MICROWAVE DIRECTIONS: Grease 12-cup microwave-safe fluted tube pan; sprinkle with graham cracker crumbs. Lightly spoon flour into measuring cup; level off. In medium bowl, combine flour, raisins, walnuts, baking soda, pumpkin pie spice and cloves; mix well. Set aside. In large bowl, combine brown sugar, preserves, ½ cup margarine, 2 tablespoons rum and eggs; beat well. Alternately add flour mixture and buttermilk to brown sugar mixture, beating well after each addition. Pour batter carefully over crumbs in greased pan.

Microwave on MEDIUM for 10 minutes, rotating pan once halfway through cooking. Microwave on HIGH for 4 to 8 minutes, rotating pan once halfway through cooking. Cake is done when toothpick inserted in center comes out clean and cake begins to pull away from sides of pan. Cool upright in pan on flat surface 5 minutes. Invert onto serving plate. Cool completely. In small bowl, blend powdered sugar, 1 teaspoon margarine, 1/2 teaspoon rum and enough milk for desired drizzling consistency. Drizzle over cake. Store cake loosely covered. **16 servings.**

TIP: *To substitute for buttermilk, use 2 teaspoons vinegar or lemon juice plus milk to make 2/3 cup.

HIGH ALTITUDE—Above 3500 Feet: No change.

NUTRIENTS PER 1/16 OF RECIPE

Calories	270	Protein	6% U.S. RDA
Protein	4g	Vitamin A	6% U.S. RDA
Carbohydrate	42g	Vitamin C	<2% U.S. RDA
Fat	10g	Thiamine	8% U.S. RDA
Cholesterol	70mg	Riboflavin	6% U.S. RDA
Sodium	150mg	Niacin	4% U.S. RDA
Potassium	170mg	Calcium	6% U.S. RDA
Dietary Fiber	<1g	Iron	8% U.S. RDA

Japanese Fruit Marble Cake

Flora H. Grantham, Maryland
Bake-Off® 31, 1984

2 cups sugar
1 cup margarine or butter, softened
1 teaspoon vanilla
1 teaspoon lemon extract
4 eggs
3 cups all purpose or unbleached flour
3 teaspoons baking powder
1/8 teaspoon salt
1 cup milk
2 teaspoons cinnamon
2 teaspoons nutmeg
1 teaspoon lemon extract
1 tablespoon flour
1/2 cup chopped pecans or walnuts
1/2 cup raisins
1/4 cup coconut

GLAZE
1 cup powdered sugar
4 to 6 teaspoons lemon juice

Heat oven to 350°F. Grease and flour 10-inch tube pan or 12-cup fluted tube pan. In large bowl, beat sugar, margarine, vanilla and 1 teaspoon lemon extract until light and fluffy. Add eggs, 1 at a time, beating well after each addition. Lightly spoon flour into measuring cup; level off. In medium bowl, combine 3 cups flour, baking powder and salt; mix well. Add flour mixture and milk to egg mixture. Blend at low speed until moistened; beat 2 minutes at medium speed. Pour 2/3 of batter into greased and floured pan. To remaining batter, stir in cinnamon, nutmeg and 1 teaspoon lemon extract until well blended. In small bowl, combine 1 tablespoon flour, pecans, raisins and coconut; mix well. Fold pecan mixture into spice batter. Spoon spice batter over batter in pan. To marble, pull knife through batter in folding motion, turning pan while folding.

Bake at 350°F. for 50 to 60 minutes or until toothpick inserted in center comes out clean. Cool upright in pan 10 minutes; remove from pan. Place on serving plate, top side up. In small bowl, blend powdered sugar and enough lemon juice for desired drizzling consistency. Drizzle over warm cake. Cool completely. **16 servings.**

HIGH ALTITUDE—Above 3500 Feet: Increase flour to 3 cups plus 3 tablespoons. Bake at 375°F. for 45 to 55 minutes.

NUTRIENTS PER 1/16 OF RECIPE

Calories	390	Protein	8% U.S. RDA
Protein	5g	Vitamin A	10% U.S. RDA
Carbohydrate	56g	Vitamin C	<2% U.S. RDA
Fat	16g	Thiamine	10% U.S. RDA
Cholesterol	70mg	Riboflavin	10% U.S. RDA
Sodium	230mg	Niacin	6% U.S. RDA
Potassium	125mg	Calcium	8% U.S. RDA
Dietary Fiber	1g	Iron	8% U.S. RDA

Japanese Fruit Marble Cake

Regional American foods continue their popularity as a part of the Bake-Off® Contests. This pleasant lemon-and-spice-flavored cake is a variation of fruitcake traditionally served during the holidays in Southeastern United States.

Caramel Pear Upside-Down Cake

Caramel Pear Upside-Down Cake

We've added new-fashioned ease to this old-fashioned cake by using a cake mix. The unique upside-down layer is a yummy combination of pears and caramel.

Margaret Faxon, Missouri
Bake-Off® 5, 1953

29-ounce can pear halves, drained, reserving ½ cup liquid
28 caramels
2 tablespoons margarine or butter
1 package pudding-included yellow cake mix
1 cup water
⅓ cup oil
3 eggs
¼ cup chopped nuts
Whipped cream, if desired

Heat oven to 350°F. Generously grease 13 × 9-inch pan. Slice pear halves; arrange over bottom of greased pan. In small saucepan over medium heat, melt caramels in reserved pear liquid, stirring until smooth. Stir in margarine; blend well. Pour mixture evenly over pears. In large bowl, combine cake mix, water, oil and eggs at low speed until moistened; beat 2 minutes at *highest* speed. Carefully pour batter evenly over pear mixture.

Bake at 350°F. for 35 to 55 minutes or until toothpick inserted in center comes out clean. Cool 5 minutes; invert onto cookie sheet or large serving plate. Sprinkle with nuts. Serve warm or cold with whipped cream. **12 servings.**

HIGH ALTITUDE—Above 3500 Feet: Add 3 tablespoons flour to dry cake mix. Bake at 375°F. for 35 to 45 minutes.

NUTRIENTS PER 1/12 OF RECIPE

Calories	440	Protein	6% U.S. RDA
Protein	5g	Vitamin A	4% U.S. RDA
Carbohydrate	58g	Vitamin C	<2% U.S. RDA
Fat	21g	Thiamine	10% U.S. RDA
Cholesterol	80mg	Riboflavin	10% U.S. RDA
Sodium	370mg	Niacin	4% U.S. RDA
Potassium	130mg	Calcium	8% U.S. RDA
Dietary Fiber	2g	Iron	8% U.S. RDA

Double Lemon Streusel Cake

Betty Engles, Michigan
Bake-Off® 28, 1978

CAKE
1 package pudding-included lemon cake mix
⅓ cup margarine or butter, softened
½ cup milk
2 eggs

TOPPING
8-ounce package cream cheese, softened
¼ cup sugar
4 teaspoons lemon juice
½ teaspoon grated lemon peel
½ cup chopped nuts

Heat oven to 350°F. Generously grease and flour 13 × 9-inch pan. In large bowl, combine cake mix and margarine at low speed until crumbly. Reserve 1 cup of crumb mixture for topping. Add remaining cake ingredients; beat 2 minutes at *highest* speed. Pour batter into greased and floured pan.

In small bowl, combine all topping ingredients except nuts; beat until smooth. Drop by teaspoonfuls onto batter; carefully spread evenly to cover. In second small bowl, blend reserved 1 cup crumb mixture and nuts. Sprinkle over cream cheese mixture. Bake at 350°F. for 30 to 40 minutes or until top springs back when touched lightly in center. Cool completely. **15 servings.**

HIGH ALTITUDE—Above 3500 Feet: Add 4 tablespoons flour to dry cake mix. Bake at 375°F. for 30 to 40 minutes.

NUTRIENTS PER 1/15 OF RECIPE

Calories	280	Protein	6% U.S. RDA
Protein	4g	Vitamin A	8% U.S. RDA
Carbohydrate	32g	Vitamin C	<2% U.S. RDA
Fat	16g	Thiamine	8% U.S. RDA
Cholesterol	50mg	Riboflavin	8% U.S. RDA
Sodium	320mg	Niacin	4% U.S. RDA
Potassium	75mg	Calcium	6% U.S. RDA
Dietary Fiber	<1g	Iron	4% U.S. RDA

Orange Kiss-Me Cake

Lily Wuebel, California
Bake-Off® 2, 1950

CAKE

    1 orange
    1 cup raisins
 1/3 cup walnuts
    2 cups all purpose or unbleached
      flour
    1 cup sugar
    1 teaspoon baking soda
    1 teaspoon salt
    1 cup milk
 1/2 cup shortening
    2 eggs

TOPPING

 1/3 cup sugar
    1 teaspoon cinnamon
 1/4 cup finely chopped walnuts

Heat oven to 350°F. Grease and flour 13 × 9-inch pan. Squeeze orange, reserving 1/3 cup juice. Grind together orange peel and pulp, raisins and 1/3 cup walnuts; set aside.* Lightly spoon flour into measuring cup; level off. In large bowl, combine flour, 1 cup sugar, baking soda, salt, milk, shortening and eggs at low speed until moistened; beat 3 minutes at medium speed. Stir in orange-raisin mixture. Pour batter into greased and floured pan. Bake at 350°F. for 35 to 45 minutes or until toothpick inserted in center comes out clean.

Drizzle reserved 1/3 cup orange juice over warm cake in pan. In small bowl, combine 1/3 cup sugar and cinnamon; mix well. Stir in 1/4 cup walnuts; sprinkle over cake. Cool completely.
12 to 16 servings.

TIP: *A blender or food processor can be used to grind orange-raisin mixture.

HIGH ALTITUDE—Above 3500 Feet: Increase flour to 2 cups plus 2 tablespoons. Bake at 375°F. for 35 to 40 minutes.

NUTRIENTS PER 1/16 OF RECIPE

Calories	260	Protein	6% U.S. RDA
Protein	4g	Vitamin A	<2% U.S. RDA
Carbohydrate	38g	Vitamin C	4% U.S. RDA
Fat	10g	Thiamine	10% U.S. RDA
Cholesterol	35mg	Riboflavin	6% U.S. RDA
Sodium	220mg	Niacin	4% U.S. RDA
Potassium	150mg	Calcium	4% U.S. RDA
Dietary Fiber	1g	Iron	6% U.S. RDA

Caramel Apple Cake

Josephine DeMarco, Illinois
Bake-Off® 27, 1976

 1 3/4 cups all purpose or unbleached
      flour
 1 1/2 cups firmly packed brown sugar
   1/2 teaspoon baking powder
   1/2 teaspoon baking soda
   1/2 teaspoon salt
 1 1/2 teaspoons cinnamon
   3/4 cup margarine or butter,
      softened
    1 teaspoon vanilla
    3 eggs
 1 1/2 cups finely chopped peeled
      apples
   1/2 to 1 cup chopped nuts
   1/2 cup raisins, if desired

FROSTING

    2 cups powdered sugar
   1/4 teaspoon cinnamon
   1/4 cup margarine or butter, melted
   1/2 teaspoon vanilla
    4 to 5 teaspoons milk

Heat oven to 350°F. Grease and flour 13 × 9-inch pan. Lightly spoon flour into measuring cup; level off. In large bowl, combine flour, brown sugar, baking powder, baking soda, salt, 1 1/2 teaspoons cinnamon, 3/4 cup margarine, 1 teaspoon vanilla and eggs at low speed until moistened; beat 3 minutes at medium speed. By hand, stir in apples, nuts and raisins. Pour batter into greased and floured pan. Bake at 350°F. for 30 to 40 minutes or until toothpick inserted in center comes out clean. Cool completely. In small bowl, blend powdered sugar, 1/4 teaspoon cinnamon, 1/4 cup margarine, 1/2 teaspoon vanilla and enough milk for desired spreading consistency. Frost cooled cake. **15 servings.**

HIGH ALTITUDE—Above 3500 Feet: Decrease brown sugar to 1 cup. Bake at 375°F. for 25 to 35 minutes.

NUTRIENTS PER 1/15 OF RECIPE

Calories	390	Protein	6% U.S. RDA
Protein	4g	Vitamin A	10% U.S. RDA
Carbohydrate	53g	Vitamin C	<2% U.S. RDA
Fat	18g	Thiamine	10% U.S. RDA
Cholesterol	60mg	Riboflavin	6% U.S. RDA
Sodium	280mg	Niacin	4% U.S. RDA
Potassium	210mg	Calcium	8% U.S. RDA
Dietary Fiber	1g	Iron	10% U.S. RDA

Orange Kiss-Me Cake

Time-proven and "classic" in status, this moist, fresh orange-tasting cake is as popular today as when it won top honors more than thirty-five years ago. It continues to be one of the most requested Bake-Off® recipes.

Black Bottom Cups

Black Bottom Cups

Doris Geisert, California
Bake-Off® 13, 1961

2 (3-ounce) packages cream cheese, softened
¹⁄₃ cup sugar
1 egg
6-ounce package (1 cup) semi-sweet chocolate chips
1¹⁄₂ cups all purpose or unbleached flour
1 cup sugar
¹⁄₄ cup unsweetened cocoa
1 teaspoon baking soda
¹⁄₂ teaspoon salt
1 cup water
¹⁄₃ cup oil
1 tablespoon vinegar
1 teaspoon vanilla
¹⁄₂ cup chopped almonds, if desired
2 tablespoons sugar, if desired

Heat oven to 350°F. Line 18 muffin cups with paper baking cups. In small bowl, beat cream cheese, ¹⁄₃ cup sugar and egg until smooth. By hand, stir in chocolate chips; set aside. Lightly spoon flour into measuring cup; level off. In large bowl, combine flour, 1 cup sugar, cocoa, baking soda and salt; mix well. Add water, oil, vinegar and vanilla; beat 2 minutes at medium speed. Fill paper-lined muffin cups ¹⁄₂ full. Top each with tablespoonful of cream cheese mixture. In small bowl, combine almonds and 2 tablespoons of sugar; sprinkle evenly over cream cheese mixture. Bake at 350°F. for 20 to 30 minutes or until cream cheese mixture is light golden brown. Cool 15 minutes; remove from pans. Cool completely. Store in refrigerator.
18 cupcakes.

HIGH ALTITUDE—Above 3500 Feet: No change.

NUTRIENTS PER 1 CUPCAKE

Calories	250	Protein	4% U.S. RDA
Protein	3g	Vitamin A	2% U.S. RDA
Carbohydrate	31g	Vitamin C	<2% U.S. RDA
Fat	13g	Thiamine	4% U.S. RDA
Cholesterol	25mg	Riboflavin	6% U.S. RDA
Sodium	160mg	Niacin	4% U.S. RDA
Potassium	90mg	Calcium	2% U.S. RDA
Dietary Fiber	2g	Iron	6% U.S. RDA

Mardi Gras Party Cake

Eunice Surles, Louisiana
Bake-Off® 11, 1959

CAKE
6-ounce package (1 cup) butterscotch chips
1/4 cup water
2 1/4 cups all purpose or unbleached flour
1 1/4 cups sugar
1 teaspoon baking soda
1 teaspoon salt
1/2 teaspoon baking powder
1 cup buttermilk*
1/2 cup shortening
3 eggs

FILLING
1/2 cup sugar
1 tablespoon cornstarch
1/2 cup half-and-half or evaporated milk
1/3 cup water
1 egg, slightly beaten
2 tablespoons margarine or butter
1 cup coconut
1 cup chopped nuts

SEAFOAM CREAM
1 cup whipping cream
1/4 cup firmly packed brown sugar
1/2 teaspoon vanilla

Heat oven to 350°F. Generously grease and flour two 9-inch round cake pans.** In small saucepan over low heat, melt 2/3 cup of the butterscotch chips in 1/4 cup water, stirring until smooth. Cool. Lightly spoon flour into measuring cup; level off. In large bowl, combine flour, all remaining cake ingredients and cooled butterscotch mixture at low speed until moistened; beat 3 minutes at medium speed. Pour batter into greased and floured pans. Bake at 350°F. for 20 to 30 minutes or until toothpick inserted in center comes out clean. Cool 10 minutes; remove from pans. Cool completely.

In medium saucepan, combine 1/2 cup sugar and cornstarch; stir in half-and-half, 1/3 cup water, 1 egg and remaining 1/3 cup butterscotch chips. Cook over medium heat until mixture thickens, stirring constantly. Remove from heat. Stir in margarine, coconut and nuts; cool.

In small bowl, beat whipping cream until soft peaks form. Gradually add brown sugar and vanilla, beating until stiff peaks form.

To assemble cake, place 1 cake layer on serving plate. Spread top with half of filling mixture. Top with remaining layer; spread remaining filling on top to within 1/2 inch of edge. Frost sides and top edge of cake with seafoam cream. Refrigerate at least 1 hour before serving. Store in refrigerator. **16 servings.**

TIPS: *To substitute for buttermilk, use 1 tablespoon vinegar or lemon juice plus milk to make 1 cup.

**Cake can be baked in 13 × 9-inch pan; grease bottom of pan only. Bake at 350°F. for 30 to 35 minutes or until toothpick inserted in center comes out clean. Cool completely. Spread top of cooled cake with filling mixture. Serve topped with seafoam cream.

HIGH ALTITUDE—Above 3500 Feet: Bake at 350°F. for 30 to 35 minutes. Cool 7 minutes; remove from pans. Cool completely.

NUTRIENTS PER 1/16 OF RECIPE

Calories	450	Protein	8% U.S. RDA
Protein	6g	Vitamin A	8% U.S. RDA
Carbohydrate	50g	Vitamin C	<2% U.S. RDA
Fat	25g	Thiamine	10% U.S. RDA
Cholesterol	90mg	Riboflavin	10% U.S. RDA
Sodium	270mg	Niacin	4% U.S. RDA
Potassium	140mg	Calcium	6% U.S. RDA
Dietary Fiber	<1g	Iron	8% U.S. RDA

Mardi Gras Party Cake

A delicate butterscotch-flavored cake with a scrumptious coconut-butterscotch-nut filling and fluffy brown sugar frosting. This recipe reflects the longtime Southern tradition of serving foods rich in flavor and especially appealing in appearance.

Chocolate Orange Cream Torte

Dorine K. Firestone, Ohio
Bake-Off® 32, 1986

CAKE
1 package pudding-included devil's food cake mix
1/2 cup water
1/2 cup orange juice
1/3 cup oil
3 eggs

FILLING
8-ounce package cream cheese, softened
1/3 cup whipping cream
2 tablespoons powdered sugar
8-ounce bar milk chocolate, chopped

FROSTING
2 cups whipping cream
1 teaspoon powdered sugar
2 teaspoons orange marmalade
1/2 teaspoon orange extract

Heat oven to 350°F. Grease and flour two 8 or 9-inch round cake pans. In large bowl, combine all cake ingredients at low speed until moistened; beat 2 minutes at *highest* speed. Pour batter into greased and floured pans. Bake at 350°F. for 25 to 35 minutes or until toothpick inserted in center comes out clean. Cool 10 minutes; remove from pans. Cool completely.

In small bowl, combine cream cheese, 1/3 cup whipping cream and 2 tablespoons powdered sugar at low speed until smooth and fluffy. Fold in chocolate.

In large bowl, beat 2 cups whipping cream and 1 teaspoon powdered sugar until thickened. Add orange marmalade and orange extract; beat until stiff peaks form.

To assemble torte, slice each cake layer in half horizontally to make 4 layers. Place 1 layer on serving plate. Spread top with 1/3 of filling mixture. Repeat with 2 more layers and remaining filling. Top with fourth layer; frost sides and top of cake with frosting mixture. Refrigerate until serving time. Store in refrigerator. **16 servings.**

HIGH ALTITUDE—Above 3500 Feet: Add 5 tablespoons flour to dry cake mix. Increase water to 2/3 cup. Bake at 375°F. for 25 to 35 minutes.

NUTRIENTS PER 1/16 OF RECIPE

Calories	450	Protein	8% U.S. RDA
Protein	6g	Vitamin A	15% U.S. RDA
Carbohydrate	36g	Vitamin C	4% U.S. RDA
Fat	31g	Thiamine	4% U.S. RDA
Cholesterol	120mg	Riboflavin	10% U.S. RDA
Sodium	340mg	Niacin	2% U.S. RDA
Potassium	210mg	Calcium	15% U.S. RDA
Dietary Fiber	<1g	Iron	8% U.S. RDA

Streamlined Hungarian Torte

Feather-light meringue tops flaky pastry layers filled with nuts and apricot preserves in this torte. It is not as time-consuming as it looks!

Rose Manske, Wisconsin
Bake-Off® 18, 1967

1 package active dry yeast
1/4 cup warm water
3 1/2 cups all purpose, unbleached, or self-rising flour
1 1/3 cups margarine or butter
1/2 cup dairy sour cream
4 eggs, separated
1 3/4 cups chopped walnuts
3/4 cup sugar
1 teaspoon cinnamon
10-ounce jar (3/4 cup) apricot preserves*
1/2 cup sugar

Heat oven to 350°F. Grease 13 × 9-inch pan. In small bowl, dissolve yeast in warm water (105 to 115°F.). Lightly spoon flour into measuring cup; level off. In large bowl, using pastry blender or fork, cut margarine into flour until mixture resembles coarse crumbs. Stir in sour cream, egg yolks and dissolved yeast just until a soft dough forms.

Shape dough into a ball; divide into 3 equal parts. On well-floured surface, roll each part to 13 × 9-inch rectangle. Place 1 rectangle in bottom of greased pan. Reserve 1/4 cup of the walnuts. In small bowl, combine remaining 1 1/2 cups walnuts, 3/4 cup sugar and cinnamon; sprinkle over rectangle in pan. Top with second rectangle; spread evenly with preserves. Top with remaining rectangle. Bake at 350°F. for 40 to 50 minutes or until light golden brown.

In large bowl, beat egg whites until foamy. Gradually add 1/2 cup sugar;

beat until stiff peaks form, about 3 minutes. Spread egg white mixture over baked pastry, covering completely. Sprinkle with reserved 1/4 cup walnuts. Bake an additional 10 to 15 minutes or until egg white mixture is golden brown. Cool. **16 servings.**

TIP: *Other flavors of preserves can be substituted for apricot preserves.

HIGH ALTITUDE—Above 3500 Feet: No change.

NUTRIENTS PER 1/16 OF RECIPE

Calories	480	Protein	10% U.S. RDA
Protein	7g	Vitamin A	15% U.S. RDA
Carbohydrate	52g	Vitamin C	<2% U.S. RDA
Fat	27g	Thiamine	15% U.S. RDA
Cholesterol	70mg	Riboflavin	10% U.S. RDA
Sodium	200mg	Niacin	8% U.S. RDA
Potassium	150mg	Calcium	4% U.S. RDA
Dietary Fiber	1g	Iron	10% U.S. RDA

Raspberry Ribbon Torte

Frances A. Neilsen, California
Bake-Off® 6, 1954

PASTRY
> 2 cups all purpose or unbleached flour
> 1/4 teaspoon salt
> 1 cup margarine or butter, softened
> 4 to 6 tablespoons cold water
> 2 to 4 tablespoons sugar

FILLINGS
> 1 1/2 cups milk
> 3 1/2-ounce package instant vanilla pudding and pie filling mix
> 2 tablespoons cornstarch
> 1/4 cup water
> 10-ounce package frozen raspberries with syrup, thawed, undrained
> 1/4 cup finely ground almonds

FROSTING
> 1 cup whipping cream
> 2 tablespoons powdered sugar
> 1/4 teaspoon almond extract

Lightly spoon flour into measuring cup; level off. In medium bowl, blend flour and salt. Using pastry blender or fork, cut margarine into flour mixture until mixture resembles coarse crumbs. Sprinkle flour mixture with water, 1 tablespoon at a time, while tossing and mixing lightly with fork. Add water until dough is just moist enough to hold together. Shape dough into a ball; wrap in plastic wrap. Cover and refrigerate 30 minutes or until dough is easy to handle.

Heat oven to 450°F. Divide dough into 6 equal parts. Shape each into a ball; flatten and smooth edges. On well-floured surface, roll 1 ball lightly from center to edge into 9-inch circle; cut around an inverted 9-inch pie pan to even edges. Place on ungreased *cool* cookie sheet; prick generously with fork. Sprinkle with 1 to 2 teaspoons of the sugar. Bake at 450°F. for 5 to 7 minutes or until light golden brown. (Watch carefully, as pastry browns quickly.) Remove from cookie sheet. Cool completely. Repeat with remaining balls of dough.

In small bowl, combine milk and pudding mix at low speed until slightly thickened; cover and refrigerate. In medium saucepan, blend cornstarch and water; add raspberries. Cook over medium heat until mixture becomes thick and clear, stirring constantly. Cool slightly; refrigerate.

Assemble torte 2 to 4 hours before serving. Place 1 pastry layer on serving plate; spread thinly with 1/3 of the raspberry filling. Top with second pastry layer; spread thinly with 1/3 of the vanilla filling. Repeat with remaining 4 layers, ending with vanilla filling. Sprinkle almonds over top of torte. In small bowl, beat whipping cream until soft peaks form. Blend in powdered sugar and almond extract; beat until stiff peaks form. Frost sides of torte with whipped cream mixture. If desired, pipe rim or rosettes of whipped cream around top edge of cake. Refrigerate until serving time. **16 servings.**

HIGH ALTITUDE—Above 3500 Feet: No change.

NUTRIENTS PER 1/16 OF RECIPE

Calories	290	Protein	4% U.S. RDA
Protein	3g	Vitamin A	15% U.S. RDA
Carbohydrate	30g	Vitamin C	4% U.S. RDA
Fat	18g	Thiamine	8% U.S. RDA
Cholesterol	20mg	Riboflavin	8% U.S. RDA
Sodium	210mg	Niacin	4% U.S. RDA
Potassium	105mg	Calcium	6% U.S. RDA
Dietary Fiber	1g	Iron	6% U.S. RDA

Raspberry Ribbon Torte

When making this stunning dessert, prepare everything early in the day. Then assemble the six baked pastry layers, raspberries and creamy vanilla filling two hours before serving.

Mocha Cream Chocolate Torte

Mocha Cream
Chocolate Torte

Natalie C. Glomb, Pennsylvania
Bake-Off® 32, 1986

CAKE
> 1 package pudding-included
> German chocolate cake mix
> 1¼ cups water
> ⅓ cup oil
> 3 eggs

FROSTING
> ½ cup sugar
> ¼ cup cornstarch
> 2 tablespoons instant coffee
> granules or crystals
> 1¼ cups milk
> 1 cup margarine or butter,
> softened
> ¼ cup powdered sugar
> Chocolate sprinkles, if desired
> Whole blanched almonds, if
> desired

Heat oven to 350°F. Grease and flour 13 × 9-inch pan. In large bowl, combine all cake ingredients at low speed until moistened; beat 2 minutes at *highest* speed. Pour batter into greased and floured pan. Bake at 350°F. for 30 to 40 minutes or until toothpick inserted in center comes out clean. Cool 15 minutes; remove from pan. Cool completely.

Meanwhile, in heavy saucepan combine sugar, cornstarch and instant coffee; blend well. Gradually stir in milk. Cook over medium heat until mixture thickens and boils, stirring constantly. Remove from heat; cover with plastic wrap. Refrigerate 30 minutes or until cool. (Mixture will be very thick.) In large bowl, beat margarine and powdered sugar until well blended. Gradually add cooled coffee mixture; beat until light and fluffy.

To assemble torte, cut cooled cake in half lengthwise. Slice each half in half horizontally to make 4 layers. Place 1 layer on serving tray. Spread top with frosting mixture. Repeat with remaining layers and frosting. Frost sides and top of cake. Sprinkle top of torte with chocolate sprinkles; garnish with almonds. Store in refrigerator. **12 servings.**

HIGH ALTITUDE—Above 3500 Feet: Add 2 tablespoons flour to dry cake mix. Bake at 375°F. for 25 to 35 minutes.

NUTRIENTS PER 1/12 OF RECIPE

Calories	470	Protein	6% U.S. RDA
Protein	5g	Vitamin A	15% U.S. RDA
Carbohydrate	50g	Vitamin C	<2% U.S. RDA
Fat	28g	Thiamine	8% U.S. RDA
Cholesterol	70mg	Riboflavin	10% U.S. RDA
Sodium	530mg	Niacin	6% U.S. RDA
Potassium	140mg	Calcium	8% U.S. RDA
Dietary Fiber	<1g	Iron	6% U.S. RDA

Heavenly Hawaiian Cake Roll

Judy Merritt, New York
Bake-Off® 33, 1988

FILLING
Powdered sugar
1/3 cup butter or margarine, melted
1/2 cup firmly packed brown sugar
1 cup coconut
2 tablespoons chopped maraschino cherries
8-ounce can crushed pineapple in its own juice, well drained, reserving 1/2 cup liquid for cake

CAKE
3 eggs
1 cup sugar
1 cup all purpose, unbleached or self-rising flour*
1 teaspoon baking powder
1/4 teaspoon salt

TOPPING
1/2 cup whipping cream
1/2 teaspoon vanilla
2 tablespoons powdered sugar
1/4 cup chopped macadamia nuts, toasted**

Heat oven to 375°F. Line 15 × 10 × 1-inch baking pan with foil. Lightly sprinkle clean towel with powdered sugar. Spread butter evenly in bottom of foil-lined pan; sprinkle with brown sugar.

Sprinkle coconut, maraschino cherries and pineapple evenly over brown sugar; press down lightly. Set aside.

In small bowl, beat eggs at high speed until thick and lemon-colored, about 5 minutes. Gradually add sugar; beat well. If necessary, add enough water to reserved pineapple liquid to make 1/2 cup. Blend reserved pineapple liquid into egg mixture at low speed. Lightly spoon flour into measuring cup; level off. Add flour, baking powder and salt; beat at medium speed until smooth. Spread batter evenly over coconut mixture in pan.

Bake at 375°F. for 13 to 18 minutes or until top springs back when touched lightly in center. Immediately invert cake onto powdered-sugared towel; remove pan. Gently lift sides of foil from hot cake; carefully remove foil. Starting with shortest side and using towel to guide cake, roll up. (Do not roll towel into cake.) Wrap towel around rolled cake; cool completely on wire rack.

In small bowl, combine whipping cream, vanilla and 2 tablespoons powdered sugar; beat until stiff peaks form. Place cake roll seam side down on serving plate. Spread topping over sides and top of cake roll; sprinkle with nuts. Store in refrigerator. **12 servings.**

TIPS: *If using self-rising flour, omit baking powder and salt.

**To toast macadamia nuts, spread on cookie sheet; bake at 375°F. for about 3 minutes or until light golden brown, stirring occasionally.

Chopped toasted almonds or pecans can be substituted for macadamia nuts.

HIGH ALTITUDE—Above 3500 Feet: No change.

NUTRIENTS PER 1/12 OF RECIPE

Calories	300	Protein	4% U.S. RDA
Protein	3g	Vitamin A	8% U.S. RDA
Carbohydrate	41g	Vitamin C	2% U.S. RDA
Fat	14g	Thiamine	6% U.S. RDA
Cholesterol	100mg	Riboflavin	6% U.S. RDA
Sodium	140mg	Niacin	2% U.S. RDA
Potassium	120mg	Calcium	4% U.S. RDA
Dietary Fiber	1g	Iron	6% U.S. RDA

Heavenly Hawaiian Cake Roll

The cake and filling bake together in this easy-to-make jelly roll. Heavenly to eat!

Chocolate Silk Pecan Pie, page 170.

Pies, Pastries and Other Desserts

Early Bake-Off® finalists were depicted as homemakers who served made-from-scratch pies and other desserts with everyday regularity. But as time pressures have mounted, good cooks have turned to more stream-lined methods to speed preparation.

Today the fancy pies, pastries and desserts of yesterday can be made with remarkable ease and equally delicious results. A pat-in-the-pan crust allows even the most inexperienced baker to present a lovely pie for dessert. Versatile refrigerated crescent rolls form the crust for many delicious sweets. The latest advancement, all ready pie crusts, takes the worry and work out of pastry making altogether so that anyone can prepare favorite heirloom Bake-Off® desserts like Cherry-Berry Pie and Peacheesy Pie.

Instead of fussing over the crust, today's creative Bake-Off® entrants spend their time dreaming up "designer" fillings—a tart flavored with tangy lemon and hazelnuts, a cherry pie with an almond-coconut topping, a deliciously rich dessert featuring whipped cream, caramel and pecan filling drizzled with chocolate. Complex, traditional recipes for flans and cheesecakes are turned into quick modern-day versions. And indulgent new treats like Italian Crescent Crostata are gilded with ethnic touches of faraway places and times gone by.

At the same time, certain ingredients are cherished for their time-tested appeal. Among the favorite flavors are apple, cherry, lemon, pumpkin and chocolate teamed ever so skillfully with sweet spices, nuts, coconut and caramel as well as the creamy goodness of sour cream and whipping cream.

So, when it's time for a reward, turn to these pies, pastries and desserts. They offer sweetly satisfying answers for all types of special dessert occasions—even when preparation time is limited.

Cherry-Berry Pie

Eva Carter, Wisconsin
Bake-Off® 7, 1955

15-ounce package refrigerated pie
crusts
1 teaspoon flour

FILLING
¾ cup sugar
2 tablespoons quick-cooking
tapioca
2 tablespoons cornstarch
¼ teaspoon salt
16-ounce can pitted tart red
cherries, drained, reserving
liquid
10-ounce package frozen
strawberries with syrup, thawed,
drained, reserving syrup
1 tablespoon lemon juice
Sugar

Prepare pie crust according to package directions for *two-crust pie* using 9-inch pie pan. Heat oven to 400°F.

In medium saucepan, combine ¾ cup sugar, tapioca, cornstarch and salt; mix well. Stir in reserved cherry and strawberry liquids. Cook over medium heat 5 to 10 minutes or until mixture becomes thick and clear, stirring constantly. Remove from heat. Stir in cherries, strawberries and lemon juice. Spoon fruit mixture into pie crust-lined pan. Top with second crust; seal and flute. Sprinkle with sugar. Cut slits in several places. Bake at 400°F. for 30 minutes or until golden brown. Cool.
8 servings.

NUTRIENTS PER 1/8 OF RECIPE
Calories	430	Protein	2% U.S. RDA
Protein	2g	Vitamin A	8% U.S. RDA
Carbohydrate	69g	Vitamin C	20% U.S. RDA
Fat	16g	Thiamine	<2% U.S. RDA
Cholesterol	15mg	Riboflavin	2% U.S. RDA
Sodium	390mg	Niacin	2% U.S. RDA
Potassium	115mg	Calcium	<2% U.S. RDA
Dietary Fiber	2g	Iron	6% U.S. RDA

Topsy Turvy Apple Pie

This is a fun-to-serve upside-down pie. Traditional apple filling is baked between two flaky crusts and topped off with a rich pecan glaze. Preparation is simplified by using refrigerated pie crusts.

Topsy Turvy Apple Pie

Ronelva Gaard, Minnesota
Bake-Off® 3, 1951

GLAZE AND CRUST
¼ cup firmly packed brown sugar
1 tablespoon margarine or butter,
melted
1 tablespoon corn syrup
¼ cup pecan halves
15-ounce package refrigerated pie
crusts
1 teaspoon flour

FILLING
⅔ cup sugar
2 tablespoons flour
½ teaspoon cinnamon
4 cups sliced peeled apples

Whipped cream, if desired

In 9-inch pie pan, combine brown sugar, margarine and corn syrup; spread evenly over bottom of pan. Arrange pecans over mixture in pan. Prepare pie crust according to package directions for *two-crust pie*; place bottom crust over mixture in pan. Heat oven to 425°F.

In small bowl, combine sugar, 2 tablespoons flour and cinnamon; mix well. Arrange half of apple slices in pie crust-lined pan; sprinkle with half of sugar mixture. Repeat with remaining apple slices and sugar mixture. Top with second crust; seal and flute. Cut slits in several places. Bake at 425°F. for 8 minutes. Reduce oven temperature to 375°F. Bake an additional 25 to 35 minutes or until apples are tender and crust is golden brown. (Place pan on foil or cookie sheet during baking to catch any spillage.) Loosen edge of pie; carefully invert onto serving plate. Serve warm or cold with whipped cream.
8 servings.

NUTRIENTS PER 1/8 OF RECIPE
Calories	440	Protein	2% U.S. RDA
Protein	2g	Vitamin A	4% U.S. RDA
Carbohydrate	59g	Vitamin C	2% U.S. RDA
Fat	22g	Thiamine	4% U.S. RDA
Cholesterol	25mg	Riboflavin	2% U.S. RDA
Sodium	350mg	Niacin	<2% U.S. RDA
Potassium	130mg	Calcium	2% U.S. RDA
Dietary Fiber	2g	Iron	2% U.S. RDA

Topsy Turvy Apple Pie

Almond Macaroon Cherry Pie

Almond Macaroon Cherry Pie

✦

Rose Anne LeMon, Arizona
Bake-Off® 32, 1986

15-ounce package refrigerated pie crusts
1 teaspoon flour

FILLING
21-ounce can cherry fruit pie filling
¼ to ½ teaspoon cinnamon
⅛ teaspoon salt, if desired
1 teaspoon lemon juice

TOPPING
1 cup coconut
½ cup sliced almonds
¼ cup sugar
⅛ teaspoon salt, if desired
¼ cup milk
1 tablespoon margarine or butter, melted
¼ teaspoon almond extract
1 egg, beaten

Prepare pie crust according to package directions for *filled one-crust pie* using 9-inch pie pan. (Refrigerate remaining crust for later use.) Heat oven to 400°F.

In large bowl, combine all filling ingredients; mix lightly. Spoon into pie crust-lined pan. Bake at 400°F. for 20 minutes.

Meanwhile, in medium bowl combine all topping ingredients; mix well. Spread evenly over partially baked pie. Bake an additional 15 to 30 minutes or until crust and topping are golden brown. Store in refrigerator. **8 servings.**

TIP: Cover pie with foil during last 5 to 10 minutes of baking if necessary to prevent excessive browning.

NUTRIENTS PER 1/8 OF RECIPE

Calories	400	Protein	6% U.S. RDA
Protein	4g	Vitamin A	6% U.S. RDA
Carbohydrate	58g	Vitamin C	4% U.S. RDA
Fat	17g	Thiamine	2% U.S. RDA
Cholesterol	35mg	Riboflavin	6% U.S. RDA
Sodium	260mg	Niacin	2% U.S. RDA
Potassium	170mg	Calcium	4% U.S. RDA
Dietary Fiber	3g	Iron	4% U.S. RDA

Peacheesy Pie

꿍⁓

Janis Boykin, Florida
Bake-Off® 16, 1964

15-ounce package refrigerated pie crusts
1 teaspoon flour

FILLING
1/2 cup sugar
2 tablespoons cornstarch
1 to 2 teaspoons pumpkin pie spice
2 tablespoons light corn syrup
2 teaspoons vanilla
28-ounce can peach slices, drained, reserving 3 tablespoons liquid

TOPPING
1/3 cup sugar
1 tablespoon lemon juice
2 eggs, slightly beaten
3-ounce package cream cheese, softened
1/2 cup dairy sour cream
2 tablespoons margarine or butter

Allow both crust pouches to stand at room temperature for 15 to 20 minutes. Meanwhile, in medium bowl combine all filling ingredients except reserved peach liquid; mix well. Set aside.

In small saucepan, combine 2 tablespoons of the reserved peach liquid, 1/3 cup sugar, lemon juice and eggs; mix well. Cook over medium heat until mixture thickens, stirring constantly. Remove from heat. In small bowl, beat cream cheese and sour cream until smooth. Gradually beat in hot egg mixture until well blended. Heat oven to 425°F.

Prepare 1 pie crust according to package directions for *filled one-crust pie* using 9-inch pie pan. Unfold remaining pie crust; remove plastic sheets. Press out fold lines from crust. Using floured 3-inch round cutter, cut out 8 circles from crust. Brush tops with remaining 1 tablespoon peach liquid. Spoon peach filling into pie crust-lined pan; dot with margarine. Spoon cream cheese topping over filling. Arrange pie crust circles over topping. Bake at 425°F. for 10 minutes. Reduce oven temperature to 350°F. Bake an additional 35 to 40 minutes or until crust is golden brown. Cool. Store in refrigerator. **8 servings.**

NUTRIENTS PER 1/8 OF RECIPE

Calories	530	Protein	8% U.S. RDA
Protein	5g	Vitamin A	15% U.S. RDA
Carbohydrate	70g	Vitamin C	2% U.S. RDA
Fat	26g	Thiamine	<2% U.S. RDA
Cholesterol	100mg	Riboflavin	6% U.S. RDA
Sodium	310mg	Niacin	2% U.S. RDA
Potassium	190mg	Calcium	4% U.S. RDA
Dietary Fiber	2g	Iron	6% U.S. RDA

Lemon Luscious Pie

꿍⁓

Helen Gorsuch, California
Bake-Off® 14, 1962

15-ounce package refrigerated pie crusts
1 teaspoon flour

FILLING
1 cup sugar
3 tablespoons cornstarch
1 cup milk
1/4 cup lemon juice
3 egg yolks, slightly beaten
1/4 cup margarine or butter
1 tablespoon grated lemon peel
1 cup dairy sour cream
Whipped cream, if desired
Chopped walnuts, if desired

Heat oven to 450°F. Prepare pie crust according to package directions for *unfilled one-crust pie* using 9-inch pie pan. (Refrigerate remaining pie crust for later use.) Bake at 450°F. for 9 to 11 minutes or until light golden brown. Cool completely.

In medium saucepan, combine sugar and cornstarch; mix well. Stir in milk, lemon juice and beaten egg yolks; cook over medium heat until mixture thickens, stirring constantly. Remove from heat. Add margarine and lemon peel; stir until margarine is melted. Cool. Fold in sour cream. Spoon filling mixture into cooled baked crust; spread evenly. Refrigerate about 2 hours or until firm. Just before serving, garnish with whipped cream and walnuts.
8 servings.

NUTRIENTS PER 1/8 OF RECIPE

Calories	430	Protein	6% U.S. RDA
Protein	4g	Vitamin A	15% U.S. RDA
Carbohydrate	44g	Vitamin C	6% U.S. RDA
Fat	27g	Thiamine	2% U.S. RDA
Cholesterol	130mg	Riboflavin	8% U.S. RDA
Sodium	270mg	Niacin	<2% U.S. RDA
Potassium	135mg	Calcium	8% U.S. RDA
Dietary Fiber	<1g	Iron	2% U.S. RDA

Peacheesy Pie

꿍⁓

It isn't often that a $25,000 prize rewards homework well done. Yet that's just what happened in September 1964 for seventeen-year-old Janis Boykin of Melbourne, Florida. Her Home Economics assignment was to develop a new recipe at home.

"It's a new creation," she said proudly. Her five brothers liked it . . . and her Home Economics teacher, Mrs. Newman, wholeheartedly agreed and encouraged Janis to enter the recipe in the Bake-Off®. Hardly expecting to win, but daring to dream, Janis entered—and won.

Janis, now Mrs. Michael F. Risley, was the youngest contestant ever to win the top prize. Refrigerated pie crusts update this spiced peach and cheesecake pie for today's bakers.

Chocolate Caramel Satin Pie

Phelles Friedenauer, Illinois
Bake-Off® 33, 1988

15-ounce package refrigerated pie crusts
1 teaspoon flour

FILLING
24 caramels
1/3 cup water
2/3 cup firmly packed brown sugar
1/2 cup chopped walnuts
2/3 cup dairy sour cream
1 teaspoon vanilla
2 eggs, beaten
1 1/2 ounces (1/3 cup) grated sweet cooking chocolate, reserving 2 tablespoons for topping

TOPPING
1 cup vanilla milk chips*
1/4 cup milk
1 cup whipping cream
Reserved 2 tablespoons grated sweet cooking chocolate

Heat oven to 450°F. Prepare pie crust according to package directions for *unfilled one-crust pie* using 9-inch pie pan. (Refrigerate remaining pie crust for later use.) Bake at 450°F. for 8 to 9 minutes or until light golden brown. Cool slightly.

Meanwhile, in medium heavy saucepan over low heat, melt caramels in water, stirring until smooth. Remove from heat. Stir in brown sugar, walnuts, sour cream, vanilla and eggs; blend well. Pour into baked crust. Reduce oven temperature to 350°F. *Immediately* return pie to oven. Bake an additional 30 to 40 minutes or until edges of filling are set. Cool 15 minutes. Sprinkle chocolate over pie. Refrigerate until firm, about 2 hours.

In small heavy saucepan over low heat, melt vanilla milk chips in milk, stirring until smooth. Remove from heat; cool. In small bowl, beat whipping cream until stiff peaks form. Fold in cooled chip mixture. Spread over cooled filling. Sprinkle top of pie with reserved

2 tablespoons chocolate. Refrigerate until serving time. Store in refrigerator. **10 servings.**

TIP: *Do not substitute almond bark or vanilla-flavored candy coating.

NUTRIENTS PER 1/10 OF RECIPE

Calories	540	Protein	8% U.S. RDA
Protein	6g	Vitamin A	10% U.S. RDA
Carbohydrate	57g	Vitamin C	<2% U.S. RDA
Fat	32g	Thiamine	4% U.S. RDA
Cholesterol	100mg	Riboflavin	10% U.S. RDA
Sodium	240mg	Niacin	<2% U.S. RDA
Potassium	260mg	Calcium	10% U.S. RDA
Dietary Fiber	1g	Iron	8% U.S. RDA

Caramel Candy Pie

Florence Ries, Minnesota
Bake-Off® 4, 1952

15-ounce package refrigerated pie crusts
1 teaspoon flour

FILLING
1 envelope unflavored gelatin
1/4 cup cold water
1 cup milk
14-ounce package caramels
1 1/2 cups whipping cream, whipped

TOPPING
2 tablespoons sugar
1/4 cup slivered almonds

Heat oven to 450°F. Prepare pie crust according to package directions for *unfilled one-crust pie* using 9-inch pie pan. (Refrigerate remaining pie crust for later use.) Bake at 450°F. for 9 to 11 minutes or until light golden brown. Cool completely.

In small bowl, soften gelatin in water; set aside. In medium heavy saucepan, combine milk and caramels; cook over low heat until caramels are melted and mixture is smooth, stirring frequently. Add softened gelatin; stir until gelatin is dissolved. Refrigerate about 1 hour or until mixture is slightly thickened but not set, stirring occasionally. Fold caramel mixture into whipped cream. Pour into cooled baked crust; spread evenly. Refrigerate 2 hours or until firm.

In small skillet, combine sugar and almonds; cook over low heat until sugar is melted and almonds are golden

---

brown, stirring constantly. Immediately spread on foil or greased cookie sheet. Cool; break apart. Just before serving, garnish pie with caramelized almonds. **8 servings.**

NUTRIENTS PER 1/8 OF RECIPE

Calories	530	Protein	8% U.S. RDA
Protein	6g	Vitamin A	15% U.S. RDA
Carbohydrate	56g	Vitamin C	<2% U.S. RDA
Fat	32g	Thiamine	2% U.S. RDA
Cholesterol	60mg	Riboflavin	10% U.S. RDA
Sodium	310mg	Niacin	<2% U.S. RDA
Potassium	210mg	Calcium	15% U.S. RDA
Dietary Fiber	<1g	Iron	4% U.S. RDA

Grand Prize Winner

Open Sesame Pie

Mrs. B. A. Koteen, Washington, D.C.
Bake-Off® 6, 1954

PASTRY

  1 cup all purpose, unbleached or self-rising flour*
  2 tablespoons sesame seed, toasted**
  ½ teaspoon salt
  ⅓ cup shortening
  3 to 4 tablespoons cold water

FILLING

  1 envelope unflavored gelatin
  ¼ cup cold water
  1 cup chopped dates
  ¼ cup sugar
  ¼ teaspoon salt
  1 cup milk
  2 eggs, separated
  1 teaspoon vanilla
  1 cup whipping cream, whipped
  2 tablespoons sugar
  Nutmeg

Heat oven to 450°F. Lightly spoon flour into measuring cup; level off. In medium bowl, combine flour, sesame seed and ½ teaspoon salt. Using pastry blender or fork, cut shortening into flour mixture until mixture resembles coarse crumbs. Sprinkle flour mixture with water, 1 tablespoon at a time, while tossing and mixing lightly with fork. Add water until dough is just moist enough to hold together. Shape dough into a ball. Flatten ball; smooth edges. On floured surface, roll lightly from center to edge into 10½-inch circle. Fold dough in half; fit evenly in 9-inch pie pan. Do not stretch. Turn edges under; flute. Prick bottom and sides of pastry generously with fork. Bake at 450°F. for 9 to 15 minutes or until light golden brown. Cool completely.

In small bowl, soften gelatin in ¼ cup water; set aside. In medium saucepan, combine dates, ¼ cup sugar, ¼ teaspoon salt, milk and egg yolks. Cook over medium heat 6 to 10 minutes or until mixture is slightly thickened, stirring constantly. Remove from heat. Add softened gelatin and vanilla; stir until gelatin is dissolved. Refrigerate until date mixture is thickened and partially set, stirring occasionally. Fold whipped cream into date mixture. In small bowl, beat egg whites until soft peaks form. Gradually add 2 tablespoons sugar, beating until stiff peaks form. Fold into date mixture. Spoon filling into cooled baked pie shell; sprinkle with nutmeg. Refrigerate at least 2 hours before serving. Store in refrigerator. **8 servings.**

TIPS: *If using self-rising flour, omit salt.

**To toast sesame seed, spread on cookie sheet; bake at 375°F. for 3 to 5 minutes or until light golden brown, stirring occasionally. Or, spread in small skillet; stir over medium heat for about 5 minutes or until light golden brown.

HIGH ALTITUDE—Above 3500 Feet: No change.

NUTRIENTS PER 1/8 OF RECIPE

Calories	390	Protein	10% U.S. RDA
Protein	7g	Vitamin A	10% U.S. RDA
Carbohydrate	40g	Vitamin C	<2% U.S. RDA
Fat	23g	Thiamine	10% U.S. RDA
Cholesterol	110mg	Riboflavin	10% U.S. RDA
Sodium	250mg	Niacin	6% U.S. RDA
Potassium	250mg	Calcium	8% U.S. RDA
Dietary Fiber	2g	Iron	8% U.S. RDA

Open Sesame Pie

This recipe created a profitable rush to the country's supermarkets. It wasn't the date chiffon filling but the sesame seed crust that caused such commotion. Within hours after this pie was announced as the winning Bake-Off® recipe, a virtual "out of stock" was declared on sesame seed. And from that time on, it has been a regularly stocked item on most supermarket shelves.

Lemon Fudge Ribbon Pie

⸙

Harriet Mason, California
Bake-Off® 32, 1986

CRUST
15-ounce package refrigerated pie crusts
1 teaspoon flour
½ teaspoon unsweetened cocoa

FILLING
8-ounce package cream cheese, cut into 2 pieces
1 cup sugar
¼ cup lemon juice
1 teaspoon vanilla
3 eggs, beaten
½ ounce (½ square) unsweetened chocolate or 1 ounce (1 square) semi-sweet chocolate

TOPPING
1 cup whipping cream*
1 tablespoon powdered sugar*
Grated sweet cooking or semi-sweet chocolate, if desired

MICROWAVE DIRECTIONS: Prepare pie crust according to package directions for *unfilled one-crust pie* using 9-inch microwave-safe pie pan. (Refrigerate remaining crust for later use.) Sprinkle edge of crust with cocoa; rub in gently with finger tips before fluting. Generously prick crust with fork. Microwave on HIGH for 6 to 8 minutes, rotating pan ½ turn every 2 minutes. Crust is done when surface appears dry and flaky. Cool completely.

In medium microwave-safe bowl, microwave cream cheese on HIGH for 1 to 1½ minutes to soften. Stir in sugar until smooth. Add lemon juice, vanilla and eggs; blend well. Microwave on HIGH for 5 to 7 minutes, stirring every 2 minutes until smooth and thickened.

In small microwave-safe bowl, microwave unsweetened chocolate on HIGH for 2 minutes or until melted; blend in ½ cup of lemon filling. Pour into cooled cooked crust; spread evenly. Carefully spread remaining lemon filling over chocolate filling. Cover with waxed paper; refrigerate 3 to 4 hours or until firm. In small bowl, beat whip-

Cookie Crust Pecan Pie

⸙

Ever-popular pecan pie is baked in a 13 × 9-inch pan for a new shape. Refrigerated cookie dough makes a quick-to-prepare crust.

ping cream until soft peaks form. Blend in powdered sugar; beat until stiff peaks form. Spoon or pipe over filling. Garnish with grated chocolate. Store in refrigerator. **8 servings.**

TIP: *One and one-half cups frozen whipped topping, thawed, can be substituted for whipping cream and powdered sugar.

NUTRIENTS PER 1/8 OF RECIPE

Calories	490	Protein	8% U.S. RDA
Protein	6g	Vitamin A	20% U.S. RDA
Carbohydrate	43g	Vitamin C	4% U.S. RDA
Fat	33g	Thiamine	2% U.S. RDA
Cholesterol	180mg	Riboflavin	8% U.S. RDA
Sodium	290mg	Niacin	<2% U.S. RDA
Potassium	130mg	Calcium	6% U.S. RDA
Dietary Fiber	<1g	Iron	4% U.S. RDA

Cookie Crust Pecan Pie

⸙

Louise Schlinkert, California
Bake-Off® 20, 1969

20-ounce package refrigerated sliceable sugar cookie dough
3¾-ounce package instant butterscotch pudding and pie filling mix
Dash salt
¾ cup dark corn syrup
⅔ cup milk
½ teaspoon vanilla, if desired
1 egg
1½ cups pecan halves or pieces
Whipped cream or ice cream, if desired

Heat oven to 350°F. Slice cookie dough into ¼-inch slices; place in ungreased 13 × 9-inch pan. With lightly floured hands, press dough over bottom and 1 inch up sides to form crust. pressing dough as thin as possible on sides of pan. In medium bowl, combine pudding mix, salt, corn syrup, milk, vanilla and egg; mix well. Fold in pecans. Pour into crust-lined pan. Bake at 350°F. for 25 to 35 minutes or until edges are deep golden brown and filling is set. Cool completely; cut into squares. Serve with whipped cream or ice cream. **12 servings.**

NUTRIENTS PER 1/12 OF RECIPE

Calories	440	Protein	6% U.S. RDA
Protein	4g	Vitamin A	2% U.S. RDA
Carbohydrate	57g	Vitamin C	<2% U.S. RDA
Fat	22g	Thiamine	15% U.S. RDA
Cholesterol	35mg	Riboflavin	15% U.S. RDA
Sodium	270mg	Niacin	6% U.S. RDA
Potassium	170mg	Calcium	6% U.S. RDA
Dietary Fiber	1g	Iron	10% U.S. RDA

Lemon Fudge Ribbon Pie

Mystery Pecan Pie

Mary McClain, Arkansas
Bake-Off® 16, 1964

15-ounce package refrigerated pie
  crusts
1 teaspoon flour

FILLING
  8-ounce package cream cheese,
    softened
  1 teaspoon vanilla
  1 egg
  1/3 cup sugar
  1/4 teaspoon salt
  3 eggs
  1/4 cup sugar
  1 cup corn syrup
  1 teaspoon vanilla
  1 1/4 cups chopped pecans

Prepare pie crust according to package directions for *filled one-crust pie* using 9-inch pie pan. (Refrigerate remaining crust for later use.) Heat oven to 375°F.

In small bowl, beat cream cheese, 1 teaspoon vanilla, 1 egg, 1/3 cup sugar and salt at low speed until smooth and well blended; set aside. In second small bowl, beat 3 eggs. Stir in 1/4 cup sugar, corn syrup and 1 teaspoon vanilla; mix well.

Spread cream cheese mixture in bottom of pie crust-lined pan. Sprinkle with pecans. Gently pour corn syrup mixture over pecans. Bake at 375°F. for 35 to 45 minutes or until center is set. Cool. Store in refrigerator. **8 servings.**

TIP: Cover edge of pie crust with strip of foil during last 10 to 15 minutes of baking if necessary to prevent excessive browning.

NUTRIENTS PER 1/8 OF RECIPE

Calories	570	Protein	10% U.S. RDA
Protein	8g	Vitamin A	10% U.S. RDA
Carbohydrate	63g	Vitamin C	<2% U.S. RDA
Fat	32g	Thiamine	6% U.S. RDA
Cholesterol	180mg	Riboflavin	8% U.S. RDA
Sodium	320mg	Niacin	<2% U.S. RDA
Potassium	150mg	Calcium	6% U.S. RDA
Dietary Fiber	1g	Iron	15% U.S. RDA

Chocolate Silk Pecan Pie

Leonard Thompson, California
Bake-Off® 32, 1986

CRUST
  15-ounce package refrigerated pie
    crusts
  1 teaspoon flour
  1/3 cup sugar
  1/8 teaspoon salt, if desired
  1/2 cup dark corn syrup
  3 tablespoons margarine or butter,
    melted
  2 eggs
  1/2 cup chopped pecans

FILLING
  1 cup hot milk
  1/4 teaspoon vanilla
  1 1/3 cups (8 ounces) semi-sweet
    chocolate chips

TOPPING
  1 cup whipping cream
  2 tablespoons powdered sugar
  1/4 teaspoon vanilla
  Chocolate curls, if desired

Prepare pie crust according to package directions for *filled one-crust pie* using 9-inch pie pan. (Refrigerate remaining crust for later use.) Heat oven to 350°F. In small bowl, beat sugar, salt, corn syrup, margarine and eggs 1 minute at medium speed. Fold in pecans. Pour into pie crust-lined pan. Bake at 350°F. for 40 to 55 minutes or until center of pie is puffed and golden brown. Cool on wire rack 1 hour.

While filled crust is cooling, in blender container or food processor bowl with metal blade, combine all filling ingredients; blend 1 minute or until smooth. Refrigerate about 1 1/2 hours or until filling mixture is slightly thickened but not set. Gently stir mixture; pour into cooled filled crust; spread evenly. Refrigerate 1 hour or until firm.

In small bowl, beat whipping cream until soft peaks form. Blend in powdered sugar and 1/4 teaspoon vanilla; beat until stiff peaks form. Spoon or

---

Mystery Pecan Pie

Solve the mystery when you taste the smooth cream cheese filling hiding under the rich pecan filling in this extra-special pie.

Chocolate Silk Pecan Pie

In this luscious pie, smooth-as-silk chocolate crowns rich-flavored pecan pie. It is one of our favorites! For best results, be sure to measure ingredients accurately.

pipe over filling. Garnish with chocolate curls. Store in refrigerator. **8 to 10 servings.**

TIP: Cover pie with foil during last 15 to 20 minutes of baking if necessary to prevent excessive browning.

NUTRIENTS PER 1/10 OF RECIPE

Calories	490	Protein	6% U.S. RDA
Protein	5g	Vitamin A	10% U.S. RDA
Carbohydrate	46g	Vitamin C	<2% U.S. RDA
Fat	32g	Thiamine	4% U.S. RDA
Cholesterol	90mg	Riboflavin	6% U.S. RDA
Sodium	240mg	Niacin	<2% U.S. RDA
Potassium	180mg	Calcium	6% U.S. RDA
Dietary Fiber	2g	Iron	8% U.S. RDA

Raspberry Angel Cream Pie

Kay Bare, Idaho
Bake-Off® 33, 1988

15-ounce package refrigerated pie crusts
1 teaspoon flour
1/4 cup chopped walnuts or pecans

FILLING
1/2 cup milk
25 large marshmallows
1 cup whipping cream, whipped

TOPPING
1/3 cup sugar
2 tablespoons cornstarch
3/4 cup water
1 teaspoon lemon juice
1 teaspoon orange-flavored liqueur, if desired
1 teaspoon red food coloring, if desired
2 cups fresh or frozen raspberries without syrup, thawed, drained
Whipped cream
Whole raspberries

Heat oven to 450°F. Prepare pie crust according to package directions for *unfilled one-crust pie* using 9-inch pie pan. (Refrigerate remaining pie crust for later use.) Press walnuts into bottom of pie crust-lined pan. Bake at 450°F. for 9 to 11 minutes or until light golden brown. Cool completely.*

MICROWAVE DIRECTIONS: In 2-quart microwave-safe bowl, combine milk and marshmallows. Microwave on HIGH for 2 to 3 minutes or until marshmallows are melted, stirring once halfway through cooking.** With wire whisk, beat mixture until smooth. Cover; refrigerate 35 to 45 minutes or until mixture is thickened but not set. Fold in whipped cream. Spread filling mixture in cooled baked crust. Cover; refrigerate.

In medium microwave-safe bowl, combine sugar, cornstarch, water, lemon juice, liqueur and food coloring; blend well. Stir in 1 cup of the raspberries. Microwave on HIGH for 2 minutes; stir. Microwave on HIGH 2 to 5 minutes or until mixture becomes thick and clear, stirring once halfway through cooking. Refrigerate 30 to 45 minutes or until set. Fold in remaining 1 cup raspberries. Spoon topping mixture over cooled filling. Refrigerate 1 to 2 hours or until firm. Garnish with whipped cream and whole raspberries. Refrigerate before serving. Store in refrigerator. **8 servings.**

TIPS: *To microwave pie crust, prepare crust as directed above. Microwave on HIGH for 6 to 8 minutes, rotating pan once halfway through cooking. Crust is done when surface appears dry and flaky. Cool completely.

**Marshmallows puff up and do not appear melted. Stir to melt; additional cooking can toughen them.

NUTRIENTS PER 1/8 OF RECIPE

Calories	400	Protein	4% U.S. RDA
Protein	3g	Vitamin A	10% U.S. RDA
Carbohydrate	44g	Vitamin C	10% U.S. RDA
Fat	25g	Thiamine	2% U.S. RDA
Cholesterol	50mg	Riboflavin	6% U.S. RDA
Sodium	190mg	Niacin	2% U.S. RDA
Potassium	140mg	Calcium	6% U.S. RDA
Dietary Fiber	1g	Iron	2% U.S. RDA

Beginner's luck?

A woman who expressed frustration to her husband about never becoming a finalist after entering for many years found her spouse trying on his own to perfect a winning recipe. Sure enough, his creation not only took him to the Bake-Off® (along with his wife, who coached from the visitors' gallery), it gave him the distinction of becoming the first man ever to win a major prize. A U.S. Navy submarine steward, he aptly named his dessert Sub Meringue Pie.

Tangy Crescent Nut Tart
ᥬᥬ

Refrigerated crescent roll dough forms the easy flaky crust for this tart. Coconut and hazelnuts give texture and subtle flavor to the lemony filling.

Frost-on-the-Pumpkin Pie
ᥬᥬ

Kathleen S. Johnson, Ohio
Bake-Off® 29, 1980

CRUST

1¼ cups (18 squares) finely crushed graham crackers or graham cracker crumbs

3 tablespoons sugar

½ teaspoon cinnamon

¼ teaspoon nutmeg

⅛ teaspoon cloves

⅓ cup margarine or butter, melted

FILLING

1 can ready-to-spread vanilla frosting

1 cup dairy sour cream

1 cup canned pumpkin

1 teaspoon cinnamon

½ teaspoon ginger

¼ teaspoon cloves

8-ounce container (3¼ cups) frozen whipped topping, thawed

Heat oven to 350°F. In small bowl, combine all crust ingredients; stir until blended. Reserve 2 tablespoons of crust mixture for topping. Press remaining crust mixture in bottom and up sides of 9 or 10-inch pie pan. Bake at 350°F. for 6 minutes. Cool.

In large bowl, combine all filling ingredients except whipped topping; beat 2 minutes at medium speed. Fold in 1 cup of the whipped topping; pour into cooled baked crust; spread evenly. Refrigerate until firm. Spread remaining whipped topping over filling; sprinkle with reserved 2 tablespoons crust mixture. Refrigerate at least 4 hours before serving.* Store in refrigerator. **8 servings.**

TIP: *Refrigerate 6 hours or overnight before serving if substituting non-frozen whipped topping or whipped cream.

NUTRIENTS PER 1/8 OF RECIPE

Calories	560	Protein	4% U.S. RDA
Protein	3g	Vitamin A	150% U.S. RDA
Carbohydrate	64g	Vitamin C	2% U.S. RDA
Fat	32g	Thiamine	2% U.S. RDA
Cholesterol	10mg	Riboflavin	8% U.S. RDA
Sodium	320mg	Niacin	2% U.S. RDA
Potassium	190mg	Calcium	6% U.S. RDA
Dietary Fiber	1g	Iron	6% U.S. RDA

Tangy Crescent Nut Tart
ᥬᥬ

Debi Wolf, Oregon
Bake-Off® 32, 1986

8-ounce can refrigerated crescent dinner rolls

1 cup sugar

¼ cup all purpose or unbleached flour

3 to 4 tablespoons lemon juice

2 to 3 teaspoons grated lemon peel

1 teaspoon vanilla

4 eggs

1 cup coconut

1 cup finely chopped hazelnuts (filberts) or walnuts

1 to 2 tablespoons powdered sugar

Heat oven to 350°F. Lightly grease 10-inch tart pan.* Separate dough into 8 triangles. Place triangles in greased pan; press over bottom and up sides to form crust. Seal perforations. Bake at 350°F. for 5 minutes. Cool 5 minutes; gently press sides of warm crust to top of pan.

In large bowl, combine sugar, flour, lemon juice, lemon peel, vanilla and eggs; beat 3 minutes at medium speed. By hand, stir in coconut and hazelnuts. Pour hazelnut mixture into cooled partially baked crust. Bake an additional 25 to 30 minutes or until filling is set and crust is golden brown. Cool. Sprinkle with powdered sugar. Store in refrigerator. **8 to 12 servings.**

TIP: *A 10-inch pizza pan can be substituted for the tart pan. Bake filled crust 20 to 25 minutes.

NUTRIENTS PER 1/12 OF RECIPE

Calories	270	Protein	8% U.S. RDA
Protein	5g	Vitamin A	<2% U.S. RDA
Carbohydrate	32g	Vitamin C	2% U.S. RDA
Fat	14g	Thiamine	8% U.S. RDA
Cholesterol	90mg	Riboflavin	6% U.S. RDA
Sodium	180mg	Niacin	4% U.S. RDA
Potassium	135mg	Calcium	2% U.S. RDA
Dietary Fiber	2g	Iron	6% U.S. RDA

Tangy Crescent Nut Tart

Caramel Pear Pecan Flan

Caramel Pear Pecan Flan

Tillie A. Astorino, Massachusetts
Bake-Off® 32, 1986

15-ounce package refrigerated pie
   crusts
1 teaspoon flour
½ cup chopped pecans

FILLING
  8-ounce package cream cheese,
    softened
  ¾ to 1 cup caramel ice cream
    topping
  2 eggs
  29-ounce can pear halves, well
    drained, sliced*
  1½ cups frozen whipped topping,
    thawed
  3 tablespoons chopped pecans

MICROWAVE DIRECTIONS: Prepare pie crust according to package directions for *unfilled one-crust pie* using 10-inch microwave-safe tart pan or 9-inch microwave-safe pie pan. (Refrigerate remaining crust for later use.) Place prepared crust in pan; press in bottom and up sides of pan. Trim edges if necessary. Press ½ cup pecans into bottom and sides of pie crust-lined pan. Generously prick crust with fork. Microwave on HIGH for 6 to 8 minutes, rotating pan ½ turn every 2 minutes. Crust is done when surface appears dry and flaky. Cool completely.

In small bowl, beat cream cheese, ½ cup of the ice cream topping and eggs until smooth. Pour into cooled cooked pie crust; spread evenly. Arrange pear slices in single layer over cream cheese mixture. Microwave on HIGH for 6 to 9 minutes for tart pan or 9 to 11 minutes for pie pan, rotating pan ¼ turn every 3 minutes. Pie is done when center is almost set. (Cream cheese mixture will firm as it sets and cools.) Cover loosely with waxed paper; cool on flat surface 1 hour. Refrigerate 2 hours before serving. Just before serving, top with whipped topping; drizzle with remaining ¼ to ½ cup ice cream topping. Sprinkle with 3 tablespoons pecans. Store in refrigerator. **6 to 10 servings.**

TIP: *Six to 10 canned pear halves, drained, arranged with rounded sides up and narrow ends pointing toward center, can be substituted for sliced pears. If desired, for decorative garnish, score pear halves by making ⅛-inch-deep decorative cuts on rounded side.

NUTRIENTS PER 1/10 OF RECIPE

Calories	400	Protein	10% U.S. RDA
Protein	6g	Vitamin A	10% U.S. RDA
Carbohydrate	43g	Vitamin C	<2% U.S. RDA
Fat	23g	Thiamine	2% U.S. RDA
Cholesterol	90mg	Riboflavin	4% U.S. RDA
Sodium	240mg	Niacin	<2% U.S. RDA
Potassium	130mg	Calcium	2% U.S. RDA
Dietary Fiber	2g	Iron	4% U.S. RDA

Grand Prize Winner
Apple Nut Lattice Tart
❧

Mary Lou Warren, Colorado
Bake-Off® 32, 1986

15-ounce package refrigerated pie crusts
1 teaspoon flour

FILLING
3 to 3½ cups (3 to 4 medium) thinly sliced peeled apples
½ cup sugar
3 tablespoons chopped walnuts or pecans
3 tablespoons golden raisins
½ teaspoon cinnamon
2 teaspoons lemon juice
¼ to ½ teaspoon grated lemon peel
1 egg yolk, beaten
1 teaspoon water

GLAZE
¼ cup powdered sugar
1 to 2 teaspoons lemon juice

Prepare pie crust according to package directions for *two-crust pie* using 10-inch tart pan with removable bottom or 9-inch pie pan. Place 1 prepared crust in pan; press in bottom and up sides of pan. Trim edges if necessary. Heat oven to 400°F.

In large bowl, combine apples, sugar, walnuts, raisins, cinnamon, 2 teaspoons lemon juice and lemon peel; mix lightly. Spoon into pie crust-lined pan.

To make lattice top, cut remaining crust into ½-inch wide strips. Arrange strips in lattice design over apple mixture. Trim and seal edges. In small bowl, blend egg yolk and water; gently brush over lattice. Bake at 400°F. for 40 to 60 minutes or until golden brown and apples are tender. Cool 1 hour.

In small bowl, blend powdered sugar and enough lemon juice for desired drizzling consistency. Drizzle over slightly warm tart. Cool; remove sides of pan. **8 servings.**

TIP: Cover tart with foil during last 15 to 20 minutes of baking if necessary to prevent excessive browning.

NUTRIENTS PER 1/8 OF RECIPE

Calories	380	Protein	2% U.S. RDA
Protein	2g	Vitamin A	<2% U.S. RDA
Carbohydrate	50g	Vitamin C	4% U.S. RDA
Fat	19g	Thiamine	2% U.S. RDA
Cholesterol	35mg	Riboflavin	<2% U.S. RDA
Sodium	330mg	Niacin	<2% U.S. RDA
Potassium	125mg	Calcium	<2% U.S. RDA
Dietary Fiber	2g	Iron	2% U.S. RDA

Apple Nut Lattice Tart
❧

A distinctive lattice top, golden raisins, and walnuts make this updated apple pie special enough to win the top prize.

Caramel Pear Pecan Flan
❧

The subtle flavor of pears and the rich flavor of caramel combine in a microwave cheesecake pie.

Pecan Caramel Tart

Kathy Specht, California
Bake-Off® 33, 1988

Pecan Caramel Tart

Turtle candy in a crust! So unbelievably easy and so irresistibly delicious!

15-ounce package refrigerated pie crusts
1 teaspoon flour

FILLING
½ cup whipping cream
36 caramels
3½ cups pecan halves

TOPPING
¼ cup semi-sweet chocolate chips
1 teaspoon margarine or butter
1 tablespoon whipping cream

Heat oven to 450°F. Prepare pie crust according to package directions for *unfilled one-crust pie* using 10-inch tart pan with removable bottom or 9-inch pie pan. (Refrigerate remaining crust for later use.) Place prepared crust in pan; press in bottom and up sides of pan. Trim edges if necessary. Generously prick crust with fork. Bake at 450°F. for 9 to 11 minutes or until light golden brown. Cool completely.

In medium heavy saucepan, combine ½ cup whipping cream and caramels; cook over low heat until caramels are melted and mixture is smooth, stirring frequently. Remove from heat. Add pecans; stir until well coated. Spread evenly over cooled baked crust.

In small saucepan over low heat, melt chocolate chips and margarine, stirring until smooth. Stir in 1 tablespoon whipping cream until well blended. Drizzle over pecan filling. Refrigerate 1 hour or until filling is firm. If desired, garnish with sweetened whipped cream. **12 servings.**

NUTRIENTS PER 1/12 OF RECIPE

Calories	480	Protein	6% U.S. RDA
Protein	4g	Vitamin A	4% U.S. RDA
Carbohydrate	37g	Vitamin C	<2% U.S. RDA
Fat	35g	Thiamine	20% U.S. RDA
Cholesterol	15mg	Riboflavin	6% U.S. RDA
Sodium	180mg	Niacin	2% U.S. RDA
Potassium	210mg	Calcium	6% U.S. RDA
Dietary Fiber	3g	Iron	6% U.S. RDA

Praline Crescent Dessert

Marjorie Hooper, Florida
Bake-Off® 30, 1982

⅓ cup margarine or butter
½ cup firmly packed brown sugar
3 tablespoons dairy sour cream
1 cup crisp rice cereal
½ cup chopped pecans or nuts
½ cup coconut
8-ounce can refrigerated crescent dinner rolls
3-ounce package cream cheese, softened
2 tablespoons powdered sugar
Whipping cream, whipped, if desired

Heat oven to 375°F. In medium saucepan over low heat, melt margarine. Stir in brown sugar; cook 2 minutes, stirring constantly. Stir in sour cream; cook 4 minutes, stirring occasionally. Remove from heat. Add cereal, pecans and coconut; stir until evenly coated.

Separate dough into 8 triangles. Place 1 triangle in each ungreased muffin cup; press dough to cover bottom and sides, forming ¼-inch rim. In small bowl, beat cream cheese and powdered sugar until smooth. Spoon rounded teaspoonful into each dough-lined cup; spread over bottom. Spoon brown sugar mixture evenly over cream cheese mixture. Bake at 375°F. for 11 to 16 minutes or until edges of crust are deep golden brown. Cool 1 minute; remove from pan. Serve warm or cold topped with whipped cream. Store in refrigerator. **8 servings.**

TIP: To make ahead, prepare, cover and refrigerate up to 2 hours; bake as directed above.

NUTRIENTS PER 1/8 OF RECIPE

Calories	390	Protein	6% U.S. RDA
Protein	4g	Vitamin A	15% U.S. RDA
Carbohydrate	33g	Vitamin C	2% U.S. RDA
Fat	27g	Thiamine	10% U.S. RDA
Cholesterol	25mg	Riboflavin	10% U.S. RDA
Sodium	400mg	Niacin	6% U.S. RDA
Potassium	190mg	Calcium	4% U.S. RDA
Dietary Fiber	2g	Iron	8% U.S. RDA

Italian Crescent Crostata

Italian Crescent Crostata

Ann Mehl, Minnesota
Bake-Off® 31, 1984

**2 (8-ounce) cans refrigerated
crescent dinner rolls**
1½ cups raspberry preserves
¾ cup chopped walnuts or pecans
½ cup raisins or currants
Beaten egg, if desired
Powdered sugar

Heat oven to 350°F. Separate dough into 8 rectangles; separate 5 of the rectangles into 10 triangles. Place the 10 triangles in ungreased 12-inch pizza pan or 13 × 9-inch pan; press over bottom and ½ inch up sides to form crust. Seal perforations. Bake at 350°F. for 12 to 15 minutes or until light golden brown.

In medium bowl, combine preserves, walnuts and raisins. Spread over partially baked crust. To make lattice top, seal perforations of remaining 3 rectangles; cut each lengthwise into 5 strips to make 15 strips of dough. Arrange strips in lattice design over preserve mixture, pinching strips together where necessary. Gently brush beaten egg over lattice. Bake an additional 17 to 22 minutes or until golden brown. Cool; sprinkle with powdered sugar.
10 to 12 servings.

NUTRIENTS PER 1/12 OF RECIPE

Calories	330	Protein	6% U.S. RDA
Protein	4g	Vitamin A	<2% U.S. RDA
Carbohydrate	49g	Vitamin C	2% U.S. RDA
Fat	13g	Thiamine	10% U.S. RDA
Cholesterol	25mg	Riboflavin	6% U.S. RDA
Sodium	320mg	Niacin	6% U.S. RDA
Potassium	210mg	Calcium	2% U.S. RDA
Dietary Fiber	1g	Iron	8% U.S. RDA

Almond Filled Cookie Cake

ॐ€⅗

Elizabeth Meijer, Connecticut
Bake-Off® 30, 1982

Almond Filled Cookie Cake

ॐ€⅗

This special recipe is a rich almond dessert adapted from a Dutch pastry. Thinly slice this tempting dessert to serve.

CRUST

2²/₃ cups all purpose or unbleached flour
1¹/₃ cups sugar
1¹/₃ cups unsalted or regular butter or margarine, softened*
¹/₂ teaspoon salt
1 egg

FILLING

1 cup grated or finely chopped almonds
¹/₂ cup sugar
1 teaspoon grated lemon peel
1 egg, slightly beaten
Whole almonds
Powdered sugar, if desired

Heat oven to 325°F. Grease 10 or 9-inch springform pan.** Lightly spoon flour into measuring cup; level off. In large bowl, blend flour and remaining crust ingredients at low speed until a soft dough forms. Refrigerate for easier handling, if desired. Divide dough in half; spread half in bottom of greased pan.

In small bowl, blend all filling ingredients except whole almonds and powdered sugar; spread over crust to within ¹/₂ inch of sides of pan. Between waxed paper, press out remaining half of dough to 10 or 9-inch circle. Remove top layer of waxed paper; invert dough over filling. Remove bottom layer of waxed paper; press dough into place. Garnish with whole almonds.

Bake at 325°F. for 55 to 65 minutes or until light golden brown. (Place foil on rack below pan during baking to catch any spillage.) Cool 15 minutes; remove sides of pan. Cool completely. Sprinkle with powdered sugar.
24 to 32 servings.

TIPS: *If using regular butter or margarine, omit ¹/₂ teaspoon salt.

**A 9-inch round cake pan can be used. Line bottom with waxed paper; grease. Continue as directed above. Cool 30 minutes; remove from pan.

HIGH ALTITUDE—Above 3500 Feet: No change.

NUTRIENTS PER 1/32 OF RECIPE

Calories	190	Protein	4% U.S. RDA
Protein	3g	Vitamin A	6% U.S. RDA
Carbohydrate	21g	Vitamin C	<2% U.S. RDA
Fat	11g	Thiamine	4% U.S. RDA
Cholesterol	40mg	Riboflavin	6% U.S. RDA
Sodium	40mg	Niacin	4% U.S. RDA
Potassium	60mg	Calcium	2% U.S. RDA
Dietary Fiber	<1g	Iron	4% U.S. RDA

Peaches and Cream Crescent Dessert

ॐ€⅗

Marilyn Blankschien, Wisconsin
Bake-Off® 28, 1978

8-ounce can refrigerated crescent dinner rolls
8-ounce package cream cheese, softened
¹/₂ cup sugar
¹/₄ to ¹/₂ teaspoon almond extract
21-ounce can peach fruit pie filling*
¹/₂ cup all purpose or unbleached flour
¹/₄ cup firmly packed brown sugar
3 tablespoons margarine, softened
¹/₂ cup sliced almonds or chopped nuts

Heat oven to 375°F. Unroll dough into 2 long rectangles. Place in ungreased 13 × 9-inch pan; press over bottom to form crust. Seal perforations. Bake at 375°F. for 5 minutes.

Meanwhile, in small bowl beat cream cheese, sugar and almond extract until smooth. Spread over partially baked crust. Spoon fruit filling evenly over cream cheese mixture. Lightly spoon flour into measuring cup; level off. In second small bowl, blend flour, brown sugar and margarine at low speed until crumbly. Stir in almonds; sprinkle crumb mixture over fruit filling. Bake an additional 25 to 30 minutes or until golden brown. Cool completely. Cut into squares. Store in refrigerator.
12 servings.

NUTRIENTS PER 1/12 OF RECIPE

Calories	310	Protein	6% U.S. RDA
Protein	4g	Vitamin A	15% U.S. RDA
Carbohydrate	37g	Vitamin C	2% U.S. RDA
Fat	16g	Thiamine	6% U.S. RDA
Cholesterol	25mg	Riboflavin	8% U.S. RDA
Sodium	250mg	Niacin	4% U.S. RDA
Potassium	115mg	Calcium	2% U.S. RDA
Dietary Fiber	1g	Iron	15% U.S. RDA

Spicy Apple Twists

❧

Dorothy DeVault, Ohio
Bake-Off® 10, 1958

2 large baking apples, cored
1½ cups all purpose, unbleached or
  self-rising flour*
½ teaspoon salt
½ cup shortening
4 to 6 tablespoons cold water
1 tablespoon margarine or butter,
  softened

TOPPING
¼ cup margarine or butter, melted
½ cup sugar
1 teaspoon cinnamon
1 cup water

Heat oven to 425°F. Cut each apple into 8 wedges. Lightly spoon flour into measuring cup; level off. In medium bowl, blend flour and salt. Using pastry blender or fork, cut shortening into flour mixture until mixture resembles coarse crumbs. Sprinkle flour mixture with water, 1 tablespoon at a time, while tossing and mixing lightly with fork. Add water until dough is just moist enough to hold together. Shape dough into a ball. Flatten ball; smooth edges. On floured surface, roll lightly from center to edge into 12-inch square. Spread with 1 tablespoon softened margarine. Fold 2 sides to center. Roll into 16 × 10-inch rectangle. Cut crosswise into sixteen 10-inch strips. Wrap one strip around each apple wedge. Place ½ inch apart in ungreased 13 × 9-inch pan. Brush each wrapped apple wedge with melted margarine.

In small bowl, blend sugar and cinnamon; sprinkle over wrapped apples. Bake at 425°F. for 20 minutes. Pour water into pan. Bake an additional 12 to 17 minutes or until golden brown. Serve warm or cold, plain or with whipped cream. **16 servings.**

TIP: *If using self-rising flour, omit salt.

NUTRIENTS PER 1/16 OF RECIPE

Calories	170	Protein	2% U.S. RDA
Protein	1g	Vitamin A	2% U.S. RDA
Carbohydrate	18g	Vitamin C	<2% U.S. RDA
Fat	10g	Thiamine	4% U.S. RDA
Cholesterol	0mg	Riboflavin	2% U.S. RDA
Sodium	110mg	Niacin	2% U.S. RDA
Potassium	40mg	Calcium	<2% U.S. RDA
Dietary Fiber	<1g	Iron	2% U.S. RDA

Almond Brickle Dessert

❧

Louise Bork, Ohio
Bake-Off® 18, 1967

½ cup slivered almonds
⅓ cup sugar
½ cup margarine or butter
¼ cup honey
1 tablespoon milk
1¾ cups all purpose, unbleached or
  self-rising flour*
⅔ cup sugar
2 teaspoons baking powder
½ cup margarine or butter,
  softened
⅓ cup milk
1 teaspoon almond extract
2 eggs

Heat oven to 350°F. Grease 9-inch square pan. In small saucepan, combine almonds, ⅓ cup sugar, ½ cup margarine, honey and 1 tablespoon milk. Cook over medium heat 9 to 11 minutes or until mixture comes to a boil, stirring constantly. Boil 2 minutes. Remove from heat; set aside.

Lightly spoon flour into measuring cup; level off. In large bowl, combine 1 cup flour, ⅔ cup sugar, baking powder, ½ cup margarine, ⅓ cup milk, almond extract and eggs. Blend at low speed until moistened; beat 3 minutes at medium speed. By hand, stir in remaining ¾ cup flour; mix well. Spread batter in greased pan. Spoon almond mixture over batter; spread evenly to cover. Bake at 350°F. for 25 to 35 minutes or until toothpick inserted in center comes out clean. **9 servings.**

TIP: *If using self-rising flour, omit baking powder.

HIGH ALTITUDE—Above 3500 feet: No change.

NUTRIENTS PER 1/9 OF RECIPE

Calories	440	Protein	8% U.S. RDA
Protein	6g	Vitamin A	20% U.S. RDA
Carbohydrate	51g	Vitamin C	<2% U.S. RDA
Fat	25g	Thiamine	10% U.S. RDA
Cholesterol	60mg	Riboflavin	10% U.S. RDA
Sodium	330mg	Niacin	8% U.S. RDA
Potassium	125mg	Calcium	15% U.S. RDA
Dietary Fiber	2g	Iron	8% U.S. RDA

Almond Brickle Dessert

❧

Honey almond topping and a rich almond-flavored base create a small-sized dessert with homemade goodness.

Fudge Marble Cheesecake

Fudge Marble Cheesecake

Wanda Bierbaum, Illinois
Bake-Off® 32, 1986

1 package pudding-included fudge marble cake mix
¹/₃ cup oil
3 eggs
¹/₂ cup sugar
2 (8-ounce) packages cream cheese, softened
1 cup ricotta cheese or small curd cottage cheese
¹/₂ cup dairy sour cream
¹/₂ cup whipping cream

Heat oven to 350°F. Grease 13 × 9-inch pan. Reserve 1 cup of the dry cake mix and marble pouch; set aside. In large bowl, combine remaining cake mix, oil and 1 egg at low speed until a soft dough forms. Press in bottom and 1¹/₂ inches up sides of greased pan. Bake at 350°F. for 10 minutes.

In large bowl, combine reserved 1 cup cake mix, remaining 2 eggs, sugar, cream cheese, ricotta cheese, sour cream and whipping cream at low speed until blended; beat 3 minutes at medium speed. Reserve 1¹/₂ cups of cheese mixture. Spoon remaining cheese mixture over partially baked crust. Add reserved marble pouch to reserved cheese mixture; blend well. Spoon chocolate mixture randomly over cheese mixture. To marble, pull knife through mixture in wide curves; turn pan and repeat.

Bake an additional 30 to 40 minutes or until top springs back when touched lightly in center. *Do not overbake. To prevent cracking, immediately run knife around edge of pan.* Cool completely. Refrigerate until serving time. Store in refrigerator. **15 servings or 36 bars.**

HIGH ALTITUDE—Above 3500 feet: No change.

NUTRIENTS PER 1/15 OF RECIPE

Calories	410	Protein	10% U.S. RDA
Protein	7g	Vitamin A	15% U.S. RDA
Carbohydrate	38g	Vitamin C	<2% U.S. RDA
Fat	26g	Thiamine	8% U.S. RDA
Cholesterol	110mg	Riboflavin	10% U.S. RDA
Sodium	360mg	Niacin	4% U.S. RDA
Potassium	120mg	Calcium	10% U.S. RDA
Dietary Fiber	<1g	Iron	8% U.S. RDA

Peanut Chocolate Parfait Dessert

Karen Everly, Oregon
Bake-Off® 32, 1986

BASE
1 package pudding-included devil's food cake mix
1/2 cup margarine or butter, melted
1/4 cup milk
1 egg
3/4 cup peanuts

FILLING
1 1/2 cups powdered sugar
3/4 cup peanut butter
8-ounce package cream cheese, softened
2 1/2 cups milk
8-ounce container (3 1/4 cups) frozen whipped topping, thawed
5 1/4-ounce package instant vanilla pudding and pie filling mix (6-serving size)

TOPPING
1/2 cup peanuts
1.45-ounce bar milk chocolate, chilled, grated

Heat oven to 350°F. Grease and flour bottom only of 13 × 9-inch pan. In large bowl, combine all base ingredients except 3/4 cup peanuts; beat at medium speed until well blended. By hand, stir in 3/4 cup peanuts. Spread evenly in greased and floured pan. Bake at 350°F. for 20 to 25 minutes. *Do not overbake.* Cool completely.

In small bowl, combine powdered sugar and peanut buter at low speed until crumbly; set aside. In large bowl, beat cream cheese until smooth. Add milk, whipped topping and pudding mix; beat 2 minutes at low speed until well blended. Pour half of cream cheese mixture over cooled base; spread evenly. Sprinkle with half of peanut butter mixture. Repeat layers with remaining cream cheese and peanut butter mixtures. Sprinkle with 1/2 cup peanuts; gently press into filling. Sprinkle grated chocolate over peanuts.

Cover; refrigerate or freeze until serving time. Store in refrigerator or freezer. **16 servings.**

HIGH ALTITUDE—Above 3500 Feet: No change.

NUTRIENTS PER 1/16 OF RECIPE

Calories	540	Protein	20% U.S. RDA
Protein	11g	Vitamin A	10% U.S. RDA
Carbohydrate	53g	Vitamin C	<2% U.S. RDA
Fat	32g	Thiamine	10% U.S. RDA
Cholesterol	35mg	Riboflavin	10% U.S. RDA
Sodium	500mg	Niacin	20% U.S. RDA
Potassium	330mg	Calcium	20% U.S. RDA
Dietary Fiber	2g	Iron	8% U.S. RDA

Peanut Chocolate Parfait Dessert

Fudgy cake crust and fluffy peanut cream filling team up to make this heavenly dessert. Make it ahead and store in the freezer.

Microwave Honey Apple Cobbler

James Sloboden, Washington
Bake-Off® 32, 1986

4 cups thinly sliced apples
½ cup firmly packed brown sugar
1 teaspoon cornstarch
½ teaspoon cinnamon
2 tablespoons water
1 tablespoon lemon juice

CAKE

½ cup buttermilk*
¼ cup honey
2 tablespoons oil
1 egg
1 cup all purpose, unbleached or self-rising flour**
¼ cup firmly packed brown sugar
½ teaspoon baking soda
½ teaspoon ginger
¼ teaspoon baking powder
¼ teaspoon salt
¼ teaspoon nutmeg

MICROWAVE DIRECTIONS: In 8-inch (1½-quart) round microwave-safe dish or 2-quart round microwave-safe casserole, combine apples, ½ cup brown sugar, cornstarch, cinnamon, water and lemon juice; mix well. Cover with microwave-safe plastic wrap. Microwave on HIGH for 4 minutes or until apples are tender, stirring once halfway through cooking. Spread apples evenly over bottom of pan.

In small bowl, combine buttermilk, honey, oil and egg; blend until smooth. Lightly spoon flour into measuring cup; level off. Add flour and all remaining cake ingredients to buttermilk mixture.

Blend at low speed until well combined; beat 2 minutes at medium speed. Pour batter over cooked apples; tap dish on counter so batter settles evenly over apples.

Elevate dish on inverted microwave-safe dish or on shelf provided. Microwave on HIGH for 6 to 10 minutes, rotating dish ¼ turn every 2 minutes. Cake is done when toothpick inserted in center comes out clean and cake pulls away from sides of pan. Let stand on flat surface 5 minutes before serving. Serve warm or cold. If desired, top with whipped cream. Store in refrigerator. **6 to 8 servings.**

TIPS: *To substitute for buttermilk, use 1½ teaspoons vinegar or lemon juice plus milk to make ½ cup.

**If using self-rising flour, omit baking soda, baking powder and salt.

HIGH ALTITUDE—Above 3500 Feet: No change.

NUTRIENTS PER 1/8 OF RECIPE

Calories	260	Protein	4% U.S. RDA
Protein	3g	Vitamin A	<2% U.S. RDA
Carbohydrate	50g	Vitamin C	4% U.S. RDA
Fat	5g	Thiamine	8% U.S. RDA
Cholesterol	35mg	Riboflavin	6% U.S. RDA
Sodium	180mg	Niacin	4% U.S. RDA
Potassium	190mg	Calcium	4% U.S. RDA
Dietary Fiber	2g	Iron	10% U.S. RDA

Men win, too!

Food trend analysts report that more men are cooking these days, and they may be gaining greater confidence in their cooking skills as well. At the finals in 1986, there were more male prizewinners than at any other Bake-Off® Contest in history. Since 1949, there have been 128 male finalists, and twenty-three of them have been prizewinners.

Sour Cream Apple Squares

Grand Prize Winner

Sour Cream Apple Squares

ೂ☙

Luella Maki, Minnesota
Bake-Off® 26, 1975

**2 cups all purpose or unbleached
  flour**
2 cups firmly packed brown sugar
**¹⁄₂ cup margarine or butter,
  softened**
1 cup chopped nuts
1 teaspoon baking soda
1 to 2 teaspoons cinnamon
¹⁄₂ teaspoon salt
1 cup dairy sour cream
1 teaspoon vanilla
1 egg
**2 cups finely chopped peeled
  apples**

Heat oven to 350°F. Lightly spoon flour into measuring cup; level off. In large bowl, combine flour, brown sugar and margarine at low speed until crumbly. Stir in nuts. Press 2³⁄₄ cups of crumb mixture into ungreased 13×9-inch pan. To remaining crumb mixture, add baking soda, cinnamon, salt, sour cream, vanilla and egg; blend well. Stir in apples. Spoon apple mixture evenly over crumb mixture in pan. Bake at 350°F. for 30 to 40 minutes or until toothpick inserted in center comes out clean. Cut into squares. If desired, serve with whipped cream or ice cream.
12 servings.

HIGH ALTITUDE—Above 3500 Feet:
Bake at 375°F. for 25 to 35 minutes.

NUTRIENTS PER 1/12 OF RECIPE

Calories	420	Protein	6% U.S. RDA
Protein	5g	Vitamin A	10% U.S. RDA
Carbohydrate	58g	Vitamin C	2% U.S. RDA
Fat	19g	Thiamine	10% U.S. RDA
Cholesterol	30mg	Riboflavin	8% U.S. RDA
Sodium	300mg	Niacin	6% U.S. RDA
Potassium	270mg	Calcium	10% U.S. RDA
Dietary Fiber	1g	Iron	15% U.S. RDA

Ruby Razz Crunch

Achsa Myers, Colorado
Bake-Off® 8, 1956

Ruby Razz Crunch

Frozen rhubarb and raspberries bake into a delectable dessert garnished with a frozen raspberry-flavored whipped cream topping.

FILLING
10-ounce package frozen raspberries with syrup, thawed, drained, reserving syrup
16-ounce package frozen rhubarb, thawed, drained, reserving liquid
1/2 cup sugar
3 tablespoons cornstarch

TOPPING
1/2 cup whipping cream, whipped
2 tablespoons sugar
1 to 3 drops red food coloring, if desired

CRUST
1 1/4 cups all purpose or unbleached flour
1 cup quick-cooking rolled oats
1 cup firmly packed brown sugar
1 teaspoon cinnamon
1/2 cup margarine or butter, melted

Heat oven to 325°F. In measuring cup, combine reserved raspberry and rhubarb liquids. If necessary, add water to make 1 cup. In medium saucepan, combine 1/2 cup sugar and cornstarch; mix well. Stir in 1 cup reserved liquids. Cook over medium heat until mixture becomes thick and clear, stirring constantly. Remove from heat. Reserve 2 tablespoons of the raspberries for topping. Stir remaining raspberries and rhubarb into cornstarch mixture. Set aside.

Line cookie sheet with waxed paper. In small bowl, combine all topping ingredients and reserved 2 tablespoons raspberries; blend well. Make 9 mounds of topping mixture on waxed-paper-lined cookie sheet; freeze until firm.*

Lightly spoon flour into measuring cup; level off. In large bowl, combine flour, rolled oats, brown sugar and cinnamon; mix well. Add margarine; mix until crumbly. Press 2/3 of crumb mixture in bottom of ungreased 9-inch square pan. Spoon filling mixture over crumb mixture in pan; spread evenly. Sprinkle with remaining crumb mixture. Bake at 325°F. for 45 to 55 minutes or until crust is golden brown and filling bubbles around edges. Cool slightly. To serve, cut into squares; top each serving with mound of frozen topping.
9 servings.

MICROWAVE DIRECTIONS: In 4-cup microwave-safe measuring cup, combine 1/2 cup sugar and cornstarch; mix well. Measure reserved liquids as directed above; stir into cornstarch mixture. Microwave on HIGH for 4 to 4 1/2 minutes or until thick and bubbly, stirring once halfway through cooking. Reserve 2 tablespoons of the raspberries for topping. Stir remaining raspberries and rhubarb into cornstarch mixture. Set aside. Prepare topping as directed above.* Place margarine in medium microwave-safe bowl. Microwave on HIGH for 45 to 60 seconds or until melted. Add remaining crust ingredients; mix until crumbly. Press 2/3 of crumb mixture in bottom of 8-inch (2-quart) square microwave-safe dish. Spoon filling mixture over crumb mixture in pan; spread evenly. Sprinkle with remaining crumb mixture. Microwave on MEDIUM for 10 minutes, turning dish 1/4 turn halfway through cooking. Turn 1/4 turn; microwave on HIGH for 4 to 5 minutes or until filling bubbles around edges. Let cool at least 20 minutes before serving. Serve as directed above.

TIP: *If desired, topping can be prepared and served without freezing.

NUTRIENTS PER 1/9 OF RECIPE

Calories	440	Protein	6% U.S. RDA
Protein	4g	Vitamin A	25% U.S. RDA
Carbohydrate	70g	Vitamin C	8% U.S. RDA
Fat	16g	Thiamine	20% U.S. RDA
Cholesterol	20mg	Riboflavin	10% U.S. RDA
Sodium	220mg	Niacin	15% U.S. RDA
Potassium	240mg	Calcium	20% U.S. RDA
Dietary Fiber	3g	Iron	20% U.S. RDA

Ruby Razz Crunch

Chocolate Almond Frozen Mousse

Adelaide B. Shaw, New York
Bake-Off® 29, 1980

CRUST
1 cup all purpose or unbleached flour
½ cup ground almonds
½ cup firmly packed brown sugar
½ cup margarine or butter, melted

FILLING
4 eggs, separated
¼ cup milk
½ to 1 teaspoon almond extract
1 can ready-to-spread chocolate fudge frosting
1 cup whipping cream, whipped

Heat oven to 350°F. Lightly spoon flour into measuring cup; level off. In medium bowl, combine flour and all remaining crust ingredients; mix until crumbly. Spread in bottom of ungreased 13 × 9-inch pan. Bake at 350°F. for 10 to 15 minutes or until light golden brown, stirring once. Cool. Press 2 cups of crumb mixture in bottom of ungreased 9 or 10-inch springform pan or 9-inch square pan. Reserve remaining crumb mixture.

In small saucepan, slightly beat egg yolks; add milk. Cook over medium heat until thickened, stirring constantly. Remove from heat; stir in almond extract. In large bowl, fold egg yolk mixture into frosting. In small bowl, beat egg whites until stiff peaks form. Fold beaten egg whites and whipped cream into frosting mixture; pour over crumb mixture in pan.

Freeze 1 hour; sprinkle with reserved crumb mixture. Freeze an additional 3 to 4 hours or until firm. If desired, serve with whipped cream. **12 servings.**

NUTRIENTS PER 1/12 OF RECIPE

Calories	410	Protein	8% U.S. RDA
Protein	5g	Vitamin A	15% U.S. RDA
Carbohydrate	42g	Vitamin C	<2% U.S. RDA
Fat	25g	Thiamine	6% U.S. RDA
Cholesterol	120mg	Riboflavin	8% U.S. RDA
Sodium	210mg	Niacin	4% U.S. RDA
Potassium	210mg	Calcium	4% U.S. RDA
Dietary Fiber	1g	Iron	10% U.S. RDA

European Almond Crescent Cups

Debi Wolf, Oregon
Bake-Off® 31, 1984

¼ cup sugar
¼ cup ground almonds
3 tablespoons margarine or butter, softened
½ teaspoon almond extract
¼ teaspoon vanilla
1 egg, slightly beaten
8-ounce can refrigerated crescent dinner rolls
3 tablespoons apricot preserves or orange marmalade

GLAZE
½ cup powdered sugar
2 to 3 tablespoons orange-flavored liqueur or 3 to 4 teaspoons orange juice
8 candied cherry halves or whole almonds, if desired

Heat oven to 375°F. Grease 8 muffin cups. In small bowl, combine sugar, almonds, margarine, almond extract, vanilla and egg; blend well. Separate dough into 8 triangles. Place 1 triangle in each greased muffin cup; press dough to cover bottom and sides forming ¼-inch rim. Spoon about 1 tablespoonful of almond mixture into each dough-lined cup; spoon scant 1 teaspoonful of the preserves over almond mixture. Bake at 375°F. for 10 to 18 minutes or until edges of crust are deep golden brown. Cool 1 minute; remove from pan. In small bowl, blend powdered sugar and enough liqueur for desired drizzling consistency. Drizzle over cups. Garnish each with cherry half. **8 servings.**

NUTRIENTS PER 1/8 OF RECIPE

Calories	260	Protein	4% U.S. RDA
Protein	3g	Vitamin A	4% U.S. RDA
Carbohydrate	35g	Vitamin C	<2% U.S. RDA
Fat	12g	Thiamine	6% U.S. RDA
Cholesterol	35mg	Riboflavin	6% U.S. RDA
Sodium	300mg	Niacin	4% U.S. RDA
Potassium	100mg	Calcium	2% U.S. RDA
Dietary Fiber	1g	Iron	4% U.S. RDA

Appendix

⁂

Nutrition Information

To assist in planning healthful, wholesome meals, specific nutritional information is provided with each recipe. This unique NUTRI-CODED system, a computerized method designed by Pillsbury research scientists, utilizes information compiled by the U.S. Department of Agriculture in the revised Agriculture Handbook No. 8, and represents Pillsbury's strong, continuing commitment to nutrition education for the consumer. Every effort has been made to ensure accuracy of information; however, The Pillsbury Company does not guarantee its suitability for specific medically imposed diets.

The NUTRI-CODES for each recipe provide information on a per serving basis about:

calories, protein, carbohydrates, fat, cholesterol, sodium, potassium, dietary fiber, calcium, iron, and vitamins.

Protein, carbohydrates, fats, and dietary fiber are expressed in grams; cholesterol, sodium and potassium in milligrams. The amounts of vitamins, calcium, and iron are expressed as percentages needed by the body on a daily basis (U.S. Recommended Daily Allowance).

Guidelines to Use Nutrition Information:

SERVING SIZE: This has been determined as a typical serving for each recipe. If more or less is eaten, adjust nutrition information accordingly.

CALORIES: The amount of calories a person needs is determined by age, size and activity level. The recommended daily allowances generally are: 1800 to 2400 for women and children 4 to 10 years of age and 2400 to 2800 for men.

PROTEIN: The amount of protein needed daily is determined by age and size; the general U.S. RDA is 65 grams for adults and children of at least 4 years of age.

CARBOHYDRATE, FAT, CHOLESTEROL, SODIUM, AND POTASSIUM: Recommended Daily Allowances (RDA) for these nutrients have not been determined. The amounts of carbohydrates and fat needed in the daily diet are dependent upon daily caloric requirements. The amounts should be adequate so the body does not burn protein for energy. The American Heart Association recommendation for those who wish to restrict dietary cholesterol is for a daily intake that is less than 100 milligrams per 1000 calories and not exceeding a total of 300 milligrams.

DIETARY FIBER: Nutritionists recommend a dietary fiber intake of 20 to 35 grams per day from a variety of foods.

PERCENT U.S. RDA PER SERVING: For a nutritionally balanced diet, choose recipes which will provide 100% of the U.S. Recommended Daily Allowance for each nutrient.

Guidelines Used in Calculating Nutrition Information:

- When the ingredient listing gives one or more options, the first ingredient listed is the one analyzed.
- When a range is given for an ingredient, the larger amount is analyzed.
- When ingredients are listed as "if desired," these ingredients are included in the nutrition information.
- Serving suggestions listed in the ingredients are calculated in the nutrition information.
- When each bread recipe is analyzed, a serving of yeast-leavened bread is a 1-oz. slice and a quick bread serving is 1/16 of the loaf. Recipes that vary are indicated.
- Symbols used in relation to nutrition data:

  $<$ Less than 2% of the nutrient
  <1 Less than one gram (or milligram) of the nutrient

Any questions regarding nutrition information in this book should be addressed to:

The Pillsbury Company
Pillsbury Center—Suite 2866
Minneapolis, Minnesota 55402

Pillsbury Products Used in Bake-Off® Contest Recipes

DRY GROCERY PRODUCTS:

Canned Vegetables

Green Giant® Cut Green Beans
Green Giant® Mexicorn® Whole Kernel Golden
  Sweet Corn with Red and Green Sweet Peppers
Green Giant® Niblets® Whole Kernel
  Golden Sweet Corn
Green Giant® Sliced Mushrooms
Green Giant® Sweet Peas
Green Giant® Whole Kernel Golden Sweet Corn
Green Giant® Whole Mushrooms
Le Sueur® Early Peas

Flour

Pillsbury's BEST® All Purpose Flour
Pillsbury's BEST® Bread Flour
Pillsbury's BEST® Self-Rising Flour
Pillsbury's BEST® Unbleached All Purpose Flour
Pillsbury's BEST® Whole Wheat Flour

Frosting

Pillsbury Ready to Spread Chocolate Fudge
  Frosting Supreme
Pillsbury Ready to Spread Cream Cheese
  Frosting Supreme
Pillsbury Ready to Spread Milk Chocolate
  Frosting Supreme
Pillsbury Ready to Spread Vanilla Frosting Supreme

Mixes

Cake:

Pillsbury Plus Butter Recipe Cake Mix
Pillsbury Plus Dark Chocolate Cake Mix
Pillsbury Plus Devil's Food Cake Mix
Pillsbury Plus Fudge Marble Cake Mix
Pillsbury Plus German Chocolate Cake Mix
Pillsbury Plus Lemon Cake Mix
Pillsbury Plus White Cake Mix
Pillsbury Plus Yellow Cake Mix

Specialty:

Hungry Jack® Buttermilk Pancake
  and Waffle Mix
Hungry Jack® Buttermilk Complete
  Pancake Mix
Hungry Jack® Extra Lights®
  Complete Pancake Mix
Hungry Jack® Mashed Potato Flakes
Pillsbury Au Gratin Potatoes
Pillsbury Creamy White Sauce
  Scalloped Potatoes
Pillsbury Date Quick Bread Mix
Pillsbury Hot Roll Mix
Pillsbury Real Cheese Sauce Scalloped Potatoes

REFRIGERATED PRODUCTS:

Hungry Jack® Refrigerated Flaky Biscuits
Pillsbury All Ready Pie Crusts
Pillsbury's BEST® Refrigerated Sugar Cookies
Pillsbury Refrigerated Biscuits
Pillsbury Refrigerated Quick Crescent Dinner Rolls

FROZEN PRODUCTS:

Side Dishes

Green Giant® Rice Originals® Frozen Rice Medley

Vegetables

Green Giant® Frozen Broccoli Cuts
Green Giant® Frozen Cut Green Beans
Green Giant® Frozen Mixed Vegetables
Green Giant® Frozen Sweet Peas
Green Giant® Harvest Fresh®
  Frozen Chopped Spinach
Green Giant® Harvest Fresh® Frozen Cut Broccoli
Green Giant® Harvest Fresh®
  Frozen Mixed Vegetables
Green Giant® Harvest Fresh® Frozen Sweet Peas
Green Giant® Niblets® Frozen Corn
Green Giant® Valley Combinations®
  Frozen Broccoli Cauliflower Supreme

Index

F*resh* has been inspired by my friendship with Gary and Naty King, a local couple who have farmed organically on a four-and-a-half-acre plot of land in the Hazelmere Valley, just one hour south of Vancouver, for more than twenty years. When I first met the Kings about fourteen years ago, introduced by my chef Dennis Green, I was able to see and taste firsthand the incredible array of vegetables they grow. The flavour and quality of this produce, grown without the use of chemicals or pesticides, was far superior to what we had been buying for Bishop's to that point—and I was hooked. Little did I realize what an impact that first brief meeting would have on my outlook and on my restaurant.

Visiting Hazelmere Organic Farm changed my whole way of thinking about sourcing locally grown produce. More than ever before, I realized the importance of knowing where the food we consume comes from. Chefs are very busy people with little time to visit their suppliers personally to see what is available, fresh and in season. In the past, I, like other chefs, would get on the telephone and place my orders with wholesalers who could provide ready-peeled vegetables, pre-made salads, even cleaning fluids and paper products. Everything arrived in one convenient delivery.

The problem with this system is that I had no real idea where the produce was coming from, who had grown it and how far it had travelled.

Today, at Bishop's, we know all the growers and farmers who provide our food. Our menus are in harmony with the seasons and much of our produce is grown in the Hazelmere Valley, which is rich with clean water, abundant sunshine and, most of all, fertile soils. It is

A L HARVEY

located so close to city life, I marvel that the area is still able to support
not only this family, but a community of several other small farming
families. The soils are nurtured and protected by traditional farming
practices, such as composting, mulching, companion planting and
crop rotation, and wildlife abounds.

Over the years, our collaboration with the Kings has grown. In the
late fall or early spring, Bishop's chef Dennis Green and I sit down with
farmer Gary King to plan the crops that can be grown for us, and the
fruits and vegetables we might feature on the upcoming year's menus.
We have also started to give cooking classes at the farm. It's great to
get city dwellers to attend, to get them out into the country so they
can meet the farmers, experience firsthand what is growing and better understand the whole idea of seasonality. These classes are also an
opportunity for us, as chefs, to speak about our passion for food, to
tell the story of the partnership we have formed with the Kings and to
share how much we have learned from them about food production

on small plots like theirs. I call this "the circle"—we know the people who grow the food, and we usually know or get to know the people we cook it for.

The best part of this story for me is that the Kings and their organic farm—and the produce that they grow for us—have become the very underpinnings of my restaurant. In some ways, it feels like a return to my roots: my own father was an avid gardener, and we had a backyard garden. As a child I don't think I fully appreciated what that garden brought to us as a family, but I certainly remember fondly how it looked with flowers, vegetables and even hens with eggs.

This book is divided into three broad categories: spring and early summer—fresh and light, late summer and early fall—abundant and satisfying, and late fall and winter—hearty and comforting. The recipes within each section are inspired by the ingredients that these seasons bring to us. You will see there are lots of easy-to-prepare soups and salads, vegetable dishes, and rustic homemade casseroles and pies. Some of these foods I remember from my childhood.

Good food to me means shopping and seeking out the very best and freshest of seasonal ingredients, and then preparing them in as simple a way possible. Although this book highlights products from the Northwest, feel free to adapt the recipes using whatever you have in your local area. At Bishop's, we are fortunate to be able to buy directly from the growers. For my own home supply, I enjoy visiting area farmers' markets. These are exciting places and very reminiscent of marketplaces in Europe. Here you will find the kinds of ingredients that I like to cook with, and shopping this way also provides an opportunity to meet and connect with local farmers. I encourage you to go early in the day, as the more popular items sell out fast, and do not forget to bring your own shopping bag. Along the same lines, more and more people are planting community gardens, and these small plots on inner city land are capable of producing an extraordinary amount of fresh fruits and vegetables for local tables.

I hope these recipes and the stories that accompany them will give you a real sense of being in the garden, a feeling of being energized and inspired to create your own delicious dinners by using fresh and locally grown ingredients. Enjoy.

John Bishop

THE SUSTAINABLE KITCHEN

Sustainability is a much-used word these days. Throughout this book and in my culinary life, I find myself thinking about my actions and how sustainable they are. In hotel school I was taught the three C's of a kitchen, which are keep it *clean*, keep it *cool* and keep it *covered*. Now we should also include the three R's, which are *reduce*, *reuse* and *recycle*. These are words that we all should try to live by.

I try to avoid wasting food as much as possible by storing leftovers for later use. When I first started cooking, I cannot recall that there was aluminum foil or plastic wrap in anyone's kitchen. Now, however, we have become all too used to reaching for them. There are alternative ways to store food. A glass or ceramic or plastic container with a lid is recyclable even though it has to be washed with detergents and is, I think, better for our environment long term. Waxed paper or parchment paper held in place with elastic bands can also act as lids for bowls and be reused. Food scraps that cannot be stored go into the kitchen compost, which feeds my garden.

In my kitchen, I use clean tea towels in place of paper towels when mopping up messes or draining food. This cuts down on the amount of paper waste, though it does mean a few more items for the laundry.

When shopping for groceries, it is a good idea to take along your own reusable bags in order to cut down on the use of plastic bags. Also, I try not to use individual plastic bags to separate fruit and vegetables unless it's absolutely necessary, or I bring along some plastic bags from home to serve this purpose.

To help our environment, we can also cut out the use of harsh chemicals for cleaning, and instead seek out more natural yet effective cleaners such as borax, vinegar or ammonia. At the restaurant we use a biodegradable compound for cleaning wall tiles and other surfaces.

These are small actions, but if we all get involved I think we can make a noticeable difference to the world we leave for our kids.

COOKING TEMPERATURES

FOR MEAT AND POULTRY

W E recommend that you check the doneness of cooked beef, poultry, lamb and pork with an instant-read meat thermometer. Insert the thermometer into the thickest part of the meat, away from fat or bones, and read off the temperature. When the meat reaches the temperature specified in the recipe (or the temperature corresponding to the doneness you wish, see chart below), remove it from the oven and allow it to rest in a warm spot, such as beside the stove. Small steaks and roasts should rest uncovered, but a large roast or whole turkey will benefit from being covered lightly with aluminum foil. Resting times vary depending on the size of the meat, but allow about 5 minutes for small steaks and chicken breasts, 15 to 20 minutes for medium-sized roasts and 30 to 45 minutes for large roasts and whole turkeys.

This resting time is very important. Meat continues to cook once it is removed from the heat, as the temperature adjusts and the juices in the meat are redistributed, making the meat easier to carve and preventing all the juices from running out when cut. Depending on the size and shape of the piece of meat, its internal temperature will rise by an additional 5°F to 15°F once it is removed from the heat. We refer to this effect as "carry-over cooking," and it must be taken into account when calculating the desired doneness of the meat. As a rule of thumb, allow 5°F for individual steaks or chicken breasts, 10°F for medium-sized roasts or whole chicken or duck, and 15°F for large roasts such as a prime rib or whole turkey.

MEAT	TARGET TEMPERATURE (when removed from oven, before resting)	FINAL RESTED TEMPERATURE (after resting)
BEEF OR LAMB		
rare	110°F–120°F	125°F
medium rare	120°F–130°F	135°F
medium	130°F–140°F	145°F
medium well	140°F–150°F	155°F
well done	150°F–160°F	165°F
PORK		
medium	130°F–140°F	145°F
medium well	140°F–150°F	155°F
well done	150°F–160°F	165°F
DUCK		
medium rare	120°F–130°F	135°F
medium	130°F–140°F	145°F
medium well	140°F–150°F	155°F
well done	150°F–160°F	165°F
CHICKEN OR TURKEY		
boneless breast	155°F–160°F	165°F
whole bird	160°F–170°F	175°F

FRESH & LIGHT

SPRING & EARLY SUMMER

LATE SPRING AND EARLY SUMMER are an anxious time, a time of anticipation, when chefs and home cooks look to the food growers to see what exciting early-season produce they will bring to us. Farmers like Gary and Naty King from Hazelmere Farm will have planted almost one hundred thousand tiny seedlings in the hopes of producing a bumper crop of vegetables for the coming year. It is a sense of optimism that surrounds us at this time of year.

The words "fresh" and "light" best describe the recipes in this section. After the long winter, it is good to have such a range of ingredients to work with, including first-of-the-season ocean-caught fish, sweet early-harvest berries and tender, young vegetables. Menus include tempura zucchini blossoms stuffed with Dungeness crabmeat, salad greens lightly dressed and served with locally crafted artisan goat cheese or paired with freshly picked berries, braised fennel and greens, fresh asparagus tips and roasted fingerling potatoes, sablefish in mussel chowder and a brimming bowl of fresh seasonal fruits. As the weather brightens, it is an opportunity to begin cooking and eating outdoors—and a reminder that backyard barbecuing season is just around the corner.

TEMPURA ZUCCHINI BLOSSOMS

WITH DUNGENESS CRAB, MASCARPONE CHEESE
AND TOMATO VINAIGRETTE

TOMATO VINAIGRETTE

2 Tbsp olive oil

¼ cup shallots or onions, sliced

1 tsp minced garlic

1 cup diced tomatoes

¼ cup red wine vinegar

1 tsp liquid honey

½ cup olive oil

FILLED ZUCCHINI BLOSSOMS

1 Tbsp butter

¼ cup minced shallots

1 tsp minced garlic

1 cup mascarpone cheese

8 oz fresh Dungeness crabmeat

1 Tbsp chopped fresh parsley

12 zucchini blossoms
(each 4 inches)

WHEN the zucchini plants begin to flower in early summer, we are blessed with this seasonal treat. Anyone who has grown zucchini knows full well how prolific these plants tend to be. In order to limit the number of zucchini each plant produces, Gary King of Hazelmere Farm picks the early blossoms. They are wonderful stuffed, fried in a light tempura batter and served as an appetizer. For a vegetarian version, I sometimes substitute 1 cup of toasted pine nuts for the crabmeat in the filling. *Serves 4*

TOMATO VINAIGRETTE Heat the 2 Tbsp of olive oil in a medium saucepan on medium heat. Add shallots (or onions) and garlic and sauté until lightly coloured, about 5 minutes. Stir in tomatoes and cook on medium heat until soft, about 5 minutes. Remove from the heat, then add wine vinegar and honey.

Transfer the tomato mixture to a food processor or blender. Purée, adding the ½ cup of olive oil in a slow, continuous stream, until the vinaigrette is smooth. Strain through a fine-mesh sieve into a bowl, discarding any solids. Season with salt and pepper to taste.

FILLED ZUCCHINI BLOSSOMS Heat butter in a small saucepan on medium heat. Sauté shallots and garlic until tender, 2 to 3 minutes. Add mascarpone cheese and stir together until well combined. Transfer to a large bowl. Stir in crabmeat and parsley. Cover and refrigerate for at least 1 hour.

Place the crab mixture into a piping bag with a large plain tip. Open each zucchini blossom and fill ¾ full with the crabmeat mixture, twisting the end of the blossom to seal in the filling. Set stuffed blossoms on a baking sheet and refrigerate until needed.

TEMPURA BATTER   Preheat a deep fryer to 350°F. In a medium bowl, mix flour, cornstarch and salt. Add mineral water and whisk lightly until just combined.

Dip blossoms in the batter, one at a time, then remove and shake off any excess. Deep-fry blossoms until golden brown, 2 to 3 minutes. Place on paper towels to absorb excess oil and season lightly with salt.

TO SERVE   Drizzle 2 Tbsp of the vinaigrette on each of 4 plates. Top the vinaigrette with 3 blossoms and serve immediately.

TEMPURA BATTER

1 cup all-purpose flour

1 cup cornstarch

1 tsp salt

1¾ cups sparkling
   mineral water

SMOKED SOCKEYE
SALMON & LEEK TART

1 Tbsp butter

2 cups sliced leeks

one 9-inch tart shell, pre-baked

4 oz smoked salmon, chopped

1 Tbsp chopped dill

1 Tbsp chopped chives

2 cups light cream (or 1 cup
 milk + 1 cup whipping cream)

4 eggs

A QUICHE by any other name, this tart is a great way to use up little bits of smoked salmon left over from a cocktail party. Serve it as a breakfast or brunch entrée, a light lunch with a tossed salad or as the first course to a more formal dinner. At the restaurant, we sometimes make miniature versions in individual tart shells and serve them as an hors d'oeuvre. *Serves 8*

PREHEAT THE OVEN to 350°F. Heat butter in a large sauté pan on medium heat. Add leeks and sauté until tender, about 5 minutes. Transfer to the bottom of the tart shell. Top leeks with smoked salmon, dill and chives.

In a small bowl, whisk together cream (or milk and whipping cream) and eggs. Pour over the leek-salmon mixture. Bake for 45 minutes, until the top is puffed and golden. Cool slightly before serving.

TO SERVE Cut into 8 wedges and serve on individual plates.

GRILLED SPOT PRAWNS

WITH RICE NOODLE SALAD AND

SESAME-LIME VINAIGRETTE

ONE of my favourite Japanese dishes is sunomono salad, with its refreshing combination of noodles, light dressing and fresh shrimp. This recipe builds on that concept and makes a more substantial first course with similar characteristics. The sweetness of spot prawns (found in the Northern Pacific from California to Alaska) is balanced with a combination of honey, slightly acidic rice vinegar and mirin, a sweetened Japanese cooking wine. The contrast of the cool salad and warm prawns is a delight on a warm evening. *Serves 4*

5 oz rice vermicelli or
    bean thread noodles

Juice of 2 limes

¼ cup sesame oil

1 Tbsp liquid honey

2 Tbsp mirin

2 Tbsp rice vinegar

1 Tbsp vegetable oil for grilling

1 lb spot prawns, peeled
    and deveined, tail on

PLACE RICE VERMICELLI (or bean thread noodles) in a large bowl. Cover with boiling water and allow to stand for 10 minutes, until softened. Drain noodles in a colander and rinse well under cold water. Return them to the large bowl and set aside.

Using a whisk, combine lime juice, sesame oil, honey, mirin and rice vinegar in a small bowl. Add half of the vinaigrette to the noodles and toss well. Place ¼ of the noodle salad onto each plate.

Preheat the grill or barbecue to medium heat. Place vegetable oil in a small bowl. Toss prawns in oil and grill until they turn pink and are cooked through, 1 to 2 minutes per side.

TO SERVE Arrange 4 to 5 grilled prawns on top of the noodles on each plate. Drizzle with the remaining vinaigrette.

SMOKED SALMON

THESE delicious cakes are sushi with a twist! The rice cakes are made from the seasoned rice that is used in traditional sushi, mixed with a few sesame seeds and panfried until crisp. Here they're topped with smoked salmon to make canapés. Dress them up with garnishes of capers, pickled ginger or onion, or sprigs of dill. *Serves 6 (Yield: 12 cakes)*

1 cup sushi rice

1 cup water

2 Tbsp rice vinegar

1 Tbsp sugar

½ tsp salt

2 Tbsp sesame seeds

¼ cup vegetable oil for frying

4 oz thinly sliced smoked salmon

PLACE RICE IN a strainer and rinse well under running water. Drain, transfer to a medium pot with a lid, add the 1 cup of water and soak for 30 minutes. Bring to a boil on medium heat, then reduce to very low, cover and cook for 15 minutes. Turn off the heat and allow to stand for 10 minutes before lifting the lid.

While the rice is cooking, combine rice vinegar, sugar and salt in a small bowl.

Turn rice into a large bowl, add half the dressing and stir with a cutting and turning motion. Add the remaining dressing and continue to stir until rice has cooled to room temperature. Store at room temperature, covered with a damp towel, until you are ready to make the rice cakes.

Add sesame seeds to sushi rice and combine. Using a spoon, form rice into small cakes, each about 2 inches in diameter and ½ inch thick.

Heat vegetable oil in a nonstick pan on medium heat. Fry cakes until golden brown and crisp on both sides, 3 to 5 minutes. Drain on paper towels.

TO SERVE Top each cake with a small slice of smoked salmon and arrange on a serving platter.

SPINACH & NETTLE SOUP
WITH GOAT CHEESE AND HAZELNUT SWIRL

THIS early in the year, soup made from a combination of tender spinach leaves and some foraged tops of young nettles makes for a delicious and earthy-tasting treat that can be served either hot or cold. Both spinach and nettles are good sources of vitamins and minerals. Wild nettle purée is sometimes available in vegetarian whole food stores in the freezer department. If you are unable to locate nettles, a good substitute is watercress. We had a great deal of fun creating the goat cheese swirl; I particularly like the combination of lemon and chives with grated hazelnuts on top. Any leftovers can be used as a spread for toast or crackers. *Serves 4 to 6*

SPINACH AND NETTLE SOUP

- 4 packed cups nettle tops, washed
- 2 Tbsp butter
- 1 onion, chopped
- 2 cloves garlic, chopped
- 2 stalks celery, chopped
- ½ cup white wine
- 4 cups chicken or vegetable stock
- 2 cups whipping cream
- 1 large bunch spinach, washed and coarsely chopped

GOAT CHEESE AND HAZELNUT SWIRL

- ¼ cup soft goat cheese
- ¼ cup whipping cream
- 1 tsp lemon zest
- 1 tsp chopped chives
- ¼ tsp salt
- 2 tsp freshly grated hazelnuts

SPINACH AND NETTLE SOUP Place a steamer in a saucepan filled ¼ full with water. Bring the water to a boil on medium-high heat, place nettles in the steamer basket, cover tightly and cook for 5 to 6 minutes. Remove from the heat and allow nettles to cool. Drain nettle tops in a colander, shaking out any excess water. Transfer to a blender and purée. Set aside.

Melt butter in a stockpot on medium heat. Add onions, garlic and celery and sauté until tender, about 5 minutes. Add wine, chicken (or vegetable) stock and cream, increase the heat to medium-high and bring to a boil, then add nettle purée and spinach. Reduce the heat to low and simmer for 20 to 30 minutes, or until vegetables are tender. Season with salt and pepper to taste, then allow soup to cool for 15 minutes.

Transfer soup to a blender or food processor and purée until smooth.

GOAT CHEESE AND HAZELNUT SWIRL Place goat cheese and cream in a small bowl. Whisk together lightly until smooth and without lumps. Add lemon zest and chives and season with salt. Refrigerate for 5 to 10 minutes before serving to allow the flavours to meld.

TO SERVE Ladle hot soup into warmed soup bowls. Spoon 1 Tbsp of the goat cheese mixture into the centre of each bowl of soup. Top with grated hazelnuts.

CHILLED CUCUMBER BUTTERMILK SOUP

6 to 7 cucumbers,
  peeled and seeded

1 large sweet onion
  (such as Walla Walla)

4 cups buttermilk

3 to 4 Tbsp chopped fresh mint

Pinch of sugar

8 sprigs fresh mint, for garnish

THERE is nothing more refreshing on a hot day than a bowl of chilled cucumber buttermilk soup. The simplicity of the preparation and the combination of flavours make this recipe one of my absolute summer must-haves. *Serves 8*

PLACE A FINE-MESH sieve over a bowl.

Using a box grater, grate cucumbers and onion into a large bowl. Transfer the mixture to the sieve and allow to drain for 5 to 10 minutes.

Process drained vegetables in a food processor or blender until smooth. Strain puréed vegetables through the sieve, pressing out any excess liquid and discarding any solids. Whisk in buttermilk, chopped mint, sugar and salt to taste. Cover and refrigerate for 2 to 24 hours.

TO SERVE Ladle 8 oz of soup into each of 8 chilled bowls and garnish with fresh mint.

BUTTER LETTUCE SALAD

WITH STRAWBERRY VINAIGRETTE AND
TOASTED HAZELNUTS

During the course of the summer, we make a habit of preparing fruit vinegars and purées with the berries that come into season at different times. The fruit vinegars make delicious salad dressings that find their way into menus throughout the year. This recipe uses strawberry vinegar and olive oil for the vinaigrette, but feel free to use any combination of fruit vinegar and oil that you prefer. *Serves 4*

4 strawberries

¼ cup strawberry vinegar (page 57)

½ cup olive oil

½ tsp salt

2 heads butter lettuce, washed

½ cup toasted hazelnuts

Place strawberries and strawberry vinegar in a food processor. Purée, adding olive oil in a slow, continuous stream, until the vinaigrette is smooth. Season with salt.

Cut lettuce heads into quarters and place in a bowl. Add vinaigrette and toss until well covered.

To serve Place 2 lettuce quarters on each plate. Garnish each serving with 2 Tbsp of the toasted hazelnuts.

CUCUMBER SALAD

WITH SPICY SALSA

HAVE not always been the biggest fan of cucumber, even though I grew up in the land that is famous for its summertime cucumber sandwiches. This salad, however, is cooling on a hot summer's day. The tomatoes that I like to use in this recipe are the heirloom varieties grown by Milan Djordjevich from Stoney Paradise—they are sweet and juicy, just as real tomatoes should be. Serve this salad on individual plates or as a platter for the centre of the table. *Serves 6*

SPICY SALSA Combine salsa ingredients in a mixing bowl. Stir well to combine. Set aside.

CUCUMBER SALAD Arrange 10 to 12 cucumber slices on individual plates, overlapping each slice around the edge of the dish. Using 2 to 3 inner leaves arranged in the centre of each plate, create lettuce cups for the salsa.

TO SERVE Spoon 2 Tbsp of the salsa into each lettuce cup. Garnish the cucumber with freshly chopped chives.

SPICY SALSA

3 large, ripe field-grown
   tomatoes, finely diced

1 small red onion, finely chopped

1 clove garlic, pressed

1 jalapeño pepper, chopped
   and deseeded

2 Tbsp cilantro, coarsely chopped

1 Tbsp mint, coarsely chopped

2 Tbsp lime juice

3 Tbsp olive oil

1 tsp salt

CUCUMBER SALAD

1 English cucumber, washed,
   peeled and thinly sliced

1 head butter lettuce,
   leaves washed and dried

1 Tbsp freshly chopped
   chives, for garnish

MARINATED GOAT CHEESE

WITH SEASONAL SALAD GREENS

6 oz fresh soft goat cheese

1 tsp chopped parsley

1 tsp chopped thyme

1 tsp chopped rosemary

½ cup olive oil

4 cups seasonal salad greens
(such as arugula, watercress,
baby mustards or a mixture)

¼ cup aged balsamic vinegar

DAVID Wood from Salt Spring Island Cheese Company supplies us with fresh goat cheese all year long. In the spring and summer months we like to marinate his chèvre with herbs and olive oil and serve it on a seasonal salad with a light vinaigrette. This is a simple salad at its best, so buy the freshest greens you can find, give them a good soak in cold water and spin them dry in a salad spinner. Wrap the washed greens in a clean dry towel and allow them to crisp up in the refrigerator for the afternoon. *Serves 4*

CUT GOAT CHEESE into 4 even pieces. Roll each piece into a ball, then form it into a disk ½ inch thick. Transfer goat cheese discs to a shallow dish and sprinkle with parsley, thyme and rosemary. Cover with olive oil and refrigerate uncovered, allowing them to marinate for at least 2 hours. (The cheese can be prepared to this stage and refrigerated, covered, for up to 2 days.)

Wash and dry salad greens and place them in a large bowl.

Remove cheese from the oil and transfer to a plate. To the oil, add balsamic vinegar. Whisk together until well combined and set aside.

TO SERVE Divide salad greens among individual plates. Drizzle each serving with 1 to 2 Tbsp of the vinaigrette and top with a piece of goat cheese. Serve with a shake of freshly ground pepper.

TRI-TIP STEAK

BARBECUE DINNER

THIS inexpensive cut of meat from the sirloin part of the beef is usually available in the meat department on request. Also called just "tip steak" or "tip roast," it is lean, tender and great for barbecuing whole. Although this cut is very often sliced into small steaks and grilled, we use the whole piece for this particular dinner. After it has been barbecued, we allow the meat to rest. I would also recommend using a meat thermometer to check the temperature accurately. *Serves 6*

SPICE RUB   Combine all spice rub ingredients in a small bowl. Using a mortar and pestle or an electric spice mill, grind this mixture coarsely. Transfer to an airtight jar and store for 1 to 2 weeks in a cool pantry. This rub can be used to season other meats as well, such as chicken or pork.

SPICE RUB

1 Ibsp black peppercorns

1 tsp pink or green
   peppercorns

1 tsp dill seed

1 tsp fennel seeds

1 tsp coriander seeds

1 tsp yellow or brown
   mustard seeds

TRI-TIP STEAK   Preheat the oven to 375°F. Heat an ovenproof frying pan on medium heat. Add the 4 Tbsp of olive oil and potatoes, and season with rosemary, thyme and 1 tsp of the salt. Panfry gently until golden brown, about 5 minutes. Transfer to the oven and roast for about 40 minutes. Keep warm.

Prepare the steak while the potatoes are cooking. Preheat the barbecue to high heat. Coat steak on both sides with the 1 Tbsp olive oil and spice rub. Grill steak for 10 to 15 minutes per side, until nicely charred all over. Check for doneness with a meat thermometer: for rare meat, the internal temperature should be 125°F. For medium, cook 5 minutes more per side, or until the thermometer reads 145°F. Turn off the barbecue and transfer seared steak to a small ovenproof pan. Allow it to rest above the warm grill with the barbecue cover partially propped open (about an inch) for at least 30 minutes after cooking.

While the steak is resting, heat a skillet on medium heat. Add butter and onions and cook for 5 minutes, stirring occasionally. Reduce the heat to its lowest setting. Cover tightly with a lid and gently cook onions for 30 to 40 minutes. Season with the remaining salt.

TO SERVE   Thinly slice the steak on a diagonal across the grain. Arrange potatoes and onions on preheated plates, then top with 3 to 4 slices of steak.

TRI-TIP STEAK

4 Tbsp olive oil

2 lbs small new potatoes, scrubbed and halved

1 Tbsp chopped fresh rosemary and thyme

2 tsp salt

1½ to 2 lbs tri-tip steak whole roast

1 Tbsp olive oil

2 Tbsp spice rub

2 Tbsp butter

3 large sweet onions, in ½-inch slices

BARBECUED

LEG OF LOCAL LAMB

WITH MINT SAUCE

THIS lamb is delicious served with warm crusty bread, steamed and minted new potatoes, a simple green salad and an assortment of grilled vegetables. To prepare the vegetables, simply slice some zucchini, fennel bulb and ripe red bell peppers, drizzle with olive oil, season with freshly chopped mixed herbs, toss well, then grill lightly. Serve with a slightly chilled red wine such a Cabernet Sauvignon or a Merlot. *Serves 4 to 6*

MINT SAUCE

1 packed cup mint leaves, washed

½ cup sugar

¼ cup boiling water

½ cup red or white wine vinegar

BARBECUED LAMB

½ cup olive oil

1 sprig fresh rosemary, finely chopped

¼ cup finely chopped fresh basil leaves

2 to 3 cloves garlic, finely chopped

3 to 4 lbs boneless leg of lamb, trimmed of excess fat and butterflied

1 Tbsp salt

1 Tbsp coarsely ground pepper

1 Tbsp coriander seeds, toasted and ground

MINT SAUCE Place mint and sugar on a cutting board and chop together. Transfer the mint-sugar mixture to a small heatproof bowl and scald with boiling water. Allow leaves and sugar to steep for 5 to 10 minutes. Add wine vinegar and stir. Serve the sauce immediately or transfer it to a glass jar and refrigerate for up to 1 week.

BARBECUED LAMB Preheat the barbecue to medium-high heat. In a small bowl, whisk together olive oil, rosemary, basil and garlic until well combined.

Season lamb with salt, pepper and coriander. Place on the grill, skin side down, and brush the meat with half the herb-oil mixture. Sear lamb for 15 to 20 minutes. Turn the lamb over, placing it to one side of the grill and away from the direct flame. Brush the skin side with the remaining herb-oil mixture and cook slowly, with the cover down, for 30 minutes. Check for doneness with a meat thermometer: for rare to medium-rare meat, the internal temperature should be 130°F. Remove lamb from the grill, keep warm on the upper rack of the barbecue or in a warm spot beside it and allow to rest for 20 to 30 minutes before carving.

TO SERVE Place 3 to 4 thin slices of barbecued lamb on individual plates. Spoon 2 to 3 tsp of the mint sauce over each serving.

VENISON CHOPS

W E ARE fortunate to have a good supply of local fallow deer available from the Nicola Valley. The meat is quite tender and mild, and because it is much leaner than beef, it is at its best when served nice and pink. Game meats are always accented by bold flavours in a marinade or sauce, so juniper and rosemary are two of my favourite ingredients in any venison preparation. I like to serve these chops with freshly steamed vegetables and new potatoes. *Serves 4*

PLACE VENISON in a shallow dish. Combine juniper berries, garlic, rosemary, mustard seeds, fennel seeds, pepper and vegetable oil in a small bowl. Whisk until well combined, then pour over venison. Cover and refrigerate from 4 to 24 hours.

Preheat the grill or barbecue to medium heat. Remove venison from the marinade and brush off any excess oil to prevent it flaring up on the grill. Season lightly with salt.

Grill venison for 3 to 4 minutes per side for medium rare, or until cooked to desired doneness. Remove from the heat and allow to rest for 5 minutes before serving.

TO SERVE Arrange venison chops on a serving platter and decorate with rosemary branches.

2 lbs venison racks, frenched and cut into chops

1 Tbsp juniper berries

1 tsp garlic

1 Tbsp chopped rosemary

1 tsp yellow mustard seeds

1 tsp fennel seeds

1 tsp cracked pepper

1 cup vegetable oil

2 tsp coarse sea salt

3 to 4 branches rosemary, for garnish

(ON THE FARM)

GARY KING

photos by AL HARVEY

Hazelmere organic farm is a sustainable family-managed working vegetable farm that my wife, Naty, and I started more than 20 years ago in Surrey. The farm is more of a lifestyle choice than a for-profit-only business: we raise and harvest crops, but it's also a gathering place where we educate people about the food they eat and where it comes from and where we nourish our family, patrons and community.

On any given day, I might guide a school group on a walking tour of the farm; harvest a few of the 100+ varieties of vegetables, fruit, berries or culinary herbs that we grow; attend to a neighbour's needs at the farm-gate sales barn; put together an assortment of products for delivery to Bishop's Restaurant or walk with John in the garden as he prepares for a cooking class at the farm or elsewhere.

In the last week of February, as spring arrives in the Pacific Northwest, we are busy on the farm. We are turning under the fall rye and applying compost to enrich the soil and we're planting potatoes, lettuce, onions and leeks. When rhubarb starts to grow, we

begin to plant the peas. At this time of year, we are harvesting only kale buds, culinary herbs and leeks. Some of the best local fruits and vegetables still come from jars, cellars and freezers (last year's bounty canned, preserved or frozen) and we enjoy these until we start to harvest the first early-season crops.

In late April, after the first major outdoor planting, we fill the greenhouse once again with seeded flats. The work on the farm slows down for a few weeks, and there is time to visit friends and follow the routes that foods travel as they move from farm to plate. I like to drive the scenic, curvy road across the Sechelt Peninsula to Egmont, where Mario and Angie Agosti smoke salmon and gather wild mushrooms. John and I visit these friends as part of an agri-culinary tour, in which we learn about coastal products and share meals made with John's recipes and local fish from Gus and Dana Angus.

By late May, when backyard gardeners are starting their planting, we are harvesting the early-season lettuces, spinach, rhubarb and new potatoes and planting such heat-loving vegetables as tomatoes, corn, peppers and squash. The farmer's markets begin, and we start to see a dramatic increase in customers. I always look forward to this time, to sharing this food grown with love, effort and dedication and respect for the wilderness from which it comes, so that it can sustain our bodies and our communities.

PORK RACK BARBECUE

BRINED PORK

8 cups water

½ cup salt

½ cup brown sugar

Pinch of pepper

one 3-lb rack of pork

PORK is a favourite meat in our house. I like to cook small roasts from the rib, either a rack or rib-end roasts, which have the ribs cut off and tied back on. Either way, you get the best of both worlds: nice tender pork, brined overnight to keep it moist and to season it well all the way through, and a few ribs to nibble on afterwards.

Whenever you cook a roast or a larger piece of meat on the barbecue, it is important to use indirect heat. With a gas barbecue, the easiest way to do this is to turn one side of the barbecue on and place the meat on the other. With a charcoal grill you have to be a little more strategic and arrange the coals in a doughnut shape around the edge, allowing the heat to distribute evenly but keeping the direct flame away from the centre of the grill. Place the meat in the centre and cook with the cover down. *Serves 6*

BRINED PORK Place water, salt, brown sugar and pepper in a medium saucepan on high heat. Bring to a boil, turn off the heat and allow to cool completely.

Place pork in a deep container or a large resealable freezer bag and cover with brine. Refrigerate for 24 hours.

MAPLE SYRUP GLAZE Combine all glaze ingredients in a small bowl and whisk together until well combined. Set aside.

TO FINISH PORK Preheat the barbecue to medium heat. Remove pork from brine and pat dry with a clean tea towel.

Place pork on the barbecue over indirect heat. Using a basting brush, baste the top of the rack with 2 Tbsp of the glaze. Baste the top again in 15 minutes. After cooking for 30 minutes, turn pork rack over and baste again. Cook, basting every 15 minutes and turning pork over every 30 minutes, for 1 hour longer. Check for doneness on a meat thermometer: the internal temperature of the meat should be 140°F. Remove from the heat and allow pork to rest for 15 minutes before carving.

TO SERVE Cut the pork rack into individual chops and place on a serving platter.

MAPLE SYRUP GLAZE
½ cup maple syrup
¼ cup apple cider vinegar
1 Tbsp grainy Dijon mustard
1 Tbsp minced garlic
½ tsp freshly ground pepper
1 tsp fennel seeds, crushed

CHICKEN BREAST

WITH FRESH BREAD CRUMBS AND LEMON

½ cup all-purpose flour

1 egg, beaten

2 cups fresh bread crumbs

1 Tbsp chopped parsley

1 tsp lemon zest (reserve
the lemon for garnish)

4 chicken breasts,
boneless and skinless

¼ cup vegetable oil

CRISP chicken cutlets, or scaloppine, are a nice easy spring dinner. I like to put a bit of fresh lemon into the breading with some herbs, and serve with fresh lemon wedges on the side. An interesting salad with a simple vinaigrette and a loaf of fresh bread make great accompaniments. *Serves 4*

Place flour on a plate and egg in a small shallow bowl. Combine bread crumbs, parsley and lemon zest in another small shallow bowl.

Pound chicken breasts lightly to ¼ inch thickness. Season with salt and pepper. Dredge each chicken breast in flour, then in the beaten egg, then finally in the bread crumb mixture.

Heat vegetable oil in a large sauté pan on medium heat. Add chicken breasts and panfry until golden on both sides, about 5 minutes per side.

TO SERVE Drain chicken on paper towels and transfer to a serving platter. Chop the lemon into 8 wedges and set them around the platter.

> *Served with Yukon Gold Herbed Potato Dumplings (page 53)*

CHICKEN BURGERS

WITH SUNFLOWER SEEDS, CILANTRO AND GINGER

BEET KETCHUP

1 onion, diced

1 Tbsp minced garlic

2 cups red wine vinegar

1 cup sugar

3 cups cooked diced beets

CHICKEN burgers are a lot lighter tasting than beef burgers. These ones use Asian herbs and spices for lots of added flavour and sunflower seeds for a healthy crunch. Make sure the burgers are thoroughly cooked if you barbecue them. Serve with a tossed salad of mixed greens and watercress. *Serves 4*

BEET KETCHUP Combine all ingredients in a medium saucepan on medium heat. Bring to a boil, reduce the heat to a simmer and cook for 45 minutes, until vegetables are tender. Allow to cool slightly, transfer to a blender or food processor and purée until smooth. Transfer to an airtight container and refrigerate until cool.

This recipe makes 4 cups of beet ketchup. Will keep refrigerated in an airtight container for up to 1 month.

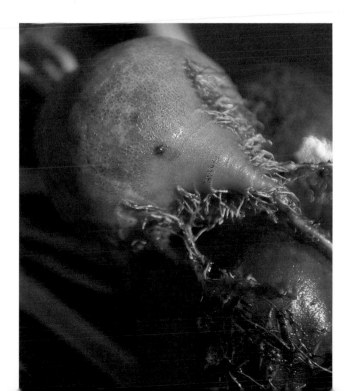

CHICKEN BURGERS Line a baking sheet with parchment paper.

Place chicken, sunflower seeds, green onions, ginger, cilantro and soy sauce in a large bowl and mix by hand until well combined (or combine using an electric mixer, if you prefer). Place a 4-inch ring mould or cookie cutter onto the baking sheet. Spoon enough of the chicken mixture into the mould (or cookie cutter) to fill it ½ inch full. Repeat until you have 4 equal rounds. The burgers can be covered and refrigerated for up to 3 hours.

Preheat the barbecue to high heat. Just before grilling, brush burgers with olive oil and season with salt and pepper. Reduce the heat to medium and grill burgers for 5 to 6 minutes per side. Check for doneness with a meat thermometer: the internal temperature of the meat should be 160°F.

If you prefer, these burgers can also be fried. Preheat a frying pan on medium heat, then add 2 Tbsp of oil. Place the burgers in the pan and cook until the bottoms are browned, 4 to 5 minutes. Turn them over and continue cooking until they are firm to the touch, another 5 to 8 minutes.

In a small bowl, combine mayonnaise and wasabi paste. Set aside.

Gently toast hamburger buns on the grill. Spread each half with some of the wasabi-mayonnaise mixture, then place a hot burger on the bottom half of each bun. Top the burgers with 1 Tbsp of the alfalfa sprouts, a dollop of beet ketchup, a few slices of pickled ginger and the top half of the bun.

TO SERVE Place 1 chicken burger on each plate. Serve immediately.

CHICKEN BURGERS

2 large free-range chicken breasts, boneless and skinless and coarsely ground (about 1¼ lbs total)

3 Tbsp husked sunflower seeds

¼ cup chopped green onions

1 tsp grated ginger

1 Tbsp chopped cilantro leaves

1 Tbsp soy sauce

2 Tbsp olive oil

½ tsp salt

½ tsp freshly ground pepper

¼ cup mayonnaise

1 tsp wasabi paste

4 hamburger buns, sliced in half

½ cup alfalfa sprouts

2 Tbsp pickled ginger

GRILLED CHICKEN BREASTS

WITH BRAISED GREENS
AND GRAINY MUSTARD VINAIGRETTE

CHICKEN BREASTS

4 boneless free-range chicken
  breasts (about 1½ lbs)
  skin removed

1 Tbsp extra-virgin olive oil

¼ tsp salt

¼ tsp pepper

WE EAT chicken at home at least once, if not twice a week. It also is very popular at the restaurant—in part, I am sure, because we try to only purchase free-range chicken, and from Thomas Reid farms when possible. The flavour of this chicken is very different from what you buy at the grocery store, and the meat is so rich and dense that you really don't need as much per person. In fact, one breast, sliced thinly, could feed two people. The braised greens with grainy mustard vinaigrette can also be served as an accompaniment to grilled spring salmon or fresh halibut.

Make the vinaigrette ahead of time. Once it's cooled, refrigerate it in an airtight container for up to three days. Whisk to blend the ingredients before you serve it. *Serves 4*

CHICKEN BREASTS Preheat the grill or barbecue to medium-high heat. Brush chicken breasts with olive oil, then sprinkle with salt and pepper. Place on the rack. Close the cover and grill, turning once, until browned and no longer pink inside, about 35 minutes. Check for doneness with a meat thermometer: the internal temperature of the meat should be 160°F. Remove to a plate and keep warm.

GRAINY MUSTARD VINAIGRETTE   In a small saucepan, combine wine, wine vinegar, shallots, mustard and honey on medium heat. Simmer, stirring occasionally, until reduced by half, about 15 minutes. Gradually whisk in olive oil, then set aside.

BRAISED GREENS   In a skillet, heat butter on medium-high heat. Add garlic and ginger and cook for 1 minute. Add chard, salt and pepper, then cover and cook until chard is wilted and tender, about 8 minutes. Drain off any excess liquid.

TO SERVE   Mound chard in the centre of each warmed plate. Top with a chicken breast and drizzle with 2 Tbsp of the vinaigrette.

GRAINY MUSTARD VINAIGRETTE

½ cup white wine

¼ cup white wine vinegar

1 Tbsp chopped shallots

1 Tbsp grainy mustard

2 tsp liquid honey

¼ cup extra-virgin olive oil

BRAISED GREENS

1 Tbsp butter

1 large clove garlic, minced

1 tsp minced ginger

1 bunch Swiss chard, destemmed

¼ tsp salt

¼ tsp pepper

THIS vegetable broth scented with Asian five-spice is an amazingly simple dish with very complex flavours. You can prepare the broth a few days ahead of time and store it in the refrigerator until you have time to buy a nice selection of fresh shellfish to cook in it.

Whenever you are using a variety of shellfish that have differing cooking times, begin by cooking those that will need the most time (such as clams and scallops), then add those that require less cooking a few minutes later (mussels and prawns). The variety of shell shapes adds visual interest to this dish and complements the array of textures and flavours that are present. *Serves 6 to 8*

FIVE-SPICE VEGETABLE BROTH Place all broth ingredients in a large stockpot on medium-high heat. Bring to a simmer and cook for 1 hour, until flavour is developed. Strain through a fine-mesh sieve, discarding any solids, and reserve.

HOTPOT Place broth in a large stockpot on medium heat and bring to a simmer. Add shellfish, starting with clams or swimming scallops, cover and cook for 2 minutes, add mussels or prawns, and cook for 2 to 3 minutes more. Using a slotted spoon, remove shellfish from the broth and divide evenly among serving dishes.

To the broth, add mushrooms and green onions. Bring to a simmer, remove from the heat and pour over the shellfish. Serve immediately.

FIVE-SPICE VEGETABLE BROTH

8 cups water

1 cup sliced onions

1 cup sliced carrots

1 cup sliced celery

2 cloves garlic, sliced

1 Tbsp chopped ginger

1 pod star anise

1 tsp whole cloves

1 tsp whole black peppercorns

1 tsp coriander seeds

1 tsp cardamom seeds

¼ cup soy sauce

½ cup white wine

HOTPOT

1 recipe five-spice vegetable broth

2 lbs mixed shellfish (such as clams, swimming scallops, mussels, prawns)

1 cup sliced shiitake mushrooms

¼ cup thinly sliced green onions

‹ *Served with Sticky Rice Parcels (page 52)*

BARBECUED SPOT PRAWNS

WITH WILD RICE CASSEROLE AND BRAISED FENNEL

WILD RICE CASSEROLE

3 Tbsp butter

1 cup finely chopped onions

1 cup finely chopped celery

1 cup wild rice, washed

3 cups fish or vegetable stock

1 tsp lemon zest

1 tsp salt

¼ tsp pepper

¼ cup finely chopped parsley

½ cup fresh or frozen peas

SPOT prawns have a very short season, only about two months, so most of them are frozen at sea immediately after being caught. They are one of the few seafoods that do not suffer from being frozen, and, to quote a fishmonger friend of mine, they are very often fresher tasting than fresh prawns that are stored on ice. In this recipe the seasoning is very basic—just fresh garlic and herbs—because we do not want to mask the sweet flavour of the prawns. Using two skewers for each brochette makes them easier to turn and prevents the prawns from slipping around.

Wild rice has evolved naturally over thousands of years in northern lakes. It is still harvested by aboriginal peoples and is considered wild and organic. As for the fresh fennel, occasionally you will see brown staining on the outside of the bulb, which indicates that it may not be very fresh. Fennel is expensive, so don't be tempted to remove the leaves; simply remove the stained bits with a peeler. You can prepare the rice and the fennel at the same time. *Serves 4*

WILD RICE CASSEROLE Preheat the oven to 375°F. Melt butter in a frying pan on medium heat. Add onion and celery and sauté until tender, about 5 minutes. Add rice, then stir in fish (or vegetable) stock, lemon zest, salt and pepper. Increase the heat to medium-high, bring to a boil, then remove from the heat. Transfer the rice mixture to an ovenproof casserole with a lid. Bake covered for 35 minutes.

Remove the casserole from the oven and add parsley and peas. Cover, then return to the oven and cook for 10 to 15 minutes, or until rice is tender.

BRAISED FENNEL BULB Preheat the oven to 375°F. Place fennel quarters into a medium bowl, then pour butter over them. Sprinkle with fennel fronds and season with salt. Toss lightly to coat well.

Transfer the seasoned fennel to a shallow roasting pan and cook for about 45 minutes, turning the vegetables occasionally until caramelized and tender. Remove from the oven, set aside and keep warm.

BARBECUED SPOT PRAWNS Preheat the barbecue to medium-high heat. Place 6 prawns side by side on a plate. Thread a single skewer through one end of each of these prawns to create a skewer with 6 prawns on it. Thread a second skewer through the other end of each of the 6 prawns. Repeat with the remaining skewers and prawns. Place the skewers on a baking sheet and brush both sides with olive oil. Rub the prawns with garlic and season with the herbs and a light shake of salt. Grill the prawns for 2 to 3 minutes per side, or until lightly charred and colour changes.

TO SERVE Mound 1½ cups of wild rice on each warmed plate. Top with a prawn skewer and arrange braised fennel around the edges. Garnish with a wedge of lemon.

BRAISED FENNEL BULB

1 lb fresh fennel bulb
  (1 large or 2 medium),
  cut in quarters, lengthwise

2 Tbsp melted butter

2 Tbsp chopped fennel fronds

1 tsp salt

BARBECUED SPOT PRAWNS

24 spot prawns (about 1¼ lbs),
  peeled and deveined, tail on

8 wooden skewers, soaked in
  cold water for 2 to 3 hours

¼ cup olive oil

2 cloves fresh garlic, crushed

2 Tbsp finely chopped mixed
  fresh herbs (such as basil,
  thyme, tarragon)

4 lemon wedges, for garnish

SPRING SALMON
ROASTED IN CORN HUSKS

HERB BUTTER

½ cup butter, softened

1½ tsp coarse salt

¼ tsp ground pepper

2 tsp chopped fresh chives

2 tsp chopped fresh basil

¼ cup chopped fresh parsley

SPRING SALMON

4 large ears corn

8 fillets spring salmon, boneless (each 2 oz)

4 lemon wedges, for garnish

THIS dish is fun to prepare. It is a North American version of cooking *en papillote,* which means "steamed in paper." I like the fact that we encase the salmon in corn husks so the sugars from the corn permeate the salmon and the fish steams in its own juices. It is not necessary to soak fresh corn husks—if you do, they tend to curl up and will be difficult to fill. Any salmon will work in this recipe, but spring salmon is preferable simply because it tends to be more moist.

When cooking the shucked corn on its own, I always follow the sage advice of farmer Gary King, who says to pick the corn only when your water has boiled. You can also serve this dish with steamed new potatoes. *Serves 4*

HERB BUTTER Combine butter, salt, pepper, chives, basil and parsley in a small bowl. Set aside and chill.

SPRING SALMON Preheat the barbecue to medium-high heat. Shuck corn, setting aside the whole cobs and reserving the husks. Remove and discard the silk from the husks. Set aside 3 to 4 of the inner husks and tear them lengthwise into ½-inch strips. These will be used to tie the salmon bundles together. Reserve 16 of the larger inner husks to use in bundling the salmon.

Lay out one inner husk with the top narrow part pointing away from you. Place a salmon fillet lengthwise onto the centre of the corn husk and dot with a generous tablespoon of herb butter. Place a second inner husk on top of the salmon and butter, tucking the sides around the salmon so that the bottom husk overlaps the top one. Fold over the top narrow part of the husks to seal in the salmon and tie in place with one of the inner husk strips. Fold over the bottom part of the husks and tie in

place with another of the inner husk strips. This will prevent the salmon juices from escaping. Repeat with the remaining husks and salmon fillets until you have 8 bundles. The salmon bundles can be made 3 to 4 hours ahead and refrigerated.

Place the salmon bundles on the grill but away from the flames, close the cover and cook for 15 to 20 minutes, turning the bundles once after 8 to 10 minutes. To check for doneness, remove one of the bundles from the grill. Untie one of the ends. If the salmon is firm to the touch and opaque in colour, it is done. Remove the remaining bundles from the grill. If the fish is not cooked, retie the corn husks and return the bundle to the grill for 5 to 6 minutes more.

To prepare the corn, fill a large stockpot with water and bring it to a boil on high heat. Turn off the heat, place the ears of corn into the hot water, cover the pot with a lid and allow the corn to sit in the hot water for just 5 minutes. Remove corn from the water, transfer to a serving platter and serve immediately.

TO SERVE Arrange the corn-wrapped salmon bundles on one platter and the freshly cooked corn on another. Garnish the salmon platter with lemon wedges. Have guests help themselves to 2 salmon bundles and one ear of corn.

PAN-ROASTED SABLEFISH
WITH MUSSEL CHOWDER

MUSSEL CHOWDER

2 cups water

½ cup white wine

2 sprigs thyme

1 clove garlic, crushed

1 lb fresh mussels, cleaned and beards removed

1 Tbsp olive oil

½ cup diced onions

½ cup diced celery

½ cup diced carrots

½ cup diced red bell peppers

1 tsp minced garlic

½ cup peeled and diced potatoes

½ cup whipping cream

1 Tbsp chopped parsley

SABLEFISH

4 fillets fresh sablefish, boneless and skin removed (each 6 oz)

1 tsp salt

2 Tbsp vegetable oil

SABLEFISH is one of those exceptional ingredients that makes cooking a pleasure. The flavour is delicate and the texture sublime, a reason it finds its way onto the menu all year long. I like to panfry fresh sablefish fillets on one side only, so that the top becomes crispy while the underside of the fillet remains delicate and soft. Although a chowder might seem like a heavy accompaniment, this is the lightest of seafood broths finished with a touch of cream and fresh parsley, accenting the beautifully sweet flavour of our local mussels. *Serves 4*

MUSSEL CHOWDER Place water, wine, thyme and crushed garlic in a saucepan on high heat and bring to a boil. Reduce the heat to medium-low and simmer for 15 minutes. Add mussels and cook until they just open, 3 to 5 minutes.

Remove from the heat. Use a slotted spoon to lift mussels from the cooking liquid and place them on a large platter or tray. Remove mussels from their shells and set meat aside. Discard the shells. Strain the cooking liquid through a fine-mesh sieve, discarding the solids, and reserve.

Heat olive oil in a medium saucepan on medium-high heat. Add onions, celery, carrots, bell peppers and minced garlic and sauté until onions are translucent and slightly softened, 5 to 7 minutes. Add the reserved mussel cooking liquid and bring to a simmer. Add potatoes, reduce the heat to medium-low and cook until vegetables are tender, 15 to 20 minutes. Stir in cream and cook for 10 minutes more. Season with salt and pepper to taste and keep the chowder warm on low heat, covered with a lid, while the sablefish cooks.

SABLEFISH Preheat the oven to 450°F. Season sablefish with
salt and set aside.

Heat an ovenproof sauté pan on medium-high heat, then
add vegetable oil. Place sablefish in the pan and cook on one side
until browned around the edge, 1 to 2 minutes. Transfer the
pan to the oven and cook for 5 to 7 minutes, or until fish is just
opaque in the centre.

Remove the pan from the oven.

TO SERVE Just before serving, stir parsley into the mussel
chowder. Ladle chowder into bowls, then top each serving
with a fillet of sablefish.

FINGERLING POTATOES

WITH LEMON THYME AND CHIVE FLOWERS

1½ lbs fingerling potatoes, washed and cut in half lengthwise

¼ cup olive or vegetable oil

2 Tbsp finely chopped lemon thyme

6 chive flowers, for garnish

THESE thumb-size white or red potatoes are similar to their little cousin, the new potato. They are very waxy and their flavour is buttery rich, which makes them a nice accompaniment to meat or fish. *Serves 6*

PREHEAT THE OVEN to 375°F. Place potatoes, olive (or vegetable) oil and lemon thyme in a bowl. Toss well, then season with salt and pepper.

Heat a frying pan on medium-high heat. Spoon potatoes into the hot pan and sauté until lightly browned, 5 to 6 minutes. Transfer potatoes to a roasting pan and cook for 20 to 30 minutes, until tender. Garnish with chive flowers.

HAZELMERE KALE BUDS

WITH ASIAN SOY-GINGER VINAIGRETTE

KALE buds form after the kale plant has fully matured, when it "goes to seed." It is the yellow seed that provides all of the goodness. Kale contains the highest levels of beta-carotene of any green vegetable. It is high in vitamin C and has lots of calcium as well. Best of all, kale is delicious.

Kale buds can be found in produce markets in the early spring. I love cooking and eating these tasty buds, especially after they have had a touch of winter frost (the frost makes them really sweet.) Cooked this way, kale buds make a good accompaniment to roast chicken or seafood and they are wonderful served on their own as a first course, like a warm salad. *Serves 4*

¼ cup rice vinegar

1 Tbsp soy sauce

1 tsp grated ginger

¼ cup sesame oil

4 cups kale buds, freshly washed

PLACE RICE VINEGAR, soy sauce and ginger in a small bowl. Whisk until well combined.

Heat sesame oil in a frying pan on medium heat. Add kale buds and sauté for 2 to 3 minutes. Add the soy-ginger vinaigrette and toss lightly to wilt the kale. Serve immediately.

STICKY RICE PARCELS

3 cups cooked Japanese
rice, cooled

6 sheets rice paper
(each 8 inches square)

6 wild lime (kaffir lime) leaves

2 Tbsp vegetable oil

RICE paper is easily found in almost any Asian food store. There are many brands available but they're all made with rice, water and salt and you can use any of them. A popular brand is Bánh Tráng. Since the translucent sheets must be immersed in simmering water before using them, these parcels must be assembled one at a time. They are a great side dish with fish. *Serves 6*

PLACE A WIDE pan of simmering water on very low heat. Slide 1 sheet of rice paper into the water and allow to simmer for about 20 seconds, until pliable. Using metal tongs, transfer the softened rice paper to a clean, dry work surface. Lay a lime leaf in the centre of the sheet. Gently press ½ cup rice on top of the leaf, forming a 2 × 4-inch rectangle.

Fold the bottom and top edges of the rice paper over the filling (they will meet in the middle), then fold in the sides as if you were wrapping a gift. The rice paper will stick to itself to seal the parcel. Repeat with the remaining rice paper and filling ingredients until you have 6 parcels.

Place 2 Tbsp of the vegetable oil in a wide shallow nonstick pan on medium heat. Arrange rice parcels in the pan in one layer (cook them in two batches, if necessary) and panfry on one side until crispy and brown, about 4 minutes. Gently turn parcels over and sear for another 4 minutes, until browned, crisp and heated through. Keep cooked parcels warm in a 300°F oven, if need be, until served.

POTATO DUMPLINGS

THESE delicious little dumplings are really worth the effort. When I make them at home, it is usually a family affair, with one or more of my kids helping me to roll out the dough. The dumplings are very tasty as a vegetarian option served with a fresh tomato sauce, or as a side dish to accompany barbecued meat. *Serves 4*

1 lb Yukon Gold
  potatoes, unpeeled

1 egg

1½ cups all-purpose flour

2 Tbsp finely chopped mixed
  fresh herbs (such as rosemary,
  basil, thyme)

1 tsp salt

2 Tbsp vegetable oil

2 cloves garlic, peeled
  and chopped

PLACE POTATOES in a large saucepan of water on medium-high heat. Boil potatoes until cooked, 25 to 30 minutes. Drain, then allow to cool to room temperature. Peel potatoes, discarding the peels. Mash potatoes well or put through a potato ricer, removing any lumps. Stir in egg, flour, mixed herbs and salt, until well combined. Form the mixture into a smooth ball of dough.

Lightly dust a baking sheet and a clean, dry work surface with flour. Divide the dough into four equal parts. Form each piece of dough into a log 12 to 14 inches long and ¾ inch in diameter. Cut each log into 1-inch slices. Place the rounds on the tray.

Line another baking sheet with waxed paper and fill a large bowl with ice cold water. Fill a large pot ¾ full with salted water and bring it to a simmer on medium-high heat. Place the rounds, 1 log's worth at a time, into the pot. Cook until they float to the surface, 4 to 5 minutes. Using a slotted spoon, transfer the cooked dumplings to the bowl of ice water and allow them to cool for 2 minutes. Transfer the cooled dumplings to the wax-papered baking sheet. Repeat with the remaining rounds, until all the dumplings are cooked and cooled.

Heat vegetable oil in a large frying pan on medium-high heat. Add dumplings and garlic and season lightly with salt and pepper. Panfry until golden brown on all sides, 8 to 10 minutes, and serve.

STEAMED ASPARAGUS

WITH ORANGE BUTTER SAUCE

NOTHING says spring quite like freshly steamed asparagus. The first asparagus spears arrive in the market just after the peak of citrus season, so we like to combine the two flavours as an homage to spring. This asparagus can be served as a course unto itself, like a warm salad, or as a side dish to accompany grilled meats or seafood.

Tradition has it that asparagus stems should be peeled, which is especially important if the spears are thicker than your finger. Use a vegetable peeler, but don't use too much pressure while peeling or you will trim away more than just the fibrous outer layer. If the chives in your garden are flowering, sprinkle some of the flower petals over the finished dish. *Serves 4*

½ cup fresh orange juice

½ cup butter, in ½-inch cubes

1 lb asparagus spears, woody ends trimmed

¼ tsp salt

2 Tbsp chive flower petals, for garnish (optional)

PLACE ORANGE JUICE in a small saucepan on medium heat and bring to a simmer. Cook until reduced by half, 3 to 5 minutes. Whisk in butter, 1 cube at a time, until well incorporated.

Place a bamboo steamer over a large saucepan on high heat. When water is simmering, place asparagus in the steamer and cook until tender, 3 to 5 minutes.

TO SERVE Divide asparagus among plates, sprinkle lightly with salt and top each serving with 1 Tbsp of the sauce. Garnish with chive flower petals.

‹ *Shown with Roasted Fingerling Potatoes with Lemon Thyme and Chive Flowers (page 50)*

MAKING FRUIT PURÉES AND VINEGARS

FRUIT PURÉE
2 lbs fresh fruit or berries

FRUIT VINEGAR
1 cup berry seeds and pulp

3 cups white or red wine vinegar

D URING the summer, when berries and other fruits are abundant, is the perfect time to preserve some for the winter. Fruit purées are best made with soft fruits or berries that do not require cooking to become soft enough to purée. We freeze the strained purées in amounts small enough to use in a single recipe (about 2 cups). Purées will keep frozen in an airtight container for up to 1 year.

Instead of discarding the strained seeds and pulp, we use them to make fruit vinegars. Depending on the fruit you are using for the vinegar, you may choose either red or white wine vinegar. I prefer to use red wine vinegar for darker, more robust fruits such as raspberries and blackberries and white wine vinegar for lighter fruits such as strawberries. Refrigeration is not necessary to preserve fruit vinegars, as the vinegar has a residual acidity that makes them shelf stable. We have found, however, that refrigerating fruit vinegars prevents them from browning over time.

FRUIT PURÉE Wash fruit (or berries). Remove and discard any thick skins, large pits and stems. Transfer fruit (or berries) to a food processor and purée until smooth. Strain the purée through a fine-mesh sieve, reserving the pulp and seeds to make fruit vinegar. This recipe should make 4 cups. Divide purée evenly into 2 individual airtight containers and freeze until needed, up to 1 year.

FRUIT VINEGAR Place seeds and pulp in a large glass jar with a lid and cover with vinegar. Refrigerate with the lid on for at least 1 month. This recipe will make about 3 cups. Strain through a fine-mesh sieve as needed.

BUTTERMILK PANNA COTTA
WITH ORANGE AND DRIED CRANBERRY COMPOTE

ORANGE AND DRIED CRANBERRY COMPOTE

2 cups orange juice

2 cups water

1 cup sugar

1 cinnamon stick

2 whole cloves

1 whole allspice berry

Pinch of nutmeg

2 cups dried cranberries

BUTTERMILK PANNA COTTA

2 cups whipping cream

¾ cup sugar

½ vanilla bean, split and
seeds removed

7 sheets gelatin, softened
in cold water

2½ cups buttermilk

PANNA cotta is an eggless Italian custard thickened with gelatin. It is silky smooth and its subtle flavour complements this tart compote. Dried cranberries are easily available year-round and are a good choice when fresh berries are not yet available.

Silicone moulds are ovenproof, and freezer and dishwasher safe. They're available at most kitchen supply stores and come in many different shapes and sizes. Since silicone moulds are very flexible, place them on a baking sheet before filling them. *Serves 12*

ORANGE AND DRIED CRANBERRY COMPOTE Place orange juice, water, sugar, cinnamon, cloves, allspice and nutmeg in a medium saucepan on medium heat. Bring to a boil. Add cranberries and simmer, covered, for 5 minutes. Remove from the heat and allow to cool to room temperature.

Refrigerate, covered, overnight before serving.

BUTTERMILK PANNA COTTA Place cream, sugar and vanilla bean seeds in a large saucepan on medium heat. Scald for about 7 minutes, or until simmering. Add gelatin and stir until dissolved, then stir in buttermilk.

Pour the panna cotta mixture into 2-inch round silicone moulds and refrigerate until set, about 30 minutes. Once the panna cotta is set, cover the moulds with plastic wrap and freeze for 8 hours.

Three hours before serving, unwrap the frozen panna cottas, flex the moulds to loosen the panna cottas and invert them onto a serving tray or baking sheet. Allow to defrost in the refrigerator.

TO SERVE Using an offset spatula, gently place panna cottas onto individual plates and garnish each serving with ½ cup of the fruit compote.

STRAWBERRY
RHUBARB FOOL

1 cup rhubarb, sliced

½ cup sugar

½ cup water

1 cup fresh strawberries, hulled

2 cups whipping cream

AS SPRING rhubarb season is finishing, strawberry season is just beginning. This quick and easy recipe is perfect for that time, and results in a dessert that is a lovely shade of pink. *Serves 8*

PLACE RHUBARB, sugar and water in a small pot on medium heat. Bring to a boil, reduce the heat to low and simmer, covered, until tender, about 20 minutes. Add strawberries and cook for 5 minutes more, until softened.

Transfer the fruit mixture to a food processor and purée. Pour into a bowl and set aside to cool slightly. Cover and refrigerate for 20 minutes.

Place cream in a mixing bowl and whip until stiff peaks form. Gently fold whipped cream into chilled purée.

TO SERVE Spoon ½ cup of the fool into each serving dish. Chill until needed or for up to 8 hours.

RICE PUDDING

WITH RHUBARB COMPOTE

THIS delicious rice pudding is served chilled. It appears light but is really rather decadent. The sweetened whipped cream is optional, as is the caramelization.

Pearl rice is short-grain rice, also called glutinous rice. It has a high starch content, and the grains are fat and round. It makes a very creamy pudding.

RHUBARB COMPOTE   Place compote ingredients in a small saucepan on medium heat. Simmer, covered, until tender, 25 to 30 minutes. Serve it warm or cold. Will keep refrigerated in an airtight container for up to 4 days.

RICE PUDDING   Place rice, milk, 1 cup of the cream, the ¼ cup + 2 Tbsp of granulated sugar, butter, vanilla bean and salt in a medium saucepan on medium-low heat. Simmer, uncovered, until rice is tender, about 45 minutes. Remove the vanilla pod. Transfer the pudding to a bowl, then cover with a lid and refrigerate for 1 hour, or until chilled.

If desired, place 1 cup of the cream and the 2 Tbsp of granulated sugar in a mixing bowl and whip until soft peaks form. Gently fold whipped cream into the chilled pudding.

Spoon ¾ cup of the pudding into each of eight 3-inch ring moulds or gratin dishes. Sprinkle brown sugar evenly over the individual puddings. If desired, caramelize sugar either by using a propane or butane torch, or by placing the moulds (or dishes) under the broiler just until the sugar melts and is golden.

TO SERVE   Spoon compote over pudding and serve.

RHUBARB COMPOTE

2 cups rhubarb, sliced

1 cup sugar

Zest of 1 orange

RICE PUDDING

½ cup pearl rice

3½ cups homogenized milk

1 cup whipping cream

¼ cup + 2 Tbsp granulated sugar

¼ cup butter

1 vanilla bean, split
   and seeds removed

Pinch of salt

1 cup whipping cream
   (optional)

2 Tbsp granulated sugar
   (optional)

¼ cup brown sugar

FRUIT SALAD BOWL

WITH GRANOLA TOPPING

IMAGINE a bowl brimming with locally harvested fresh fruits and berries so naturally juicy, ripe and sweet that all they require is to be cut up and lightly tossed with just a hint of fresh chopped mint. You just arrange the mixture in one of your best bowls and serve. Certain varieties of apples and pears will go brown shortly after cutting, so when I make this salad I usually cut those fruits last, then toss them into the mix.

This topping is the best-ever granola recipe from Lisa Miki, our former pastry assistant. On its own, it's an excellent breakfast with a bit of milk or a perfect mid-day snack.

Leftover fruit salad can be made into a galette by simply placing the cut fruit onto the middle of a dinner plate–sized pastry disc, folding up the sides of the pastry to encase it, and baking the filled pastry in a 400°F oven until golden. *Serves 4*

GRANOLA Preheat the oven to 350°F. Line two baking sheets with parchment paper.

In a large bowl, combine oatmeal, oat bran, flax, almonds, pumpkin seeds, cinnamon and cardamom.

In a large bowl, mix together honey, apple juice and vanilla extract. Stir the honey mixture into the oatmeal mixture and toss to combine. Spread granola on baking sheets, then bake for 30 to 40 minutes, stirring occasionally. Remove from the oven and allow to cool. Add dried fruit. Will keep in an airtight container for up to 2 weeks at room temperature.

Recipe continued overleaf...

GRANOLA

5 cups large-flake oatmeal

½ cup oat bran

¼ cup milled flax

½ cup sliced almonds

½ cup raw, hulled pumpkin seeds

½ tsp ground cinnamon

½ tsp ground cardamom

½ cup liquid honey

½ cup apple juice

1 tsp vanilla extract

1 cup mixed dried fruit (such as cherries, cranberries, raisins, diced apricots)

FRUIT SALAD

3 peaches, pitted and
cut in eighths

6 apricots, pitted and
cut in quarters

6 plums, pitted and cut in
quarters

1 cup cherries, pitted

2 cups strawberries, sliced

2 cups whole red and
green grapes

2 cups honeydew melon, peeled
and cut in large chunks

¼ cup chopped mint leaves

Juice of 1 orange

2 apples

2 pears

1 cup fresh berries (such as
raspberries, blueberries
and/or red currants)

4 sprigs fresh mint, for garnish

FRUIT SALAD Combine peaches, apricots, plums, cherries, strawberries, grapes and melon in a large fruit bowl. Add chopped mint
and orange juice, toss well and refrigerate for up to 3 hours.

Just before serving, wash and core the apples and pears. Cut
each fruit into eighths and toss together with the rest of the fruit
salad. Scatter berries on top to add to the wonderful array of
colours in the bowl. Garnish with sprigs of fresh mint.

TO SERVE Ladle fruit salad into individual bowls and top each
serving with 2 Tbsp of the granola.

THIS sorbet is tart verging on sour, and spicy from the liberal use of fresh ginger. *Serves 16 (Yield: about 8 cups)*

IN A MEDIUM saucepan, combine water, sugar and glucose (or corn syrup) on medium heat until sugar dissolves. Increase the heat to medium-high and bring to a rapid boil. Add ginger and allow to boil for 2 minutes. Remove from the heat and set aside to infuse for about 1 hour.

Stir in lime juice and allow to cool completely. Strain through a fine-mesh sieve into an airtight 8-cup container. Chill for 4 hours.

Process in an ice cream maker according to the manufacturer's directions. Will keep in the freezer in an airtight container for up to 2 weeks.

TO SERVE Remove the sorbet from the freezer and allow to sit at room temperature for about 10 minutes. Using an ice cream scoop warmed in hot water, scoop one ball of sorbet into each chilled cocktail glass or small dish.

3 cups water

2 cups sugar

2½ oz glucose or white corn syrup

two 3-inch pieces fresh ginger, peeled and thinly sliced

2¾ cups freshly squeezed lime juice

STRAWBERRY SOUP
WITH FROZEN YOGURT

THIS beautifully coloured soup makes a lovely first course or a light, refreshing dessert, especially served with frozen yogurt, a tangy and bright-tasting alternative to vanilla ice cream. For a softer texture, temper frozen yogurt in the refrigerator for about half an hour before serving. This recipe makes 8 cups of frozen yogurt. *Serves 16*

FROZEN YOGURT

2 cups whole milk

2 cups light cream

1 vanilla bean (optional)

¾ cup sugar

9 egg yolks

4 cups plain, unsweetened yogurt

FROZEN YOGURT Heat milk and cream in a medium saucepan on medium heat and bring to a simmer. Slice vanilla bean in half lengthwise, scrape out seeds and add them to the cream mixture, discarding pod.

While the cream mixture is heating, whisk together sugar and egg yolks in a stainless steel bowl until pale yellow and thick. Carefully whisk ½ cup of the cream mixture into the yolk mixture to temper it. Gradually add the rest of the cream mixture.

Place the custard in a saucepan on medium heat, stirring constantly, until the mixture is thick enough to coat the back of a spoon. Strain custard through a fine-mesh sieve into a medium bowl. Discard any solids. Stir in yogurt, then refrigerate for 4 hours.

Process in an ice cream maker according to the manufacturer's directions. Will keep in the freezer in an airtight container for up to 2 weeks.

STRAWBERRY SOUP Combine strawberries, water, wine and sugar in a medium saucepan on medium-low heat. Bring to a simmer and cook until the strawberries burst, 10 to 15 minutes. Remove from the heat and allow to cool.

   Strain soup through a fine-mesh sieve into a medium bowl, pressing the berries gently with the back of a spoon to push the pulp through but leave the seeds behind. Discard the seeds. Stir in balsamic vinegar and yogurt. Refrigerate, covered, for about 4 hours.

TO SERVE Ladle 1 cup of soup into each bowl and garnish with a scoop of frozen yogurt.

STRAWBERRY SOUP

2 cups strawberries

1½ cups water

½ cup red wine

½ cup sugar

1 Tbsp balsamic vinegar,
   or to taste

¾ cup plain yogurt

ABUNDANT & SATISFYING

LATE SUMMER & EARLY FALL

LATE SUMMER TO EARLY FALL is the most splendid time for cooks, with so much abundance, so much to cook with and enjoy. When we harvest the summer bounty, it is also a time when we think about such country traditions as canning and preserving, so we can savour the produce from these long summer days all winter long.

Here you will find recipes for harvest-ripe green figs gently wrapped in pastry, stuffed with local blue cheese and then drizzled with saffron honey, and naturally sweet heirloom tomato soup with fresh sage and apple biscuits. There are also barbecued porterhouse steak and a whole Dungeness crab feast with pickled ginger mayonnaise, plus lighter dishes such as summer vegetable galettes served with roasted tomato sauce. Desserts reflect the tree-fruit harvests, with cider-poached Asian pears, oven-roasted fruits with local cheeses and all kinds of summer pie variations. This truly is my favourite time of the year.

FRESH FIGS

BAKED IN PUFF PASTRY WITH BLUE CHEESE
AND SAFFRON HONEY

1 cup liquid honey

Large pinch of saffron

½ lb puff pastry

1 egg, beaten

12 fresh figs

4 oz blue cheese,
    in 12 pieces

THE inspiration for this dish came a few years ago when my Italian neighbour gave me a fig tree to plant in my garden, along with a basket of fresh figs from that year's harvest. Figs have an uncanny way of ripening all at once, so we look forward to the week in August when we can make this dish. The figs on my tree are the large green figs, but you can substitute black Mission figs, which are a bit smaller and firmer but will work just as well. *Serves 12 as an hors d'oeuvre, 4 as an appetizer*

PLACE HONEY in a small saucepan on medium heat. Bring to a boil, add saffron, then stir and remove from the heat. Cool to room temperature.

Strain the spiced honey through a fine-mesh sieve into a small bowl. Discard solids. Will keep refrigerated in an airtight container indefinitely.

On a clean, dry work surface, roll out puff pastry into an 8-inch square, about ⅛ inch thick. Using a sharp knife, cut into strips ½ inch wide and brush the tops with beaten egg.

With a sharp knife, cut an X into the stem end of each fig, reaching about ⅔ of the way through each fruit. Stuff the incision with a piece of blue cheese. Place a fig at one end of a pastry strip. Wind the pastry around the fruit, starting at the bottom and working towards the top, slightly overlapping each turn so the entire fig is covered with pastry. Pinch the end of the pastry to secure it. Repeat with the remaining figs and pastry strips. Place wrapped figs on a baking sheet and refrigerate for 1 hour, or until pastry is chilled.

Preheat the oven to 400°F. Bake figs until pastry is golden and crisp, 10 to 15 minutes. Pour the honey into a jug.

TO SERVE Transfer the figs to a serving platter or place 3 wrapped figs on each plate. Drizzle with saffron honey.

SALMON FRITTERS

WITH GREEN ONIONS, GINGER
AND CITRUS MAYONNAISE

WHEN cutting fillets of salmon into dinner-size portions, there is usually a bit of trimmed fish left over, and it's always nice to find a way to make something delicious with it. This fritter recipe is inspired by a Southeast Asian dish I saw that was prepared with whitefish and prawns. You can certainly substitute a different fish for the salmon if you like, but try to avoid using anything too firm, such as tuna, as it will have a tendency to dry out. If you want to serve these fritters as an hors d'oeuvre, make them smaller by using a teaspoon instead of a tablespoon to form them. *Serves 4 as an appetizer (Yield: 12 fritters)*

CITRUS MAYONNAISE In a small bowl, whisk together lemon juice, lime juice, orange juice, mayonnaise and cayenne pepper. Will keep refrigerated in an airtight container for 2 to 3 days.

SALMON FRITTERS Heat a deep fryer to 350°F. Place salmon in a food processor with green onions, ginger, lemon juice and egg whites. Season with salt and pepper. Pulse until well minced.

Using two tablespoons, roughly form the fish mixture into 2 Tbsp balls and drop them into the hot vegetable oil. Fry until the fritters are puffed, golden and cooked through, 3 to 5 minutes. Using a slotted metal spoon, remove from the oil and drain on paper towels.

TO SERVE Arrange fritters on individual plates or on a serving platter. Place the citrus mayonnaise in a dipping bowl and serve on the side. Serve immediately.

CITRUS MAYONNAISE

Juice of 1 lemon, 1 lime and 1 orange

½ cup mayonnaise

Pinch of cayenne pepper

SALMON FRITTERS

½ lb salmon, trimmed and diced

4 green onions, chopped

1 tsp grated ginger

Juice of 1 lemon

2 egg whites

4 cups vegetable oil for deep-frying

FRESH GOAT CHEESE

WITH OVEN-DRIED TOMATOES, ARUGULA
AND BALSAMIC VINAIGRETTE

OVEN-DRIED TOMATOES

12 ripe, thick-skinned tomatoes
(such as Cascades or Romas)

1 Tbsp olive oil

1 tsp salt

BALSAMIC VINAIGRETTE

¼ cup balsamic vinegar

¾ cup olive oil

1 tsp honey

GOAT CHEESE AND ARUGULA

5 oz fresh goat cheese

5 oz fresh arugula

THE combination of sweet oven-dried tomatoes; nutty, spicy arugula, and earthy fresh goat cheese, all served with balsamic vinaigrette, is a marriage made in heaven. We prefer to use ripe, thick-skinned tomatoes, such as Cascades or Romas, for oven drying, as they are fleshy and retain some moisture even after a few hours in the oven. A good oven-dried tomato has a concentrated sweetness that is like candy. Once dried, the tomatoes can be stored in the refrigerator for a few days, or even frozen for use in pasta dishes or risotto later in the year. *Serves 4*

OVEN-DRIED TOMATOES Preheat the oven to 300°F. Line a baking sheet with parchment paper.

Slice tomatoes in half lengthwise and drizzle with olive oil. Sprinkle with salt, then arrange cut side up on the baking sheet. Bake for 2 hours, until semi-dry. Cool. Can be refrigerated for up to 3 days.

BALSAMIC VINAIGRETTE Place vinaigrette ingredients in a small bowl and whisk until well combined. Set aside until needed. Will keep refrigerated in an airtight container for up to 1 week.

GOAT CHEESE AND ARUGULA Cut goat cheese into 4 pieces and mould each into a circle by pressing it into a 2-inch ring mould.

Wash and dry arugula and mound on individual plates.

TO SERVE Top arugula with 6 oven-dried tomatoes and drizzle with vinaigrette. Place 1 round of goat cheese on each salad.

SWEET ONION SOUP

WITH HERBED CHEDDAR
CHEESE BISCUITS

**HERBED CHEDDAR
CHEESE BISCUITS**

2 cups all-purpose flour

1 Tbsp baking powder

1 tsp baking soda

1 tsp salt

⅓ cup butter

1 Tbsp finely chopped
fresh thyme

2 tsp finely chopped
fresh rosemary

¾ cup grated Cheddar cheese

¾ cup plain yogurt

1 Tbsp milk

I LIKE to make this rich, country-style soup because it uses the naturally large, sweet onions that Gary and Naty King grow on their farm in the Hazelmere Valley. There are several varieties, with names such as Ailsa Craig, Walla Walla, Vidalia or Maui. In this recipe, I keep the spicing as simple as possible to allow the natural flavour of the onions to come through. The added cream enriches the soup, but is optional. *Serves 6*

HERBED CHEDDAR CHEESE BISCUITS Preheat the oven to 375°F. Line a baking sheet with parchment paper.

In a large bowl, combine flour, baking powder, baking soda and salt. Add butter and work into the flour mixture with your fingers until the dough has the consistency of cornmeal. Stir in thyme and rosemary. Make a well in the centre of the dry ingredients.

Place cheese, yogurt and milk in a small bowl and stir to combine. Pour the yogurt mixture into the well and combine lightly until the dough forms a ball. Turn the dough onto a lightly floured surface and knead 10 times.

Roll out the dough to a thickness of 1 inch. Using a 2-inch round cookie cutter, cut out 12 biscuits. Arrange biscuits 2 inches apart on the baking sheet and bake in the top third of the oven for 15 to 20 minutes, until lightly golden. Transfer to a cooling rack.

SWEET ONION SOUP Melt butter in a stockpot on medium heat. Add onions and garlic. Cover, reduce the heat to low and cook for 15 to 20 minutes. Remove the lid, stir in flour and cook for 5 to 6 minutes. Deglaze the pot with wine.

Add chicken (or vegetable) stock, salt, pepper and sugar and increase the heat to medium-high. Bring to a boil, reduce the heat to low and simmer uncovered for 30 minutes. Stir in cream and simmer for another 10 minutes.

TO SERVE Ladle soup into warm bowls. Sprinkle with chopped parsley.

SWEET ONION SOUP

3 Tbsp butter

6 cups thinly sliced
  sweet onions

3 to 4 cloves garlic, chopped

¼ cup all-purpose flour

½ cup dry white wine

6 cups chicken or
  vegetable stock

2 tsp salt

½ tsp pepper

1 Tbsp sugar

½ cup whipping cream
  (optional)

2 Tbsp chopped fresh
  parsley, for garnish

ROASTED TOMATO SOUP

WITH SAGE AND APPLE BISCUITS

WHEN tomato season is at its peak, we make this soup with the tomatoes that are too ripe to slice for salads. I find that if you use a combination of red and yellow tomatoes you get a beautiful orange soup. *Serves 6*

SAGE AND APPLE BISCUITS Preheat the oven to 375°F. Line a baking sheet with parchment paper.

In a large bowl, combine flour, baking powder, baking soda and salt. Add butter and work into the flour mixture with your fingers until the dough has the consistency of a coarse meal. Stir in sage. Make a well in the centre of the dry ingredients.

Place apple, yogurt and milk in a small bowl and stir to combine. Pour the yogurt mixture into the well and combine lightly until the dough forms a ball. Divide the dough into 3 pieces. Turn onto a lightly floured surface and knead each piece gently.

Pat the dough into 3 rounds, each 1 inch thick. Using a sharp knife, score the top of each round into quarters, place on the baking sheet and bake in the top third of the oven for 15 to 20 minutes, until lightly golden. Transfer to a cooling rack.

ROASTED TOMATO SOUP Preheat the oven to 450°F. Place tomatoes, onion and garlic in a roasting pan. Drizzle with olive oil and sprinkle with salt, then roast until softened, 45 minutes to 1 hour.

Transfer to a large saucepan on medium heat. Add sherry, water and sugar (or honey) and bring to a simmer. Cook for 30 minutes, stirring occasionally, then add basil. Cook for another 10 minutes. Allow to cool slightly, then transfer to a blender or food processor and purée until smooth.

Strain soup through a fine-mesh sieve. Discard any solids. Season to taste with salt.

TO SERVE Ladle the soup into individual warmed bowls. Break the biscuits into quarters and serve on the side.

SAGE AND APPLE BISCUITS

2 cups all-purpose flour

1 Tbsp baking powder

1 tsp baking soda

1 tsp salt

⅓ cup butter

1 Tbsp finely chopped fresh sage

¾ cup grated apple

¾ cup plain yogurt

2 Tbsp milk

ROASTED TOMATO SOUP

2 lbs very ripe tomatoes

1 small onion

2 cloves garlic, peeled

2 Tbsp olive oil

1 tsp salt

½ cup dry sherry

3½ cups water

2 Tbsp sugar or honey

1 bunch basil, roughly chopped

SWEET CORN SOUP

WITH CORN FRITTERS

CORN COB BROTH

2 ears corn

8 cups water

2 tsp salt

SWEET CORN SOUP

2 Tbsp butter

1 cup onions, chopped

1 cup diced celery root

2 cloves garlic, chopped

2 Tbsp chopped fresh thyme

6 cups corn cob broth

1 cup diced potatoes

2 cups corn kernels

1 cup whipping cream

CORN FRITTERS

½ cup all-purpose flour

½ cup cornmeal

2 tsp sugar

1 tsp baking powder

½ tsp baking soda

½ tsp salt

2 eggs

½ cup buttermilk

2 Tbsp chopped green onions

¼ cup corn kernels

4 cups vegetable oil
for deep-frying

THIS dish is a satisfying way to celebrate the corn season, with a soup made from both the kernels and cobs of the corn, and a crisp cornmeal fritter floating on top. The corn broth has such a pure sweet flavour that it carries through the whole dish. We use celery root and potato as additions in the soup to give it body and depth of flavour, along with a velvety texture. *Serves 8*

CORN COB BROTH Cut the kernels from the cobs, reserving them for the soup and fritters. Combine corn cobs, water and salt in a large stockpot on medium-low heat and simmer for 1 hour. Strain through a fine-mesh sieve and discard the solids.

SWEET CORN SOUP Heat butter in a large saucepan on medium-high heat. Add onions, celery root, garlic and thyme and sauté until onions are translucent. Add broth and potatoes, reduce the heat to medium-low and simmer until vegetables are cooked thoroughly, about 30 minutes. Allow to cool slightly, then transfer to a blender or food processor and purée. Return purée to the saucepan, add corn and cream and simmer for 10 minutes. Add more salt, if desired. Keep warm until needed.

CORN FRITTERS Heat a deep fryer to 350°F. Combine flour, cornmeal, sugar, baking powder, baking soda and salt in a large bowl and mix well. In a small bowl, beat eggs with buttermilk. Add the buttermilk mixture to the dry ingredients and mix lightly. Fold in green onions and corn.

Drop the batter by teaspoonfuls into hot vegetable oil and fry until the fritters are golden brown, 3 to 5 minutes. Using a slotted metal spoon, remove from the oil and drain on paper towels.

TO SERVE Ladle hot soup into individual bowls. Place the fritters in a basket and pass them around so each person can float a fritter in their soup. Serve immediately.

SUMMER SALAD BOWL

WITH ACCOMPANIMENTS

THIS salad feast is a complete meal that's not only nourishing and visually appealing but also celebrates the bounty that summer brings to the table. I love the combination of greens with the sweet fruit flavours. Serve this dish on its own or as part of a summer buffet. *Serves 6*

CREAMY DRESSING Combine the dressing ingredients in a large bowl, then whisk until creamy and smooth. Will keep refrigerated in a glass container for up to 1 week.

SUMMER SALAD Preheat the oven to 375°F. Bake potatoes for about 1 hour, or until cooked. The potatoes are cooked when a sharp knife poked into the flesh comes out hot to the touch. Remove potatoes from the oven and set aside.

Place lettuce in a large salad bowl. Arrange each of the other ingredients in its own small bowl.

TO SERVE Pour all of the salad dressing onto the greens and toss well. Place the salad bowl in the centre of the table. Arrange the small bowls around it. Slice potatoes open lengthwise and dab butter in the middle. Place 1 potato on each plate and allow guests to help themselves to greens and the various accompaniments.

CREAMY DRESSING

½ cup mayonnaise

½ cup sour cream or plain yogurt

¼ cup white wine vinegar

2 Tbsp fresh orange juice

1 Tbsp liquid honey

1 clove garlic, crushed

¼ tsp salt

¼ tsp pepper

SUMMER SALAD

6 large russet potatoes, scrubbed

2 heads lettuce, washed, spun dry and hand-torn into bite-size pieces

1 cup coarsely grated carrot

1 cup thinly sliced celery or fresh fennel bulb

1 English cucumber, peeled and chopped

4 heirloom tomatoes, cut in quarters

2 roasted beets, peeled and sliced

1 cup raisins

2 sweet apples, peeled, cored and quartered

1 cup coarsely grated Cheddar cheese

1 cup sliced almonds or chopped walnuts

3 Tbsp butter

WARM SHIITAKE MUSHROOM AND SPINACH SALAD

WITH ROASTED PEAR DRESSING

ROASTED PEAR DRESSING

1 tsp butter

1 pear, peeled, cored and quartered

¼ cup cider vinegar

¾ cup vegetable oil

WARM SALAD

¼ cup olive oil

1 lb shiitake mushrooms, destemmed and quartered

½ cup sliced shallots

1 bunch spinach, washed and destemmed (about 4 cups)

Once the fall begins to bring cooler temperatures, I start to think about making warm salads. Spinach is one of the few salad greens that can stand up to the heat of warm mushrooms being poured over them, and it is very complementary to the nutty flavour of the shiitakes. *Serves 4*

ROASTED PEAR DRESSING Melt butter in a small sauté pan on medium-high heat. Add pears and cook until tender and caramelized, 5 to 7 minutes. Remove from the heat and allow to cool to room temperature.

Place pears in a food processor with cider vinegar. Purée, adding vegetable oil in a slow, continuous stream, until the dressing is smooth and emulsified. Strain through a fine-mesh sieve into a small bowl and refrigerate for up to 2 days.

WARM SALAD Heat olive oil in a frying pan on medium heat. Add mushrooms and shallots and sauté until golden brown and tender, about 5 minutes.

Place spinach leaves in a large bowl and toss with 1 to 2 Tbsp of the pear vinaigrette.

TO SERVE Divide spinach evenly among plates and spoon the warm mushroom mixture on top. Serve immediately.

SUMMER VEGETABLE AND
GOAT CHEESE GALETTE
WITH ROASTED TOMATO SAUCE

THIS individual galette, the simplest of one-crust pies, makes a delicious vegetarian entrée served with some freshly braised greens. The vegetable filling can be prepared ahead of time, as can the pastry rounds—refrigerate them separately, to be assembled and baked fresh later. *Serves 4*

ROASTED TOMATO SAUCE

4 large ripe tomatoes

2 tsp olive oil

½ tsp salt

½ cup coarsely chopped onions

2 cloves garlic

1 cup water

1 tsp sugar

GALETTE PASTRY

¾ cup all-purpose flour

¼ cup cornmeal

1 tsp sugar

½ tsp salt

¼ cup butter, in ½-inch pieces

2 Tbsp cold water

ROASTED TOMATO SAUCE Preheat the oven to 450°F. Place tomatoes in an ovenproof dish or a frying pan and drizzle with olive oil and salt. Add onions and garlic and toss lightly. Roast for 30 minutes, until tomatoes are softened and lightly coloured.

Transfer the tomato mixture to a small saucepan on medium heat. Add water and sugar and simmer for 15 minutes. Cool slightly, then transfer to a blender or a food processor and purée. Strain through a fine-mesh sieve. Discard any solids. Keep warm on low heat until needed.

GALETTE PASTRY In a medium bowl, combine flour, cornmeal, sugar and salt. Add butter and cut in with a knife or mix with your hands, combining well until the dough has the consistency of coarse meal. Add water and stir until just combined. Cover with a tea towel and allow to rest for 20 minutes.

Divide the dough into 4 pieces. On a lightly floured board, roll out each ball to a thickness of ⅛ inch. With a pastry cutter, trim each piece to a 6-inch circle. Set aside.

SUMMER VEGETABLE AND GOAT CHEESE FILLING Heat olive oil in a large sauté pan on medium-high heat. Add garlic and onions and sauté until softened, 3 to 5 minutes. Stir in green and yellow zucchini, leeks, bell peppers and beans and cook until just tender, 5 to 7 minutes. Add basil, parsley and thyme and allow the filling to cool to room temperature.

TO ASSEMBLE THE GALETTES Preheat the oven to 375°F. Line each of four 4-inch tart shells with a pastry circle. The pastry should extend slightly up the sides of the tart shell.

Spoon ½ cup of the filling into individual shells with a slotted spoon. Dot each galette with fresh goat cheese. Fold and tuck the sides of the pastry around the filling, leaving a 1-inch area of unencased filling in the centre. Bake until golden and cooked through, about 20 minutes.

BRAISED GREENS Place butter in a large shallow pan on medium-high heat. Add garlic and sauté until golden, 1 to 2 minutes. Add chard (or kale), vegetable stock (or water) and salt to taste. Cover and cook until tender, 2 to 5 minutes. Drain well in a colander.

TO SERVE Spoon ¼ cup of the tomato sauce into the centre of each plate. Remove the galettes from the tart shells and set on the sauce. Serve greens on the side.

SUMMER VEGETABLE AND GOAT CHEESE FILLING

1 Tbsp olive oil

2 cloves garlic, minced

½ cup diced onions

1 cup diced green zucchini

1 cup diced yellow zucchini

½ cup thinly sliced leeks

½ cup diced red bell peppers

1 cup green or yellow beans, thinly sliced

2 Tbsp chopped fresh basil

1 Tbsp chopped fresh parsley

1 Tbsp chopped fresh thyme

4 oz fresh goat cheese

BRAISED GREENS

1 Tbsp butter

1 clove garlic, chopped

1 bunch chard or kale, washed, destemmed and lightly chopped

½ cup vegetable stock or water

CHANTERELLE AND PEAR POT PIES

FRESH chanterelle mushrooms and ripe pears make for a perfect pairing that is sweet and earthy. These little pies are perfect for lunch, simply served with a salad of mixed fall greens. *Serves 4*

CHANTERELLE AND PEAR FILLING Preheat the oven to 375°. Place mushrooms, shallots and pears in a roasting pan. Add olive oil and toss well. Season with salt and pepper. Roast for 45 minutes, stirring occasionally.

While the mushroom mixture is roasting, prepare the white sauce. Melt butter in a heavy saucepan on medium heat. Add flour and cook gently, stirring constantly until the flour is well incorporated. You will know it is ready when it leaves the sides of the pan and becomes slightly lighter in colour. Remove the butter and flour mixture from the heat and add milk and thyme.

Return the pan to medium heat and bring the sauce to a boil, stirring constantly for 5 minutes. Season to taste with salt and pepper.

Combine the roasted mushroom mixture with the white sauce. Spoon into four 8-oz ramekins. Allow to cool.

POT PIE PASTRY Preheat the oven to 375°F. Divide the dough into 4 balls.

On a lightly floured board, roll out each ball to a thickness of ¼ inch. With a pastry cutter, cut out four 5-inch circles. Cover each ramekin with a circle of pastry, allowing it to overlap the edges.

In a small bowl, lightly whisk together egg and milk (or water). Brush the pastry with the egg wash. Place the ramekins on a baking sheet and bake for 35 to 40 minutes, or until tops are golden brown.

TO SERVE Place one pot pie on each salad-sized plate.

CHANTERELLE AND PEAR FILLING

¾ lb fresh chanterelle mushrooms, sliced

2 large shallots, chopped

1 ripe Bartlett pear, peeled, cored and sliced

2 Tbsp olive oil

1 Tbsp butter

1 Tbsp all-purpose flour

1½ cups milk

1 tsp chopped fresh thyme

POT PIE PASTRY

1 recipe pâte brisée dough (page 119)

1 egg

1 Tbsp milk or water

VEGETABLE FRITTATA

2 Tbsp olive oil

1 cup diced potatoes

1 cup diced onions

½ cup diced red bell peppers

1 cup diced summer zucchini

1 cup thinly sliced mushrooms

1 cup fresh peas

12 eggs

1 cup light cream or milk

1 tsp salt

½ tsp freshly ground pepper

2 Tbsp chopped fresh basil

FRITTATAS make ideal and quite substantial brunch main courses for small groups. The fillings can be varied depending on the season; this one is vegetarian, but it can also be served with slices of crispy cooked bacon and country sausages. Sometimes I make a quick fresh tomato sauce to accompany the frittata. *Serves 6 to 8*

PREHEAT THE OVEN to 375°F. Butter a 10-inch springform pan, then line the bottom of the pan with a circle of parchment paper that has been cut to fit. Place a sheet of aluminum foil on a baking sheet, set the springform pan on top, then fold the foil up around the bottom and sides of the pan. This will prevent any leakage from the pan.

Heat olive oil in a large frying pan on medium heat. Add potatoes, onions and bell peppers, then cover and cook for 8 minutes, stirring occasionally. Add zucchini, mushrooms and peas and cook for another 5 to 6 minutes. Remove from the heat and spoon the cooked vegetables into the springform pan.

In a medium bowl, whisk eggs, cream (or milk), salt and pepper until well combined. Stir in basil, then pour the egg mixture over the vegetables. Bake for 20 to 30 minutes, or until eggs are set and have risen. Allow to cool for 10 to 15 minutes.

TO SERVE Remove the aluminum foil and place the springform pan on a large serving platter. Remove the sides of the springform pan and cut the frittata into pie-shaped wedges. Serve on individual plates.

ROASTED PRIME RIB

WITH MUSHROOM JUS

A PRIME rib roast is certainly the focal point of many a big family dinner. Most butchers will sell what we refer to as a banquet rib, which has had the cap separated from the eye of the meat, and then tied back on to protect and tenderize during the long cooking process. When seasoning the roast, rub olive oil, salt and pepper both on top and underneath the cap to fully season the meat. *Serves 8 to 10*

PRIME RIB Preheat the oven to 400°F. Rub prime rib with olive oil and season very well with salt and pepper. Cook for 45 minutes, then reduce the heat to 350°F and roast for 2 hours longer. Check for doneness with a meat thermometer; the internal temperature should be 125°F.

Remove from the oven and allow to rest for 30 minutes before carving.

MUSHROOM JUS Heat butter in a large sauté pan on medium-high heat. Add mushrooms, shallots and garlic and sauté until golden and caramelized, about 10 minutes.

Deglaze the pan with wine. Cook until reduced by half, about 5 minutes. Add beef stock and cook until reduced again by half, 15 to 20 minutes. Season with salt and pepper to taste.

TO SERVE Place the prime rib on a large cutting board with the bones facing away from you. Cut the string that ties the cap to the rib and remove the cap. Pull out the string and discard. Slice the meat away from the bones, so that the eye of the roast is in one piece. Cut crosswise into thin slices and arrange on a large serving platter. (The cap may also be sliced and placed on the platter, as many people have a penchant for the crisp cap.) Serve mushroom jus in a sauceboat on the side.

PRIME RIB

1 prime rib roast
   (about 8 to 10 lbs)

2 Tbsp olive oil

MUSHROOM JUS

2 Tbsp butter

1 lb portobello or other
   mushrooms

2 shallots, peeled

1 tsp minced garlic

1 cup red wine

4 cups beef stock

DRY-RUB PORK RIBS

WITH CORN MUFFINS
AND SPLIT PEA—GINGER PURÉE

CORN MUFFINS

2 cups cornmeal

3 cups all-purpose flour

½ cup sugar

2 Tbsp baking powder

1½ tsp salt

1 cup fresh or frozen
   corn kernels

¼ cup chopped
   green onions

3 eggs

2 Tbsp vegetable oil

1 cup plain yogurt

2 cups whole milk

DRY-RUB PORK RIBS

1 Tbsp brown sugar

1 tsp coarse salt

½ tsp pepper

1 Tbsp chili powder

1 tsp fennel seeds

1 tsp coriander seeds

1 tsp yellow mustard seeds

1 tsp minced garlic

1 tsp minced ginger

2 racks pork back ribs
   (each 1½ lbs)

THERE are few things as satisfying as ribs with freshly baked corn muffins and a side dish of split peas with a hint of ginger. Make sure you buy the pork back ribs, which are cut from the loin, rather than the side ribs, which come from the belly and have less meat.

The corn muffin recipe makes enough for twenty-four muffins. Leftover muffins will keep in an airtight container at room temperature for two days or frozen for up to one month. *Serves 4*

CORN MUFFINS Preheat the oven to 400°F. Butter muffin tins, then lightly dust with flour.

Place cornmeal, flour, sugar, baking powder and salt in a large bowl and stir well to combine. Add corn kernels and green onions and mix lightly. Make a well in the centre of the dry ingredients. Set aside.

In a medium bowl, whisk eggs with vegetable oil until well combined. Whisk in yogurt, then milk. Pour the egg-milk mixture into the well and stir with a spatula until ingredients are fairly well combined. Do not overmix or your muffins will be tough.

Fill muffin tins two-thirds full with batter and bake for about 20 minutes, or until a skewer inserted in the centre comes out clean. Transfer to a cooling rack.

DRY-RUB PORK RIBS Combine brown sugar, salt, pepper, chili powder, fennel seeds, coriander and mustard seeds in a small bowl. Using a mortar and pestle or an electric spice mill, grind this mixture finely. Add garlic and ginger and mix well.

Rub ribs on both sides with the dry rub, place in a shallow pan and allow to marinate in the refrigerator for 1 hour.
Recipe continued overleaf…

SPLIT PEA–GINGER PURÉE

1 Tbsp butter

½ cup diced onions

¼ cup chopped celery

1 Tbsp minced ginger

1 tsp minced garlic

1 tsp ground coriander

1 tsp ground cumin

1 tsp chopped fresh thyme

½ cup dried split green peas,
  washed thoroughly

4 cups vegetable or
  chicken stock

Preheat the oven to 350°F. Line a baking sheet with parchment paper. Place ribs on the baking sheet and bake for 1½ to 2 hours, until tender when pierced with a fork between the bones. Remove from the oven and allow to rest for 15 minutes before serving.

SPLIT PEA–GINGER PURÉE Heat butter in a medium saucepan on medium-high heat. Add onions, celery, ginger and garlic and sauté until golden brown, about 5 minutes. Add coriander, cumin, thyme and peas and cook until peas are lightly coated with spices, 1 to 2 minutes.

Add vegetable (or chicken) stock and salt to taste. Increase the heat to high and bring to a simmer. Reduce the heat to low, cover and cook for 1 hour, until peas are tender. Cool slightly, then transfer to a blender or a food processor. Purée until smooth. Strain through a coarse sieve. Discard solids

TO SERVE Cut the ribs into individual servings and arrange them on a large platter. Serve split pea–ginger purée in a bowl on the side along with a basket of corn muffins.

PORTERHOUSE STEAK

MY MEMORIES of eating this cut of steak go back to my days as a young merchant marine. On leave for a few days in Buenos Aires, where the ship I was cooking on had tied up in an area known as La Boca el Puente, I joined the dockworkers as they ate their daily meals seated at wooden tables in the small cantinas that lined the docks. In those humble places and for very little money, I tasted the famous Argentinian grass-fed beef of the pampas, cooked on an open and very hot wood-burning grill. All these years later, meat still always seems to taste better when cooked on the bone like this, rustic and delicious.

At Bishop's, we really look forward to the time of year when farmer Gary King and his wife, Naty, start to bring in cippolini onions. These small, flat, button-shaped, sweet onions are totally unlike any of the other onion varieties; we like to prepare them very simply—just oven-braised and lightly seasoned—which allows their natural sweetness to come through and take the place of a sauce for beef. Freshly grated horseradish is a good spicy accompaniment to this dish. *Serves 4*

BRAISED CIPPOLINI ONIONS

2 Tbsp butter

1½ lbs whole cippolini onions, peeled and ends trimmed

¼ cup white wine

2 cups hot chicken or vegetable stock

1 tsp salt

1 Tbsp finely chopped fresh thyme

BRAISED CIPPOLINI ONIONS Preheat the oven to 350°F. Melt butter in a frying pan on medium-high heat. Add onions and sauté and lightly brown for about 5 minutes. Deglaze the pan with wine and cook for 2 to 3 minutes more.

Transfer onions into a small ovenproof casserole. Pour in chicken (or vegetable) stock. Season with salt and thyme. Loosely cover the casserole with parchment paper and bake for 40 to 50 minutes, until onions are tender. *Recipe continued overleaf...*

PORTERHOUSE STEAK Preheat the barbecue to high heat. Rub steak with mustard, then brush with olive oil and season with salt and pepper.

Place steak directly on the hot barbecue and grill over direct heat for 10 minutes per side. When charred on both sides, move the steak off the direct heat and away from the flame. Cook for another 6 to 8 minutes. Remove the steak from the grill and allow to rest for 15 minutes before carving.

TO SERVE Remove the meat from the bone and cut across the grain into ¼-inch slices. Place 1 slice of the striploin and 1 slice of the tenderloin onto each warmed dinner plate and serve with the cippolini onions on the side.

PORTERHOUSE STEAK

2 lbs porterhouse steak, cut 2 to 3 inches thick and trimmed of excess fat

1 Tbsp Dijon mustard

1 Tbsp olive oil

1 Tbsp kosher salt

2 tsp coarsely ground pepper

‹ *Served with "Not Baked Potatoes" (page 113)*

PAN-ROASTED LAMB LOIN

WITH QUINCE AND SWEET VERMOUTH SAUCE

PAN-ROASTED LAMB LOIN

2 racks or loins lamb
(2 lbs total), deboned
(reserve bones for sauce)

1 tsp minced garlic

Zest of 1 lemon

¼ cup vegetable oil

½ tsp pepper

1 tsp chopped thyme
(reserve stems for sauce)

1 tsp chopped rosemary
(reserve stems for sauce)

QUINCE AND SWEET
VERMOUTH SAUCE

Bones from lamb loins or racks

1 onion, diced

2 stalks celery, sliced

2 carrots, sliced

2 cloves garlic

2 quince, diced

8 cups water

Thyme and rosemary stems

1 bay leaf

½ cup sweet vermouth or port

You will find fresh quince, which look and taste like a cross between apples and pears, in the fall for only a few weeks. They have a very intriguing perfume, sweet and complex, but they are very firm and their flavour is not too sweet, which is why you will find them used in both savoury and sweet recipes. Look for quince that are bright yellow in colour and have a strong fragrance, but no soft spots.

When making this dish, I prefer to debone the lamb and make the stock for the sauce the day before. This extra time allows the lamb to marinate overnight, which makes it more flavourful and tender and makes the job of skimming the fat from the stock a bit easier. *Serves 4*

PAN-ROASTED LAMB LOIN Place lamb in a shallow dish with all the remaining ingredients, cover and marinate for several hours or overnight.

QUINCE AND SWEET VERMOUTH SAUCE Preheat the oven to 450°F. Place the lamb bones, onions, celery, carrots, garlic and quince in a shallow roasting pan and roast until nicely browned, about 30 minutes.

Transfer to a medium saucepan, add water and heat on medium heat. Add thyme and rosemary stems and bay leaf and bring to a simmer. Reduce the heat to low and simmer for 2 hours, or until the bones are falling apart.

Strain the liquid from bones and vegetables (discard bones and vegetables), then skim and discard fat from the surface. Strain the stock through a fine-mesh sieve. (At this point, you may want to refrigerate the broth overnight. The next day, remove the fat from the surface before proceeding.)

Increase the heat to high and bring the broth back to a boil in the saucepan. Cook until the broth is reduced to 1 cup, about 30 minutes. Using a ladle, skim the top of the broth often to remove any impurities that rise to the surface.

TO FINISH LAMB Preheat the oven to 450°F. Lightly season lamb with salt. Heat a heavy ovenproof frying pan on high heat, then sear lamb on all sides, 3 to 5 minutes.

Roast lamb for 5 to 7 minutes. Check for doneness with a meat thermometer; the internal temperature should be 125°F. Remove lamb from the pan and allow to rest for 5 minutes while you finish the sauce.

TO FINISH SAUCE Deglaze the frying pan by adding sweet vermouth (or port) and stirring to loosen the browned bits on the bottom. Add the lamb stock, then simmer until slightly thickened, about 5 minutes.

TO SERVE Thinly slice each lamb loin across the grain into 8 slices. Arrange 4 slices on individual plates. Serve the sauce in a sauceboat on the side.

ROASTED

CORNISH GAME HENS

WITH MUSHROOM AND HAZELNUT STUFFING

CORNISH game hens really do have a different taste than chicken. And if you can get them fresh, they somehow manage to taste quite sweet and juicy, almost like a cross between wild game birds and free-run chickens. One bird is certainly more than enough for one person, or can be split in half for two served with the stuffing on the side. Simple accompaniments would be creamy mashed potatoes and ears of fresh-picked corn. *Serves 4*

MUSHROOM AND HAZELNUT STUFFING
Heat butter in a frying pan on medium heat. Add shallots, garlic, celery and ginger and sauté until tender, 2 to 3 minutes. Add mushrooms and hazelnuts and sauté until they begin to brown, 3 to 4 minutes. Remove from the heat and add bread crumbs, cilantro and salt and pepper to taste.

ROASTED CORNISH GAME HENS
Preheat the oven to 400°F. Spoon about 1 cup of the mushroom and hazelnut stuffing into each hen. Rub hens with olive oil and season with salt, pepper and thyme. Place hens into a roasting pan, leaving 1 inch around each one so the skin can brown.

Roast for 20 minutes per pound, or roughly 45 to 50 minutes total for these stuffed birds. Check for doneness with a meat thermometer; the internal temperature should be 170°F. Transfer hens to a warmed platter and allow to rest for 10 to 15 minutes before serving.

TO SERVE Each person gets a whole hen, unless you are splitting them in half. Serve on warmed plates and garnish with sprigs of fresh thyme.

MUSHROOM AND HAZELNUT STUFFING

2 Tbsp butter

2 Tbsp finely chopped shallots

2 cloves garlic, finely chopped

1 stalk celery, chopped

½ tsp grated ginger

2 cups chopped button or shiitake mushrooms

½ cup coarsely chopped hazelnuts

2 cups fresh bread crumbs

2 Tbsp chopped fresh cilantro

ROASTED CORNISH GAME HENS

4 fresh Cornish game hens (each about 1lb)

1 Tbsp olive oil

1 tsp coarse salt

1 tsp freshly ground pepper

1 tsp chopped fresh thyme leaves

SALT-CRUSTED CHICKEN

3 egg whites

¾ cup coarse salt

2 double chicken breasts, bone in (each 1 lb)

BAKING meat or poultry in a crust of salt serves a dual purpose: it seasons the meat and it allows the meat to cook in its own juices. For this dish, I prefer to take the breasts from a whole chicken intact, not split in half, as you would usually find them, as the breastbone protects the centre of the meat and allows the chicken to cook more gently. Once the chicken has cooked, the salt crust will be quite hard, allowing you to break it off and separate it easily from the meat. Serves 4

PREHEAT THE OVEN to 400°F. Place egg whites in a mixing bowl and whip until stiff peaks form. Fold in salt.

Place chicken breasts, skin side up, in an ovenproof dish. Using a rubber spatula, spread the egg white mixture evenly over chicken breasts. Bake for 1 hour. Check for doneness with a meat thermometer: the internal temperature of the meat should be 170°F. Remove chicken from the oven and allow it to rest for 15 minutes.

Using your hands, break and lift off the salt crust from the chicken. The skin will most likely be stuck to the salt crust, so remove any remaining skin as well. With a sharp knife, cut along either side of the breastbone, and, following the bone, lift the breasts away from the rib cage.

TO SERVE Place a single chicken breast on each plate.

WHOLE CHICKEN

ON THE BARBECUE WITH ROASTED POTATOES

ROASTED POTATOES

6 potatoes, peeled and
   cut in 1-inch dice

2 Tbsp olive oil

2 cloves garlic, chopped

1 Tbsp chopped fresh thyme

1 tsp salt

CHICKEN

1 whole chicken
   (about 3 to 4 lbs)

1 Tbsp olive oil

1 tsp salt

½ tsp coarsely ground pepper

6 sprigs fresh thyme

THIS whole roasted chicken recipe was inspired by a really hot day and a brand new barbecue. The chicken cooks by itself in its own juices without having to be turned or prodded. Roasting the potatoes below the chicken allows the chicken juices to collect and caramelize. Occasionally I add other vegetables to the potatoes, such as onions, diced squash or sweet potato.

Serves 4 to 6

ROASTED POTATOES In a large bowl, toss potatoes with olive oil, garlic, thyme, salt and pepper. Heat a large frying pan on medium-high heat. Add potatoes and sauté until they start to brown, about 10 minutes. Transfer the potatoes to a metal roasting pan.

CHICKEN Preheat the barbecue to medium-high heat (light only the front burner, if you have a dual burner).

Rub chicken with olive oil and season with salt and pepper. Stuff the chicken cavity with the sprigs of thyme. Place chicken, breast side up, onto the raised cooking grate at the back of the grill and away from direct flame. Place the pan of potatoes on the barbecue under the roasting chicken in such a way that it collects the roasting juices from the chicken.

Close the cover on the barbecue and roast chicken and potatoes for about 1¾ hours, stirring potatoes occasionally. Check for doneness with a meat thermometer: the internal temperature of the chicken should be 170°F in the thickest part of the thigh. Turn off the barbecue and allow chicken to stand for 15 minutes before carving.

TO SERVE Portion the chicken by first removing the leg meat. Cut each leg into two pieces and carve the breast meat into thin slices. Place pieces of both leg and breast meat onto warmed plates and serve with roasted potatoes.

CRAB FEAST

DUNGENESS crabs are found along the Pacific coast of North America. They can weigh anywhere from 1½ pounds up to 4 pounds. They are mostly sold live, but are also sold as crabmeat, which is primarily used in the preparation of salads, seafood cocktails or crab cakes. The meat is very delicate and sweet in flavour. I prefer to serve the whole crab, especially when I have visitors who may not have experienced eating a feast such as this. It's a little bit of work to get at the meat, but people always find the effort worthwhile, and I think this dish truly defines West Coast cuisine.

Don't be tempted to throw out the yellow gooey stuff in the top shell. This is known as crab mustard, or tomalley, and it can be used to make a delicious concoction for spreading onto slices of warm baguette. The recipe for the crab spread is courtesy of Gus and Dana Angus from Totem Sea Farms on the Sunshine Coast. The other accompaniments I like to serve are a bowl of steamed new potatoes and locally harvested sea asparagus or fiddlehead ferns, just lightly steamed and tossed with melted butter. *Serves 4*

PICKLED GINGER MAYONNAISE Combine mayonnaise, mustard, lemon juice and ginger in a medium bowl. Cover and refrigerate for 2 to 3 hours until well chilled. Will keep in an airtight container in the refrigerator for 5 or 6 days.

DUNGENESS CRAB Fill a large stockpot with 2 gallons of water and bring to a boil on high heat. Add salt, then carefully place the crabs into the water. Bring the water back to a boil, then reduce the heat to medium, partially cover the pot with a lid and cook for 15 to 20 minutes, until the crab shells turn bright red. Using a pair of long barbecue tongs, remove the crabs from the water and set aside to cool for 15 minutes. *Recipe continued overleaf...*

PICKLED GINGER MAYONNAISE

2 cups mayonnaise

2 Tbsp mild Dijon mustard

Juice of ½ lemon

2 Tbsp finely chopped pickled ginger

DUNGENESS CRAB

½ cup coarse salt

2 live Dungeness crabs (each 2 to 3 lbs)

4 large lemon wedges

CRAB SPREAD

2 slices day-old white bread,
  toasted and dried

Cooked tomalley from
  2 crab shells

¼ cup finely chopped
  red bell peppers

1 clove garlic, minced

1 Tbsp Worcestershire sauce

1 Tbsp balsamic vinegar

¼ cup olive oil

1 tsp finely chopped fresh
  jalapeno peppers (optional)

1 baguette, warmed and
  cut in 1-inch slices

When cool, pry off the top shell by holding the base of the crab in one hand and placing the thumb of the other hand under the edge of the shell. Pull up to loosen and remove the shell. Inside the top shell, you will find a yellowish substance, which is the tomalley, or crab mustard. Scrape the tomalley into a bowl and strain off any excess liquid. Reserve the tomalley for the crab spread. Reserve the top shell to hold the debris as you disassemble the crab.

Remove all of the gills that are now exposed on the top side of the crab and the triangular piece of shell that sits on the underside. Rinse the whole crab thoroughly under cold water to remove any other inedible bits

Using your hands or a sharp knife, split the body of the crab in half lengthwise, and then into quarters, leaving the legs attached.

CRAB SPREAD Place the bread between 2 sheets of parchment paper. With a rolling pin, crush the slices to form fine bread crumbs. Transfer the crumbs to a large bowl, then add tomalley, bell peppers, garlic, Worcestershire sauce, balsamic vinegar, olive oil and jalapeño peppers. Stir well to combine. The mixture should be of a spreading consistency. If it is not, add a bit more olive oil. Scoop the spread into an airtight container and refrigerate for up to 3 days.

TO SERVE Place the crab onto a large platter in the centre of the table. Arrange lemon wedges on a plate and scoop the pickled ginger mayonnaise into a small serving bowl. Spoon the crab spread into a small bowl and serve with a basket of warm baguette slices.

GARLIC BUTTER BEANS

WITH FRESH TOMATO SAUCE

DRIED beans are a valuable pantry staple, and I particularly like large butter beans, also called lima beans, which are a lot meatier than their smaller counterparts. Delicious as a side dish with barbecued chicken or steak, these beans are baked and the fresh tomatoes take the place of a sauce. If you can find heirloom tomatoes, which are sweeter and tastier than other varieties, it will make a big difference. *Serves 4 to 6*

PREHEAT THE OVEN to 350°F. Place beans in a medium bowl, cover with cold water and allow them to soak overnight in a cool place. (Alternatively, place beans in a saucepan, cover with cold water and slowly bring to a boil on medium heat. Simmer uncovered on medium heat for 10 minutes. Remove from the heat, cover and allow to cool for 15 to 20 minutes.) Drain beans in a colander. Remove and discard the tougher outer husks and set beans aside.

Heat olive oil in an ovenproof frying pan on medium heat. Add onions and garlic, cover and sauté until onions are translucent, 2 to 3 minutes. Add beans, tomatoes, honey, salt and thyme (or basil). Cover and bake for 1¾ hours, until beans are tender.

1 cup dried butter beans

¼ cup olive oil

1 onion, chopped

3 large cloves garlic, chopped

12 large ripe tomatoes, blanched, peeled and chopped

1 Tbsp liquid honey

2 tsp salt

2 sprigs fresh thyme or basil, destemmed and chopped

❨ ON THE FARM ❩

GARY KING

photos by AL HARVEY

E VERYTHING IS PLENTIFUL during the summers at Hazelmere . . . everything except the rain! From June through September, the farm is thick with ripening fruit and vegetables and we are busy watering, weeding, planting and harvesting the crops. There's a steady flow of visitors: some drop by the sales barn to buy field-fresh produce, others tour the farm to learn about our organic practices. We also welcome foodies who come to take cooking classes with John Bishop and Dennis Green.

During these warm, sunny months, I often walk through the garden with these visitors. We stop to admire the healthy plants and discuss why squash, corn and beans are planted together as companions and how they help each other to grow. In another area, we see tomatoes and parsley growing happily together because parsley roots release nutrients for tomato plants to feed on. We share a drink of water from the irrigation hose and, as the group moves to the back of the farm, we stop for a few moments to harvest thyme, sage and rosemary.

The farm is a haven for wildlife, and often we listen for bird songs and try to spot species in their natural habitat (including the sparrows that nest among our beets). Someone usually points

out what appear to be broken trees in the greenway behind our house and I explain that they have been pruned for bird habitat as well as for our safety. Our attention returns to the garden when the barn cat is seen on rodent patrol in the sunroot patch.

One of the joys of summer is eating fresh-picked food grown on the farm and prepared right in the backyard. And it doesn't hurt that it's cooked by award-winning chefs from Bishop's Restaurant! On days when John and Dennis come to the farm to give a class, our visitors learn about the ingredients as a meal is prepared. John might talk about ducks from Cowichan Bay on Vancouver Island. My wife, Naty, might discuss the nutritional values saved in the produce due to its freshness. And while Dennis cooks up these ingredients, John will emphasize how important it is to have local organic ingredients for use at Bishop's, from our farm as well as from producers in the Okanagan, the Similkameen Valley and in Washington State. John and I have visited many of these farms together to learn about their farming techniques and to cook up and share meals made with their local foods.

The proof, as they say, is in the eating, and soon we all sit down to a home-grown meal served at long scrubbed tables. There is bread made by pastry chef Dawne Gourley and brought from the restaurant, and platters of local meats or fish served with fruits and vegetables from the farm. This, for me, is summer just as it should be, a true partnership between farmer and cook.

ZUCCHINI RAGOUT

WITH TOMATOES AND BASIL

2 Tbsp olive oil

2 shallots, peeled and sliced

2 cloves garlic, peeled and chopped

4 cups zucchini, washed and cut in 2-inch sticks

3 large ripe field tomatoes, blanched, skins removed and chopped (liquid reserved)

1 Tbsp liquid honey

1 tsp salt

¼ cup chopped fresh basil

THIS ragout can be made using any type of soft-skinned summer squash, such as pattypan or baby marrow. It goes well with fish or grilled meats or can be served cold as part of an antipasto platter. *Serves 4 to 6*

HEAT OLIVE OIL in a frying pan on medium heat. Add shallots, garlic and zucchini and sauté for 10 to 15 minutes. Add tomatoes and their liquid, honey and salt. Reduce the heat to low, cover and cook gently for 30 minutes, until tender. Remove from the heat and stir in basil. Serve hot or at room temperature.

VEGETABLE FRITTERS

THESE vegetable fritters are so versatile they can be served as a snack with a dipping sauce, as a starch with a meat like the salt-crusted chicken (page 99) or as the basis for a vegetarian meal. Firm vegetables that retain their texture when cooked, such as turnips, parsnips, celery root or cauliflower, work best. *Serves 6*

IN A MEDIUM bowl, whisk together flour and salt. Add egg yolks, beer and vegetable oil and mix well. Fold in egg whites and set the batter aside.

Preheat a deep fryer to 350°F. Dip vegetable slices in the batter and fry until golden and tender, 3 to 5 minutes. Using a slotted metal spoon, remove from the oil and drain on paper towels. Serve immediately.

1 cup all-purpose flour

½ tsp salt

2 egg yolks

½ cup beer

¼ cup vegetable oil

2 egg whites, beaten
to form stiff peaks

2 cups firm vegetables (such as
turnips, parsnips, celery root,
cauliflower), in ⅛-inch slices

4 cups vegetable oil
for deep-frying

VEGETABLE CURRY

WITH CAULIFLOWER AND POTATOES

3 Tbsp butter

1 large onion, coarsely chopped

3 to 4 cloves garlic, chopped

1 Tbsp finely chopped ginger

2 stalks celery, coarsely chopped

2 carrots, peeled and sliced
in ¼-inch rounds

2 cups small cauliflower florets

1 Yukon Gold potato, peeled
and cut in large dice

1 sweet apple, peeled, cored,
and cut in large dice

¾ tsp turmeric

1 tsp ground cumin

1 tsp ground coriander

1 tsp garam masala

¼ tsp cayenne pepper

2 Tbsp toasted brown
mustard seeds

14 oz canned coconut milk

2 cups vegetable stock or water

2 Tbsp tomato paste

¼ cup red lentils

2 large field tomatoes, cored
and cut in large dice

½ cup fresh peas

2 Tbsp coarsely chopped
fresh cilantro

EVER since I went to India for the filming of *Deconstructing Supper,* a documentary on global food production, I've had a longing for the flavours of curry. This version can be made with all sorts of vegetables, depending on the season. For example, when tomatoes and peas are no longer in season, use some of the many different squashes. I like to serve this curry with warm naan, steamed basmati rice and a fruit chutney. *Serves 4 to 6*

MELT BUTTER in a 10-inch straight-sided sauté pan on medium heat. Add onions, garlic and ginger. Cover and cook for 5 minutes. Add celery, carrots, cauliflower, potatoes and apples and cook for 3 to 4 more minutes. Stir in turmeric, cumin, coriander, garam masala, cayenne pepper and mustard seeds, and cook uncovered for 2 to 3 minutes. Add coconut milk, vegetable stock (or water), tomato paste and lentils. Stir well to combine all ingredients and simmer uncovered for 20 to 25 minutes. Add tomatoes and peas, and cook for another 10 to 15 minutes. Season with salt and pepper. Garnish with cilantro.

OVEN-ROASTED BEETS

WITH WARMED DILL BUTTER

2 large red or yellow beets

2 tsp olive oil

¼ cup butter, warmed

1 Tbsp freshly chopped dill

¼ tsp salt

ALL beets are naturally high in sugar and they become even sweeter when roasted. You could also roast several different varieties of beets and then combine them for a visual treat. I particularly like the yellow, or golden, beets because they don't stain like red beets. Roasted beets also pair very well with a topping of crumbled feta or other fairly soft goat cheeses. *Serves 4*

PREHEAT THE OVEN to 375°F. Rub beets with olive oil, place on a baking sheet and roast for 1½ hours, until beets are tender and cooked. Remove from the oven and allow to cool.

While the beets are cooling, melt butter in a small saucepan on medium heat. Add dill and salt. Set aside.

Scrape the surface of the beets with a knife to remove the skin. Cut beets into quarters and toss with warmed dill butter. Serve hot.

"NOT BAKED POTATOES"

THESE are meant to mimic baked potatoes but without the skin. We serve them mixed and mashed with butter as you would prepare a baked potato, but formed with a ring mould for a clean, more formal presentation. Top with the traditional garnishes: chopped chives, sour cream and crisp bacon or pancetta. *Serves 4*

1 lb Yukon Gold potatoes, peeled and quartered

¼ to ½ cup butter

PLACE POTATOES in a medium saucepan and cover with cold water. Boil on medium-high heat until tender, about 20 minutes. Drain well.

Using a fork, mash potatoes, adding butter 1 Tbsp at a time until smooth. Season with salt to taste.

Place a 3-inch ring mould on a plate. Spoon mashed potatoes into the mould, then remove the mould to leave a cylinder of potato on the plate. Repeat with the remaining mashed potatoes.

PRESERVING HERBS

3 packed cups low-moisture   OR   6 packed cups high-moisture
fresh herbs (such as sage   fresh herbs (such as basil, mint,
or rosemary)   oregano, parsley)

LONG after the summer's flourish has passed and the winter season sets in, I am able to conjure up those long sunny days by cooking with some of the herbs I've picked and hung to dry in our south-facing basement window. I like to dry the herbs I use most frequently, such as oregano, thyme, sage and parsley.

The softer herbs such as basil I usually make into pesto and freeze in ice cube trays. These blocks can then be popped into soups and stews at the last minute. Herbs such as chives or tarragon can be bundled together in small amounts and frozen in reusable freezer bags. *Makes 2 oz*

DRYING HERBS Locate a brown paper bag (I recycle the long, narrow ones from the local wine store). Keeping the stems or branches as long as possible, cut the herbs to about the length of the paper bag. Place the herbs in the paper bag, leaving a few ends exposed. Tightly tie the open end of the bag around the exposed herbs with a piece of twine. The twine will secure the herbs and the bag protects them from dust.

Use thumbtacks to hang a string from one side of a little-used window to the other. Attach the bag to the string using clothes pegs. I usually leave them to hang and dry for a good month.

Once the herbs are dry, simply rub the bag between your hands. This not only removes the leaves from the stems, but it also crushes the dry leaves into small usable pieces. Untie the bag, remove and discard the branches or stems, then scoop the dried herbs into individual jars (leftover herb jars or resealable plastic bags work well for this purpose).

BASIL PESTO

2 packed cups fresh basil leaves

1 to 2 cloves garlic, peeled

¼ cup pine nuts, walnuts or
blanched almonds, toasted

¼ cup extra-virgin olive oil

½ cup Parmesan cheese,
freshly grated

IF YOU are freezing the pesto, do not add the Parmesan cheese, as it does not freeze well. Simply blend all the ingredients except the cheese and spoon the pesto into an ice cube tray. Freeze for 3 or 4 hours, or up to 24 hours. When the pesto is frozen, pop the cubes out of the tray. Place them in resealable freezer bags. Will keep frozen for up to 6 months. If you want to add the Parmesan, thaw the cubes, then stir in 1 Tbsp of freshly grated Parmesan per cube just before serving. *Yield: 1¼ cups, or 6 cubes*

PLACE BASIL, garlic and nuts in a food processor and blend until roughly chopped. With the machine running, add ½ of the olive oil in a continuous stream. Turn off the food processor and add Parmesan cheese. Process to mix, then add the remaining oil in a continuous stream. Process until the mixture is finely chopped and pasty. Season with salt and pepper to taste. Transfer to an airtight container and refrigerate. Will keep refrigerated for up to 6 days.

ASIAN PEARS

1¾ cups apple cider
or scrumpy

2 cups water

1½ cups sugar

½ vanilla bean, split and
seeds removed

one 1-inch piece fresh ginger,
smashed flat

1 star anise pod

1 cinnamon stick

Juice and zest of 1 lemon

8 Asian pears, peeled,
core and stem intact

THESE pears make a light dessert that is delicious served with a little crème fraîche (page 176). Make sure to choose pears that are ripe and firm. At the restaurant, we like to use cider from the Merridale Estate Cidery on Vancouver Island, but any scrumpy or apple cider will work well. These poached pears will keep, refrigerated and stored in their poaching liquid, up to two weeks. *Serves 8*

CUT A CIRCLE of parchment paper the diameter of a large saucepan. Poke a hole in the centre of the paper to act as a vent. Set aside.

In the saucepan, combine cider (or scrumpy), water, sugar, vanilla, ginger, star anise, cinnamon and lemon juice and zest. Bring to a boil on high heat and boil hard for 1 minute. Reduce the heat to low until the syrup is simmering. Using a spoon, carefully lower pears into the liquid.

Place parchment directly on the pears and liquid. (Some liquid will cover the top of the parchment paper; this is fine.) Simmer pears for 15 to 20 minutes, until tender but firm. Check for doneness: a skewer should easily pierce the fruit but the pears should remain intact. Remove from the heat, discard parchment paper and allow pears to cool in the saucepan. Serve warm or chilled.

APPLE CROSTADA

P INK Lady apples are tart and crisp and hold their shape
well during baking. Feel free to substitute another apple.
Serve this crostada with dollops of freshly whipped
cream. *Serves 10*

LINE AN 11 × 17-inch baking sheet with parchment paper. Roll
pastry around a rolling pin and unroll across the baking sheet.
Set aside.

Place apples, flour, granulated sugar, salt and cinnamon in a
large bowl and mix well. Carefully pile apples in the centre of the
pastry, leaving a 3-inch border between the fruit and the edge of
the pastry all the way around. Dot apples with butter.

Fold and tuck the sides of the pastry around the fruit. You will
have a 4-inch area of exposed filling in the centre. Refrigerate the
crostada, uncovered, for 30 minutes.

Preheat the oven to 425°F. Brush pastry crust with cream,
then sprinkle with turbinado (or coarse) sugar. Bake for 20 minutes, then reduce the heat to 350°F. Bake for another 40 minutes,
or until juices are bubbling. Allow to cool for at least 20 minutes.

TO SERVE Cut the crostada into 10 equal wedges and serve on
individual plates.

½ recipe pâte brisée dough
(page 119), rolled to 14-inch
diameter

8 Pink Lady apples, peeled,
cored and sliced

¼ cup flour

⅓ cup granulated sugar,
or to taste

Pinch of salt

¼ tsp ground cinnamon

2 Tbsp unsalted butter,
in pieces

2 Tbsp whipping cream

2 Tbsp turbinado sugar
or coarse sugar

Made with the ripe fruits of summer, these pies are simply the best. Choose fruit with a heady perfume and handle your pastry carefully, and your efforts will be well rewarded. These pies are best served with vanilla ice cream. Pâte brisée is a French term for "short pastry." It's a rich, flaky dough that can be used for sweet and savoury pies and tarts. *Serves 10 (Yield: one 9-inch pie)*

PÂTE BRISÉE Combine flour, granulated sugar and salt in a medium bowl. Add butter and work into the flour mixture with your fingers until the dough has the consistency of a coarse meal. Add the ⅓ cup of cold water and knead lightly until well combined.

Cover with a clean towel and allow to rest for 20 minutes. This will relax the dough, which makes it easier to roll.

Divide the dough into two pieces, one slightly larger than the other. Lightly dust a clean dry work surface with flour. Roll out the smaller piece into a circle 11 inches in diameter and ¼ inch thick. Fit this disc in a 9-inch pie plate.

Roll out the larger piece into a 10 × 12-inch rectangle about ¼ inch thick. Cut into strips ½ inch wide. Set these aside to create a lattice top. *Recipe continued overleaf...*

PÂTE BRISÉE

2 cups all-purpose flour

1 Tbsp granulated sugar

½ tsp salt

⅔ cup cold butter

⅓ cup cold water

1 egg

1 Tbsp water

2 Tbsp whipping cream (optional)

2 Tbsp coarse sugar (optional)

STRAWBERRY-RHUBARB FILLING

2½ cups strawberries, washed, hulled and halved if large

2½ cups rhubarb, in ½-inch dice

1½ cups sugar

¼ cup cornstarch

2 Tbsp unsalted butter, cubed

BING CHERRY FILLING

5 cups pitted Bing cherries

1 cup sugar

¼ cup cornstarch

2 Tbsp unsalted butter, cubed

SOUR CHERRY FILLING

4 cups pitted sour cherries, juice reserved

1 cup sugar

Pinch of salt

1 tsp pure almond extract

3 Tbsp cornstarch

2 Tbsp unsalted butter, cubed

STRAWBERRY-RHUBARB FILLING In a large bowl, combine strawberries, rhubarb, sugar and cornstarch. Scoop the filling into the pie shell and dot with butter.

BING CHERRY FILLING In a large bowl, combine cherries, sugar and cornstarch. Scoop the filling into the pie shell and dot with butter.

SOUR CHERRY FILLING In a large bowl, combine cherries and their juice, sugar, salt, almond extract and cornstarch. Toss together gently and carefully scoop into the pie shell. Dot with butter.

TO ASSEMBLE THE PIES In a small bowl, whisk together egg and the 1 Tbsp of water. Brush the edges of the pie with this mixture, then arrange pastry strips in a lattice pattern on top of the filling. Crimp the edges where the lattice meets the crust. Refrigerate the pie for 30 minutes.

Preheat the oven to 425°F. Brush the lattice with cream, if desired and bake for 20 minutes. Reduce the heat to 350°F and bake for another 35 minutes, or until juices are thick and bubbling. Allow to cool to room temperature before serving.

TO SERVE Cut the pie into wedges and serve on individual plates. There will be plenty of fruit juices, so make sure to scoop those up onto the plate and serve with the pie.

ROASTED PUMPKIN TART

AUTUMN brings beautiful bright orange sugar pumpkins! They are small, and heavy for their size. I often roast a lot more pumpkin than I need, as the purée can be used for breads, soups and other desserts—not just pies or tarts. Serve this tart with a drizzle of maple syrup or fresh whipped cream . . . or both. *Serves 12 (Yield: one 10-inch tart)*

PREHEAT THE OVEN to 400°F. Line a baking sheet with parchment paper.

Place whole pumpkin, skin on and stem removed, on the baking sheet. Bake for 1½ hours. Remove from the oven, carefully cut in half and allow to cool. Using a sharp knife, peel away and discard the skin. Scoop out the seeds and membrane and discard.

Place the flesh in a food processor and purée until smooth. Measure 1¾ cups pumpkin purée for the tart filling. Reserve any extra purée for another use, such as making bread or waffles. (Purée may be frozen in an airtight container for up to 3 months.)

Preheat the oven to 350°F. In a large bowl, whisk eggs with brown sugar. Stir in pumpkin purée, cinnamon, nutmeg, ginger, cardamon and salt. Add cream and mix to combine.

Pour the filling into the tart shell and bake for 55 minutes, or until set. A skewer inserted in the filling should come out clean. Allow to cool.

TO SERVE Cut the tart into wedges and serve on individual plates.

1 whole small sugar pumpkin

2 eggs

1 cup brown sugar

1 tsp ground cinnamon

½ tsp ground nutmeg

¼ tsp ground ginger

⅛ tsp ground cardamom

¼ tsp salt

¾ cup whipping cream

1 parbaked 10-inch tart shell

ROASTED PEARS

WITH BLUE CHEESE

4 ripe Bosc or other pears

1 Tbsp melted butter

Pinch of fresh thyme leaves

4 oz blue cheese, crumbled

AT THE restaurant, roasting pears is something we do as an accompaniment to blue cheese in the fall, making a nice segue from the savoury to the sweet. Choose pears that are blemish free and just ripe for best results. If the pears are too ripe, they will not caramelize well before becoming too delicate to handle. *Serves 4*

PREHEAT THE OVEN TO 400°F. Line a baking sheet with parchment paper. Peel, halve and core pears and arrange them cut side down on the baking sheet. Brush pears with butter and sprinkle with thyme, then roast until caramelized, about 30 minutes. Allow to cool to room temperature.

TO SERVE Place 2 pear halves, cut side up, in each bowl. Top with blue cheese.

APPLE CINNAMON CAKE

1 cup granulated sugar

½ cup brown sugar

½ cup butter, softened

1 tsp vanilla extract

¼ cup cream cheese

½ cup mascarpone cheese

2 large eggs

1½ cups all-purpose flour

1½ tsp baking powder

¼ tsp salt

3 cups peeled and diced apples

¼ cup granulated sugar

2 tsp ground cinnamon

JUST as delicious when made with pears, this cake is excellent all by itself, eaten out of your hand. It will fill your home with the intoxicating smell of cinnamon and apples (or pears) as it bakes. The cake is easiest to slice when cool, but it is possible to slice it warm if you just can't wait! Serve with whipped cream or ice cream. *Serves 10*

PREHEAT THE OVEN to 350°F. Grease a 9-inch springform pan and lightly dust with flour.

Place the 1 cup of granulated sugar, brown sugar, butter, vanilla extract, cream cheese and mascarpone cheese in the bowl of an electric mixer. Beat until well blended. Add eggs, one at a time, and mix well.

In a large bowl, combine flour, baking powder and salt. Add the cheese mixture to the flour mixture and stir until just combined.

Place apples in another large bowl. In a small bowl, combine the ¼ cup of granulated sugar and cinnamon and mix well. Add 2 Tbsp of the cinnamon sugar to the apples. Reserve any extra cinnamon sugar for the topping. Toss the apples to coat with sugar, then stir the apple mixture into the batter.

Pour the batter into the springform pan and sprinkle the top with the remaining cinnamon sugar. Bake for 1 hour, or until the cake pulls away from the sides of the pan. Cool the cake on a rack until serving.

TO SERVE This cake is best served in generous pieces. Place on individual plates or eat by hand.

NECTARINES
POACHED IN WINE SYRUP

FRESH tree fruits are always a staple of late summer dessert menus. I try to use a late-harvest wine with a flavour complementary to the nectarines, such as a Riesling or a Gewürztraminer, for the syrup. The fruit, once poached, will keep for up to a week in the refrigerator and can be served with ice cream and a little of the poaching syrup. *Serves 4*

4 nectarines

2 cups late-harvest white wine

1 cup sugar

2 cups water

1 cinnamon stick

1-inch piece ginger, peeled and thinly sliced

1 star anise pod

FILL A BOWL with ice cold water. Bring a large pot of water to a boil on high heat. Blanch nectarines for 30 seconds, then immerse in ice water to stop the cooking. Peel and discard the skins.

Using a sharp knife, halve nectarines and remove the pits. Discard the pits.

Place wine, sugar, water, cinnamon, ginger and star anise in a large saucepan and bring to a boil on high heat. Reduce the heat to low and simmer for 15 minutes to infuse. Add nectarines and poach for 15 minutes, until tender. Remove from the heat, transfer nectarines and syrup to a bowl and refrigerate for at least 2 hours.

TO SERVE Place 2 nectarine halves in each bowl. Spoon 2 Tbsp of the syrup over the nectarines.

HEARTY & COMFORTING
LATE FALL & WINTER

LATE FALL AND WINTER are magical times. At the onset, harvesting is almost completed, trees are starting to drop their leaves, and nights are cooler and getting longer. Local farms are seas of orange pumpkins and roadside stands are filled with colourful squashes, winter cabbages and root vegetables of all kinds. Gary and Naty King at Hazelmere Farm bring us celery roots and several different organic beets. Martin Rothe in Oliver is busy packing and carefully storing apples and other tree fruits to overwinter, and local hazelnut and walnut trees are bearing fruit.

At this time of year, we start to crave dishes that are comforting and hearty, such as Cowichan Valley duck confit with warm Asian vinaigrette, a rich stew prepared with large oysters from Fanny Bay on Vancouver Island, hot crusty breads, and hearty casseroles made with free-range chicken and soft polenta. For dessert, there is hazelnut tart, chocolate and dried pear loaf or steamed pudding with egg-nog custard—all of which suggest winter.

COWICHAN VALLEY

DUCK LEG CONFIT

WITH WILTED GREENS

AND WARM ASIAN VINAIGRETTE

DUCK CONFIT

4 duck legs, deboned
(about 2 lbs total)

1 tsp coarse salt

Pinch of cracked pepper

2 cloves garlic, sliced

WILTED GREENS
AND VINAIGRETTE

¼ cup rice vinegar

1 Tbsp soy sauce

1 tsp grated ginger

¼ cup + 1 Tbsp sesame oil

4 cups spinach or chard
or pea tops

Duck confit is traditionally made by poaching seasoned duck legs slowly in rendered duck fat. This alternative method involves roasting them slowly in the oven, which renders the fat and allows them to become tender, then cooking them for a short period of time at a higher heat to crisp up the skin. When arranging the duck legs in the roasting pan, place them close together so that they don't colour too much during the initial stage of cooking. *Serves 4*

DUCK CONFIT Preheat the oven to 325°F. Line an 8-inch square cake pan with parchment paper.

Season duck legs with salt, pepper and garlic and place in the cake pan. Cook for 1½ hours, to allow most of the fat to render from the legs. Increase the heat to 400°F and cook for another 30 minutes, until the skin is crisp. Remove duck legs from the oven, transfer them to a plate and allow to rest for 5 minutes while you prepare the greens.

WILTED GREENS AND VINAIGRETTE Whisk together rice vinegar, soy sauce, ginger and ¼ cup of the sesame oil in a small bowl until well combined.

Heat the remaining 1 Tbsp of sesame oil in a medium sauté pan on medium-high heat. Add spinach (or chard or pea tops) and 2 Tbsp of the vinaigrette, and toss to wilt.

TO SERVE Divide the wilted greens among 4 warmed plates. Top each portion of greens with a leg of duck confit and drizzle with an additional 1 Tbsp of the vinaigrette.

FANNY BAY OYSTERS

THE Pacific Northwest is renowned for its fresh seafood, especially the incredible variety of oysters that are found here. They are exported around the globe and often appear on menus in some of the world's finest restaurants. Oysters are available fresh almost all year round, but they are best in winter and early spring when the water is at its coldest. At this time, they become fat, plump and briny tasting and just perfect for panroasting.

Panko are also known as Japanese bread crumbs and are available in specialty stores. They are great for crusting chicken or seafood. *Serves 4*

ROASTED RED PEPPER SAUCE

1 red bell pepper, roasted, deseeded and finely chopped

½ cup mayonnaise

½ cup sour cream

1 Tbsp fresh lime or lemon juice

1 tsp freshly grated horseradish

OYSTERS

½ cup cold water

½ cup cornstarch

2 Tbsp chopped mixed herbs (such as parsley, thyme, chives)

2 cups panko or dry bread crumbs

12 large Fanny Bay or other beach oysters, shucked

½ cup vegetable oil for frying

Sprigs of herbs (such as parsley, thyme, chives), for garnish

ROASTED RED PEPPER SAUCE Place bell peppers, mayonnaise, sour cream, lime (or lemon) juice and horseradish in a blender or food processor. Blend lightly until the sauce has a smooth consistency. Transfer to a small bowl and refrigerate covered for 2 to 3 hours before serving.

OYSTERS In a medium bowl, whisk water and cornstarch together to form a slurry mixture. Combine mixed herbs and panko (or bread crumbs) in a shallow bowl.

Dip and coat oysters in the cornstarch water, then roll them in the bread crumb mixture until they are evenly coated.

Heat a large frying pan on medium heat. Add vegetable oil to a depth of ½ inch. Place oysters in hot oil and cook for about 4 minutes per side, or until firm to the touch. Using a slotted spoon, remove oysters from the oil and drain on paper towels.

TO SERVE Spoon a dollop of roasted red pepper sauce onto each plate. Top with 3 oysters and garnish with sprigs of parsley, thyme and chives.

FRESH beach oysters, together with potatoes and leeks, make for a hearty winter stew. John Bishop has long been making himself a quick lunch by poaching freshly shucked oysters in the soup of the day, and it has inspired this dish, which is a soup with oysters as the base. You can make the base ahead of time if you like, adding the remaining oysters when you reheat the stew. *Serves 4*

2 Tbsp butter

1 tsp chopped garlic

½ cup sliced onions

½ cup chopped celery

½ cup sliced leeks

24 medium beach oysters, shucked

½ cup white wine

4 cups water

½ cup diced potatoes

1 cup whipping cream

1 Tbsp chopped parsley

HEAT BUTTER in a medium saucepan on medium heat. Add garlic, onions, celery and leeks and sauté until softened, about 5 minutes. Stir in 12 oysters.

Deglaze the pan with wine. Add water and bring to a simmer. Add potatoes and cook for about 30 minutes, until vegetables are tender. Stir in cream and season with salt to taste. Remove from the heat, allow to cool slightly, then transfer to a blender or food processor and purée until smooth.

Strain soup through a fine-mesh sieve and return to the saucepan on medium heat. Discard any solids. Add the remaining oysters and simmer for 5 minutes, until oysters are cooked and plump. Add parsley.

TO SERVE Spoon 3 oysters into each of 4 warmed bowls and top with a ladleful of the remaining stew.

ROASTED GARLIC, WINTER KALE AND
WHITE BEAN SOUP

THIS hearty winter soup is meant to be rustic and can be a meal in itself when served with warm crusty bread and extra-virgin olive oil for dipping on the side. The bean I like to use for this soup is the small white Northern bean, which cooks up quite quickly. The oven-roasted garlic can also be chopped and spread onto slices of warm baguette with a light drizzle of olive oil and a sprinkle of your favourite salt. *Serves 6*

OVEN-ROASTED GARLIC

1 head garlic

SOUP

3 Tbsp olive oil

1 cup finely chopped
 onions or leeks

1 cup finely chopped celery *celery root*

1 cup peeled and diced potatoes *also butternut squash.*

½ cup dried white beans,
 presoaked overnight *Great Northern*
 and drained

1 head garlic cloves, roasted,
 peeled and chopped *4 cloves.*

1 Tbsp chopped fresh thyme

4 cups chicken or vegetable stock

~~1 cup whipping cream~~

1 bunch kale, washed
 and coarsely chopped

3 tsp extra-virgin olive oil

OVEN-ROASTED GARLIC Preheat the oven to 375°F. Place whole head of garlic on a baking sheet and bake for 20 to 30 minutes, until garlic becomes tender and roasted. Allow to cool and peel off the outer skins.

SOUP Heat olive oil in a stockpot on medium-high heat. Add onions (or leeks) and celery, cover and cook until transparent and tender, about 5 minutes. Stir in potatoes, beans, garlic, thyme and chicken (or vegetable) stock. Bring to a boil, then reduce the heat to medium and simmer partially covered for 35 to 40 minutes. To finish the soup, stir in cream and kale and cook uncovered for another 15 minutes. Season with salt and pepper to taste.

TO SERVE Pour soup into warmed bowls and drizzle each serving with extra-virgin olive oil.

CHILI SOUP

MAKE a vegetarian version of this hearty soup by substituting ½ cup of dried red lentils and 1 cup of finely chopped mushrooms for the ground beef. *Serves 4 to 6*

HEAT OLIVE OIL in a stockpot on medium-high heat. Add ground beef and fry until cooked, about 10 minutes. Add onions, celery, carrots, garlic and chili peppers, and cook for 5 to 6 minutes until tender. Stir in tomatoes, kidney beans and tomato paste. Season with chili powder and cumin, then salt and pepper to taste. Pour in the chicken (or vegetable) stock and bring to a boil. Reduce the heat to low, skim off any foam from the surface, cover and simmer for 30 to 40 minutes.

TO SERVE Ladle soup into warmed soup plates. Top with a good dollop of sour cream and garnish with lots of chopped cilantro.

2 Tbsp olive oil

½ lb ground beef

1 onion, chopped

2 stalks celery, finely chopped

1 carrot, peeled and finely chopped

2 cloves garlic, crushed

1 green chili pepper, deseeded and chopped

2 large tomatoes, blanched, skinned and chopped

1 cup red kidney beans, cooked

2 Tbsp tomato paste

2 Tbsp chili powder

1 Tbsp ground cumin

6 cups chicken or vegetable stock

½ cup sour cream, for garnish

½ cup chopped fresh cilantro, for garnish

GREEN LENTIL SOUP

WITH SPICY CHORIZO SAUSAGE
AND MULTIGRAIN BREAD

C HEF Dennis Green has become an expert at making chorizo sausage ever since we started to use local lamb on the menu at Bishop's. He mixes the lamb trimmings with spices and stuffs them into real sausage casings. When the sausages are filled, he simply hangs the links in the walk-in cooler to dry and mature for a few weeks. We then serve thinly shaved slices of these sausages on plain toast, as a starter when guests arrive. Serve this soup with hot crusty bread. And if you have leftovers, this multigrain bread makes excellent, crunchy-textured crumbs when ground. *Serves 4 to 6*

MULTIGRAIN BREAD In the bowl of an electric mixer, combine water, yeast and sugar. Allow to stand for 2 to 5 minutes, until the mixture is creamy. Add flour, multigrain cereal, salt and olive oil and mix, using the dough hook, for 7 to 10 minutes. The dough will pull away from the sides of the bowl. Transfer the dough to a large, lightly oiled bowl, cover with a damp tea towel and allow to rise for 2 to 3 hours, until the dough has doubled in volume.

Line a baking sheet with parchment paper. Lightly dust a clean, dry work surface with flour. Turn out the dough onto this surface and divide it into two equal pieces. Shape each piece into a ball, rounding it by cupping it with both hands while continually tucking the dough under its bottom until a smooth ball is formed. If the dough becomes sticky, dust your hands with flour, but use as little as possible. Pinch together the seam on the bottom of each ball.

Place the two round loaves, or boules, on the baking sheet. Cover gently with a damp tea towel and allow to rise a second time, about 2 hours. To test if the bread is ready to be baked, gently press on one of the loaves with your finger. If the dough holds the indentation, it's ready to go into the oven; if it springs back slightly it needs to rise for a little longer. *Recipe continued overleaf...*

MULTIGRAIN BREAD

2 cups + 2 Tbsp water, room temperature

2 Tbsp active dry yeast

2 Tbsp sugar

1½ lbs bread flour or all-purpose flour

1¼ cups multigrain cereal

4 tsp salt

⅓ cup olive oil

GREEN LENTIL SOUP

¼ cup olive oil

2 onions, chopped

2 cloves garlic, chopped

1 tsp freshly grated ginger

2 stalks celery, chopped

1 potato, peeled and cubed

1½ cups green lentils,
    washed and drained

6 cups vegetable or chicken stock

1 Tbsp chopped lovage leaves

1 tsp ground roasted
    coriander seeds

3 dried spicy chorizo sausages,
    in bite-size chunks

Preheat the oven to 400°F. Using a sharp knife, score the top of each loaf two or three times to a depth of ¼ inch, then carefully slide the baking sheet into the oven. Bake for about 40 minutes, or until the bread is a dark golden brown and sounds hollow when tapped on the bottom. Transfer to a cooling rack.

GREEN LENTIL SOUP Heat olive oil in a stockpot on medium heat. Add onions, garlic, ginger, celery and potatoes and sauté until soft, about 5 minutes. Stir in lentils, vegetable (or chicken) stock, lovage and coriander, and bring to a simmer. Reduce the heat to low and simmer for 40 to 45 minutes. Allow to cool slightly, then transfer to a blender or food processor and purée until smooth. Season to taste with salt and pepper.

Add chorizo and simmer gently on medium heat for 5 minutes to heat the sausage.

TO SERVE Ladle hot soup into warmed bowls and serve with thick slices of warm multigrain bread.

SOBA NOODLE SALAD

WITH CRANBERRIES AND APPLE

SOBA noodles are made from buckwheat, which is gluten-free and contains no wheat, and are readily available at most Asian food markets. This colourful noodle salad really is easy to prepare. Any sweet apple will work for this recipe, but my personal preference is the Gala because of its snappy flavour. Breaking the noodles in half before cooking makes them easier to eat. This salad is beautiful by itself but could also be served as an accompaniment to meat or seafood dishes. *Serves 4*

IN A LARGE SAUCEPAN, bring water to a boil on medium-high heat. Add noodles and cook for 5 minutes, stirring occasionally. Remove from the heat, drain noodles in a strainer and allow to cool under cold running water. Drain noodles well and transfer to a large bowl.

Add sesame oil and wine vinegar and toss to coat noodles. Stir in cranberries, apples, green onions and sesame seeds until well combined.

TO SERVE Swirl one-quarter of the noodles around a dinner fork. Using another fork, push the noodles off the dinner fork onto the centre of a salad plate, creating a turban-like mound. Repeat with the remaining noodles. Sprinkle each serving with chopped nuts (or sunflower seeds) and garnish with a sprig of cilantro. Serve immediately.

4 cups water

4 oz dried soba noodles, broken in half

1 Tbsp sesame oil

1 Tbsp rice wine vinegar

¼ cup coarsely chopped dried cranberries

½ cup coarsely grated apple, unpeeled but cored

¼ cup coarsely chopped green onions

1 Tbsp black or white sesame seeds

¼ cup coarsely chopped roasted peanuts or whole sunflower seeds

4 sprigs fresh cilantro

BOILED EGG AND
HALIBUT PIE

FRESH halibut and farm-fresh eggs seem like an unlikely pairing, but, in fact, they do taste very good together. I like to serve this pie with a steamed green vegetable such as broccoli or French beans, but you can vary the vegetables depending on the season. Try fresh peas in the early summer, fennel in midsummer, and corn kernels or a small dice of squash in the late summer.

As an alternative to the pastry topping, you could pipe creamy mashed potatoes over the halibut mixture. Drizzle the potatoes with olive oil and dust lightly with your favourite sea salt. *Serves 6*

PIE

2 Tbsp butter

1 cup finely sliced leeks,
   white part only

1 stalk celery, finely chopped

1 carrot, peeled and diced

1 cup shiitake
   mushrooms, sliced

1 clove garlic, chopped

1 lb boneless halibut fillet,
   in 1-inch cubes

1 cup white wine

1 cup water

1 bay leaf

6 black peppercorns

3 eggs, hard-boiled, peeled
   and sliced in half lengthwise

3 cups white wine and
   parsley sauce

1½ recipes pâte brisée
   dough (page 119)

½ tsp coarse sea salt

PIE Lightly butter a 9-inch pie plate.

Melt butter in a frying pan on medium heat. Add leeks, celery, carrots, mushrooms and garlic. Cover and sauté until tender, 10 to 15 minutes. Pour the vegetables into the pie plate. Set aside.

Place halibut, wine and water in a saucepan on medium-high heat. Add bay leaf and peppercorns and bring to a boil. Poach halibut for 5 to 6 minutes, until just cooked. Remove from the heat.

Set a fine-mesh sieve over a small bowl. Drain fish, reserving the poaching liquid. Discard the bay leaf and peppercorns. Set poaching liquid aside to use for parsley sauce.

Place fish on top of the vegetables in the pie plate. Arrange eggs, cut side down, on the fish.

WHITE WINE AND PARSLEY SAUCE Melt butter in a heavy sauce-pan on medium heat. Add flour and cook gently, stirring constantly until the flour is well incorporated. Remove from the heat. Stir in cream, poaching liquid and parsley. Return the pan to medium heat and bring the sauce to a simmer, stirring constantly with a whisk or a wooden spoon, for 5 minutes, or until the sauce is thick. Season with salt and pepper.

TO FINISH PIE Pour white wine and parsley sauce over the eggs. Set aside and allow to cool completely.

Preheat the oven to 375°F. Lightly dust a clean, dry work surface with flour. Roll out dough into a circle 9 inches in diameter and ¼ inch thick. Cover pie with the crust, sprinkle with sea salt and bake for about 45 minutes.

TO SERVE Portion the pie into 6 servings and serve on warmed plates.

WHITE WINE AND
PARSLEY SAUCE

2 Tbsp butter

2 Tbsp unbleached
   all-purpose flour

1 cup whipping cream

2 cups poaching liquid from fish

2 Tbsp chopped fresh parsley

SALMON CORNISH PASTIES

PASTRY

2 cups all-purpose flour

1 tsp sugar

1 tsp salt

⅔ cup shortening

1 egg, beaten

1 tsp white vinegar

2 Tbsp cold water

THE traditional Cornish pasty is a handheld pie that resembles a small football in shape and is filled with meat and vegetables, a satisfying lunch for a miner working deep in the coal mines of Cornwall. We have given this pasty a West Coast twist by using salmon instead of meat in the filling. These can be made vegetarian by substituting more vegetables, such as carrot or turnip, for the salmon, or they can be made in the traditional way by substituting diced lamb or beef for the salmon and using thyme or rosemary in place of the dill. I have been told that in some regions bakers put meat and vegetables in one end of the pasty and jam in the other, so you can start with lunch and have dessert by the time you are finished! Serve these pasties with a tossed side salad. *Serves 4*

PASTRY Combine flour, sugar and salt in a medium bowl. Add shortening and work it into the flour mixture with your fingers until the dough has the consistency of coarse meal.

In a small bowl, combine egg, white vinegar and water, then add to dry ingredients and knead lightly until well combined. Cover with a tea towel and allow to rest for 20 minutes. This will relax the dough, which makes it easier to roll.

Divide the dough into 8 pieces. On a lightly floured board, roll out each ball to a thickness of ⅛ inch. With a pastry cutter, trim each piece to a 6-inch circle.

SALMON FILLING Combine the filling ingredients in a medium bowl. Season with salt to taste.

TO ASSEMBLE THE PASTIES Preheat the oven to 375°F. Spoon ⅛ of the filling into the centre of each pastry circle. Fold the top half of each circle over the bottom half to make a half-moon shape, being careful to completely enclose the filling. Using a fork, crimp the edges together, then transfer the filled pasties, seam side up, to a baking sheet. Flatten the base of the pasties slightly so they do not fall over while baking. With a small knife, cut a small slit in each side of the pasties to allow steam to escape while baking. Bake for 45 minutes, until the sides are golden and the vegetables in the filling are cooked.

TO SERVE Place 2 pasties per person on individual plates.

SALMON FILLING

1 lb salmon, diced

1 onion, diced

1 potato, diced

1 stalk celery, diced

1 tsp chopped parsley

1 tsp chopped dill

LENTIL
SHEPHERD'S PIE

FILLING

1 Tbsp butter

1 Tbsp olive oil

1 onion, finely chopped

1 clove garlic, finely chopped

1 stalk celery, finely chopped

1 carrot, peeled and
   finely chopped

6 mushrooms, quartered
   and sliced

¼ cup yellow bell peppers,
   finely chopped

1 tsp chopped fresh thyme

1½ tsp ground cumin

½ tsp ground cardamom

1 cup dried brown lentils, rinsed

1 large ripe field tomato,
   cored and finely diced

2 cups vegetable stock

1 Tbsp tomato paste

½ Tbsp honey or sugar

4 dashes Worcestershire sauce

1 Tbsp balsamic vinegar

1 Tbsp lemon juice

1 tsp lemon zest

2 Tbsp chopped fresh
   basil leaves

ALWAYS thought shepherd's pie had to be made with ground-up meat leftovers from the weekend roast, but my sister Cherry Hunt inspired me with this lentil alternative. She is totally committed to a meat- and fish-free diet and to growing all her produce organically in the small vegetable garden she maintains. It does take an incredible amount of work, but this small garden plot (called an allotment in Britain) provides enough fruits and vegetables for her family, and also enables her to give some of the bounty to friends. It also means she is very connected to the land for most of the year.

Cut the rutabaga for the topping in smaller pieces than the potato so they take about the same time to cook. Serve this shepherd's pie with steamed green vegetables or a tossed green salad. *Serves 4 to 6*

FILLING Melt butter with olive oil in a large saucepan on medium heat. Add onions, garlic, celery, carrots, mushrooms and bell peppers. Sauté the vegetables for 3 to 5 minutes, until softened. Add thyme, cumin and cardamom, and cook for 2 to 3 more minutes. Add lentils, tomatoes, vegetable stock, tomato paste, honey (or sugar), Worcestershire sauce, balsamic vinegar, lemon juice, lemon zest and basil. Season with salt and freshly ground pepper to taste. Bring to a boil, then reduce the heat to low. Cover and simmer for about 40 minutes. *Recipe continued overleaf…*

1½ lbs Yukon Gold potatoes,
   peeled and quartered

1 cup rutabaga, peeled
   and cut in large dice

1 Tbsp butter

½ cup light or whipping cream

1 Tbsp olive oil

TOPPING   Place potatoes and rutabaga in a large saucepan. Cover with water and boil on medium-high heat until tender, 25 to 30 minutes. Drain well.

Mash potatoes and rutabaga well or put through a potato ricer to remove any lumps. Add butter and cream and mix well to make the topping light and fluffy. Season with salt and pepper.

TO ASSEMBLE THE PIE   Preheat the oven to 375°F. Grease a 9-inch ovenproof baking dish. Pour the lentil filling into the baking dish. Allow to cool.

Spread the mashed potato mixture evenly over the top of the filling. Brush with olive oil. Bake uncovered for 40 to 45 minutes, until golden brown.

TO SERVE   Portion the pie into 4 to 6 servings and serve on warmed plates.

PORK AND APPLE MEATLOAF
WITH YELLOW TOMATO SAUCE

F ANYTHING defines country comfort food, this pork and apple meatloaf does, especially late in the year when the weather tends to be cooler. The yellow tomato sauce can be made from tomatoes that were frozen earlier in the summer. (To store ripe whole tomatoes for winter use, simply wash and freeze the whole tomatoes in freezer bags. When the tomatoes are defrosted, the skins come off easily.) The combination of yellow tomato and yellow bell pepper makes for a sweet and chunky companion sauce for this dish. Serve with creamy mashed potatoes and a green vegetable. *Serves 4 to 6*

PORK AND APPLE MEATLOAF Preheat the oven to 350°F. Lightly oil a 5 × 9-inch loaf pan. In a large bowl, combine eggs and cream (or milk). Stir in bread crumbs (or panko), green onions, garlic, apples, coriander, ginger, salt and pepper. Add ground pork and mix well.

Pat meatloaf into the pan and bake for 1¼ hours.

YELLOW TOMATO SAUCE Melt butter in a medium saucepan on medium heat. Add shallots (or sweet onions) and garlic and sauté until shallots are translucent, about 5 minutes. Add tomatoes, bell peppers, rice (or wine) vinegar and honey. Season with salt and pepper. Reduce the heat to low, cover and cook for 30 to 40 minutes. Remove from the heat and coarsely blend using a hand blender. The sauce is meant to be chunky, so do not overprocess.

TO SERVE Pour ⅓ cup of sauce onto the centre of each warmed plate. Unmould the meatloaf and slice it into pieces 1 inch thick. Place a slice of meatloaf onto the sauce on each plate.

PORK AND APPLE MEATLOAF

2 eggs

½ cup light cream or milk

½ cup dry bread crumbs or panko

⅓ cup finely chopped green onions

1 clove garlic, minced

1 green apple, peeled and finely diced

1 tsp freshly ground coriander seeds

1 tsp grated fresh ginger

1 tsp salt

¼ tsp pepper

1½ lbs ground lean pork loin

YELLOW TOMATO SAUCE

2 Tbsp butter

1 cup coarsely chopped shallots or sweet onions

2 cloves garlic

2 lbs yellow tomatoes (about 6 large), blanched, skinned and chopped

1 yellow bell pepper, roasted, skinned and chopped

¼ cup rice vinegar or wine vinegar

1 Tbsp honey

1 tsp salt

½ tsp pepper

IRISH SODA BREAD

2 cups all-purpose flour

2 cups whole wheat flour

½ cup large-flake oatmeal

¼ cup whole raw pumpkin
seeds, hulled

1 tsp baking soda

¾ tsp salt

¼ cup unsalted butter, melted

2 Tbsp brown sugar

1 cup buttermilk

1 cup whole milk

THE name for this stew came about because of my daughter. Whenever I made meat stews in the usual way, her plate in particular kept coming back to the kitchen with most of the chunks of meat still on it. Being the deceptive home cook that I have become—especially when it comes to feeding two children with different eating preferences—I decided to take a different tack. To make a stew that would appeal to both our on-the-cusp-of-vegetarian daughter and our meat-eating teenaged son, plus suit our own attention to protein intake, I didn't actually cut back very much on the meat, I just cut it into smaller pieces. Cut this way and combined with lots of extra veggies, the meat seems to have less of a presence in the dish as a whole . . . and my strategy worked.

I usually like to serve this stew with hot crusty bread rolls, brown rice or mashed potatoes and perhaps a bowl of steamed greens, such as Swiss chard or kale, on the side. The soda bread takes just minutes to measure and mix together. The pumpkin seeds and oatmeal add lovely texture and crunch, but if you don't have any pumpkin seeds in your pantry, use another seed or nut or omit them altogether. This bread keeps very well in an airtight container for one to two days. *Serves 6*

IRISH SODA BREAD Preheat the oven to 425°F. In a large bowl, combine all-purpose and whole wheat flours, oatmeal, pumpkin seeds, baking soda and salt. Set aside.

In a medium bowl, whisk together butter and brown sugar. Whisking constantly, add buttermilk and whole milk in a slow, continuous stream. Pour the milk mixture into the dry ingredients, using a spatula to mix well. The dough will be sticky.

Liberally dust a clean, dry work surface with flour. Turn the dough onto the surface and divide into 2 equal pieces. Gently shape each piece into a round 6 inches in diameter.

Place the two loaves on a baking sheet and bake for 15 minutes. Reduce the heat to 350°F and continue to bake for about 30 minutes longer, or until the loaf sounds hollow when tapped on the bottom. Transfer to a cooling rack. Allow the loaves to cool for 1 hour before slicing.

BEEF STEW Heat vegetable and olive oils in a large stockpot on medium heat. Add steak and sauté until lightly browned, about 5 minutes. Add onions, leeks, garlic, celery, carrots, turnips (or rutabaga), mushrooms, squash, celery root and bell peppers and cook for 10 to 15 minutes, until tender.

Stir in tomato paste, star anise and cardamom. Cover with stock (or water), season with salt and pepper, and bring to a boil. Reduce the heat to low, skim off any fat or impurities that rise to the surface, cover and simmer until meat is tender, 40 to 50 minutes. Remove from the heat.

TO SERVE Ladle stew into warmed soup bowls and top with freshly chopped parsley.

BEEF STEW

1 Tbsp vegetable oil

1 Tbsp olive oil

8 oz top sirloin steak,
    in ½-inch cubes

1 onion, chopped

1 leek, white part only, sliced

3 cloves garlic, chopped

1 stalk celery, chopped

3 baby carrots, in ½-inch lengths

½ white turnip or rutabaga,
    in ½-inch dice

1 cup mushrooms, quartered

1 cup butternut squash,
    in ½-inch dice

½ cup celery root, in ½-inch dice

½ small red bell pepper, chopped

1 Tbsp tomato paste

1 star anise pod

1 tsp cardamom seeds

6 cups chicken or beef stock
    or water to cover

¼ cup chopped fresh parsley,
    for garnish

(ON THE FARM)

GARY KING

photos by AL HARVEY

I T IS mid-November in the Pacific Northwest and there are leeks, celeriac, beets, culinary herbs, chard, kale, spinach and squashes in the fields waiting to be harvested. Most of the produce, though, has already been picked and either canned, cellared or frozen for use over the winter. Many of the fields have cover crops and, at this time of year, there are very few visitors.

Near the ocean, where Hazelmere Organic Farm is located, heat-loving fruits and vegetables do not grow as well as they do in the interior of the province. We are very successful with potatoes, carrots, kale, beets and leeks and so, late each fall, when the work on the farm slows down I travel east to trade coastal products for interior ones. I like to visit the Similkameen Valley, especially around Cawston, B.C., where 65 per cent of the farms are organic. The local farmers and I compare notes about our farming methods and, on occasion, John Bishop joins us to celebrate a successful season by enjoying a home-grown meal together.

In December or January, John and I sit at the kitchen table to pore over seed catalogues and discuss what we will plant for harvest next year. Our attention is drawn to the window,

where outside we see a coyote in the field next door searching and then pouncing, probably on a large vole. A visiting heron is hunting for worms much closer to the farmhouse. Once again we are reminded that food for all species is provided by healthy soil, and that the local farmland is where we get our food. Both of us agree that the taste and sustainability of local organic products are our preference, but that even those that are non-certified will make their way onto our table, as long as they are locally raised with care, but without genetically modified organisms (GMOs) or chemical sprays.

We are both committed to bringing nutritious food to the table, and we know each other well enough that I can deliver produce I know John and Dennis Green will like, even if they haven't called me to order it. Likewise, they are happy to help me out and put something on the menu if I happen to have a bumper crop of it. Especially in the leaner winter months, it is the strength and flexibility of this relationship between farmers and cooks that allows us both to thrive and to conserve natural resources, build community and cultivate positive change.

LAMB SHOULDER

L AMB shoulder is an inexpensive cut that is one of my favourites for a family meal. It does require a long cooking process to become tender, but once it is done, it is almost falling apart, allowing you to mix it into the lentil stew with a fork. Puy lentils are a small dark brown variety that is named for the town in France where they originated. They are grown widely on the Prairies, and are readily available at specialty food stores. *Serves 6*

SLOW-ROASTED LAMB Preheat the oven to 450°F. Rub lamb shoulder all over with olive oil, salt and pepper. Score the skin lightly and press garlic slices into the meat.

Roll and tuck lamb into a cylinder shape 6 inches in diameter and tie with butcher's twine every 2 inches to secure the meat and ensure it retains its shape while cooking. Place in a roasting pan and roast for 45 minutes, until lamb is golden brown and the skin is crispy. Remove lamb from the oven.

Reduce the heat to 350°F. Cover the pan of lamb with two layers of aluminum foil and seal tightly. (This will allow steam to build up inside the pan, cooking the lamb in its own juices.) Bake lamb for 2 hours, until very tender when pierced with a knife. Allow to rest for 15 to 30 minutes before slicing.

PUY LENTIL STEW Heat olive oil in a medium saucepan on medium-high heat. Add onions, garlic, celery root, carrots and parsnips and sauté until lightly coloured, about 5 minutes. Stir in paprika, cumin and lentils until well combined. Add wine, mix well and pour in vegetable (or chicken) stock. Bring to a simmer, reduce the heat to medium-low and cook for 1 hour, or until lentils and vegetables are tender. Season with salt to taste.

TO SERVE Ladle lentil stew into warmed bowls. Cut lamb into ½-inch thick slices and place two slices on top of each bowl of stew. Serve immediately.

SLOW-ROASTED LAMB

1 boneless lamb shoulder (about 3 lbs)

2 Tbsp olive oil

1 tsp coarse salt

1 tsp pepper

2 Tbsp sliced garlic

PUY LENTIL STEW

2 Tbsp olive oil

½ cup diced onions

1 tsp minced garlic

½ cup diced celery root

½ cup diced carrots

½ cup diced parsnips

1 tsp paprika

1 tsp ground cumin

1 cup Puy lentils, washed well and drained

½ cup red wine

4 cups vegetable or chicken stock

BEEF TENDERLOIN

SPICE RUB

1 Tbsp black peppercorns

1 tsp pink or green peppercorns

1 tsp dill seeds

1 tsp fennel seeds

1 tsp coriander seeds

1 tsp Szechuan peppercorns

1 tsp yellow mustard seeds

1 tsp brown mustard seeds

½ tsp chili flakes

TENDERLOIN

2 lbs centre-cut beef tenderloin

1 Tbsp olive oil

2 Tbsp spice rub

6 sprigs fresh
watercress, for garnish

THE centre cut of beef tenderloin is the most expensive cut of beef you can buy, so I usually reserve it for special occasions like holidays or when friends come over for dinner. Beef tenderloin is a cut that is extremely lean and every bit of the roast is servable. I think it's a good idea to telephone your butcher ahead of time to make sure you get a piece that's exactly the right size. Be sure to specify that you would like a centre cut, not the thinner tail end. Leftovers can be thinly sliced for roast beef sandwiches or cold cuts.

I suggest that you roast the yams along with the tenderloin for the last ten minutes of its cooking. Then reduce the oven temperature to 375°F for the remaining fifteen to twenty minutes to finish the frites. *Serves 4 to 6*

SPICE RUB Combine spice rub ingredients in a small bowl. Using a mortar and pestle or an electric spice mill, grind this mixture finely. Spice rub can be stored in an airtight jar for up to 2 weeks. It can also be used to season chicken or pork.

TENDERLOIN Preheat the oven to 400°F. Brush the tenderloin with olive oil and season with spice rub.

Heat a frying pan on high heat. Place beef into the hot pan and sear on all sides until lightly browned, 8 to 10 minutes. Transfer seared beef to a roasting pan and roast for 25 to 30 minutes. Check doneness with a meat thermometer: the internal temperature should be 125°F. Remove from the oven and allow the meat to rest for 15 minutes before carving.

HORSERADISH CREAM Combine whipped cream, lemon juice and horseradish in a small bowl with a lid. Cover and refrigerate for up to 2 hours.

YAM FRITES Line a baking sheet with parchment paper. Cut each ½ yam in 4 wedges. Place yam wedges in a medium bowl. Season with salt. Pour in vegetable oil and toss until well coated. Transfer yams to the baking sheet. Ten minutes before the tenderloin has finished cooking, place frites in the oven. When the tenderloin is removed, reduce the heat to 375°F and bake for 15 to 20 minutes more, turning frites occasionally, until they are cooked and crispy. (If you are making the frites on their own, bake in a preheated oven at 375°F for 25 to 30 minutes total, turning yams occasionally, until they are cooked and crispy.)

TO SERVE Carve beef tenderloin into ½-inch slices. Place 2 beef slices onto each warmed dinner plate along with 4 to 6 yam frites and a dollop of horseradish cream. Garnish each plate with sprigs of fresh watercress.

HORSERADISH CREAM

1 cup whipped cream

Juice of ½ lemon

1 Tbsp horseradish root, freshly grated
or 1 tsp prepared horseradish sauce

YAM FRITES

4 yams, peeled, cut in wedges lengthwise

1 tsp salt

3 Tbsp vegetable oil

BRAISED RABBIT

WITH RED WINE AND BAY LEAVES

1 fryer rabbit or chicken
  (about 3 lbs), in 8 pieces

2 cups red wine

2 bay leaves

2 sprigs fresh thyme

1 sprig fresh rosemary

4 cloves garlic

1 tsp freshly ground pepper

2 Tbsp olive oil

1 cup diced onions

½ cup sliced celery

1 cup sliced carrots

1 cup mushrooms, quartered

1 tsp minced garlic

4 cups chicken stock

FRESH rabbit always brings to mind country cooking. Rabbit is quite similar to chicken in flavour and texture, which is why we have prepared it much as you would the traditional French *coq au vin*, a hearty chicken stew cooked in red wine with lots of vegetables and herbs. If you cannot find fresh rabbit, you may substitute a fresh frying chicken. Serve with boiled potatoes or savoury bread pudding (page 166). *Serves 4*

PLACE RABBIT (or chicken) in a medium bowl or a resealable container. Add wine, bay leaves, thyme, rosemary, garlic cloves and pepper, then cover and allow to marinate, refrigerated, for up to 24 hours.

Remove meat from the marinade, pat dry with paper towels and set aside. Strain the marinade through a fine-mesh sieve into a small bowl. Discard any solids and set aside.

Heat olive oil in a medium saucepan on high heat. Add meat and sauté until golden brown. Remove meat from the pot and set aside.

To the saucepan, add onions, celery, carrots, mushrooms and minced garlic. Sauté until onions are lightly coloured and translucent, about 10 minutes. Return rabbit (or chicken) to the saucepan. Add the reserved marinade.

Add enough chicken stock to cover the meat and vegetables and bring to a simmer. Reduce the heat to low and cook for 2 hours, until tender and almost falling off the bone.

TO SERVE Divide rabbit (or chicken) and vegetables among 4 plates, allowing 2 pieces of meat per person.

OVEN-FRIED CHICKEN

WITH MASHED NEW POTATOES,
SOUR CREAM AND CHIVES

I'M ALWAYS looking for easy chicken dishes that my children will like, and this one certainly fits the bill. Who doesn't like crispy fried chicken drumsticks (in this case baked rather than fried) served with freshly boiled potatoes mashed lightly with sour cream and fresh chives? A number of years ago, one of the cooks made this for a staff dinner at the restaurant, and I've been making it at home ever since. *Serves 6*

OVEN-FRIED CHICKEN Preheat the oven to 400°F. Line a baking sheet with parchment paper. Season chicken with salt and pepper and set aside.

Place bread crumbs in a shallow bowl. In another shallow bowl, whisk together mustard and olive oil. Dip chicken in the mustard-oil mixture, coating it well, then roll in bread crumbs. Place coated chicken on the baking sheet. Bake for 30 minutes, turning once, until golden and crisp.

MASHED NEW POTATOES Place potatoes in a medium saucepan, cover with water and cook on medium heat until tender, about 25 minutes. Drain well.

Add sour cream and chives (or green onions). Using a fork, mash together coarsely. Season with salt and pepper to taste.

TO SERVE Arrange chicken drumsticks on a serving platter and place mashed new potatoes in a bowl. Serve immediately, allowing guests to help themselves.

OVEN-FRIED CHICKEN

12 chicken drumsticks,
   knuckle removed

2 cups fresh bread crumbs

¼ cup Dijon mustard

¼ cup olive oil

MASHED NEW POTATOES

1 lb new potatoes,
   washed and scrubbed

½ cup sour cream

¼ cup chopped chives
   or green onions

CHICKEN WITH VEGETABLES

AND CREAMY POLENTA CASSEROLE

VEGETABLES AND CREAMY POLENTA

¼ cup olive oil

¼ cup finely minced onions

1 clove garlic, finely chopped

2 cups vegetable or chicken stock

1 cup whipping cream

1 cup coarse ground organic cornmeal

1 Tbsp finely chopped thyme leaves

¼ cup grated Parmesan cheese

1 tsp salt

½ tsp cracked pepper

1 stalk celery, chopped

2 carrots, peeled and chopped

1 cup chopped fresh fennel bulb

1 cup chopped celery root

T HIS casserole is an all-in-one meal, and cooking the chicken on top of the polenta allows for the skin to become crispy and the juices from the chicken to flavour the casserole even further. Cornmeal cooked in this way defines comfort, perhaps even more than the creamy mashed potatoes I love. The coarse, ground organic cornmeal from the bulk section at the grocery store works well in this recipe; buy lots, because it is useful as a breading for poultry or for seafood such as oysters, and as a staple ingredient in baked goods such as cornmeal muffins or bread. Serve this casserole with a steaming bowl of freshly cooked chard or kale greens. *Serves 6 to 8*

VEGETABLES AND CREAMY POLENTA Heat olive oil in a saucepan on medium heat. Add onions and garlic and sauté until onions are translucent, about 5 minutes. Add vegetable (or chicken) stock and cream and bring to a boil. Whisk in cornmeal and thyme.

Reduce the heat to low, cover and cook gently until the mixture thickens, about 15 minutes. Remove from the heat and add Parmesan cheese. Season with salt and pepper. If the polenta becomes too thick to pour, add more vegetable (or chicken) stock or water to thin it down.

Fold in celery, carrots, fennel and celery root. Pour into a 9 × 13-inch baking pan. Set aside.

CHICKEN Season chicken with salt, pepper and paprika and dust lightly with flour. Discard any leftover flour.

Heat vegetable oil in a large frying pan on medium-high heat. Add chicken and brown on both sides, about 10 minutes. Remove from the heat.

TO ASSEMBLE THE CASSEROLE Preheat the oven to 400°F. Place chicken on top of the vegetables and polenta. Bake for 35 to 40 minutes, until the chicken is cooked.

TO SERVE Spoon 2 large serving spoonfuls of this casserole onto each warmed soup plate. Serve 1 piece of chicken per person.

CHICKEN

8 free-range chicken thighs, boneless (about 1¼ lbs total)

1 tsp salt

1 tsp pepper

1 tsp paprika

½ cup all-purpose flour

2 Tbsp vegetable oil

FIVE-SPICE DUCK BREAST

WITH SHIITAKE MUSHROOM RISOTTO

FIVE-SPICE POWDER

1 Tbsp whole cloves

1 Tbsp ground cinnamon

1 Tbsp Szechuan peppercorns

1 Tbsp star anise pods

1 Tbsp coriander seeds

RISOTTO

4 cups chicken stock

2 Tbsp butter

1 cup onions, in ¼-inch dice

1 tsp minced garlic

2 cups shiitake mushrooms, whole (or halved if large)

2 cups carnaroli or arborio rice

½ cup dry sherry

¼ cup grated Parmesan cheese

DUCK

4 boneless duck breasts (each 6 oz)

1 tsp salt

1 Tbsp five-spice powder

W E BUY all of our ducks from Cowichan Bay Farm on Vancouver Island. Lyle and Fiona Young raise pasture-fed ducks, chickens, cattle and lamb on a heritage farm that has been in the family for more than eighty years. Preparing duck with a nod to Asian flavours is a natural, so we like to roast it seasoned with five-spice powder—a combination of cinnamon, star anise, Szechuan peppercorns, coriander and cloves. If you don't have all the spices to make the five-spice powder yourself, it is readily available in Asian markets. *Serves 4 to 6*

FIVE-SPICE POWDER Combine ingredients in a small bowl. Using a mortar and pestle or an electric spice mill, grind this mixture finely. Five-spice powder can be stored indefinitely in an airtight jar at room temperature.

RISOTTO Place chicken stock in a medium saucepan and bring to a simmer on low heat. Keep hot.

Melt butter in a large saucepan on medium heat. Add onions and garlic and sauté until onions are almost translucent, about 5 minutes. Add mushrooms and sauté until lightly coloured, 2 to 3 minutes. Stir in rice and sauté until grains are covered with butter and are slightly translucent, 2 to 3 minutes. Season with salt and pepper.

Deglaze the pan with sherry, stirring to loosen the browned bits on the bottom. Add enough of the hot chicken stock to cover rice by ½ inch. Simmer, uncovered, on medium heat, stirring constantly and adding chicken stock ½ cup at a time as necessary to keep rice covered. After 20 minutes, check rice for doneness: it should be tender but not mushy. If rice is still crunchy, add more stock and cook up to 10 minutes more.

When rice is done, stir in Parmesan cheese. Cook until the risotto is still creamy but thick enough to mound slightly on a plate, 2 to 3 minutes. Serve hot.

DUCK Preheat the oven to 450°F. Season duck breasts with salt
and five-spice powder and score skin every ¼ inch for best results.

Heat a medium ovenproof frying pan on medium heat. Add
duck breasts, skin side down, and cook for 5 minutes, until lightly
coloured and skin begins to render. Turn duck over and cook in
the oven for 5 minutes. Turn duck over again (it should be skin
side down) and cook 5 minutes more. Check for doneness with
a meat thermometer: the internal temperature should be 140°F.
Remove from the oven and allow to rest for 5 minutes before
slicing. Cut duck into slices ⅛ inch thick.

TO SERVE Place 1 cup of risotto on each plate. Top each serving
with 6 to 8 slices of duck breast.

SOCKEYE SALMON FILLET
WITH CHOPPED EGG SAUCE

SALMON baked lightly this way is a favoured alternative to grilling, and so simple to do. The farm-fresh egg sauce is irresistible to almost everyone, especially young people. A good vegetable side to serve with this dish is slices of oven-roasted fresh fennel bulb. *Serves 4*

EGG SAUCE Melt butter in a heavy saucepan on medium heat. Add flour and cook gently, stirring constantly until the flour is well incorporated. You will know it is ready when it leaves the sides of the pan and becomes slightly lighter in colour. Remove the butter and flour mixture from the heat and pour in milk.

Return the pan to the heat and bring to a boil, stirring constantly for 5 minutes. Add eggs, parsley and lemon zest and season with salt and pepper to taste. Cover, set aside and keep warm.

SALMON Preheat the oven to 375°F. Season salmon fillets with salt and pepper. In a medium bowl, whisk water and cornstarch together to form a slurry mixture. Place bread crumbs in a shallow bowl.

Dip fillets in the cornstarch water, then roll them in the bread crumbs until they are evenly coated.

Heat vegetable oil in a large ovenproof frying pan on medium heat. Place salmon in hot oil and gently fry for 3 to 4 minutes per side. Set the frying pan in the oven and bake for 5 to 6 minutes, until salmon is just cooked and firm to the touch.

TO SERVE Ladle ⅓ to ½ cup of the egg sauce onto warmed dinner plates. Top with salmon fillets and garnish with lemon wedges.

EGG SAUCE

2 Tbsp butter

2 Tbsp all-purpose flour

2¼ cups milk

2 hard-boiled eggs,
    coarsely chopped

1 Tbsp chopped parsley

1 tsp lemon zest

SALMON

4 fillets salmon (each 6 oz),
    boneless and skin removed

½ cup cold water

½ cup cornstarch

1½ cups fresh
    white bread crumbs

¼ cup vegetable oil

4 lemon wedges

SAVOURY BREAD PUDDING

WITH HEIRLOOM TOMATO SAUCE

HEIRLOOM TOMATO SAUCE

3 Tbsp olive oil

2 shallots, chopped

2 cloves garlic, chopped

1 red bell pepper, quartered
and deseeded

6 large field tomatoes
(about 1½ lbs), cored,
blanched, skinned and
chopped

2 Tbsp liquid honey

1 tsp salt

THIS savoury bread pudding is an easy-to-prepare brunch item. It is the creation of one of our former chefs, Gavin Craig, who made it and served it occasionally as a part of our staff meal. For a vegetarian version, simply omit the ham or bacon and add ½ cup of sun-dried tomatoes. Serve either version with freshly grated Parmesan cheese.

Heirloom tomatoes are the sweetest and most flavoursome of the tomato varieties grown in this part of the world. They are great served as a summer salad or in a simple sauce like this. Their season, however, is relatively short, so I always try to put away a few pounds of whole tomatoes in the freezer so that I can make this sauce even in the middle of winter. *Serves 6 to 8*

HEIRLOOM TOMATO SAUCE Heat olive oil in a large saucepan on medium heat. Add shallots, garlic and bell peppers and sauté, covered, until tender, 5 to 6 minutes. Add tomatoes, honey and salt. Cover and cook on medium heat for about 30 minutes. Remove from the heat and allow to cool.

Transfer to a blender or food processor and process lightly. (There should still be chunks in the sauce.)

SAVOURY BREAD PUDDING   Preheat the oven to 350°F. Grease
a 10-inch springform pan or loaf pan well with melted butter
(or oil).

Combine bread and all remaining ingredients in a large mixing bowl. Season with salt and pepper. Spoon the bread mixture
into the springform (or loaf) pan and place it on a baking sheet.
Cover the pan with aluminum foil and bake for 30 minutes.

Remove the foil and increase the oven temperature to 450°F.
Bake bread pudding, uncovered, for about 15 minutes, or until
brown and set. Remove from the oven and allow to cool for
15 minutes. Unmould from the pan and transfer to a warmed
plate before serving.

TO SERVE   Just before serving, reheat the tomato sauce. Spoon
1 thick slice of the pudding onto each warmed plate. Top with
⅓ to ½ cup of the tomato sauce.

SAVOURY BREAD PUDDING

1 loaf sliced bread, crusts
   removed, in ¼-inch cubes

2 cups milk

5 eggs

2 shallots, chopped

1 small leek (white part only),
   washed and sliced

2 cloves garlic, chopped

1 cup shiitake mushrooms, sliced

4 slices pancetta ham or
   back bacon, chopped

3 Tbsp grated Parmesan cheese

1 Tbsp chopped fresh basil

1 Tbsp chopped fresh oregano

PICKLING VEGETABLES

2 lbs green beans,
strings removed

OR 2 lbs asparagus, woody
ends trimmed, cut to the
length of the jar

OR 4 cups cooked beets,
peeled and sliced ¼ inch thick

2 cups water

2 cups white or
red wine vinegar

1 cup sugar

2 Tbsp pickling spice

1 tsp salt

PICKLING vegetables is a great way to preserve summer's bounty for the winter. At the restaurant, I prefer to make what is referred to as a refrigerator (or fridge) pickle, which is preserved in the traditional manner using a vinegar-and-sugar solution but is not "canned." I find this makes the pickles crisper, especially when using thin pieces of vegetable. If you wish to store your pickles in the pantry (or anywhere outside of the refrigerator), you will have to process the sealed jars in a water bath for 20 minutes. *Makes 2 qts*

STERILIZE TWO 4-cup or four 2-cup wide-mouth glass jars with tight-fitting lids by submerging them in boiling water for 1 to 2 minutes. Remove the jars from the water and allow them to cool and air dry on a rack at room temperature.

Wash vegetables, if you have not already. Fill jars with vegetables, leaving ½ inch free below the rim.

Combine water, wine vinegar, sugar, pickling spice and salt in a medium saucepan on high heat. Bring to a boil and pour over vegetables. Allow to cool to room temperature. Cover tightly with a lid, refrigerate and allow flavours to combine for at least 2 weeks. Will keep refrigerated in an airtight container for up to 6 months.

CASSEROLE

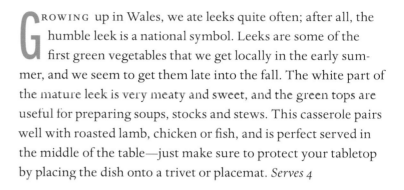

GROWING up in Wales, we ate leeks quite often; after all, the humble leek is a national symbol. Leeks are some of the first green vegetables that we get locally in the early summer, and we seem to get them late into the fall. The white part of the mature leek is very meaty and sweet, and the green tops are useful for preparing soups, stocks and stews. This casserole pairs well with roasted lamb, chicken or fish, and is perfect served in the middle of the table—just make sure to protect your tabletop by placing the dish onto a trivet or placemat. *Serves 4*

3 leeks, white part only, washed and cut in 1-inch rounds

½ cup water or chicken stock

2 Tbsp olive oil

1 Tbsp butter

2 cloves garlic, chopped

1½ cups diced white bread

2 Tbsp chopped parsley

PREHEAT THE OVEN to 400°F. Grease an 8-inch square pan.

Place leeks into the pan, lying flat and season lightly with salt and pepper. Pour water (or chicken stock) over the leeks, cover tightly with a lid or parchment cover and bake until tender, about 30 minutes.

While leeks are baking, prepare the topping. Heat a frying pan on medium heat. Add olive oil, butter and garlic and sauté lightly for 2 to 3 minutes. Add bread and fry until golden brown. Remove from the heat, toss with parsley and set aside.

Just before serving, sprinkle the leeks with the bread topping.

CASSEROLE

SLOW-COOKED vegetable casseroles are easy to make, and once assembled and in the oven they can be left to cook gently in their own time. They are a nourishing accompaniment to almost any meal. Serve these beans as a vegetable-only dish or vary the basic recipe by adding, for example, diced chicken or chopped bacon. I sometimes like to sprinkle in a few chili pepper seeds to spice it up. You can also make this hearty dish a day ahead and refrigerate it. Reheated in the oven the next day with a little added stock, it will taste even better. Serve the casserole in a preheated serving bowl in the centre of the table. *Serves 4 to 6*

PREHEAT THE OVEN to 325°F. Heat olive oil in an ovenproof casserole dish (one with a lid) on medium heat. Add onions, garlic, celery, carrots and bell peppers and sauté for 5 to 6 minutes. Add beans, tomatoes, basil, lentils and cornmeal. Cover with chicken (or vegetable) stock and bring to a simmer. Season with cayenne pepper, salt and coarsely ground pepper. Skim off any impurities that come to the surface. Cover and bake in the oven for 2 hours, until beans are tender.

3 Tbsp olive oil

1 cup chopped onions

3 cloves garlic, chopped

½ cup chopped celery

½ cup chopped carrots

1 green bell pepper, seeded and chopped

1 cup dry white beans, presoaked overnight in the refrigerator and drained

3 large field tomatoes, cored and finely chopped

6 fresh basil leaves, chopped

¼ cup dried red lentils

¼ cup stone-ground cornmeal

6 cups chicken or vegetable stock

½ tsp cayenne pepper (optional)

POTATO HASH

¼ cup olive oil

1 Tbsp sesame oil

½ head small napa
cabbage, finely sliced

2 large potatoes, cooked
and chopped

1 carrot, grated

1 stalk celery, thinly sliced

2 green onions, chopped

1 tsp caraway seeds

1 tsp herbes de Provence

WAS once asked in a phone interview by *Food & Wine* magazine to name some of my favourite dishes to cook. I quickly replied, "Fry-ups," which is the British term for hashes. The line seemed to go dead, then the bewildered interviewer said, "I am sorry, I don't think I heard you properly." I'm sure she had no clue what I was talking about! I then went on to say that I love local seafood and whatever happens to be in season, but I do in fact love putting together leftovers in the form of a hash, especially for lunch. You can create your own hash, or fry-up, with all sorts of things—leftover rice, cooked vegetables, chopped spinach or bok choy seasoned with fresh herbs and ginger. This version is an Asian hash. The flavour of caraway seeds pairs well with pork dishes and, of course, with poultry. Garnish this dish with cilantro leaves. *Serves 4 to 6*

HEAT OLIVE and sesame oils in a large frying pan on medium-high heat. Add cabbage, potatoes, carrots, celery and green onions. Season with caraway seeds, herbes de Provence and salt and pepper. Sauté, stirring often, until vegetables are nicely browned and cabbage is cooked, 20 to 30 minutes. Adjust seasonings if necessary and serve.

ARSNIPS are members of the same vegetable family as parsley; in fact, parsley root can be roasted as well. Winter is the peak season for these root vegetables, and they taste particularly sweet after they have had a touch of frost. Parsnips are also good cooked alongside roasted chicken, turkey or pork. *Serves 4*

4 parsnips, peeled
  and cut in half lengthwise

1 Tbsp olive oil

1 Tbsp melted butter

1 tsp salt

PREHEAT THE OVEN to 375°F. Place parsnips in a shallow roasting pan. Drizzle with olive oil and butter and season with salt and toss well. Arrange parsnips cut side down and roast for 45 minutes, until tender.

CHERRY'S NUT ROAST

WITH MUSHROOM AND SWEET ONION GRAVY

MUSHROOM AND
SWEET ONION GRAVY

1 Tbsp butter

1 Tbsp olive oil

1 small sweet onion, chopped

3 cloves garlic, chopped

2 cups brown mushrooms,
    halved and sliced

1½ Tbsp all-purpose flour

½ cup red wine

1 Tbsp tomato paste

2¼ cups vegetable stock

MY SISTER Cherry Hunt's recipe for nut roast is vegetarian and, if you substitute olive oil for the butter, can also be vegan. It is a good source of vegetable protein, and is easy to prepare with readily available pantry items. Make this roast in the fall when nuts are at their freshest and serve it as part of a buffet with the mushroom sauce, or take it on a country picnic with some assorted grilled vegetables and pickles. You can also use this recipe to make veggie burgers: just form the dough into patties and panfry them. The nuts can be varied according to availability. I suggest a selection of almonds, walnuts, hazelnuts and cashews. Whichever ones you choose, just be sure that no one is allergic.

I love mushrooms in any form, and in fact they're what I call my vegetable comfort food. When I was a kid growing up in Wales, in the early fall we would get up at the crack of dawn to go mushroom picking. We nearly always ended up with baskets full of pink-gilled field mushrooms, and then we would hurry home to fry them up for breakfast to eat with warm bread and butter. Sometimes we would cook them in a mushroom soup with double cream topped with lots of freshly chopped parsley and a twist of freshly ground pepper. Brown mushrooms are available year-round in local grocery stores, but if you are feeling a bit more adventurous, try this recipe prepared with wild and seasonal mushrooms, such as the very tasty and earthy morel mushrooms or the beautiful and fragrant yellow chanterelles. Serve with steamed green vegetables. *Serves 4*

MUSHROOM AND SWEET ONION GRAVY Heat butter and olive oil in a medium saucepan on medium heat. Add onions, garlic and mushrooms and cook for 15 minutes. Stir in flour and cook until golden brown, 3 to 4 minutes. Add wine, tomato paste and vegetable stock and bring to a simmer. Reduce the heat to low and cook uncovered for 35 to 40 minutes, until gravy is reduced. Remove from the heat, allow to cool slightly, then transfer to a blender and purée. Season with salt and freshly ground pepper to taste.

NUT ROAST Preheat the oven to 375°F. Grease a 5 × 9-inch loaf pan with butter, then line it with the 2 Tbsp of panko (or dry bread crumbs) to prevent sticking and to give the loaf a nice crispy outer coating.

Heat olive oil in a frying pan on medium heat. Add onions and garlic and sauté until onions are translucent and tender, about 3 minutes. Remove from the heat. Pour vegetable stock over onions and set aside.

Place nuts, parsley, thyme and basil in a blender and chop finely. Transfer the nut mixture to a large mixing bowl. Add the 4 oz of bread crumbs and the stock mixture and combine well. Season with salt and pepper to taste. Spoon the nut batter into the loaf pan. Bake uncovered for about 1 hour. Remove from the oven and allow to rest for 5 minutes.

To unmould, slip a knife around the edges of the pan to loosen the loaf. Turn it out onto a warmed plate.

TO SERVE Slice the nut loaf into ½-inch pieces. Serve 2 slices on each warmed plate. Drizzle with mushroom and sweet onion gravy.

NUT ROAST

2 Tbsp panko or
  dry bread crumbs

2 Tbsp olive oil

1 small onion, finely chopped

1 clove garlic, finely chopped

1 cup vegetable stock

8 oz mixed nuts

1 Tbsp parsley

1 tsp thyme leaves

3 fresh basil leaves

4 oz fresh bread crumbs

HAZELNUT TART
WITH CHOCOLATE GANACHE

CRÈME FRAÎCHE

2 Tbsp buttermilk

1¾ cups whipping cream

DELICIOUS organic hazelnuts are grown in the eastern Fraser Valley near Chilliwack, and we use them regularly for a variety of desserts, as well as using the oil for salad dressings. To roast and remove skins from fresh hazelnuts, bake them on a baking sheet in a 400°F oven for five to ten minutes, or until the skins are chocolate brown. Transfer them to a cool tray and place in the freezer for 5 to 10 minutes, then transfer to a clean towel and rub them vigorously to remove the skins. Make sure you use a good-quality dark chocolate for the ganache, such as Callebaut, Lindt or Valrhona.

Make the crème fraîche two days before you plan to serve it. This thick cream is rich and tangy and extremely versatile. In the restaurant we use dairy products from Avalon Dairy, a Vancouver-based dairy run by the Crowley family, who for one hundred years have been supplying fresh dairy products in traditional glass bottles. If Avalon Dairy products are not available in your area, use another organic cream with a butter fat content of at least 32 per cent. This recipe makes 2 cups. *Serves 12*

CRÈME FRAÎCHE Combine buttermilk and cream in a clean 1 pint jar or container with a tight-fitting lid. Cover and allow to sit at room temperature overnight or for up to 2 days. Check the crème fraîche after 24 hours: it should have the consistency of yogurt. If it is not quite thick enough, allow to sit another 24 hours. Will keep refrigerated in an airtight container for up to 1 week.
Recipe continued overleaf...

HAZELNUT TART

1½ cups chopped hazelnuts

3 eggs

¾ cup brown sugar

½ cup melted butter

½ cup liquid honey

1 tsp vanilla extract

¾ tsp salt

1 parbaked 10-inch tart shell

GANACHE

4 oz dark chocolate, chopped

6 Tbsp whipping cream

HAZELNUT TART Preheat the oven to 350°F. Place hazelnuts, eggs, brown sugar, butter, honey, vanilla and salt in a large bowl and mix until well combined. Pour the batter into the tart shell. Bake for 30 to 40 minutes, until set. Allow to cool to room temperature.

GANACHE Place chocolate in a stainless steel bowl.

Place cream in a small saucepan on medium heat and bring to a simmer. Pour hot cream over chocolate and stir well until chocolate is dissolved and smooth.

TO ASSEMBLE THE TART Pour ganache over cooled tart and spread evenly overtop with a metal spatula. Refrigerate for at least 1 hour to set the ganache.

TO SERVE Cut the tart into 12 wedges and place on individual plates. Serve with a dollop of crème fraîche.

THIS luxurious loaf is moist and full of flavour. It is great served for afternoon tea or given to a friend as a gift. It is also simple to make and freezes extremely well. We like to buy our dried fruits from the Zebroff family in Oliver. Their pears, apples and Bing cherries are some of the best you will find. We also recommend that you use a good-quality chocolate, such as Valrhona or Callebaut. This loaf will keep in an airtight container for up to one week. *Serves 6*

PREHEAT THE OVEN to 350°F. Grease a 5 × 9-inch loaf pan and dust with flour.

Place pears in a medium bowl. Cover with boiling water and allow to stand for 10 minutes. Drain well and set aside.

In the bowl of an electric mixer, cream butter, cream cheese and sugar until fluffy. Add eggs and almond extract and beat well. Add flour, baking powder and salt and beat again. Stir in pears and chocolate, mixing briefly to combine.

Turn the stiff batter into the loaf pan and bake on the centre rack of the oven for 1 hour, or until golden on top and a knife inserted in the loaf comes out clean. Allow to cool in the pan or on a rack.

With a knife, loosen the edges of the loaf and carefully invert onto a board. Cut into ½-inch slices and serve.

1½ cups chopped dried
  pears (about 6 oz)

½ cup unsalted butter,
  softened

⅓ cup cream cheese

¾ cup sugar

2 eggs

¼ tsp almond extract

1½ cups all-purpose flour, sifted

1 Tbsp baking powder

½ tsp salt

3 oz bittersweet chocolate,
  chopped

BREAD PUDDING

WITH PEARS, CHOCOLATE AND RAISINS

BREAD pudding is a great way to transform that half loaf of French bread from last night's dinner into a glorious dessert. I like to add diced fruit and chunks of chocolate, any variety, because they add another dimension to the dish. Bread pudding is very much a dessert of opportunity, so feel free to use what you have, whether apples, pears, bananas or dried fruits. Serve this pudding warm with lightly whipped cream. *Serves 8*

PREHEAT THE OVEN to 350°F. Grease a 2-qt casserole or soufflé dish. Set bread in a large bowl.

Place milk, eggs, sugar and cinnamon in a medium bowl and whisk until well combined. Pour the milk mixture over the bread. Add pears, chocolate and raisins and stir to combine.

Spoon the batter into the casserole (or soufflé) dish and bake for 1 hour, until puffed and golden. Allow to set for 15 minutes.

TO SERVE Spoon 1 cup of the bread pudding onto individual plates. Serve warm.

4 cups day-old crusty white French or Italian bread, in large cubes

2 cups milk

4 eggs

1 cup sugar

1 tsp cinnamon

4 pears, peeled, cored and diced

1 cup chocolate chunks or chips

1 cup raisins

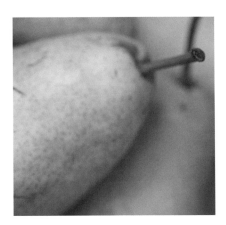

STEAMED PUDDING

WITH EGGNOG CUSTARD

EGGNOG CUSTARD

4 egg yolks

2 Tbsp dark rum

3 Tbsp sugar

1½ cups whipping cream

½ cup milk

Pinch of ground nutmeg

Pinch of cinnamon

STEAMED puddings are a staple of traditional English cuisine. Most of the time they are cooked in a pudding basin or large ceramic bowl, wrapped with cheesecloth and tied with string, then steamed in a large pot on the stove for several hours. This recipe makes individual puddings, cooked in the oven in buttered ramekins and served with an eggnog-flavoured custard sauce as a holiday dessert. *Serves 6*

EGGNOG CUSTARD Place egg yolks, rum and sugar in a medium bowl and whisk lightly until sugar is dissolved.

Combine cream, milk, nutmeg and cinnamon in a small saucepan on medium heat; bring almost to the boiling point. Carefully whisk ½ cup of the cream mixture into the yolk mixture to temper it. Gradually add the rest of the cream mixture, all the while whisking gently so as not to create any foam on the surface.

Pour custard back into the saucepan. Reduce the heat to medium-low and cook, uncovered, stirring constantly, until the mixture is thick enough to coat the back of a spoon, 3 to 4 minutes. Strain custard through a fine-mesh sieve into a medium bowl. Cover and refrigerate in an airtight container for up to 3 days.

STEAMED PUDDING Preheat the oven to 375°F. Lightly butter eight 4-oz ramekins.

Place dried fruit in a small bowl. Cover with boiling water and allow to cool to room temperature. Do not drain any unabsorbed water.

In the bowl of an electric mixer, cream butter and brown sugar until fluffy. Add eggs, one at a time, until well combined.

Sift flour, baking powder, baking soda, nutmeg, cinnamon, ginger and salt into a medium bowl. Set aside.

Add the fruit to the butter mixture and mix well. Stir in the dry ingredients until just combined, then divide batter among the ramekins.

Place the filled ramekins in a roasting pan. Fill the pan ⅔ full with hot water and cover with a sheet of parchment paper. Cover the parchment-covered pan with a layer of aluminum foil and bake for 45 minutes. Remove the ramekins from the hot water and allow to cool slightly.

TO SERVE Invert the steamed puddings onto individual plates. Spoon ¼ cup of the eggnog custard on top of each pudding.

STEAMED PUDDING

1 cup chopped dried fruit (such as raisins, apricots, cherries, apples or a mixture)

½ cup butter

1 cup brown sugar

3 eggs

2 cups all-purpose flour

1 tsp baking powder

½ tsp baking soda

Pinch of ground nutmeg

Pinch of cinnamon

Pinch of ground ginger

½ tsp salt

DAWNE'S RUM POT

1 lb fresh strawberries,
  washed, hulled and dried

sugar (equal weight of fruit
  at each stage)

26 oz dark rum (1 bottle), or more

1 lb fresh cherries, unpitted,
  washed, destemmed and dried

1 lb fresh raspberries, washed
  and dried

1 lb fresh blueberries, washed,
  destemmed and dried

FRIENDS of mine eagerly await their Christmas jar of rum pot. In fact, I buy five bottles of rum every year, just for this project. The recipe is easily doubled or quintupled.

As soon as strawberries appear at the market, I begin. Then come raspberries, blueberries, cherries and blackberries, and I add them to the rum pots in progress. I use a combination of berries and cherries in my rum pot, adding them as they become ripe; however, you can make rum pot with 4 lbs of a single type of berry or cherry, if you prefer. Do not be tempted to pit the cherries, or you will produce a cloudy rum pot.

For this recipe, use only fresh unblemished berries, not frozen ones, and have on hand a kitchen scale, as the fruit and sugar are measured by weight. Your summer's labour picking berries will be rewarded! Serve with ice cream, or sip on its own as a liqueur or added to sparkling wine for a version of kir royale. *Makes 4 qts*

STERILIZE A 16-CUP earthenware pot or wide mouth jar by submerging it in boiling water for 1 to 2 minutes. Remove from the water and allow to cool and air dry on a rack at room temperature.

Weigh strawberries and place them in the earthenware pot (or wide-mouth jar). Measure out an equal weight of sugar. Sprinkle sugar over the berries. Add rum, ensuring that the fruit and sugar are completely submerged. Seal the pot (or jar) tightly with a lid and set aside in a cool, dark place. *Recipe continued overleaf...*

When cherries come into season, unseal the pot (or jar). Weigh cherries and add them to the strawberries. Measure out an equal weight of sugar. Sprinkle sugar over the berries and cherries. If the fruit and sugar are not completely submerged in the rum, add more rum. Reseal the pot (or jar) tightly and set aside in a cool, dark place. Repeat with the raspberries and blueberries, as they come into season. (The sugar will dissolve into a syrup over time; however, if you notice any lumps of sugar, stir gently, being careful not to damage the fruit.) Allow the rum pot to age for several months.

For gift giving, strain the rum pot through a fine-mesh sieve and discard the solids. Pour the strained rum pot into individual 6-oz decorative bottles with tight-fitting lids. For home use, store the strained rum pot in your earthenware pot (or wide mouth jar). Just before serving, strain the rum pot through a fine-mesh sieve and discard the solids. Will keep indefinitely in an airtight container in a cool, dark place.

THIS pound cake is made exceptionally moist because of the honey. The top is dark gold and a little sticky, as it should be. It has a pronounced flavour and is best made with a runny honey. This recipe makes two loaves—I suggest you wrap one well in plastic wrap when cooled and freeze it. It keeps very well for up to one month in the freezer. Serve it with a little crème fraîche (page 176), a drizzle of honey and a cup of hot tea. *Serves 8 to 10 (per loaf)*

1 cup butter

1 cup sugar

1¼ cups liquid honey

4 eggs

3 cups all-purpose flour

1 tsp baking powder

1 cup milk

Zest of 1 lemon

PREHEAT THE OVEN to 350°F. In the bowl of an electric mixer, cream butter, sugar and honey. Add eggs and mix well.

Sift flour and baking powder into a bowl. Add to the butter mixture in two stages, alternating with the milk. Stir in lemon zest.

Pour the batter into a 10-inch deep-sided cake pan (or a springform pan) or into two 8-inch cake tins. Bake for 45 minutes, or until a knife inserted in the cake comes out clean.

TO SERVE Cut this pound cake into 10 slices and place on individual plates. If you cut nice, thick slices, there may only be enough for 8!

METRIC CONVERSIONS

(ROUNDED OFF TO THE NEAREST WHOLE NUMBER)

WEIGHT

IMPERIAL OR U.S.	METRIC
1 oz	30 g
2 oz	60 g
3 oz	85 g
4 oz	115 g
5 oz	140 g
6 oz	170 g
7 oz	200 g
8 oz (½ lb)	225 g
9 oz	255 g
10 oz	285 g
11 oz	310 g
12 oz	340 g
13 oz	370 g
14 oz	400 g
15 oz	425 g
16 oz (1 lb)	455 g
2 lbs	910 g

VOLUME

IMPERIAL OR U.S.	METRIC
⅛ tsp	0.5 mL
¼ tsp	1 mL
½ tsp	2.5 mL
¾ tsp	4 mL
1 tsp	5 mL
1 Tbsp	15 mL
1½ Tbsp	23 mL
⅛ cup	30 mL
¼ cup	60 mL
⅓ cup	80 mL
½ cup	120 mL
⅔ cup	160 mL
¾ cup	180 mL
1 cup	240 mL
1 qt	960 mL
1 gallon	3.84 L

BAKING UTENSILS

IMPERIAL OR U.S.	METRIC
5 × 9-inch loaf pan	2 L loaf pan
9 × 13-inch cake pan	4 L loaf pan
11 × 17-inch baking sheet	30 × 45-cm baking sheet

LINEAR

IMPERIAL OR U.S.	METRIC
⅛ inch	3 mm
¼ inch	6 mm
½ inch	12 mm
¾ inch	2 cm
1 inch	2.5 cm
1¼ inches	3 cm
1½ inches	3.5 cm
1¾ inches	4.5 cm
2 inches	5 cm
3 inches	7.5 cm
4 inches	10 cm
5 inches	12.5 cm
6 inches	15 cm
7 inches	18 cm
8 inches	20 cm
9 inches	23 cm
10 inches	25 cm
11 inches	27.5 cm
12 inches	30 cm

LIQUID MEASURES (FOR ALCOHOL)

IMPERIAL OR U.S.	METRIC
1 oz	30 mL
1½ oz	45 mL
2 oz	60 mL
3 oz	90 mL
4 oz	120 mL

OVEN TEMPERATURE

IMPERIAL OR U.S.	METRIC
110°F	43°C
120°F	49°C
125°F	52°C
130°F	54°C
135°F	57°C
140°F	60°C
145°F	63°C
150°F	66°C
155°F	68°C
160°F	71°C
165°F	74°C
170°F	77°C
175°F	79°C
300°F	150°C
325°F	160°C
350°F	180°C
375°F	190°C
400°F	200°C
425°F	220°C
450°F	230°C

INDEX

CONTENTS

Dedicated to Saskatchewan farmer Percy Schmeiser

Douglas & McIntyre Ltd.
2323 Quebec Street, Suite 201
Vancouver, British Columbia
Canada v5t 4s7
www.douglas-mcintyre.com

Library and Archives Canada Cataloguing in Publication
Bishop, John, 1944
Fresh : seasonal recipes made with local foods / John Bishop and
Dennis Green ; with Dawne Gourley ; stories by Gary King.
Includes index.

ISBN 978-1-55365-245-8

1. Cookery, Canadian—British Columbia style. 2. Cookery—British
Columbia—Vancouver. 3. Bishop's (Restaurant). I. Green, Dennis, 1969–
II. Gourley, Dawne III. King, Gary, 1944– IV. Title.
TX945.5.B58B585 2007   641.509711'33   C2006-906528-4

Editing by Lucy Kenward
Cover design by Peter Cocking
Interior design by Naomi MacDougall and Peter Cocking
Cover image by Cornelia Ritter/Getty Images
Photos by John Sherlock except as indicated
Printed and bound in Canada by Friesens
Printed on acid-free paper

We gratefully acknowledge the financial support of the Canada Council
for the Arts, the British Columbia Arts Council, and the Government
of Canada through the Book Publishing Industry Development
Program (BPIDP) for our publishing activities.

FRESH

SEASONAL RECIPES
MADE WITH LOCAL INGREDIENTS

 JOHN BISHOP

DENNIS GREEN & DAWNE GOURLEY

STORIES BY GARY KING

PRINCIPAL PHOTOGRAPHY BY JOHN SHERLOCK

Douglas & McIntyre

VANCOUVER/TORONTO

To
Cheryl Steinhauer
Thanks for shopping at Hazelmere

Gary A. King

(FRESH)

Smoo beret, scarf & Rambler legwarmers (*shown here with Macmillan gloves*) – These are the accessories you need to wear to have fun in the snow. The decorative effect is produced by using drop stitch.

Knitted in Soft Tweed, shown here in Bramble. Pattern instructions page 74, 86 & 75

Knitted in Soft Tweed, shown here in Oatmeal, Sprig, Slate Blue & Blanket. Pattern instructions page 82

Scott – This zip-up cardigan was inspired by bowling jackets and the fairisle design gives it a Nordic feel. Wear it for a spot of tobogganing.

Macmillan – Brrr, it's cold! With these mittens, your hands stay warm and you can still lace up your walking boots.

Knitted in Soft Tweed, shown here in Slate Blue. Pattern instructions page 75

Both knitted in Soft Tweed, shown here in Thistle [Ladies] & Sprig [Man]. Pattern instructions page 76

Macdonald – Chunky cable and herringbone stitch sweater, for men or women.
Keep warm, keep happy but watch out – here comes a snowball!

Knitted in Soft Tweed, shown here in Thistle. Pattern instructions page 60

Arran – True to its name, Arran has the bold cabling we associate with Celtic design. With a big bardot neckline, this sweater teams warmth with a glamourous look.

Barra – Taking its name from an island famous for lovely beaches, Barra is a simple, one-button jacket knitted up in moss stitch. It's the ideal garment to throw on for a winter walk in the woods.

Knitted in Soft Tweed, shown here in Antique. Pattern instructions page 58

Knitted in Soft Tweed, shown here in Thistle, Blanket & Slate Blue. Pattern instructions page 68

Firth – Unstructured and designed to be fastened with a handcrafted pin, this jacket has a striking striped effect that flatters the figure.

Campbell – This jacket wraps over and is held with a belt. The defining feature is the rich cabled trim. Wear it with a cloche hat to complete the look.

Knitted in Soft Tweed, shown here in Oatmeal. Pattern instructions page 72

Bruce (*left*) – Sorry
chaps, but this was
the only name for this
hunky, chunky sweater!
Don't leave it around or
the girls will grab it.

Clyde (*right*) – Our
sleeveless slipover has
moss stitch cabling and
a ribbed edging.
A design inspired by a
classic male design, you
will look bonny in Clyde!

Knitted in Soft Tweed, shown here in Blanket.
Pattern instructions page 80 & 66

Both knitted in Soft Tweed, shown here in Slate Blue [Man] & Twig [Ladies]. Pattern instructions page 78

Nevis – These sweaters, with their Alpine-style cable and rib patterning, mean business.
Is that Scotland's highest mountain I can see?

Both knitted in Soft Tweed, shown here in Oatmeal, Twig, Blanket [Scarf] & Blanket [Hat]. Pattern instructions page 85

Whisky hat and scarf – If cutting wood is men's work, then men deserve these chunky rib accessories to beat cold. Look he's smiling!

Knitted in Soft Tweed, shown here in Sprig. Pattern instructions page 62

Croft – This cape is so clever – it has a scarf attached. Worn inside or outside, it promises to keep you cosy.

Knitted in Soft Tweed, shown here in Bramble. Pattern instructions page 70

Macgregor – Remember Peter Rabbit's exploits in the greenhouse in the children's classic? This simple crew-neck sweater will never go out of style.

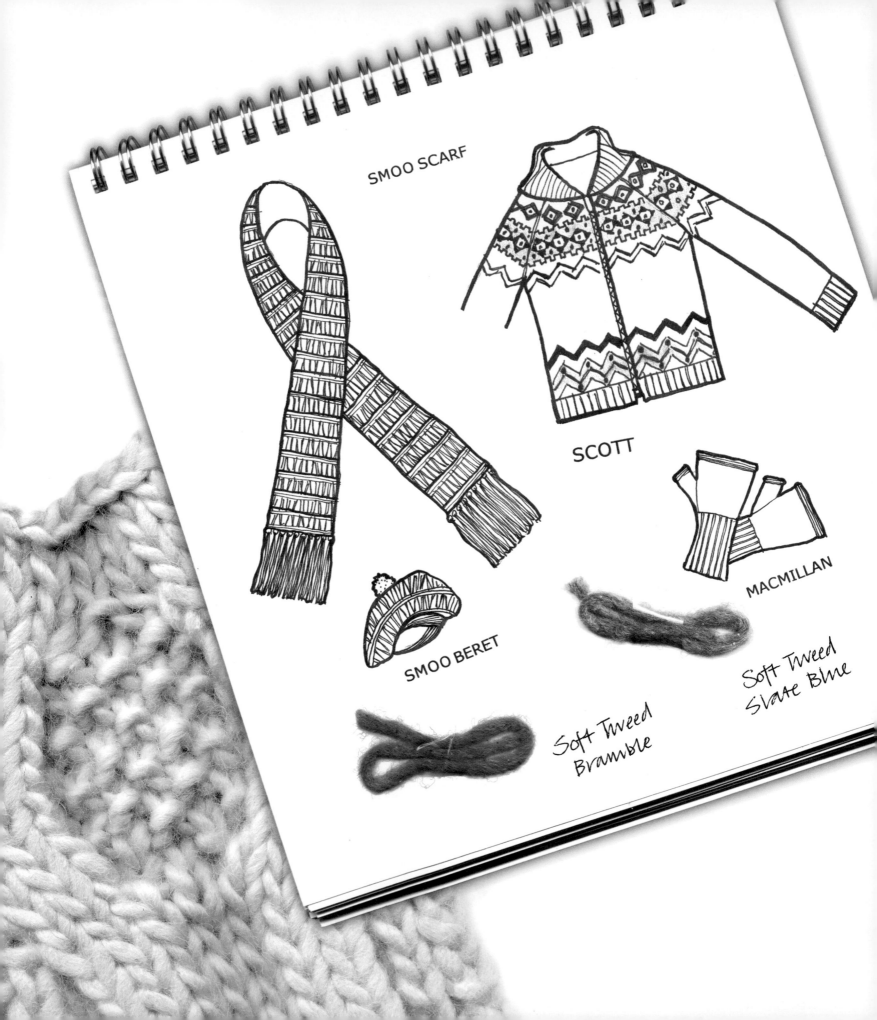

SMOO SCARF

SCOTT

MACMILLAN

SMOO BERET

Soft Tweed
Slate Blue

Soft Tweed
Bramble

Tension

Obtaining the correct tension is perhaps the single factor which can make the difference between a successful garment and a disastrous one. It controls both the shape and size of an article, so any variation, however slight, can distort the finished garment. Different designers feature in our books and it is **their** tension, given at the **start** of each pattern, which you must match. We recommend that you knit a square in pattern and/or stocking stitch (depending on the pattern instructions) of perhaps 5 - 10 more stitches and 5 - 10 more rows than those given in the tension note. Mark out the central 10cm square with pins. If you have too many stitches to 10cm try again using thicker needles, if you have too few stitches to 10cm try again using finer needles. Once you have achieved the correct tension your garment will be knitted to the measurements indicated in the size diagram shown at the end of the pattern.

Sizing and Size Diagram Note

The instructions are given for the smallest size. Where they vary, work the figures in brackets for the larger sizes. **One set of figures refers to all sizes**. Included with most patterns in this magazine is a **'size diagram'**, or sketch of the finished garment and its dimensions. The size diagram shows the finished width of the garment at the under-arm point, and it is this measurement that the knitter should choose first; a useful tip is to measure one of your own garments which is a comfortable fit. Having chosen a size based on width, look at the corresponding length for that size; if you are not happy with the total length which we recommend, adjust your own garment before beginning your armhole shaping - any adjustment after this point will mean that your sleeve will not fit into your garment easily - don't forget to take your adjustment into account if there is any side seam shaping. Finally, look at the sleeve length; the size diagram shows the finished sleeve measurement, taking into account any top-arm insertion length. Measure your body between the centre of your neck and your wrist, this measurement should correspond to half the garment width plus the sleeve length. Again, your sleeve length may be adjusted, but remember to take into consideration your sleeve increases if you do adjust the length - you must increase more frequently than the pattern states to shorten your sleeve, less frequently to lengthen it.

Chart Note

Many of the patterns in the book are worked from charts. Each square on a chart represents a stitch and each line of squares a row of knitting. Each colour used is given a different letter and these are shown in the **materials** section, or in the **key** alongside the chart of each pattern. When working from the charts, read odd rows (K) from right to left and even rows (P) from left to right, unless otherwise stated.

Knitting with colour

There are two main methods of working colour into a knitted fabric: **Intarsia** and **Fairisle** techniques. The first method produces a single thickness of fabric and is usually used where a colour is only required in a particular area of a row and does not form a repeating pattern across the row, as in the fairisle technique.

Intarsia: The simplest way to do this is to cut short lengths of yarn for each motif or block of colour used in a row. Then joining in the various colours at the appropriate point on the row, link one colour to the next by twisting them around each other where they meet on the wrong side to avoid gaps. All ends can then either be darned along the colour join lines, as each motif is completed or then can be "knitted-in" to the fabric of the knitting as each colour is worked into the pattern. This is done in much the same way as "weaving-in" yarns when working the Fairisle technique and does save time darning-in ends. It is essential that the tension is noted for **Intarsia** as this may vary from the stocking stitch if both are used in the same pattern.

Fairisle type knitting: When two or three colours are worked repeatedly across a row, strand the yarn **not** in use loosely behind the stitches being worked. If you are working with more than two colours, treat the "floating" yarns as if they were one yarn and always spread the stitches to their correct width to keep them elastic. It is advisable not to carry the stranded or "floating" yarns over more than three stitches at a time, but to weave them under and over the colour you are working. The "floating" yarns are therefore caught at the back of the work.

Finishing Instructions

After working for hours knitting a garment, it seems a great pity that many garments are spoiled because such little care is taken in the pressing and finishing process. Follow the following tips for a truly professional-looking garment.

Pressing

Block out each piece of knitting and following the instructions on the ball band press the garment pieces, omitting the ribs. Tip: Take special care to press the edges, as this will make sewing up both easier and neater. If the ball band indicates that the fabric is not to be pressed, then covering the blocked out fabric with a damp white cotton cloth and leaving it to stand will have the desired effect. Darn in all ends neatly along the selvage edge or a colour join, as appropriate.

Stitching

When stitching the pieces together, remember to match areas of colour and texture very carefully where they meet. Use a seam stitch such as back stitch or mattress stitch for all main knitting seams and join all ribs and neckband with mattress stitch, unless otherwise stated.

Construction

Having completed the pattern instructions, join left shoulder and neckband seams as detailed above. Sew the top of the sleeve to the body of the garment using the method detailed in the pattern, referring to the appropriate guide:

Shallow set-in sleeves: Place centre of cast-off edge of sleeve to shoulder seam. Join cast-off sts at beg of armhole shaping to cast-off sts at start of sleeve-head shaping. Sew sleeve head into armhole, easing in shapings.

Set-in sleeves: Place centre of cast-off edge of sleeve to shoulder seam.
Set in sleeve, easing sleeve head into armhole.

Join side and sleeve seams.
Slip stitch pocket edgings and linings into place.
Sew on buttons to correspond with buttonholes.
Ribbed welts and neckbands and any area of garter stitch should not be pressed.

Abbreviations

K	knit	**psso**	pass slipped stitch over
P	purl		
st(s)	stitch(es)	**tbl**	through back of loop
inc	increas(e)(ing)		
dec	decreas(e)(ing)	**M1**	make one stitch by picking up horizontal loop before next stitch and working into back of it
st st	stocking stitch (1 row K, 1 row P)		
g st	garter stitch (K every row)		
beg	begin(ning)		
foll	following	**yrn**	yarn round needle
rem	remain(ing)		
rep	repeat	**yfwd**	yarn forward
alt	alternate	**meas**	measures
cont	continue	**o**	no stitches, times, or rows
patt	pattern		
tog	together	**-**	no stitches, times or rows for that size
mm	millimetres		
cm	centimetres		
in(s)	inch(es)	**approx**	approximately
RS	right side	**rev st st**	reverse stocking stitch (1 row P, 1 row K)
WS	wrong side		
sl 1	slip one stitch		

= Easy, straight forward knitting

= Suitable for the average knitter

= For the more experienced knitter

informationpage

Barra

YARN

	XS	S	M	L	XL	
To fit bust	81	86	91	97	102	cm
	32	34	36	38	40	in
RYC Soft Tweed						
	9	9	10	10	11	x 50gm

(photographed in Antique 002)

NEEDLES

1 pair 7mm (no 2) (US 10½) needles
1 pair 8mm (no 0) (US 11) needles
7mm (no 2) (US 10½) circular needle

BUTTONS – 1 x 00334

TENSION

12 sts and 19 rows to 10 cm measured over moss stitch using 8mm (US 11) needles.

BACK

Using 7mm (US 10½) needles cast on 53 [55: 59: 61: 65] sts.
Row 1 (RS): K1, *P1, K1, rep from * to end.
Row 2: As row 1.
These 2 rows form moss st.
Work in moss st for a further 2 rows, ending with RS facing for next row.
Change to 8mm (US 11) needles.
Cont in moss st, dec 1 st at each end of 15th [17th: 17th: 19th: 19th] and every foll 8th row until 47 [49: 53: 55: 59] sts rem.
Work 7 rows, ending with RS facing for next row.
Inc 1 st at each end of next and every foll 8th row until there are 53 [55: 59: 61: 65] sts.
Work 7 rows, ending with RS facing for next row.
(Back should meas 35 [36: 36: 37: 37] cm.)
Shape raglan armholes
Cast off 3 sts at beg of next 2 rows.
47 [49: 53: 55: 59] sts.
Dec 1 st at each end of next and foll 9 [9: 12: 12: 15] alt rows, then on every foll 4th row until 17 [19: 19: 21: 21] sts rem.
Work 1 row, ending with RS facing for next row.
Shape back neck
Next row (RS): K3 and turn, leaving rem sts on a holder.
Work each side of neck separately.
Dec 1 st at beg of next row.

Next row (RS): K2tog and fasten off.
With RS facing, rejoin yarn to rem sts, cast off centre 11 [13: 13: 15: 15] sts, moss st to end.
Complete to match first side, reversing shapings.

LEFT FRONT

Using 7mm (US 10½) needles cast on 27 [28: 30: 31: 33] sts.
Row 1 (RS): *K1, P1, rep from * to last 1 [0: 0: 1: 1] st, K1 [0: 0: 1: 1].
Row 2: K1 [0: 0: 1: 1], *P1, K1, rep from * to end.
These 2 rows form moss st.
Work in moss st for a further 2 rows, ending with RS facing for next row.
Change to 8mm (US 11) needles.
Cont in moss st, dec 1 st at beg of 15th [17th: 17th: 19th: 19th] and every foll 8th row until 24 [25: 27: 28: 30] sts rem.
Work 7 rows, ending with RS facing for next row.
Inc 1 st at beg of next row. 25 [26: 28: 29: 31] sts.
Work 5 rows, ending with RS facing for next row.
Shape front slope
Dec 1 st at end of next and 2 foll 6th rows **and at same time** inc 1 st at beg of 3rd and foll 8th row. 24 [25: 27: 28: 30] sts.
Work 5 rows, ending with RS facing for next row.
(Left front should now match back to beg of raglan armhole shaping.)
Shape raglan armhole
Cast off 3 sts at beg and dec 1 st at end of next row. 20 [21: 23: 24: 26] sts.
Work 1 row.
Dec 1 st at raglan armhole edge of next and foll 9 [9: 12: 12: 15] alt rows, then on 4 [4: 3: 3: 2] foll 4th rows **and at same time** dec 1 st at front slope edge of 7th [5th: 5th: 5th: 5th] and 0 [3: 2: 5: 5] foll 6th rows, then on every foll 8th [8th: 8th: 0: 0] row. 2 sts rem.
Work 3 rows, ending with RS facing for next row.
Next row (RS): K2tog and fasten off.

RIGHT FRONT

Using 7mm (US 10½) needles cast on 27 [28: 30: 31: 33] sts.
Row 1 (RS): K1 [0: 0: 1: 1], *P1, K1, rep from * to end.
Row 2: *K1, P1, rep from * to last 1 [0: 0: 1: 1] st, K1 [0: 0: 1: 1].

These 2 rows form moss st.
Work in moss st for a further 2 rows, ending with RS facing for next row.
Change to 8mm (US 11) needles.
Cont in moss st, dec 1 st at end of 15th [17th: 17th: 19th: 19th] and every foll 8th row until 24 [25: 27: 28: 30] sts rem.
Complete to match left front, reversing shapings, working an extra row before beg of raglan armhole shaping.

SLEEVES

Using 7mm (US 10½) needles cast on 30 [30: 34: 34: 34] sts.
Row 1 (RS): K2, *P2, K2, rep from * to end.
Row 2: P2, *K2, P2, rep from * to end.
These 2 rows form rib.
Work in rib for a further 14 rows, inc [inc: dec: inc: inc] 1 st at centre of last row and ending with RS facing for next row.
31 [31: 33: 35: 35] sts.
Change to 8mm (US 11) needles.
Work in moss st as given for back, shaping sides by inc 1 st at each end of next and every foll 14th [14th: 14th: 20th: 14th] row to 39 [39: 39: 43: 41] sts, then on every foll 16th [16th: 16th: -: 16th] row until there are 41 [41: 43: -: 45] sts.
Cont straight until sleeve meas 45 [45: 46: 46: 46] cm, ending with RS facing for next row.
Shape raglan
Cast off 3 sts at beg of next 2 rows.
35 [35: 37: 37: 39] sts.
Dec 1 st at each end of next and every foll alt row to 15 sts, then on every foll 4th row until 5 sts rem, ending with **WS** facing for next row.
Left sleeve only
Dec 1 st at beg of next row and at same edge on foll 2 rows.
Right sleeve only
Dec 1 st at end of next row and at same edge on foll 2 rows.
Both sleeves
Next row (RS): K2tog and fasten off.

MAKING UP

Press as described on the information page.
Join raglan seams using back stitch, or mattress stitch if preferred.

Front band

With RS facing and using 7mm (US 10½) circular
needle, beg and ending at cast-on edges, pick up
and knit 31 [32: 32: 33: 33] sts up right front
opening edge to beg of front slope shaping,
38 [38: 40: 40: 42] sts up right front slope, 5 sts
from right sleeve, 18 [20: 20: 22: 22] sts from
back, 5 sts from left sleeve, 38 [38: 40: 40: 42] sts
down left front slope to beg of front slope
shaping, then 31 [32: 32: 33: 33] sts down left

front opening edge. 166 [170: 174: 178: 182] sts.
Beg with row 2, work in rib as given for sleeves
for 8 rows, ending with **WS** facing for next row.
Row 9 (WS): Rib to last 31 [32: 32: 33: 33] sts,
cast off 2 sts (to make a buttonhole – cast on 2 sts
over these cast-off sts on next row), rib to end.
Work in rib for a further 5 rows, ending with **WS**
facing for next row.
Cast off in rib (on **WS**).
See information page for finishing instructions.

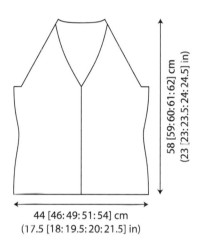

58 [59: 60: 61: 62] cm
(23 [23: 23.5: 24: 24.5] in)

44 [46: 49: 51: 54] cm
(17.5 [18: 19.5: 20: 21.5] in)

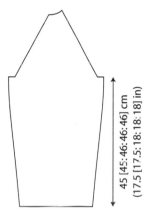

45 [45: 46: 46: 46] cm
(17.5 [17.5: 18: 18: 18] in)

🧶🧶🧶 **Arran**

YARN

	XS	S	M	L	XL	
To fit bust	81	86	91	97	102	cm
	32	34	36	38	40	in

RYC Soft Tweed

| | 9 | 9 | 10 | 10 | 11 | x 50gm |

(photographed in Thistle 003)

NEEDLES

1 pair 7mm (no 2) (US 10½) needles
1 pair 8mm (no 0) (US 11) needles
7mm (no 2) (US 10½) circular needle
8mm (no 0) (US 11) circular needle
Cable needle

TENSION

12 sts and 16 rows to 10 cm measured over stocking stitch using 8mm (US 11) needles.

SPECIAL ABBREVIATIONS

Cr3R = slip next st onto cable needle and leave at back of work, K2, then P1 from cable needle; **Cr3L** = slip next 2 sts onto cable needle and leave at front of work, P1, then K2 from cable needle; **Cr4R** = slip next st onto cable needle and leave at back of work, K3, then P1 from cable needle; **Cr4L** = slip next 3 sts onto cable needle and leave at front of work, P1, then K3 from cable needle; **C4B** = slip next 2 sts onto cable needle and leave at back of work, K2, then K2 from cable needle; **C4F** = slip next 2 sts onto cable needle and leave at front of work, K2, then K2 from cable needle; **C5F** = slip next 2 sts onto cable needle and leave at front of work, K3, then K2 from cable needle; **dec 4** = sl 1, K1, psso, K3tog, then lift 2nd st on right needle over first st and off right needle – 4 sts decreased; **inc 2** = (K1 tbl, K1) into next st, insert left needle point behind vertical strand that runs downwards from between 2 sts just made and K this strand tbl – 2 sts increased; **bind 2** – yrn, P2, then lift the "yrn" over these 2 sts and off right needle.

BACK

Using 7mm (US 10½) needles cast on 53 [55: 59: 61: 65] sts.
Row 1 (RS): K1 [2: 0: 0: 1], P3 [3: 1: 2: 3], *K3, P3, rep from * to last 1 [2: 4: 5: 1] sts, K1 [2: 3: 3: 1],

P0 [0: 1: 2: 0].
Row 2: P1 [2: 0: 0: 1], K3 [3: 1: 2: 3], *P3, K3, rep from * to last 1 [2: 4: 5: 1] sts, P1 [2: 3: 3: 1], K0 [0: 1: 2: 0].
These 2 rows form rib.
Work in rib for a further 10 rows, ending with RS facing for next row.
Change to 8mm (US 11) needles.
Beg with a K row, work in st st, dec 1 st at each end of 3rd and foll 8th row, then on foll 6th row. 47 [49: 53: 55: 59] sts.
Work 7 rows, ending with RS facing for next row.
Inc 1 st at each end of next and 2 foll 8th rows. 53 [55: 59: 61: 65] sts.
Cont straight until back meas 36 [37: 37: 38: 38] cm, ending with RS facing for next row.

Shape raglan armholes

Cast off 3 sts at beg of next 2 rows. 47 [49: 53: 55: 59] sts.
Next row (RS): K1, sl 1, K1, psso, K to last 3 sts, K2tog, K1.
Working all raglan armhole decreases as set by last row, dec 1 st at each end of 2nd and foll 6 [6: 9: 9: 12] alt rows, then on every foll 4th row until 25 [27: 27: 29: 29] sts rem.
Work 1 row, ending with RS facing for next row.

Shape back neck

Next row (RS): K3 and turn, leaving rem sts on a holder.
Work each side of neck separately.
Dec 1 st at beg of next row.
Next row (RS): K2tog and fasten off.

With RS facing, rejoin yarn to rem sts, cast off centre 19 [21: 21: 23: 23] sts, K to end.
Complete to match first side, reversing shapings.

FRONT

Using 7mm (US 10½) needles cast on 53 [55: 59: 61: 65] sts.
Work in rib as given for back for 11 rows, ending with **WS** facing for next row.
Row 12 (WS): Rib 15 [16: 18: 19: 21], (M1, rib 2) twice, M1, rib 3, M1, rib 9, M1, rib 3, M1, (rib 2, M1) twice, rib to end. 61 [63: 67: 69: 73] sts.
Change to 8mm (US 11) needles.
Place chart
Row 1 (RS): K14 [15: 17: 18: 20], work next 33 sts as row 1 of chart, K to end.
Row 2: P14 [15: 17: 18: 20], work next 33 sts as row 2 of chart, P to end.
These 2 rows set the sts – centre sts in patt foll chart and side sts in st st.
(**Note:** St count varies whilst working chart. All st counts given assume there are 33 sts in chart **at all times.**)
Cont as set, dec 1 st at each end of next and foll 8th row, then on foll 6th row.
55 [57: 61: 63: 67] sts.
Work 7 rows, ending with RS facing for next row.
Inc 1 st at each end of next and 2 foll 8th rows. 61 [63: 67: 69: 73] sts.
Cont straight until front matches back to beg of raglan armhole shaping, ending with RS facing for next row.

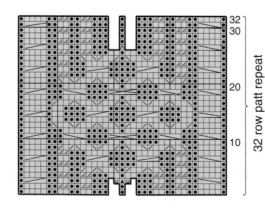

32 row patt repeat

Key

- ☐ K on RS, P on WS
- ▣ P on RS, K on WS
- ⊡ m1
- ▨ bind 2
- ☐ no st
- ▣ inc 2
- ▨ Cr3R
- ▨ Cr4R
- ▨ Cr3L
- ▨ Cr4L
- ▱ C4B
- ▱ C4F
- ▱ C5F
- ▨ dec 4

Shape raglan armholes

Cast off 3 sts at beg of next 2 rows.

55 [57: 61: 63: 67] sts.

Working all raglan armhole decreases as set by back, dec 1 st at each end of next and foll 7 [7: 10: 10: 13] alt rows, then on 2 [2: 1: 1: 0] foll 4th rows.

35 [37: 37: 39: 39] sts.

Work 1 row, ending with RS facing for next row.

Shape front neck

Next row (RS): Patt 3 sts and turn, leaving rem sts on a holder.

Work each side of neck separately.

Dec 1 st at beg of next row.

Next row (RS): K2tog and fasten off.

With RS facing, rejoin yarn to rem sts, cast off centre 29 [31: 31: 33: 33] sts dec 8 sts evenly, patt to end.

Complete to match first side, reversing shapings.

SLEEVES

Using 7mm (US 10½) needles cast on 29 [29: 31: 33: 33] sts.

Row 1 (RS): K1 [1: 2: 3: 3], *P3, K3, rep from * to last 4 [4: 5: 6: 6] sts, P3, K1 [1: 2: 3: 3].

Row 2: P1 [1: 2: 3: 3], *K3, P3, rep from * to last 4 [4: 5: 6: 6] sts, K3, P1 [1: 2: 3: 3].

These 2 rows form rib.

Work in rib for a further 10 rows, ending with RS facing for next row.

Change to 8mm (US 11) needles.

Beg with a K row, work in st st, shaping sides by inc 1 st at each end of next and every foll 10th [10th: 10th: 14th: 10th] row to 37 [37: 37: 43: 39] sts, then on every foll 12th [12th: 12th: -: 12th] row until there are 41 [41: 43: -: 45] sts.

Cont straight until sleeve meas 45 [45: 46: 46: 46] cm, ending with RS facing for next row.

Shape raglan

Cast off 3 sts at beg of next 2 rows.

35 [35: 37: 37: 39] sts.

Working all raglan armhole decreases as set by back, dec 1 st at each end of next and every foll alt row to 19 sts, then on every foll 4th row until 15 sts rem.

Work 3 rows, ending with RS facing for next row.

Left sleeve only

Dec 1 st at each end of next row.

13 sts.

Cast off 4 sts at beg of next and foll alt row.

Right sleeve only

Cast off 5 sts at beg and dec 1 st at end of next row. 9 sts.

Work 1 row.

Cast off 4 sts at beg of next row.

Work 1 row.

Both sleeves

Cast off rem 5 sts.

MAKING UP

Press as described on the information page.

Join raglan seams using back stitch, or mattress stitch if preferred.

Collar

With RS facing and using 7mm (US 10½) circular needle, beg and ending at left back raglan seam, pick up and knit 13 sts from left sleeve, 31 [33: 33: 35: 35] sts from front, 13 sts from right sleeve, then 27 [29: 29: 31: 31] sts from back.

84 [88: 88: 92: 92] sts.

Round 1 (RS): *K2, P2, rep from * to end.

Rep this round until collar meas 10 cm.

Next round: *K1, M1, K1, P2, rep from * to end.

105 [110: 110: 115: 115] sts.

Change to 8mm (US 11) circular needle.

Next round: *K3, P2, rep from * to end.

Rep last round until collar meas 21 cm from pick-up row.

Cast off in rib.

See information page for finishing instructions.

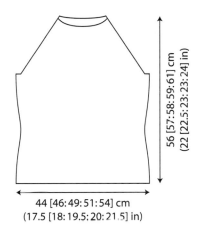

56 [57: 58: 59: 61] cm
(22 [22.5: 23: 23: 24] in)

44 [46: 49: 51: 54] cm
(17.5 [18: 19.5: 20: 21.5] in)

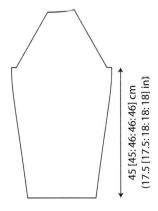

45 [45: 46: 46: 46] cm
(17.5 [17.5: 18: 18: 18] in)

 Croft

YARN

	XS-S	M	L-XL	
To fit bust	81-86	91	97-102	cm
	32-34	36	38-40	in
RYC Soft Tweed				
	9	10	11	x 50gm

(photographed in Sprig 006)

NEEDLES

1 pair 8mm (no 0) (US 11) needles

TENSION

11½ sts and 21 rows to 10 cm measured over garter stitch using 8mm (US 11) needles.

CAPE (worked sideways in one piece)

Using 8mm (US 11) needles cast on 22 sts (for first scarf section).
Work in g st for 65 cm, ending with RS facing for next row.

Shape left front edge

Cast on 52 [54: 56] sts at beg of next row.
74 [76: 78] sts.
Work 5 rows, ending with RS facing for next row.

Shape cape

Row 1 (RS): K to last 24 sts, wrap next st (by slipping next st onto right needle, bringing yarn to front of work between needles and then slipping same st back onto left needle – when working back across sts, work the st and the wrapped loop tog as one st) and turn.

Row 2: sl 1, K to end.
Row 3: K to last 32 sts, wrap next st and turn.
Row 4: sl 1, K to end.
Row 5: K to last 44 sts, wrap next st and turn.
Row 6: sl 1, K to end.
Row 7: K to last 58 sts, wrap next st and turn.
Row 8: sl 1, K to end.
Rows 9 and 10: Knit.
Rep last 10 rows 16 [17: 18] times more.
Work 8 rows, ending with RS facing for next row.
Now rep rows 1 to 10, 17 [18: 19] times more.

Shape right front edge

Cast off 52 [54: 56] sts at beg of next row.
22 sts.
Work in g st for a further 65 cm (for second scarf section).
Cast off.

MAKING UP

Press as described on the information page.
Cut 31 cm lengths of yarn and knot groups of 6 of these lengths through cast-on and cast-off edges of scarf sections to form fringe – position 9 knots evenly spaced across each end.

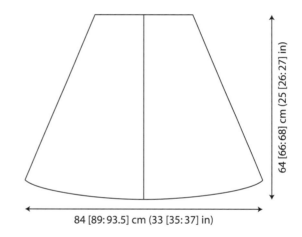

64 [66: 68] cm (25 [26: 27] in)

84 [89: 93.5] cm (33 [35: 37] in)

Cromarty

YARN

	XS	S	M	L	XL	
To fit bust	81	86	91	97	102	cm
	32	34	36	38	40	in

RYC Soft Tweed

A Antique	002	9	9	10	10	11	x 50gm
A Blanket	008	3	3	3	3	3	x 50gm
A Twig	005	3	3	3	3	3	x 50gm

NEEDLES
1 pair 7mm (no 2) (US 10½) needles
1 pair 8mm (no 0) (US 11) needles

BUTTONS – 6 x 00340

TENSION
12 sts and 16 rows to 10 cm measured over
stocking stitch using 8mm (US 11) needles.

STRIPE SEQUENCE
Beg with a K row, work in st st in stripes as folls:
Rows 1 to 6: Using yarn B.
Rows 7 to 12: Using yarn A.
Rows 13 to 18: Using yarn B.
Rows 19 to 24: Using yarn C.
Rows 25 to 30: Using yarn A.
Rows 31 to 36: Using yarn C.
These 36 rows form stripe sequence and are
repeated.

BACK
Using 7mm (US 10½) needles and yarn A cast on
58 [60: 64: 66: 70] sts.
Row 1 (RS): K0 [1: 0: 0: 0], P2 [2: 1: 2: 0], *K2, P2,
rep from * to last 0 [1: 3: 0: 2] sts, K0 [1: 2: 0: 2],
P0 [0: 1: 0: 0].
Row 2: P0 [1: 0: 0: 0], K2 [2: 1: 2: 0], *P2, K2,
rep from * to last 0 [1: 3: 0: 2] sts, P0 [1: 2: 0: 2],
K0 [0: 1: 0: 0].
These 2 rows form rib.
Work in rib for a further 14 rows, ending with RS
facing for next row.
Change to 8mm (US 11) needles.
Beg with a K row, work in st st for 20 rows,
ending with RS facing for next row.
Dec 1 st at each end of next and every foll 12th row
until 52 [54: 58: 60: 64] sts rem.
Work 3 [5: 5: 7: 7] rows, ending with RS facing for

next row.
Joining in and breaking off colours as required
and beg with row 1, cont in stripe sequence as
folls:
Inc 1 st at each end of 7th and every foll 6th row
until there are 58 [60: 64: 66: 70] sts.
Work 5 rows, ending after 6 rows using yarn C
and with RS facing for next row. (Back should
meas 54 [55: 55: 56: 56] cm.)
Shape armholes
Keeping stripes correct, cast off 4 sts at beg of
next 2 rows. 50 [52: 56: 58: 62] sts.
Dec 1 st at each end of next 3 [3: 5: 5: 7] rows, then
on foll 1 [2: 1: 2: 1] alt rows, then on foll 4th row.
40 [40: 42: 42: 44] sts.
Cont straight until armhole meas 23 [23: 24:
24: 25] cm, ending with RS facing for next row.
Shape shoulders and back neck
Cast off 4 [3: 4: 3: 4] sts at beg of next 2 rows.
32 [34: 34: 36: 36] sts.
Next row (RS): Cast off 4 [3: 4: 3: 4] sts, K until
there are 7 [8: 7: 8: 7] sts on right needle and
turn, leaving rem sts on a holder.
Work each side of neck separately.
Cast off 4 sts at beg of next row.
Cast off rem 3 [4: 3: 4: 3] sts.
With RS facing, rejoin appropriate yarn to rem sts,
cast off centre 10 [12: 12: 14: 14] sts, K to end.
Complete to match first side, reversing shapings.

POCKET LININGS (make 2)
Using 8mm (US 11) needles and yarn A cast on
20 sts.
Beg with a K row, work in st st for 26 rows,
ending with RS facing for next row.
Break yarn and leave sts on a holder.

LEFT FRONT
Using 7mm (US 10½) needles and yarn A cast on
29 [30: 32: 33: 35] sts.
Row 1 (RS): K0 [1: 0: 0: 0], P2 [2: 1: 2: 0], *K2, P2,
rep from * to last 3 sts, K2, P1.
Row 2: K1, *P2, K2, rep from * to last 0 [1: 3:
0: 2] sts, P0 [1: 2: 0: 2], K0 [0: 1: 0: 0].
These 2 rows form rib.
Work in rib for a further 14 rows, ending with RS
facing for next row.
Change to 8mm (US 11) needles.

Beg with a K row, work in st st for 20 rows,
ending with RS facing for next row.
Dec 1 st at beg of next row.
28 [29: 31: 32: 34] sts.
Work 5 rows, ending with RS facing for next row.
Place pocket
Next row (RS): K4 [4: 5: 5: 6], slip next 20 sts
onto a holder and, in their place, K across 20 sts
of first pocket lining, K to end.
Dec 1 st at beg of 6th and foll 12th row.
26 [27: 29: 30: 32] sts.
Work 3 [5: 5: 7: 7] rows, ending with RS facing for
next row.
Joining in and breaking off colours as required
and beg with row 1, cont in stripe sequence
as folls:
Inc 1 st at beg of 7th and every foll 6th row until
there are 29 [30: 32: 33: 35] sts.
Work 5 rows, ending after 6 rows using yarn C
and with RS facing for next row. (Left front should
match back to beg of armhole shaping.)
Shape armhole
Keeping stripes correct, cast off 4 sts at beg of
next row.
25 [26: 28: 29: 31] sts.
Work 1 row.
Dec 1 st at armhole edge of next 3 [3: 5: 5: 7]
rows, then on foll 1 [2: 1: 2: 1] alt rows, then on
foll 4th row.
20 [20: 21: 21: 22] sts.
Cont straight until 7 rows less have been worked
than on back to beg of shoulder shaping, ending
with **WS** facing for next row.
Shape neck
Keeping stripes correct, cast off 4 [5: 5: 6: 6] sts
at beg of next row. 16 [15: 16: 15: 16] sts.
Dec 1 st at neck edge of next 4 rows, then on foll
alt row, ending with RS facing for next row.
11 [10: 11: 10: 11] sts.
Shape shoulder
Cast off 4 [3: 4: 3: 4] sts at beg of next and foll alt
row.
Work 1 row.
Cast off rem 3 [4: 3: 4: 3] sts.

RIGHT FRONT
Using 7mm (US 10½) needles and yarn A cast on
29 [30: 32: 33: 35] sts.

Row 1 (RS): P1, *K2, P2, rep from * to last 0 [1: 3: 0: 2] sts, K0 [1: 2: 0: 2], P0 [0: 1: 0: 0].
Row 2: P0 [1: 0: 0: 0], K2 [2: 1: 2: 0], *P2, K2, rep from * to last 3 sts, P2, K1.
These 2 rows form rib.
Work in rib for a further 14 rows, ending with RS facing for next row.
Change to 8mm (US 11) needles.
Beg with a K row, work in st st for 20 rows, ending with RS facing for next row.
Dec 1 st at end of next row.
28 [29: 31: 32: 34] sts.
Work 5 rows, ending with RS facing for next row.
Place pocket
Next row (RS): K4 [5: 6: 7: 8], slip next 20 sts onto a holder and, in their place, K across 20 sts of second pocket lining, K to end.
Complete to match left front, reversing shapings, working an extra row before beg of armhole, neck and shoulder shaping.

SLEEVES
Using 7mm (US 10½) needles and yarn A cast on 32 [32: 34: 36: 36] sts.
Row 1 (RS): K0 [0: 0: 1: 1], P1 [1: 2: 2: 2], *K2, P2, rep from * to last 3 [3: 0: 1: 1] sts, K2 [2: 0: 1: 1], P1 [1: 0: 0: 0].
Row 2: P0 [0: 0: 1: 1], K1 [1: 2: 2: 2], *P2, K2, rep from * to last 3 [3: 0: 1: 1] sts, P2 [2: 0: 1: 1], K1 [1: 0: 0: 0].
These 2 rows form rib.
Work in rib for a further 14 rows, ending with RS facing for next row.
Change to 8mm (US 11) needles.
Joining in and breaking off colours as required and beg with row 3 [3: 1: 1: 1], cont in stripe sequence as folls:
Inc 1 st at each end of next and every foll 12th [12th: 12th: 16th: 12th] row to 40 [40: 40: 40: 42] sts, then on every foll 14th [14th: 14th:

18th: 14th] row until there are 42 [42: 44: 44: 46] sts.
Cont straight until sleeve meas approx 45 [45: 46: 46: 46] cm, ending after same stripe row as on back to beg of armhole shaping and with RS facing for next row.
Shape top
Keeping stripes correct, cast off 4 sts at beg of next 2 rows. 34 [34: 36: 36: 38] sts.
Dec 1 st at each end of next 3 rows, then on foll alt row, then on every foll 4th row until 20 [20: 22: 22: 24] sts rem.
Work 1 row, ending with RS facing for next row.
Dec 1 st at each end of next and foll 0 [0: 1: 1: 2] alt rows, then on foll 3 rows, ending with RS facing for next row.
Cast off rem 12 sts.

MAKING UP
Press as described on the information page.
Join both shoulder seams using back stitch, or mattress stitch if preferred.
Button band
With RS facing, using 7mm (US 10½) needles and yarn A, pick up and knit 90 [90: 94: 94: 94] sts evenly down left front opening edge, from neck shaping to cast-on edge.
Row 1 (WS): P2, *K2, P2, rep from * to end.
Row 2: K2, *P2, K2, rep from * to end.
These 2 rows form rib.
Work in rib for a further 3 rows, ending with RS facing for next row.
Cast off in rib.
Buttonhole band
With RS facing, using 7mm (US 10½) needles and yarn A, pick up and knit 90 [90: 94: 94: 94] sts evenly up right front opening edge, from cast-on edge to neck shaping.
Work in rib as given for button band for 2 rows, ending with **WS** facing for next row.

Row 3 (buttonhole row) (WS): rib 2, *work 2 tog, yrn (to make a buttonhole), rib 14 [14: 15: 15: 15], rep from * 4 times more, work 2 tog, yrn (to make 6th buttonhole), rib to end.
Work in rib for a further 2 rows, ending with RS facing for next row.
Cast off in rib.
Collar
With RS facing, using 7mm (US 10½) needles and yarn A, beg and ending halfway across top of bands, pick up and knit 19 [20: 20: 21: 21] sts up right side of neck, 20 [22: 22: 24: 24] sts from back, then 19 [20: 20: 21: 21] sts down left side of neck.
58 [62: 62: 66: 66] sts.
Row 1 (WS of body, RS of collar): P9 [11: 11: 13: 9], inc in next st, *P1, inc in next st, rep from * to last 10 [12: 12: 14: 10] sts, P to end.
78 [82: 82: 86: 90] sts.
Beg with row 1, work in rib as given for button band until collar meas 12 cm.
Change to 8mm (US 11) needles.
Cont in rib until collar meas 24 cm.
Cast off in rib.
Pocket tops (both alike)
Slip 20 pocket sts onto 7mm (US 10½) needles and rejoin yarn A with RS facing.
Row 1 (RS): K1, (P2, K2) 4 times, P2, K1.
Row 2: P1, (K2, P2) 4 times, K2, P1.
Rep last 2 rows once more.
Cast off in rib.
Belt
Using 7mm (US 10½) needles and yarn A cast on 10 sts.
Beg with row 2, work in rib as given for button band until belt meas 150 cm.
Cast off in rib.
See information page for finishing instructions, setting in sleeves using the set-in method.
Using photograph as a guide, embroider striped

sections as folls: Using yarn A, work a line of cross st along line where stripes in yarn B and yarn C meet. Using yarn C, work a line of blanket st where stripes in yarn A and yarn B meet. Using yarn B, work a line of blanket st where stripes in yarn A and yarn C meet.

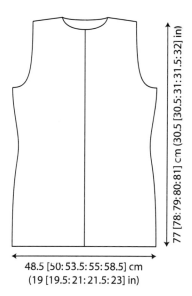

77 [78: 79: 80: 81] cm (30.5 [30.5: 31: 31.5: 32] in)

48.5 [50: 53.5: 55: 58.5] cm
(19 [19.5: 21: 21.5: 23] in)

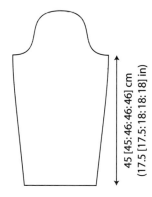

45 [45: 46: 46: 46] cm (17.5 [17.5: 18: 18: 18] in)

Clyde

YARN

	XS	S	M	L	XL	
To fit bust	81	86	91	97	102	cm
	32	34	36	38	40	in

RYC Soft Tweed

| | 5 | 6 | 6 | 6 | 7 | x 50gm |

(photographed in Blanket 008)

NEEDLES

1 pair 7mm (no 2) (US 10½) needles
1 pair 8mm (no 0) (US 11) needles
7mm (no 2) (US 10½) circular needle
Cable needle

TENSION

12 sts and 16 rows to 10 cm measured over stocking stitch using 8mm (US 11) needles.

SPECIAL ABBREVIATIONS

C10B = slip next 5 sts onto cable needle and leave at back of work, (K1, P1) twice, K1, then (P1, K1) twice, P1 from cable needle;
C10F = slip next 5 sts onto cable needle and leave at front of work, (P1, K1) twice, P1, then (K1, P1) twice, K1 from cable needle.

BACK

Using 7mm (US 10½) needles cast on 47 [49: 53: 55: 59] sts.
Row 1 (RS): K0 [0: 0: 1: 0], P0 [1: 3: 3: 1], *K2, P3, rep from * to last 2 [3: 0: 1: 3] sts, K2 [2: 0: 1: 2], P0 [1: 0: 0: 1].
Row 2: P0 [0: 0: 1: 0], K0 [1: 3: 3: 1], *P2, K3, rep from * to last 2 [3: 0: 1: 3] sts, P2 [2: 0: 1: 2], K0 [1: 0: 0: 1].
These 2 rows form rib.
Work in rib for a further 11 rows, ending with **WS** facing for next row.
Row 14 (WS): Rib 1 [2: 4: 5: 7], *(M1, rib 2) 3 times, M1, rib 7, rep from * to last 7 [8: 10: 11: 13] sts, (M1, rib 2) 3 times, M1, rib to end.
63 [65: 69: 71: 75] sts.
Change to 8mm (US 11) needles.
Beg and ending rows as indicated and repeating the 32 row patt repeat throughout, cont in patt from chart as folls:
Inc 1 st at each end of 9th and every foll 12th row until there are 69 [71: 75: 77: 81] sts.
Cont straight until back meas 33 [34: 34: 35: 35] cm, ending with RS facing for next row.

Shape armholes

Keeping patt correct, cast off 5 sts at beg of next 2 rows. 59 [61: 65: 67: 71] sts.**
Dec 1 st at each end of next 3 [3: 5: 5: 7] rows, then on foll 2 [3: 2: 3: 2] alt rows, then on foll 4th row.
47 [47: 49: 49: 51] sts.
Cont straight until armhole meas 20 [20: 21: 21: 22] cm, ending with RS facing for next row.
Shape shoulders and back neck
Cast off 4 sts at beg of next 2 rows.
39 [39: 41: 41: 43] sts.
Next row (RS): Cast off 4 sts, patt until there are 8 [7: 8: 7: 8] sts on right needle and turn, leaving rem sts on a holder.
Work each side of neck separately.
Cast off 4 sts at beg of next row.
Cast off rem 4 [3: 4: 3: 4] sts.
With RS facing, rejoin yarn to rem sts, cast off centre 15 [17: 17: 19: 19] sts, patt to end.
Complete to match first side, reversing shapings.

FRONT

Work as given for back to **.
Dec 1 st at each end of next 2 rows, ending with RS facing for next row. 55 [57: 61: 63: 67] sts.
Divide for neck
Next row (RS): Work 2 tog, patt 25 [26: 28: 29: 31] sts and turn, leaving rem sts on a holder.
Work each side of neck separately.
Keeping patt correct, dec 0 [0: 1: 1: 1] st at armhole edge of next row. 26 [27: 28: 29: 31] sts.
Dec 1 st at armhole edge on next 1 [1: 1: 1: 3] rows, then on foll 1 [2: 2: 3: 2] alt rows, then on foll 4th row **and at same time** dec 1 st at neck edge on next and every foll alt row. 19 [18: 19: 18: 19] sts.
Dec 1 st at front slope edge **only** on 2nd and every foll alt row until 12 [11: 12: 11: 12] sts rem.
Cont straight until front matches back to beg of shoulder shaping, ending with RS facing for next row.
Shape shoulder
Cast off 4 sts at beg of next and foll alt row.
Work 1 row.
Cast off rem 4 [3: 4: 3: 4] sts.
With RS facing, slip centre st onto a holder, rejoin yarn to rem sts, patt to last 2 sts, work 2 tog.
Complete to match first side, reversing shapings.

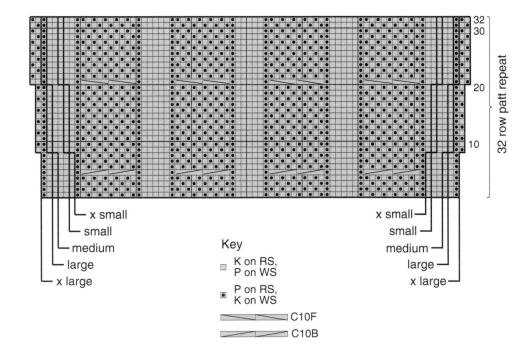

x small
small
medium
large
x large

x small
small
medium
large
x large

32 row patt repeat

Key

☐ K on RS, P on WS

▪ P on RS, K on WS

▱ C10F

▱ C10B

MAKING UP

Press as described on the information page. Join shoulder seams using back stitch, or mattress stitch if preferred.

Neckband

With RS facing and using 7mm (US 10½) circular needle, beg and ending at left shoulder seam, pick up and knit 28 [28: 32: 32: 36] sts down left side of neck, K st from front holder and mark this st with a coloured thread, pick up and knit 28 [28: 32: 32: 36] sts up right side of neck, then 18 [18: 18: 22: 22] sts from back.

75 [75: 83: 87: 95] sts.

Round 1 (RS): *K2, P2, rep from * to within 4 sts of marked st, K2, K2tog tbl, K marked st, K2tog, **K2, P2, rep from ** to end.

This round sets position of rib.

Keeping rib correct, cont as folls:

Round 2: Rib to within 2 sts of marked st, K2tog tbl, K marked st, K2tog, rib to end.

Round 3: As round 2.

Cast off in rib, still decreasing either side of marked st as before.

Armhole borders (both alike)

With RS facing and using 7mm (US 10½) needles, pick up and knit 58 [58: 62: 62: 66] sts evenly all round armhole edge.

Row 1 (WS): K2, *P2, K2, rep from * to end.

Row 2: P2, *K2, P2, rep from * to end.

Row 3: As row 1.

Cast off in rib.

See information page for finishing instructions.

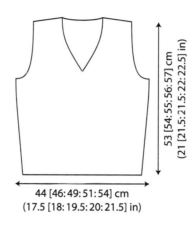

53 [54: 55: 56: 57] cm
(21 [21.5: 21.5: 22: 22.5] in)

44 [46: 49: 51: 54] cm
(17.5 [18: 19.5: 20: 21.5] in)

Firth

YARN

	XS	S	M	L	XL
To fit bust	81	86	91	97	102 cm
	32	34	36	38	40 in

RYC Soft Tweed

A Thistle	003	4	4	5	5	5	x 50gm
B Blanket	008	4	4	4	4	4	x 50gm
C Slate Blue	007	4	4	4	4	4	x 50gm

NEEDLES

1 pair 7mm (no 2) (US 10½) needles
1 pair 8mm (no 0) (US 11) needles

EXTRAS – 1 decorative kilt pin (or brooch)

TENSION

12 sts and 19 rows to 10 cm measured over
pattern using 8mm (US 11) needles.

BACK

Using 7mm (US 10½) needles and yarn A cast on
57 [59: 63: 65: 69] sts.
Row 1 (RS): P2 [3: 1: 2: 4], *K1, P3, rep from * to
last 3 [4: 2: 3: 5] sts, K1, P2 [3: 1: 2: 4].

Row 2: K2 [3: 1: 2: 4], *P1, K3, rep from * to last
3 [4: 2: 3: 5] sts, P1, K2 [3: 1: 2: 4].
Change to 8mm (US 11) needles.
Beg and ending rows as indicated, joining in
colours as required and repeating the 24 row patt
repeat throughout, cont in patt from chart as folls:
Cont straight until back meas approx 44 [44: 43:
43: 42] cm, ending after patt row 10 [10: 8: 8: 6]
and with RS facing for next row.
Shape armholes
Keeping patt correct, cast off 3 sts at beg of next
2 rows.
51 [53: 57: 59: 63] sts.
Dec 1 st at each end of next 3 rows.
45 [47: 51: 53: 57] sts.
Cont straight until armhole meas approx 20 [20:
21: 21: 22] cm, ending after patt row 24 and with
RS facing for next row.
Shape shoulders and funnel neck
Keeping patt correct, cast off 3 [3: 4: 4: 5] sts at
beg of next 2 [4: 2: 4: 2] rows, then 2 [2: 3:
3: 4] sts at beg of foll 4 [2: 4: 2: 4] rows. 31 sts.
Dec 1 st at each end of next 2 rows.
27 sts.

Work a further 3 rows, ending after patt row 11
and with **WS** facing for next row.
Cast off purlwise (on **WS**).

LEFT FRONT

Using 7mm (US 10½) needles and yarn A cast on
42 [43: 45: 46: 48] sts.
Row 1 (RS): P2 [3: 1: 2: 4], *K1, P3, rep from * to
end.
Row 2: K3, *P1, K3, rep from * to last 3 [4: 2:
3: 5] sts, P1, K2 [3: 1: 2: 4].
Change to 8mm (US 11) needles.
Beg and ending rows as indicated, cont in patt
from chart as folls:
Cont straight until left front matches back to beg
of armhole shaping, ending with RS facing for
next row.
Shape armhole
Keeping patt correct, cast off 3 sts at beg of next
row.
39 [40: 42: 43: 45] sts.
Work 1 row.
Dec 1 st at armhole edge of next 3 rows.
36 [37: 39: 40: 42] sts.

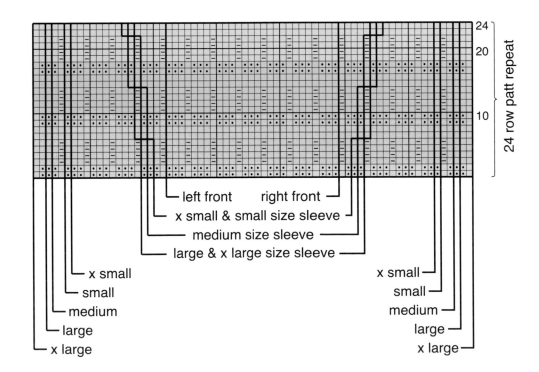

left front   right front
x small & small size sleeve
medium size sleeve
large & x large size sleeve

x small
small
medium
large
x large

x small
small
medium
large
x large

24 row patt repeat

Key

☐	A - K on RS, P on WS
⊡	A - P on RS, K on WS
▨	B - K on RS, P on WS
⊞	B - P on RS, K on WS
☐	C - K on RS, P on WS
⊡	C - P on RS, K on WS
⊟	sl 1 purlwise with yarn at WS of work

Cont straight until left front matches back to beg of shoulder shaping, ending with RS facing for next row.

Shape shoulder and funnel neck

Keeping patt correct, cast off 3 [3: 4: 4: 5] sts at beg of next and foll 0 [1: 0: 1: 0] alt row, then 2 [2: 3: 3: 4] sts at beg of foll 2 [1: 2: 1: 2] alt rows. 29 sts.

Work 1 row.

Dec 1 st at shoulder edge of next 2 rows. 27 sts.

Work a further 3 rows, ending after patt row 11 and with **WS** facing for next row.

Cast off purlwise (on **WS**).

RIGHT FRONT

Using 7mm (US 10½) needles and yarn A cast on 42 [43: 45: 46: 48] sts.

Row 1 (RS): P3, *K1, P3, rep from * to last 3 [4: 2: 3: 5] sts, K1, P2 [3: 1: 2: 4].

Row 2: K2 [3: 1: 2: 4], *P1, K3, rep from * to end.

Change to 8mm (US 11) needles.

Complete to match left front, reversing shapings, working an extra row before beg of armhole and shoulder shaping.

SLEEVES

Using 7mm (US 10½) needles and yarn A cast on 31 [31: 33: 35: 35] sts.

Row 1 (RS): P1 [1: 2: 3: 3], *K1, P3, rep from * to last 2 [2: 3: 4: 4] sts, K1, P1 [1: 2: 3: 3].

Row 2: K1 [1: 2: 3: 3], *P1, K3, rep from * to last 2 [2: 3: 4: 4] sts, P1, K1 [1: 2: 3: 3].

Change to 8mm (US 11) needles.

Beg and ending rows as indicated, cont in patt from chart as folls:

Inc 1 st at each end of 7th and every foll 8th row to 49 [49: 51: 43: 53] sts, then on every foll - [-: -: 10th: -] row until there are - [-: -: 51: -] sts, taking inc sts into patt.

Cont straight until sleeve meas approx 43 cm, ending after patt row 8 and with RS facing for next row.

Shape top

Keeping patt correct, cast off 3 sts at beg of next 2 rows. 43 [43: 45: 45: 47] sts.

Dec 1 st at each end of next and foll 2 alt rows, then on foll row, ending after patt row 16 and with RS facing for next row.

Cast off rem 35 [35: 37: 37: 39] sts.

MAKING UP

Press as described on the information page.

Join both shoulder and funnel neck seams using back stitch, or mattress stitch if preferred.

Neck edging

With RS facing, using 7mm (US 10½) needles and yarn A, pick up and knit 27 sts from cast-off edge of right front, 27 sts from cast-off edge of back, then 27 sts from cast-off edge of left front. 81 sts.

Work in g st for 2 rows, ending with **WS** facing for next row.

Cast off knitwise (on **WS**).

Front bands (both alike)

With RS facing, using 7mm (US 10½) needles and yarn A, pick up and knit 86 sts evenly along entire front opening edge, between cast-on edge and top of neck edging.

Work in g st for 2 rows, ending with **WS** facing for next row.

Cast off knitwise (on **WS**).

See information page for finishing instructions, setting in sleeves using the shallow set-in method.

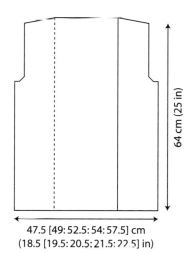

47.5 [49: 52.5: 54: 57.5] cm
(18.5 [19.5: 20.5: 21.5: 22.5] in)

64 cm (25 in)

43 cm (17 in)

Macgregor

YARN

	XS	S	M	L	XL
To fit bust	81	86	91	97	102 cm
	32	34	36	38	40 in

RYC Soft Tweed

| | 7 | 7 | 7 | 8 | 8 x 50gm |

(photographed in Bramble 004)

NEEDLES
1 pair 7mm (no 2) (US 10½) needles
1 pair 8mm (no 0) (US 11) needles
7mm (no 2) (US 10½) circular needle

TENSION
12 sts and 16 rows to 10 cm measured over
stocking stitch using 8mm (US 11) needles.

BACK
Using 7mm (US 10½) needles cast on 53 [55: 59:
61: 65] sts.
Row 1 (RS): K1 [2: 0: 0: 1], P3 [3: 1: 2: 3], *K3, P3,
rep from * to last 1 [2: 4: 5: 1] sts, K1 [2: 3: 3: 1],
P0 [0: 1: 2: 0].
Row 2: P1 [2: 0: 0: 1], K3 [3: 1: 2: 3], *P3, K3,
rep from * to last 1 [2: 4: 5: 1] sts, P1 [2: 3: 3: 1],
K0 [0: 1: 2: 0].
These 2 rows form rib.
Work in rib for a further 10 rows, ending with RS
facing for next row.
Change to 8mm (US 11) needles.
Beg with a K row, work in st st, dec 1 st at each
end of 3rd and foll 8th row, then on foll 6th row.
47 [49: 53: 55: 59] sts.
Work 7 rows, ending with RS facing for next row.
Inc 1 st at each end of next and every foll 6th row
until there are 53 [55: 59: 61: 65] sts.
Cont straight until back meas 34 [35: 35:
36: 36] cm, ending with RS facing for next row.
Shape raglan armholes
Cast off 3 sts at beg of next 2 rows.
47 [49: 53: 55: 59] sts.

Next row (RS): K1, sl 1, K1, psso, K to last 3 sts,
K2tog, K1.
Working all raglan armhole decreases as set by
last row, dec 1 st at each end of 4th [4th: 4th:
4th: 2nd] and foll 1 [1: 0: 0: 0] 4th rows, then on
every foll alt row until 19 [21: 21: 23: 23] sts rem.
Work 1 row, ending with RS facing for next row.
Shape back neck
Next row (RS): K1, sl 1, K1, psso, K1 and turn,
leaving rem sts on a holder.
Work each side of neck separately.
Dec 1 st at beg of next row.
Next row (RS): K2tog and fasten off.
With RS facing, rejoin yarn to rem sts, cast off
centre 11 [13: 13: 15: 15] sts (one st on right
needle), K2tog, K1.
Complete to match first side, reversing shapings.

FRONT
Work as given for back until 29 [31: 31: 33: 33] sts
rem in raglan armhole shaping, ending with RS
facing for next row.
Shape neck
Next row (RS): K1, sl 1, K1, psso, K7 and turn,
leaving rem sts on a holder.
Work each side of neck separately.
Dec 1 st at neck edge of next 2 rows, then on foll
alt row **and at same time** dec 1 st at raglan
armhole edge on 2nd and foll alt row. 4 sts.
Work 1 row, ending with RS facing for next row.
Next row (RS): K1, sl 1, K2tog, psso.
Next row: P2.
Next row: K2tog and fasten off.
With RS facing, rejoin yarn to rem sts, cast off
centre 9 [11: 11: 13: 13] sts, K to last 3 sts, K2tog,
K1.
Complete to match first side, reversing shapings.

SLEEVES
Using 7mm (US 10½) needles cast on 27 [27: 29:
31: 31] sts.

Row 1 (RS): K0 [0: 1: 2: 2], *P3, K3, rep from * to
last 3 [3: 4: 5: 5] sts, P3, K0 [0: 1: 2: 2].
Row 2: P0 [0: 1: 2: 2], *K3, P3, rep from * to last
3 [3: 4: 5: 5] sts, K3, P0 [0: 1: 2: 2].
These 2 rows form rib.
Work in rib for a further 10 rows, ending with RS
facing for next row.
Change to 8mm (US 11) needles.
Beg with a K row, work in st st, shaping sides by
inc 1 st at each end of next and every foll
12th [12th: 14th: 18th: 14th] row to 31 [31: 39:
37: 41] sts, then on every foll 14th [14th: -: 20th: -]
row until there are 37 [37: -: 39: -] sts.
Cont straight until sleeve meas 46 [46: 47:
47: 47] cm, ending with RS facing for next row.
Shape raglan
Cast off 3 sts at beg of next 2 rows.
31 [31: 33: 33: 35] sts.
Working all raglan armhole decreases as set by
back, dec 1 st at each end of next and every foll
alt row to 11 sts, then on every foll 4th row until
5 sts rem, ending with **WS** facing for next row.
Left sleeve only
Dec 1 st at beg of next row and at same edge on
foll 2 rows.
Right sleeve only
Dec 1 st at end of next row and at same edge on
foll 2 rows.
Both sleeves
Next row: K2tog and fasten off.

MAKING UP
Press as described on the information page.
Join raglan seams using back stitch, or mattress
stitch if preferred.
Neckband
With RS facing and using 7mm (US 10½) circular
needle, beg and ending at left back raglan seam,
pick up and knit 5 sts from left sleeve, 8 sts down
left side of neck, 9 [9: 9: 13: 13] sts from front,
8 sts up right side of neck, 5 sts from right

sleeve, then 19 [19: 19: 21: 21] sts from back.
54 [54: 54: 60: 60] sts.
Round 1 (RS): *K3, P3, rep from * to end.
Rep this round twice more.
Cast off in rib.
See information page for finishing instructions.

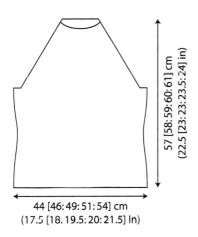

57 [58: 59: 60: 61] cm
(22.5 [23: 23: 23.5: 24] in)

44 [46: 49: 51: 54] cm
(17.5 [18: 19.5: 20: 21.5] In)

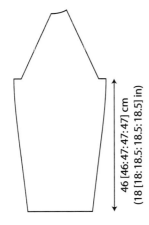

46 [46: 47: 47: 47] cm
(18 [18: 18.5: 18.5: 18.5] in)

 Campbell

YARN

	XS	S	M	L	XL
To fit bust	81	86	91	97	102 cm
	32	34	36	38	40 in

RYC Soft Tweed

| | 10 | 11 | 11 | 12 | 12 x 50gm |

(photographed in Oatmeal 001)

NEEDLES

1 pair 7mm (no 2) (US 10½) needles
1 pair 8mm (no 0) (US 11) needles
Cable needle

TENSION

12 sts and 16 rows to 10 cm measured over stocking stitch using 8mm (US 11) needles.

SPECIAL ABBREVIATIONS

Tw2 = K 2nd st on left needle tbl, then K first st and slip both sts off left needle together;
C4B = slip next 2 sts onto cable needle and leave at back of work, K2, then K2 from cable needle.

LEFT FRONT

Using 7mm (US 10½) needles cast on 39 [40: 42: 43: 45] sts.
Work in g st for 2 rows, ending with RS facing for next row.
Change to 8mm (US 11) needles.
Beg with a K row, work in st st, shaping front opening edge by dec 1 st at end of 5th [3rd: 5th: 3rd: 5th] and every foll 4th row until 25 [25: 28: 28: 30] sts rem.
Work 1 [1: 3: 3: 1] rows, ending with RS facing for next row. (Left front should meas 38 [39: 39: 40: 40] cm.)
Shape armhole
Cast off 4 sts at beg and dec 0 [0: 1: 1: 0] st at end of next row. 21 [21: 23: 23: 26] sts.
Work 1 row.
Dec 1 st at armhole edge of next 3 [3: 5: 5: 7] rows, then on foll 1 [2: 1: 2: 1] alt rows **and at same time** dec 1 st at front opening edge of next [next: 3rd: 3rd: next] and every foll 4th row. 15 [14: 15: 14: 15] sts.
Dec 1 st at front opening edge of 4th [2nd: 4th: 2nd: 4th] and every foll 4th row until 10 [9: 10: 9: 10] sts rem.

Cont straight until armhole meas 20 [20: 21: 21: 22] cm, ending with RS facing for next row.
Shape shoulder
Cast off 3 sts at beg of next and foll alt row.
Work 1 row.
Cast off rem 4 [3: 4: 3: 4] sts.

RIGHT FRONT

Using 7mm (US 10½) needles cast on 39 [40: 42: 43: 45] sts.
Work in g st for 2 rows, ending with RS facing for next row.
Change to 8mm (US 11) needles.
Beg with a K row, work in st st, shaping front opening edge by dec 1 st at beg of 5th [3rd: 5th: 3rd: 5th] and every foll 4th row until 25 [25: 28: 28: 30] sts rem.
Complete to match left front, reversing shapings, working an extra row before beg of armhole and shoulder shaping.

BACK

Using 7mm (US 10½) needles cast on 56 [58: 62: 64: 68] sts.
Work in g st for 2 rows, ending with RS facing for next row.
Change to 8mm (US 11) needles.
Beg with a K row, work in st st until back matches fronts to beg of armhole shaping, ending with RS facing for next row.
Shape armholes
Cast off 4 sts at beg of next 2 rows.
48 [50: 54: 56: 60] sts.
Dec 1 st at each end of next 3 [3: 5: 5: 7] rows, then on foll 1 [2: 1: 2: 1] alt rows.
40 [40: 42: 42: 44] sts.
Cont straight until back matches fronts to beg of shoulder shaping, ending with RS facing for next row.
Shape shoulders and back neck
Cast off 3 sts at beg of next 2 rows.
34 [34: 36: 36: 38] sts.
Next row (RS): Cast off 3 sts, K until there are 8 [7: 8: 7: 8] sts on right needle and turn, leaving rem sts on a holder.
Work each side of neck separately.
Cast off 4 sts at beg of next row.
Cast off rem 4 [3: 4: 3: 4] sts.

With RS facing, rejoin yarn to rem sts, cast off centre 12 [14: 14: 16: 16] sts, K to end.
Complete to match first side, reversing shapings.

SLEEVES

Using 7mm (US 10½) needles cast on 28 [28: 30: 32: 32] sts.
Work in g st for 2 rows, ending with RS facing for next row.
Change to 8mm (US 11) needles.
Beg with a K row, work in st st, shaping sides by inc 1 st at each end of 7th [7th: 7th: 9th: 7th] and every foll 8th [8th: 8th: 10th: 8th] row to 36 [36: 36: 40: 38] sts, then on every foll 10th [10th: 10th: 12th: 10th] row until there are 42 [42: 44: 44: 46] sts.
Cont straight until sleeve meas 44 [44: 45: 45: 45] cm, ending with RS facing for next row.
Shape top
Cast off 4 sts at beg of next 2 rows.
34 [34: 36: 36: 38] sts.
Dec 1 st at each end of next 3 rows, then on foll 2 alt rows, then on every foll 4th row until 20 [20: 22: 22: 24] sts rem.
Work 1 row, ending with RS facing for next row.
Dec 1 st at each end of next and every foll alt row to 14 sts, then on foll row, ending with RS facing for next row.
Cast off rem 12 sts.

MAKING UP

Press as described on the information page.
Join both shoulder seams using back stitch, or mattress stitch if preferred.
Front band
Using 7mm (US 10½) needles cast on 23 sts.
Row 1 (RS): P2, Tw2, P1, K4, (K1, P1) twice, P1, K2, P1, K4, P2.
Row 2: K2, P4, K1, P2, K1, (P1, K1) twice, P4, K1, P2, K2.
Row 3: P2, Tw2, P1, slip next 4 sts onto cable needle and leave at back of work, (K1, P1) twice, then K4 from cable needle, P1, K2, P1, C4B, P2.
Row 4: K2, P4, K1, P2, K1, P4, (P1, K1) twice, K1, P2, K2.
Row 5: P2, Tw2, P1, (K1, P1) twice, K4, P1, K2, P1, K4, P2.
Row 6: As row 4.

Row 7: P2, Tw2, P1, (K1, P1) twice, K4, P1, K2, P1, C4B, P2.

Rows 8 and 9: As rows 4 and 5.

Row 10: As row 4.

Row 11: As row 7.

Row 12: As row 4.

Row 13: P2, Tw2, P1, slip next 4 sts onto cable needle and leave at back of work, K4, then (K1, P1) twice from cable needle, P1, K2, P1, K4, P2.

Row 14: As row 2.

Row 15: P2, Tw2, P1, K4, (K1, P1) twice, P1, K2, P1, C4B, P2.

Row 16: As row 2.

Rows 17 and 18: As rows 1 and 2.

Row 19: As row 15.

Row 20: As row 2.

These 20 rows form patt.

Cont in patt until band, when slightly stretched, fits up entire right front opening edge, across back neck, and down entire left front opening edge, ending with RS facing for next row.

Cast off in patt.

Slip stitch band in place.

Ties (make 2)

Using 7mm (US 10½) needles cast on 5 sts.

Row 1 (RS): (K1, P1) twice, K1.

Row 2: (P1, K1) twice, P1.

Row 3: Sl 1 purlwise with yarn at back (WS) of work, P1, K1, P1, sl 1 purlwise with yarn at back (WS) of work.

Rep last 2 rows until tie meas 79 cm for right tie, or 114 cm for left tie.

Cast off.

See information page for finishing instructions, setting in sleeves using the set-in method and leaving a small opening at waist level in right side seam. Sew ends of ties to appropriate front level with opening.

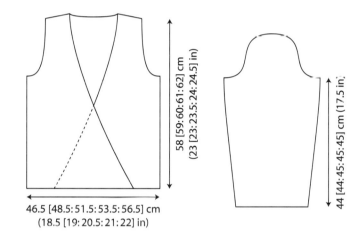

58 [59:60:61:62] cm
(23 [23:23.5:24:24.5] in)

46.5 [48.5:51.5:53.5:56.5] cm
(18.5 [19:20.5:21:22] in)

44 [44:45:45:45] cm (17.5 in)

Smoo scarf

YARN
RYC Soft Tweed
4 x 50gm
(photographed in Bramble 004)

NEEDLES
1 pair 8mm (no 0) (US 11) needles

FINISHED SIZE
Completed scarf measures 22 cm (8½ in) wide
and 254 cm (100 ins) long, excluding fringe.

TENSION
12 sts and 8½ rows to 10 cm measured over
pattern using 8mm (US 11) needles.

SCARF
Using 8mm (US 11) needles cast on 26 sts.
Row 1 (RS): Knit.
Row 2: Knit.
Row 3: K to end, winding yarn 3 times round
needle for each st.
Row 4: K to end, dropping extra loops.
These 4 rows form patt.
Cont in patt until scarf meas 254 cm, ending after
patt row 2 and with RS facing for next row.
Cast off.

MAKING UP
Press as described on the information page.
Cut 31 cm lengths of yarn and knot groups of 6 of
these lengths through cast-on and cast-off edges
to form fringe – position 9 knots evenly spaced
across each end.

Smoo beret

YARN
RYC Soft Tweed
1 x 50gm
(photographed in Bramble 004)

NEEDLES
1 pair 7mm (no 2) (US 10½) needles
1 pair 8mm (no 0) (US 11) needles

TENSION
12 sts and 16 rows to 10 cm measured over
stocking stitch using 8mm (US 11) needles.

BERET
Using 7mm (US 10½) needles cast on 54 sts.
Row 1 (RS): *K1 tbl, rep from * to end.
Rows 2 and 3: As row 1.
Row 4: K5, *inc in next st, K3, rep from * to last st,
K1. 66 sts.
Change to 8mm (US 11) needles.
Row 1 (RS): Knit.
Row 2: Knit.
Row 3: K to end, winding yarn 3 times round
needle for each st.
Row 4: K to end, dropping extra loops.
These 4 rows form patt.
Cont in patt for a further 4 rows.
Row 9: K2, *K2tog tbl, K2tog, K4, rep from * to
end. 50 sts.
Work 3 rows in patt.
Row 13: K2, *K2tog tbl, K2tog, K2, rep from * to
end. 34 sts.
Row 14: Knit.
Row 15: K2, *K2tog tbl, K2tog, K1, rep from * to
last 2 sts, K2. 22 sts.
Row 16: Knit.
Row 17: (K2tog) 11 times.
Break yarn and thread through rem 11 sts. Pull up
tight and fasten off securely.

MAKING UP
Press as described on the information page.
Join back seam using back stitch, or mattress
stitch if preferred. Make a 5 cm diameter
pom-pom and attach to top of beret.

 Macmillan

YARN

	ladies	mens	

RYC Soft Tweed

1   2   x 50gm

(photographed in Bramble 004 and Slate Blue 007)

NEEDLES

Set of 4 double-pointed 7mm (no 2) (US 10½) needles

Set of 4 double-pointed 8mm (no 0) (US 11) needles

TENSION

12 sts and 16 rows to 10 cm measured over stocking stitch using 8mm (US 11) needles.

FINISHED SIZE

Completed mitts meas 21 [24] cm around palm.

LEFT MITT

Using 7mm (US 10½) double-pointed needles cast on 24 [28] sts and distribute sts evenly over 3 needles.

Round 1 (RS): *K2, P2, rep from * to end.

This round forms rib.

Cont in rib for a further 12 [14] rounds.

Change to 8mm (US 11) double-pointed needles.

Next round (RS): Knit.

Rep last round once more.

Shape thumb gusset

Round 1 (RS): K11 [13], M1, K1, M1, K12 [14].

26 [30] sts.

Rounds 2 and 3: Knit.

Round 4: K11 [13], M1, K3, M1, K12 [14]. 28 [32] sts.

Rounds 5 and 6: Knit.

Round 7: K11 [13], M1, K5, M1, K12 [14].

30 [34] sts.

Rounds 8 and 9: Knit.

Mens size only

Round 10: K13, M1, K7, M1, K14. 36 sts.

Rounds 11 and 12: Knit.

Both sizes

Shape thumb

Next round: K11 [13] and slip these sts onto a holder, cast on and K 2 sts, K7 [9], slip rem 12 [14] sts onto a holder.

**Distribute rem 9 [11] sts over 3 needles for thumb and cont as folls:

Next round: Knit.

Rep last round twice more.

Next round: Purl.

Next round: Knit.

Cast off purlwise (on RS).

Shape palm

Next round: With RS facing pick up and knit 2 sts from base of thumb, then K sts left on second holder.

Distribute all 25 [29] sts evenly over 3 needles and cont as folls:

Next round: Knit.

Rep last round 5 [7] times more.

Next round: Purl.

Next round: Knit.

Cast off purlwise (on RS).

RIGHT MITT

Using 7mm (US 10½) double-pointed needles cast on 24 [28] sts and distribute sts evenly over 3 needles.

Round 1 (RS): *P2, K2, rep from * to end.

This round forms rib.

Cont in rib for a further 12 [14] rounds.

Change to 8mm (US 11) double-pointed needles.

Next round (RS): Knit.

Rep last round once more.

Shape thumb gusset

Round 1 (RS): K12 [14], M1, K1, M1, K11 [13].

26 [30] sts.

Rounds 2 and 3: Knit.

Round 4: K12 [14], M1, K3, M1, K11 [13].

28 [32] sts.

Rounds 5 and 6: Knit.

Round 7: K12 [14], M1, K5, M1, K11 [13].

30 [34] sts.

Rounds 8 and 9: Knit.

Mens size only

Round 10: K14, M1, K7, M1, K13. 36 sts.

Rounds 11 and 12: Knit.

Both sizes

Shape thumb

Next round: K12 [14] and slip these sts onto a holder, cast on and K 2 sts, K7 [9], slip rem 11 [13] sts onto a holder.

Complete as given for left mitt from **.

MAKING UP

Press as described on the information page.

YARN

	ladies			mens		
	S	M	L	M	L	XL
To fit bust/chest	86	91	97	102	107	112 cm
	34	36	38	40	42	44 in

RYC Soft Tweed

| | 11 | 11 | 12 | 13 | 14 | 15 x 50gm |

(ladies photographed in Thistle 003, mans in Sprig 006)

NEEDLES

1 pair 7mm (no 2) (US 10½) needles
1 pair 8mm (no 0) (US 11) needles

TENSION

12 sts and 16 rows to 10 cm measured over stocking stitch using 8mm (US 11) needles.

Pattern note: The pattern is written for the 3 ladies sizes, followed by the mens sizes in **bold**. Where only one figure appears this applies to all sizes in that group.

SPECIAL ABBREVIATIONS

Cr4B = slip next 3 sts onto cable needle and leave at back of work, K next st dropping extra loop, then K3 from cable needle; **Cr4F** = slip next st onto cable needle dropping extra loop and leave at front of work, K3, then K1 from cable needle; **C4B** = slip next 2 sts onto cable needle and leave at back of work, K2, then K2 from cable needle; **C8B** = slip next 4 sts onto cable needle and leave at back of work, K4, then K4 from cable needle; **C8F** = slip next 4 sts onto cable needle and leave at front of work, K4, then K4 from cable needle.

BACK

Using 7mm (US 10½) needles cast on 58 [62: 66: **70: 74: 78**] sts.
Row 1 (RS): K0 [**2**], *P2, K2, rep from * to last 2 [**0**] sts, P2 [**0**].
Row 2: P0 [**2**], *K2, P2, rep from * to last 2 [**0**] sts, K2 [**0**].
These 2 rows form rib.
Work in rib for a further 11 rows, ending with **WS** facing for next row.
Row 14 (WS): Rib 6 [8: 10: **3: 5: 7**], (M1, rib 6, M1,

rib 3) 2 [**3**] times, (M1, rib 2) twice, (M1, rib 1) twice, (M1, rib 2) twice, M1, (rib 3, M1, rib 6, M1) 2 [**3**] times, rib to end. 73 [77: 81: **89: 93: 97**] sts.
Change to 8mm (US 11) needles.
Row 1 (RS): P6 [8: 10: **3: 5: 7**], (K8, P3) 2 [**3**] times, K5, (P1, K1) 3 times, P1, K5, (P3, K8) 2 [**3**] times, P to end.
Row 2: K6 [8: 10: **3: 5: 7**], (P1 winding yarn twice round needle, P6, P1 winding yarn twice round needle, K3) 2 [**3**] times, P4, (K1, P1) 4 times, K1, P4, (K3, P1 winding yarn twice round needle, P6, P1 winding yarn twice round needle) 2 [**3**] times, K to end.
Row 3: P6 [8: 10: **3: 5: 7**], (Cr4F, Cr4B, P3) 2 [**3**] times, K5, (P1, K1) 3 times, P1, K5, (P3, Cr4F, Cr4B) 2 [**3**] times, P to end.
Rows 2 and 3 form patt for side sections.
Keeping side patt correct, cont as folls:
Row 4: Patt 28 [30: 32: **36: 38: 40**] sts, P4, (K1, P1) 4 times, K1, P4, patt to end.
Row 5: Patt 28 [30: 32: **36: 38: 40**] sts, K5, (P1, K1) 3 times, P1, K5, patt to end.
Row 6: As row 4.
Row 7: Patt 28 [30: 32: **36: 38: 40**] sts, C8F, K1, C8B, patt to end.
Row 8: Patt 28 [30: 32: **36: 38: 40**] sts, P17, patt to end.
Row 9: Patt 28 [30: 32: **36: 38: 40**] sts, K17, patt to end.
Rows 10 to 15: As rows 8 and 9, 3 times.
Row 16: As row 8.
Row 17: Patt 28 [30: 32: **36: 38: 40**] sts, C8B, K1, C8F, patt to end.
Rows 18 and 19: As rows 4 and 5.
Row 20: As row 4.
These 20 rows form patt for centre sts.
Cont in patt until back meas 42 [**43**] cm, ending with RS facing for next row.
Shape armholes
Keeping patt correct, cast off 3 sts at beg of next 2 rows.
67 [71: 75: **83: 87: 91**] sts.
Dec 1 st at each end of next 3 [**5**] rows, then on foll 3 [4: 5: **2: 3: 4**] alt rows, then on foll – [**4th**] row.
55 [57: 59: **67: 69: 71**] sts.
Cont straight until armhole meas 21 [22: 23: **23: 24: 25**] cm, ending with RS facing for next row.

Shape shoulders and back neck

Cast off 4 [4: 5: **6**] sts at beg of next 2 rows.
47 [49: 49: **55: 57: 59**] sts.
Next row (RS): Cast off 4 [4: 5: **6**] sts, patt until there are 8 [9: 8: **9: 10: 11**] sts on right needle and turn, leaving rem sts on a holder.
Work each side of neck separately.
Cast off 4 sts at beg of next row.
Cast off rem 4 [5: 4: **5: 6: 7**] sts.
With RS facing, rejoin yarn to rem sts, cast off centre 23 [**25**] sts dec 7 [**9**] sts evenly, patt to end.
Complete to match first side, reversing shapings.

FRONT

Work as given for back until 8 rows less have been worked than on back to beg of shoulder shaping, ending with RS facing for next row.
Shape neck
Next row (RS): Patt 19 [20: 21: **24: 25: 26**] sts and turn, leaving rem sts on a holder.
Work each side of neck separately.
Dec 1 st at neck edge of next 7 rows, ending with RS facing for next row.
12 [13: 14: **17: 18: 19**] sts.
Shape shoulder
Cast off 4 [4: 5: **6**] sts at beg of next and foll alt row.
Work 1 row.
Cast off rem 4 [5: 4: **5: 6: 7**] sts.
With RS facing, rejoin yarn to rem sts, cast off centre 17 [**19**] sts dec 7 sts evenly, patt to end.
Complete to match first side, reversing shapings.

SLEEVES

Using 7mm (US 10½) needles cast on 28 [30: 32: **32: 34: 36**] sts.
Row 1 (RS): K1 [2: 1: **1: 2: 1**], *P2, K2, rep from * to last 3 [0: 3: **3: 0: 3**] sts, (P2, K1) 1 [0: 1: **1: 0: 1**] times.
Row 2: P1 [2: 1: **1: 2: 1**], *K2, P2, rep from * to last 3 [0: 3: **3: 0: 3**] sts, (K2, P1) 1 [0: 1: **1: 0: 1**] times.
These 2 rows form rib.
Work in rib for a further 11 rows, ending with **WS** facing for next row.
Row 14 (WS): Rib 2 [3: 4: **4: 5: 6**], (M1, rib 6, M1, rib 3) twice, M1, rib 6, M1, rib to end.
34 [36: 38: **38: 40: 42**] sts.
Change to 8mm (US 11) needles.

Next row (RS): Inc in first st, P1 [2: 3: **3: 4: 5**], (K8, P3) twice, K8, P to last st, inc in last st. 36 [38: 40: **40: 42: 44**] sts.

Cont in patt as folls:

Row 1 (WS): K3 [4: 5: **5: 6: 7**], (P1 winding yarn twice round needle, P6, P1 winding yarn twice round needle, K3) twice, P1 winding yarn twice round needle, P6, P1 winding yarn twice round needle, K to end.

Row 2: P3 [4: 5: **5: 6: 7**], (Cr4F, Cr4B, P3) twice, Cr4F, Cr4B, P to end.

These 2 rows form patt.

Cont in patt, shaping sides by inc 1 st at each end of 6th [**4th: 4th: 6th**] and every foll 8th [**6th: 8th: 8th**] row to 44 [44: 44: **44: 58: 60**] sts, then on every foll 10th [**8th: -: -**] row until there are 48 [50: 52: **56: -: -**] sts, taking inc sts into rev st st. Cont straight until sleeve meas 45 [46: 47: **50: 51: 52**] cm, ending with RS facing for next row.

Shape top

Keeping patt correct, cast off 3 sts at beg of next 2 rows. 42 [44: 46: **50: 52: 54**] sts.

Dec 1 st at each end of next 5 [**9**] rows, then on every foll alt row to 16 [**20**] sts, then on foll 1 [**3**] rows, ending with RS facing for next row.

Cast off rem 14 sts.

MAKING UP

Press as described on the information page.

Join right shoulder seam using back stitch, or mattress stitch if preferred.

Neckband

With RS facing and using 7mm (US 10½) needles, pick up and knit 10 sts down left side of neck, 9 [**12**] sts from front, 10 sts up right side of neck, then 21 [**24**] sts from back.

50 [**56**] sts.

Row 1 (WS): P2, *K1, P2, rep from * to end.

Row 2: K2, *P1, M1, K2, M1, P1, K2, rep from * to end. 66 [**74**] sts.

Row 3: P2, *K1, P4, K1, P2, rep from * to end.

Row 4: K2, *P1, C4B, P1, K2, rep from * to end.

Row 5: As row 3.

Row 6: K2, *P1, K4, P1, K2, rep from * to end.

Rep rows 3 to 6 once more, then rows 3 and 4 again.

Cast off in patt (on **WS**).

See information page for finishing instructions, setting in sleeves using the set-in method.

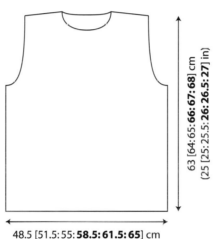

48.5 [51.5: 55: **58.5: 61.5: 65**] cm
(19 [20.5: 21.5: **23: 24: 25.5**] in)

63 [64: 65: **66: 67: 68**] cm
(25 [25: 25.5: **26: 26.5: 27**] in)

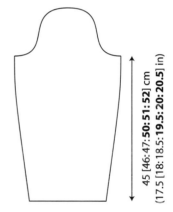

45 [46: 47: **50: 51: 52**] cm
(17.5 [18: 18.5: **19.5: 20: 20.5**] in)

🧶🧶🧶 ┊ Nevis

YARN

	ladies			mens		
	S	M	L	M	L	XL
To fit bust/chest	86	91	97	102	107	112 cm
	34	36	38	40	42	44 in

RYC Soft Tweed

| | 10 | 11 | 12 | 13 | 14 | 14 x 50gm |

(ladies photographed in Twig 005, mans in Slate Blue 007)

NEEDLES

1 pair 7mm (no 2) (US 10½) needles
1 pair 8mm (no 0) (US 11) needles
Cable needle

TENSION

15½ sts and 16 rows to 10 cm measured over pattern using 8mm (US 11) needles.

Pattern note: The pattern is written for the 3 ladies sizes, followed by the mens sizes in **bold**. Where only one figure appears this applies to all sizes in that group.

SPECIAL ABBREVIATIONS

Cr6L = slip next 4 sts onto cable needle and leave at front of work, P2, then K4 from cable needle; **C8F** = slip next 4 sts onto cable needle and leave at front of work, K4, then K4 from cable needle.

BACK

Using 7mm (US 10½) needles cast on 74 [78: 82: **88: 92: 96**] sts.
Beg and ending rows as indicated and repeating the 54 row patt repeat throughout, cont in patt from chart as folls:
Work 4 rows, ending with RS facing for next row.

Change to 8mm (US 11) needles.
Cont in patt until back meas 42 [**43**] cm, ending with RS facing for next row.
Shape armholes
Keeping patt correct, cast off 5 sts at beg of next 2 rows. 64 [68: 72: **78: 82: 86**] sts.
Dec 1 st at each end of next 3 rows, then on foll 3 [4: 5: **3: 4: 5**] alt rows, then on foll 4th row. 50 [52: 54: **64: 66: 68**] sts.
Cont straight until armhole meas 21 [22: 23: **23: 24: 25**] cm, ending with RS facing for next row.
Shape shoulders and back neck
Cast off 4 [**6**] sts at beg of next 2 rows. 42 [44: 46: **52: 54: 56**] sts.
Next row (RS): Cast off 4 [**6**] sts, patt until there are 7 [8: 9: **9: 10: 11**] sts on right needle and turn, leaving rem sts on a holder.
Work each side of neck separately.
Cast off 4 sts at beg of next row.

ladies small
ladies medium
ladies large
mens medium
mens large
mens x large

ladies small
ladies medium
ladies large
mens medium
mens large
mens x large

Key

☐ K on RS, P on WS
▣ P on RS, K on WS
▱ Cr6L
▱ C8F

Cast off rem 3 [4: 5: **5: 6: 7**] sts.
With RS facing, rejoin yarn to rem sts, cast off
centre 20 [**22**] sts dec 6 sts evenly, patt to end.
Complete to match first side, reversing shapings.

FRONT

Work as given for back until 8 rows less have
been worked than on back to beg of shoulder
shaping, ending with RS facing for next row.

Shape neck

Next row (RS): Patt 18 [19: 20: **24: 25: 26**] sts and
turn, leaving rem sts on a holder.
Work each side of neck separately.
Dec 1 st at neck edge of next 7 rows, ending with
RS facing for next row. 11 [12: 13: **17: 18: 19**] sts.

Shape shoulder

Cast off 4 [**6**] sts at beg of next and foll alt row.
Work 1 row.
Cast off rem 3 [4: 5: **5: 6: 7**] sts.
With RS facing, rejoin yarn to rem sts, cast off
centre 14 [**16**] sts dec 4 sts evenly, patt to end.
Complete to match first side, reversing shapings.

SLEEVES

Using 7mm (US 10½) needles cast on 34 [34: 36:
36: 38: 38] sts.
Row 1 (RS): K1 [1: 2: **2: 3: 3**], *P2, K4, rep from *
to last 3 [3: 4: **4: 5: 5**] sts, P2, K1 [1: 2: **2: 3: 3**].
Row 2: P1 [1: 2: **2: 3: 3**], *K2, P4, rep from * to last
3 [3: 4: **4: 5: 5**] sts, K2, P1 [1: 2: **2: 3: 3**].
These 2 rows form rib.
Work in rib for a further 2 rows, ending with RS
facing for next row.

Change to 8mm (US 11) needles.
Cont in rib, shaping sides by inc 1 st at each end
of 5th [3rd: 3rd: **3rd**] and every foll 8th [6th: 6th:
6th] row to 48 [38: 40: **50: 50: 58**] sts, then on
every foll 10th [8th: 8th: **8th**] row until there are
50 [52: 54: **58: 60: 62**] sts, taking inc sts into rib.
Cont straight until sleeve meas 46 [47: 48:
51: 52: 53] cm, ending with RS facing for next row.

Shape top

Keeping rib correct, cast off 5 sts at beg of next
2 rows.
40 [42: 44: **48: 50: 52**] sts.
Dec 1 st at each end of next 3 [**5**] rows, then on
every foll alt row to 16 [**24**] sts, then on foll 1 [**5**]
rows, ending with RS facing for next row.
Cast off rem 14 sts.

MAKING UP

Press as described on the information page.
Join right shoulder seam using back stitch, or
mattress stitch if preferred.

Neckband

With RS facing and using 7mm (US 10½) needles,
pick up and knit 10 sts down left side of neck,
9 [**12**] sts from front, 10 sts up right side of neck,
then 21 [**24**] sts from back.
50 [**56**] sts.
Row 1 (WS): K2, *P4, K2, rep from * to end.
Row 2: P2, *K4, P2, rep from * to end.
Rep last 2 rows until neckband meas 8 cm.
Cast off.
See information page for finishing instructions,
setting in sleeves using the set-in method.

47.5 [50.5: 53: **57: 59.5: 62**] cm
(18.5 [20: 21: **22.5: 23.5: 24.5**] in)

63 [64: 65: **66: 67: 68**] cm
(25 [25: 25.5: **26: 26.5: 27**] in)

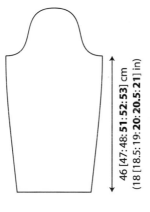

46 [47: 48: **51: 52: 53**] cm
(18 [18.5: 19: **20: 20.5: 21**] in)

Bruce

YARN

	S	M	L	XL	XXL
To fit chest	97	102	107	112	117 cm
	38	40	42	44	46 in

RYC Soft Tweed

	13	13	14	14	15 x 50gm

(photographed in Blanket 008)

NEEDLES

1 pair 7mm (no 2) (US 10½) needles
1 pair 8mm (no 0) (US 11) needles
Cable needle

TENSION

12 sts and 16 rows to 10 cm measured over
stocking stitch using 8mm (US 11) needles.

SPECIAL ABBREVIATIONS

C8B = slip next 4 sts onto cable needle and leave
at back of work, K4, then K4 from cable needle;
C8F = slip next 4 sts onto cable needle and leave
at front of work, K4, then K4 from cable needle.

BACK

Using 7mm (US 10½) needles cast on 67 [69: 73:
75: 79] sts.
Row 1 (RS): P0 [0: 2: 0: 0], K2 [3: 3: 0: 2], *P3, K3,
rep from * to last 5 [0: 2: 3: 5] sts, P3 [0: 2: 3: 3],
K2 [0: 0: 0: 2].
Row 2: K0 [0: 2: 0: 0], P2 [3: 3: 0: 2], *K3, P3,
rep from * to last 5 [0: 2: 3: 5] sts, K3 [0: 2: 3: 3],
P2 [0: 0: 0: 2].
These 2 rows form rib.
Work in rib for a further 13 rows, ending with **WS**
facing for next row.
Row 16 (WS): Rib 2 [3: 5: 6: 8], *M1, rib 3, M1,
rib 2, (M1, rib 3) twice, rep from * 4 times more,
M1, rib 3, M1, rib 2, M1, rib 3, M1, rib to end.
91 [93: 97: 99: 103] sts.
Change to 8mm (US 11) needles.
Row 1 (RS): K1 [2: 4: 5: 7], P1, (K12, P3) 5 times,
K12, P1, K to end.
Row 2 and every foll alt row: P1 [2: 4: 5: 7], K1,
(P12, K1, yfwd, K2tog) 5 times, P12, K1, P to end.
Row 3: K1 [2: 4: 5: 7], P1, (K4, C8F, P3) 5 times,
K4, C8F, P1, K to end.
Row 5: As row 1.
Row 7: K1 [2: 4: 5: 7], P1, (C8B, K4, P3) 5 times,

C8B, K4, P1, K to end.
Row 8: As row 2.
These 8 rows form patt.
Cont in patt until back meas 43 cm, ending with
RS facing for next row.
Shape armholes
Keeping patt correct, cast off 5 sts at beg of next
2 rows.
81 [83: 87: 89: 93] sts.
Dec 1 st at each end of next 5 [5: 7: 7: 9] rows,
then on foll 1 [2: 1: 2: 1] alt rows, then on foll
4th row.
67 [67: 69: 69: 71] sts.
Cont straight until armhole meas 22 [23: 24:
25: 26] cm, ending with RS facing for next row.
Shape shoulders and back neck
Cast off 6 sts at beg of next 2 rows.
55 [55: 57: 57: 59] sts.
Next row (RS): Cast off 6 sts, patt until there are
11 [10: 11: 10: 11] sts on right needle and turn,
leaving rem sts on a holder.
Work each side of neck separately.
Cast off 4 sts at beg of next row.
Cast off rem 7 [6: 7: 6: 7] sts.
With RS facing, rejoin yarn to rem sts, cast off
centre 21 [23: 23: 25: 25] sts dec 6 sts evenly,
patt to end.
Complete to match first side, reversing shapings.

FRONT

Work as given for back until 8 rows less have
been worked than on back to beg of shoulder
shaping, ending with RS facing for next row.
Shape neck
Next row (RS): Patt 24 [23: 24: 23: 24] sts and
turn, leaving rem sts on a holder.
Work each side of neck separately.
Dec 1 st at neck edge on next 3 rows, then on foll
2 alt rows, ending with RS facing for next row.
19 [18: 19: 18: 19] sts.
Shape shoulder
Cast off 6 sts at beg of next and foll alt row.
Work 1 row.
Cast off rem 7 [6: 7: 6: 7] sts.
With RS facing, rejoin yarn to rem sts, cast off
centre 19 [21: 21: 23: 23] sts dec 6 sts evenly, patt
to end.
Complete to match first side, reversing shapings.

SLEEVES

Using 7mm (US 10½) needles cast on 33 [33: 35:
37: 37] sts.
Row 1 (RS): P0 [0: 1: 2: 2], K3, *P3, K3, rep from *
to last 0 [0: 1: 2: 2] sts, P0 [0: 1: 2: 2].
Row 2: K0 [0: 1: 2: 2], P3, *K3, P3, rep from * to
last 0 [0: 1: 2: 2] sts, K0 [0: 1: 2: 2].
These 2 rows form rib.
Work in rib for a further 13 rows, ending with **WS**
facing for next row.
Row 16 (WS): Rib 7 [7: 8: 9: 9], M1, rib 3, M1,
rib 2, (M1, rib 3) 3 times, M1, rib 2, M1, rib 3, M1,
rib to end.
41 [41: 43: 45: 45] sts.
Change to 8mm (US 11) needles.
Row 1 (RS): K4 [4: 5: 6: 6], P3, (K12, P3) twice,
K to end.
Row 2: P4 [4: 5: 6: 6], K1, yfwd, K2tog,
(P12, K1, yfwd, K2tog) twice, P to end.
Row 3: K4 [4: 5: 6: 6], P3, (K4, C8F, P3) twice,
K to end.
Row 4: As row 2.
Row 5: (Inc in first st) 0 [1: 1: 1: 1] times, K4 [3: 4:
5: 5], P3, (K12, P3) twice, K to last 0 [1: 1: 1: 1] st,
(inc in last st) 0 [1: 1: 1: 1] times.
41 [43: 45: 47: 47] sts.
Row 6: P4 [5: 6: 7: 7], K1, yfwd, K2tog,
(P12, K1, yfwd, K2tog) twice, P to end.
Row 7: (Inc in first st) 1 [0: 0: 0: 0] times, K3 [5: 6:
7: 7], P3, (C8B, K4, P3) twice, K to last 1 [0: 0:
0: 0] st, (inc in last st) 1 [0: 0: 0: 0] times.
43 [43: 45: 47: 47] sts.
Row 8: P5 [5: 6: 7: 7], K1, yfwd, K2tog,
(P12, K1, yfwd, K2tog) twice, P to end.
These 8 rows form patt and beg sleeve shaping.
Cont in patt, shaping sides by inc 1 st at each end
of 7th [3rd: 3rd: 3rd: 3rd] and every foll 8th [6th:
6th: 8th: 6th] row to 55 [47: 49: 61: 57] sts, then
on every foll - [8th: 8th: -: 8th] row until there are
- [57: 59: -: 63] sts, taking inc sts into st st.
Cont straight until sleeve meas 49 [50: 50:
51: 51] cm, ending with RS facing for next row.
Shape top
Keeping patt correct, cast off 5 sts at beg of next
2 rows. 45 [47: 49: 51: 53] sts.
Dec 1 st at each end of next 5 rows, then on foll
2 alt rows, then on foll 4th row.
29 [31: 33: 35: 37] sts.

Work 1 row, ending with RS facing for next row.
Dec 1 st at each end of next and every foll alt row until 23 sts rem, then on foll 3 rows.
Cast off rem 17 sts, dec 4 sts evenly.

MAKING UP

Press as described on the information page.
Join right shoulder seam using back stitch, or mattress stitch if preferred.

Collar

With RS facing and using 7mm (US 10½) needles, pick up and knit 10 sts down left side of neck, 9 [12: 12: 15: 15] sts from front, 10 sts up right side of neck, then 22 [25: 25: 28: 28] sts from back.
51 [57: 57: 63: 63] sts.
Row 1 (WS): P3, *K3, P3, rep from * to end.
Row 2: K3, *P3, K3, rep from * to end.
These 2 rows form rib.
Cont in rib until collar meas 10 cm.
Change to 8mm (US 11) needles.

Cont in rib until collar meas 21 cm from pick-up row.
Cast off in rib.

See information page for finishing instructions, setting in sleeves using the set-in method and reversing collar seam for turn-back.

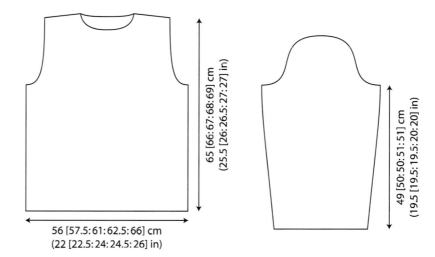

65 [66: 67: 68: 69] cm
(25.5 [26: 26.5: 27: 27] in)

56 [57.5: 61: 62.5: 66] cm
(22 [22.5: 24: 24.5: 26] in)

49 [50: 50: 51: 51] cm
(19.5 [19.5: 19.5: 20: 20] in)

Scott

YARN

		S	M	L	XL	XXL	
To fit chest		97	102	107	112	117	cm
		38	40	42	44	46	in

RYC Soft Tweed

A Oatmeal	001	8	8	8	9	10	x 50gm
B Sprig	006	2	2	2	2	2	x 50gm
C Slate Blue	007	1	1	1	1	1	x 50gm
D Blanket	008	2	2	2	2	2	x 50gm

NEEDLES

1 pair 7mm (no 2) (US 10½) needles
1 pair 8mm (no 0) (US 11) needles

ZIP – Open-ended zip to fit

TENSION

12 sts and 16 rows to 10 cm measured over stocking stitch using 8mm (US 11) needles.

BACK

Using 7mm (US 10½) needles and yarn A cast on 67 [69: 73: 75: 79] sts.
Row 1 (RS): K1, *P1, K1, rep from * to end.
Row 2: P1, *K1, P1, rep from * to end.
These 2 rows form rib.
Work in rib for a further 10 rows, ending with RS facing for next row.
Change to 8mm (US 11) needles.
Beg and ending rows as indicated and using the **fairisle** technique as described on the information page, cont in patt from chart for border, which is worked entirely in st st beg with a K row, until chart row 20 has been completed, ending with RS facing for next row.
Break off contrasts and cont using yarn A **only**.
Beg with a K row, cont in st st until back meas 43 cm, ending with RS facing for next row.
Shape raglan armholes
Beg and ending rows as indicated and using the **fairisle** technique as described on the information page, cont in patt from chart for yoke, which is worked entirely in st st beg with a K row, as folls:
Cast off 4 sts at beg of next 2 rows.
59 [61: 65: 67: 71] sts.
Dec 1 st at each end of next 7 [5: 7: 5: 7] rows, then on every foll alt row until 19 [21: 21: 23: 23] sts rem.

Work 1 row, ending with RS facing for next row.
Shape back neck
Next row (RS): K2tog, K2 and turn, leaving rem sts on a holder.
Work each side of neck separately.
Dec 1 st at neck edge of next row.
Next row (RS): K2tog and fasten off.
With RS facing, rejoin yarns to rem sts, cast off centre 11 [13: 13: 15: 15] sts, K to last 2 sts, K2tog.
Complete to match first side, reversing shapings.

LEFT FRONT

Using 7mm (US 10½) needles and yarn A cast on 34 [36: 38: 38: 40] sts.
Row 1 (RS): *K1, P1, rep from * to last 2 sts, K2.
Row 2: K2, *K1, P1, rep from * to end.
These 2 rows form rib.
Work in rib for a further 10 rows, inc 1 [0: 0: 1: 1] st at end of last row and ending with RS facing for next row. 35 [36: 38: 39: 41] sts.
Change to 8mm (US 11) needles.
Place border chart
Beg and ending rows as indicated, place chart for border as folls:

Row 1 (RS): Work first 33 [34: 36: 37: 39] sts as row 1 of border chart, using yarn A K2.
Row 2: Using yarn A K2, work last 33 [34: 36: 37: 39] sts as row 2 of border chart.
These 2 rows set the sts – front opening edge 2 sts in g st using yarn A and all other sts in patt foll chart.
Cont as set until chart row 20 has been completed, ending with RS facing for next row.
Break off contrasts and cont using yarn A **only**.
Next row (RS): Knit.
Next row: K2, P to end.
These 2 rows set the sts.
Cont as set until left front matches back to beg of raglan armhole shaping, ending with RS facing for next row.
Shape raglan armhole
Place yoke chart
Beg and ending rows as indicated, place chart for yoke as folls:
Row 1 (RS): Working first 33 [34: 36: 37: 39] sts as row 1 of yoke chart cast off 4 sts, patt to last 2 sts, using yarn A K2. 31 [32: 34: 35: 37] sts.
Row 2: Using yarn A K2, work last 29 [30: 32:

Border chart

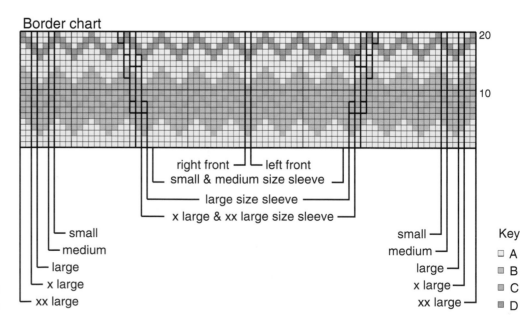

right front ⌐ ⌐ left front
⌐ small & medium size sleeve ⌐
⌐ large size sleeve ⌐
⌐ x large & xx large size sleeve ⌐

⌐ small
⌐ medium
⌐ large
⌐ x large
⌐ xx large

small ⌐
medium ⌐
large ⌐
x large ⌐
xx large ⌐

Key
☐ A
▨ B
▨ C
▨ D

Yoke chart

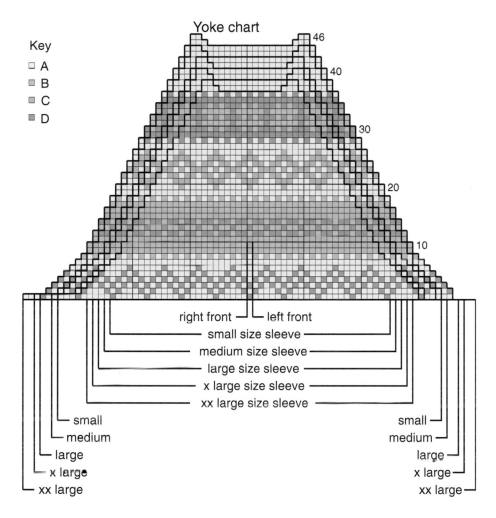

Key
- ☐ A
- ▨ B
- ▨ C
- ▨ D

46

40

30

20

10

right front ⌐⌐ left front
small size sleeve
medium size sleeve
large size sleeve
x large size sleeve
xx large size sleeve

small
medium
large
x large
xx large

small
medium
large
x large
xx large

33: 35] sts as row 2 of yoke chart.

These 2 rows set the sts – front opening edge 2 sts in g st using yarn A and all other sts in patt foll chart.

Dec 1 st at raglan armhole edge of next 7 [5: 7: 5: 7] rows, then on every foll alt row until 15 [16: 17: 18: 18] sts rem, ending with **WS** facing for next row.

Shape neck

Keeping patt correct, cast off 6 [7: 6: 7: 7] sts at beg of next row.

9 [9: 11: 11: 11] sts.

Dec 1 st at neck edge of next 3 rows, then on foll 1 [1: 2: 2: 2] alt rows **and at same time** dec 1 st at raglan armhole edge of next and every foll alt

row. 2 sts.

Work 1 row, ending with RS facing for next row.

Next row (RS): K2tog and fasten off.

RIGHT FRONT

Using 7mm (US 10½) needles and yarn A cast on 34 [36: 38: 38: 40] sts.

Row 1 (RS): K2, *P1, K1, rep from * to end.

Row 2: *P1, K1, rep from * to last 2 sts, K2.

These 2 rows form rib.

Work in rib for a further 10 rows, inc 1 [0: 0: 1: 1] st at beg of last row and ending with RS facing for next row.

35 [36: 38: 39: 41] sts.

Change to 8mm (US 11) needles.

Place chart

Beg and ending rows as indicated, place chart for border as folls:

Row 1 (RS): Using yarn A K2, work last 33 [34: 36: 37: 39] sts as row 1 of border chart.

Row 2: Work first 33 [34: 36: 37: 39] sts as row 2 of border chart, using yarn A K2.

These 2 rows set the sts – front opening edge 2 sts in g st using yarn A and all other sts in patt foll chart.

Cont as set until chart row 20 has been completed, ending with RS facing for next row.

Break off contrasts and cont using yarn A **only**.

Next row (RS): Knit.

Next row: P to last 2 sts, K2.

These 2 rows set the sts.

Complete to match left front, reversing shapings, working an extra row before beg of raglan armhole and neck shaping.

SLEEVES

Using 7mm (US 10½) needles and yarn A cast on 33 [33: 35: 37: 37] sts.

Work in rib as given for back for 12 rows, ending with RS facing for next row.

Change to 8mm (US 11) needles.

Beg and ending rows as indicated and using the **fairisle** technique as described on the information page, cont in patt from chart for border as folls:

Inc 1 st at each end of next and every foll 8th [6th: 6th: 8th: 6th] row to 39 [37: 39: 43: 45] sts, then on foll 0 [8th: 8th: 0: 0] row.

39 [39: 41: 43: 45] sts.

Work 3 [5: 5: 3: 1] rows, ending after chart row 20 and with RS facing for next row.

Break off contrasts and cont using yarn A **only**.

Beg with a K row, cont in st st, shaping sides by inc 1 st at each end of 5th [3rd: 3rd: 5th: 5th] and every foll 8th row to 45 [51: 53: 55: 57] sts, then on every foll 10th [-: -: -: -] row until there are 49 [-: -: -: -] sts.

Cont straight until sleeve meas 49 [50: 50: 51: 51] cm, ending with RS facing for next row.

Shape raglan

Beg and ending rows as indicated, cont in patt from chart for yoke as folls:

Cast off 4 sts at beg of next 2 rows.

41 [43: 45: 47: 49] sts.

Dec 1 st at each end of next and every foll alt row until 9 sts rem.

Work 1 row, ending with RS facing for next row.

Left sleeve only

Dec 1 st at each end of next row, then cast off 2 sts at beg of foll row. 5 sts.

Dec 1 st at beg of next row, then cast off 2 sts at beg of foll row.

Right sleeve only

Cast off 3 sts at beg and dec 1 st at end of next row. 5 sts.

Work 1 row.

Cast off 2 sts at beg and dec 1 st at end of next row.

Work 1 row.

Both sleeves

Cast off rem 2 sts.

MAKING UP

Press as described on the information page.

Join raglan seams using back stitch, or mattress stitch if preferred.

Left collar

Using 7mm (US 10½) needles and yarn A cast on 2 sts.

Work in g st, inc 1 st at beg of 3rd and every foll alt row until there are 22 sts.

Cont straight until shaped edge of left collar, unstretched, fits up left front neck edge (cast-on sts of collar are matched to front opening edge 2 sts of front) and across to centre back neck, ending with RS facing for next row.

Cast off very loosely knitwise.

Right collar

Work to match left collar, reversing shapings.

Join cast-off edges of collar pieces, then sew shaped edges of collar to neck edge.

See information page for finishing instructions, inserting zip into front opening.

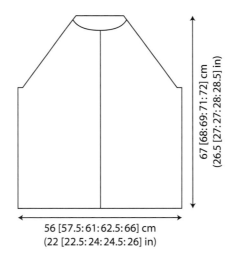

56 [57.5: 61: 62.5: 66] cm
(22 [22.5: 24: 24.5: 26] in)

67 [68: 69: 71: 72] cm
(26.5 [27: 27: 28: 28.5] in)

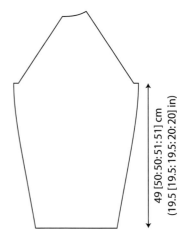

49 [50: 50: 51: 51] cm
(19.5 [19.5: 19.5: 20: 20] in)

Whisky scarf

Whisky hat

YARN
RYC Soft Tweed

A	Oatmeal	001	1	x 50gm
B	Twig	005	1	x 50gm
C	Blanket	008	4	x 50gm

NEEDLES
1 pair 8mm (no 0) (US 11) needles

FINISHED SIZE
Completed scarf measures 30 cm (12 in) wide and
246 cm (97 ins) long.

TENSION
12 sts and 16 rows to 10 cm measured over
stocking stitch using 8mm (US 11) needles.

SCARF
Using 8mm (US 11) needles and yarn A cast on
36 sts.
Row 1 (RS): Using yarn A, K4, *P4, K4, rep from *
to end.
Row 2: Using yarn A, K8, *P4, K4, rep from * to
last 4 sts, K4.
These 2 rows form patt.
Work in patt for a further 6 rows.
Join in yarn B.
**Using yarn B, work 6 rows.
Join in yarn C.
Using yarn C, work 4 rows.
Using yarn B, work 6 rows.**
Using yarn A, work 8 rows.
Break off yarn A.
Rep from ** to ** once more.
Break off yarn B and cont using yarn C only.
Cont in patt until scarf meas 216 cm, ending with
RS facing for next row.
Join in yarn B.
***Rep from ** to ** once more.
Join in yarn A.
Using yarn A, work 8 rows.
Rep from *** once more.
Cast off in patt.

MAKING UP
Press as described on the information page.

YARN
RYC Soft Tweed

		2	x 50gm

(photographed in Blanket 008)

NEEDLES
1 pair 7mm (no 2) (US 10½) needles

TENSION
13 sts and 18 rows to 10 cm measured over
stocking stitch using 7mm (US 10½) needles.

HAT
Using 7mm (US 10½) needles cast on 70 sts.
Row 1 (RS): *K3, P2, rep from * to end.
Row 2: *K2, P3, rep from * to end.
These 2 rows form rib.
Cont in rib until hat meas 19 cm, ending with RS
facing for next row.
Shape crown
Row 1 (RS): (K2tog, K1, P2, K3, P2) 7 times.
63 sts.
Row 2: (K2, P3, K2, P2) 7 times.
Row 3: (K2, P2, K2tog, K1, P2) 7 times. 56 sts.
Row 4: (K2, P2) 14 times.
Row 5: (K2, P2tog, K2, P2) 7 times. 49 sts.
Row 6: (K2, P2, K1, P2) 7 times.
Row 7: (K2, P1, K2, P2tog) 7 times. 42 sts.
Row 8: (K1, P2) 14 times.
Row 9: (K2tog, P1) 14 times. 28 sts.
Row 10: (P2tog) 14 times. 14 sts.
Row 11: (K2tog) 7 times.
Break yarn and thread through rem 7 sts. Pull up
tight and fasten off securely.

MAKING UP
Press as described on the information page.
Join back seam using back stitch, or mattress
stitch if preferred, reversing seam for turn-back.

Rambler

YARN

	ladies	mens	
RYC Soft Tweed			
Socks	3	4	x 50gm

(photographed in Antique 002 and Sprig 006)

Legwarmers	3	4	x 50gm

(photographed in Bramble 004)

NEEDLES

Set of 4 double-pointed 7mm (no 2) (US 10½) needles
Set of 4 double-pointed 8mm (no 0) (US 11) needles

TENSION

12 sts and 16 rows to 10 cm measured over stocking stitch using 8mm (US 11) needles.

SOCKS (make 2)

Using 7mm (US 10½) double-pointed needles cast on 36 [40] sts and distribute sts evenly over 3 needles.
Round 1 (RS): *K2, P2, rep from * to end.
This round forms rib.
Cont in rib for a further 5 rounds.
Change to 8mm (US 11) double-pointed needles.
Cont in rib until sock meas 48 [50] cm.**
Turn heel
Divide sts for heel as folls: slip first 18 [20] sts onto one needle for heel, and distribute rem 18 [20] sts over two needles and leave these sts for instep.
Working in **rows** on heel sts only, cont as folls:
Row 1 (RS): K17 [19], turn.
Row 2: P16 [18], turn.
Row 3: K15 [17], turn.
Row 4: P14 [16] turn.
Cont in this way, working one less st on every row before turning, until the foll row has been worked:
Next row (WS): P12, turn.
Next row: K14, pick up loop that lies immediately below next st and K tog this loop with next st, turn.
Next row: P15, pick up loop that lies immediately below next st and P tog this loop with next st, turn.
Cont in this way, working one extra st on every row before turning, until the foll row has been worked:
Next row: P17 [19], pick up loop that lies immediately below next st and P tog this loop with next st, turn.
Shape foot
Distribute all 36 [40] heel and instep sts over 3 of the 4 needles and work in rounds as folls:
Next round (RS): (K1, K2tog tbl, K12 [14], K2tog, K1) twice. 32 [36] sts.
Next round: Knit.
Rep last round until sock meas 14 [17] cm from last heel row.
Shape toe
Round 1: (K1, K2tog tbl, K10 [12], K2tog, K1) twice. 28 [32] sts.
Round 2: Knit.
Round 3: (K1, K2tog tbl, K8 [10], K2tog, K1) twice. 24 [28] sts.
Round 4: Knit.
Round 5: (K1, K2tog tbl, K6 [8], K2tog, K1) twice. 20 [24] sts.
Round 6: K10 [12].
Slip these 10 [12] sts onto one needle and rem 10 [12] sts onto another needle.
Fold sock, with RS facing, so that these 2 needles are parallel and, taking one st from front needle with one st from back needle, cast off toes sts together.

LEGWARMERS (make 2)

Work as given for socks to **.
Cast off in rib.

MAKING UP

Press as described on the information page.

BELGIUM
Pavan, Meerlaanstraat 73,
B9860 Balegem (Oosterzele).
Tel: (32) 9 221 8594
Email: pavan@pandora.be

CANADA
Diamond Yarn,
9697 St Laurent,
Montreal,
Quebec, H3L 2N1.
Tel: (514) 388 6188

Diamond Yarn (Toronto),
155 Martin Ross,
Unit 3, Toronto,
Ontario,M3J 2L9.
Tel: (416) 736 6111
Email: diamond@diamondyarn.com
Web: www.diamondyarns.com

DENMARK
Design Vaerkstedet,
Boulevarden 9, 9000 Aalborg.
Tel: (45) 9812 0713
Fax: (45) 9813 0213

Inger's, Volden 19, 8000 Aarhus.
Tel: (45) 8619 4044

Sommerfuglen, Vandkunsten 3,
1467 Kobenhavn k.
Tel/Fax: (45) 3332 8290
Email: mail@sommerfuglen.dk
Web: www.sommerfuglen.dk

Uldstedet, Fiolstraede 13,
1171 Kobenhavn k.
Tel/Fax: (45) 3391 1771

Uldstedet, G1. Jernbanevej 7,
2800 Lyngby.
Tel/Fax: (45) 4588 1088

Garnhokeren,
Karen Olsdatterstraede 9, 4000 Roskilde.
Tel/Fax: (45) 4637 2063

FINLAND
Oy Nordia Produkter Ab,
Mikkolantie 1,
00640 Helsinki.
Tel: (358) 9 777 4272
Email: info@nordiaprodukter.fi

FRANCE
Elle Tricot : 8 Rue du Coq,
67000 Strasbourg.
Tel: (33) 3 88 23 03 13.
Email: elletricot@agat.net.
Web: www.elletricote.com

GERMANY
Wolle & Design,
Wolfshovener Strasse 76,
52428 Julich-Stetternich.
Tel: (49) 2461 54735.
Email: Info@wolleunddesign.de
Web: www.wolleunddesign.de

HOLLAND
de Afstap, Oude Leliestraat 12,
1015 AW Amsterdam.
Tel: (31) 20 6231445

HONG KONG
East Unity Co Ltd, Unit B2, 7/F Block B,
Kailey Industrial Centre,
12 Fung Yip Street, Chai Wan.
Tel: (852) 2869 7110
Fax: (852) 2537 6952
Email: eastuni@netvigator.com

ICELAND
Storkurinn, Laugavegi 59,
101 Reykjavik.
Tel: (354) 551 8258
Fax: (354) 562 8252
Email: malin@mmedia.is

ITALY
D.L. srl, Via Piave, 24 – 26,
20016 Pero, Milan.
Tel: (39) 02 339 10 180.

JAPAN
Puppy Co Ltd, T151-0051,
3-16-5 Sendagaya, Shibuyaku, Tokyo.
Tel: (81) 3 3490 2017
Email: info@rowan-jaeger.com

KOREA
Coats Korea Co Ltd,
5F Kuckdong B/D,
935-40 Bangbae-Dong,
Seocho-Gu, Seoul.
Tel: (82) 2 521 6262.
Fax: (82) 2 521 5181

NORWAY
Coats Norge A/S,
Postboks 63, 2801 Gjovik.
Tel: (47) 61 18 34 00
Fax: (47) 61 18 34 20

SINGAPORE
Golden Dragon Store,
101 Upper Cross Street #02-51,
People's Park Centre.
Singapore 058357
Tel: (65) 65358454.
Email:gdscraft@hotmail.com

SOUTH AFRICA
Arthur Bales PTY,
PO Box 44644,
Linden 2104.
Tel: (27) 11 888 2401.

SPAIN
Oyambre, Pau Claris 145,
80009 Barcelona.
Tel: (34) 670 011957.
Email: comercial@oyambreonline.com

SWEDEN
Wincent, Norrtullsgatan 65,
113 45 Stockholm.
Tel: (46) 8 33 70 60
Fax: (46) 8 33 70 68
Email: wincent@chello.se
Web: www.wincentyarn.com

TAIWAN
Laiter Wool Knitting Co Ltd,
10-1 313 Lane, Sec 3,
Chung Ching North Road,
Taipei.
Tel: (886) 2 2596 0269.

Long T eh Trading Co Ltd,
3F No. 19-2,
Kung Yuan Road,
Taichung.
Tel: (886) 4 2225 6698.

Green Leave Thread Company,
No 101, Sec 4,
Chung Ching North Road,
Taipei.
Fax: (886) 2 8221 2919.

U.S.A.
Westminster Fibers Inc,
4 Townsend West,
Suite 8, Nashua,
New Hampshire 03063.
Tel: (1 603) 886 5041 / 5043.
Email: rowan@westminsterfibers.com

U.K.
Rowan, Green Lane Mill,
Holmfirth, West Yorkshire,
HD9 2DX.
Tel: 01484 681881.
Email: mail@ryclassic.com
Web: www.ryclassic.com

For All Other Countries:
Please contact Rowan for stockists details.

Shot on Location in and around The Log
Cabin, Golspie, Sutherland, Scotland
(for information on holiday lets contact
Michael Scott on 01557 814058).

With enormous thanks to:
Lord Strathnaver, The Sutherland Estate
Donald Ross, Dunrobin Glen
Betty and John Robertson (and Holly)
Dornoch and District Angling Association
Duncan Todd, Embo
Blanche Sinclair, Golspie

Photographer Mark Scott (Assisted by
Rachel Whiting and Katie Hyams)
Stylist Tara Sloggett
Make up KJ
Layout Sara Faulkner and Dan Travers
Design: Nicky Downes

First published in Great Britain in 2005
by Rowan Yarns Ltd, Green Lane Mill,
Holmfirth, West Yorkshire, England, HD9 2DX

British Library Cataloguing in
Publication Data
Rowan Yarns
RYC Winter
ISBN 1-904485-46-4